Gender and History

Series Editors
Amanda Capern
University of Hull
Hull, UK

Louella R. McCarthy
University of Wollongong
Wollongong, Australia

Gender and History is an important series of books that offers teachers and students lively and accessible surveys of the most recent research into the impact of gender and sexual orientation on the past. Exciting new methodologies and topics are covered using gender as a category of historical analysis. The series acknowledges the multiple cultural constructions and fluidity of gender and sexuality as well as intersectionality with race. Its titles aim to embed women's and LGBTQ+ histories in the curriculum while revealing some of the root causes of global inequalities of power. Culture, race, politics, economy and religion are all covered in books that use the lens of gender to excite interest in the lived and embodied experiences of people whose voices have been marginalized. Reimagining history for the twenty-first century, this series tackles questions of power and emotional life in ways that are highly engaging for the reader and that restore social justice to the historical narrative.

More information about this series at
http://www.palgrave.com/gp/series/14997

Jane Martin

Gender and Education in England since 1770

A Social and Cultural History

Jane Martin
University of Birmingham
Birmingham, UK

Gender and History
ISBN 978-3-030-79745-4   ISBN 978-3-030-79746-1 (eBook)
https://doi.org/10.1007/978-3-030-79746-1

© The Editor(s) (if applicable) and The Author(s), under exclusive licence to Springer Nature Switzerland AG 2022
This work is subject to copyright. All rights are solely and exclusively licensed by the Publisher, whether the whole or part of the material is concerned, specifically the rights of translation, reprinting, reuse of illustrations, recitation, broadcasting, reproduction on microfilms or in any other physical way, and transmission or information storage and retrieval, electronic adaptation, computer software, or by similar or dissimilar methodology now known or hereafter developed.
The use of general descriptive names, registered names, trademarks, service marks, etc. in this publication does not imply, even in the absence of a specific statement, that such names are exempt from the relevant protective laws and regulations and therefore free for general use.
The publisher, the authors and the editors are safe to assume that the advice and information in this book are believed to be true and accurate at the date of publication. Neither the publisher nor the authors or the editors give a warranty, expressed or implied, with respect to the material contained herein or for any errors or omissions that may have been made. The publisher remains neutral with regard to jurisdictional claims in published maps and institutional affiliations.

Cover illustration: Evening Standard / Stringer

This Palgrave Macmillan imprint is published by the registered company Springer Nature Switzerland AG.
The registered company address is: Gewerbestrasse 11, 6330 Cham, Switzerland

Acknowledgements

This book started life as a module I taught. It draws on various research projects of mine, and over the years, my thinking has benefited from the ideas and insights of many people including my students, past and present, colleagues and friends. Firstly, I would like to thank Gemma Banks, Bernard Barker, Marion Bowl, Elizabeth Burn, Claire Crawford, Miriam David, Rosemary Deem, Michael Fielding, Tanya Fitzgerald, David Gillborn, Joyce Goodman, Helen Gunter, Lottie Hoare, Nancy Rosoff, Stephanie Spencer, Patrick Yarker and Ruth Watts for their encouragement and support that helped keep me going in hard times. I owe a particular debt of gratitude to Elizabeth, Lottie, Marion, Miriam and Rosemary who found the time to read and offer feedback on particular chapters.

Secondly, I would like to thank the librarians and archivists at the following libraries for their invaluable help in accessing materials: Brunel University, London Metropolitan Archive, London School of Economics and UCL Institute of Education Special Collections. I would particularly like to thank the two anonymous readers for their insightful comments and feedback on an earlier draft of the manuscript and Series Editor, Amanda Capern, for her support and enthusiasm in bringing this book to press. Thanks also to Joseph Johnson and Emily Russell at Palgrave for their patience and understanding during unavoidable delays. Lastly, thanks to my Mum for inspiring me and my family for their support. Chloe made a valuable contribution in reading and commenting on my introduction. My husband Paul has lived with this research for a long time and always provided encouragement and honest reflections throughout the writing process. This book is dedicated to him.

Contents

1	**A Chronological Introduction**	1
	Theme One: Enlightenment, Industrial Capitalism and the Sexual Division of Labour	3
	Theme Two: Resistance, Socio-Political Movements and Universal Basic Education	7
	Theme Three: From Social Democracy to Neoliberal Crisis	15
	Bibliography	20
Part I	**Politics and Policies**	23
2	**Gendering the Educational Landscape**	25
	Gender and the Politics of Historical Writing	27
	Gendering the Politics of Experience	36
	Thinking Gender and Generation Through Appropriating Bourdieu	40
	Pearl Jephcott and the Gendering of British Social Science in Post-War Britain	42
	Conclusion	46
	Bibliography	47
3	**Childhood, Education and the Family**	51
	Elite Education and the Gender Order	53
	Elementary Education and the Making of Good Wives and Mothers	62
	Conclusion	73
	Bibliography	74

4	**Gender Equity and the 'Ladder of Opportunity'**	79
	Background and Inheritance: The Language of Scholarship Scripts	80
	Secondary Education for All?	87
	Failing Girls?	97
	Conclusion	102
	Bibliography	103
5	**Perspectives and Debates Since the 1970s**	107
	From Equal Opportunities to Identity Politics in a Competition State: Setting the Context	108
	The Academically Underachieving Male: The New Disadvantaged?	117
	Schooling and Its Impact on Gender Relations in New Times	121
	Conclusion	129
	Bibliography	130

Part II   Learners and Learning — 133

6	**Culture and Curriculum**	135
	Viewing Elementary Curriculum Formulations Historically	139
	Viewing Secondary Curriculum Formulations Historically	147
	The Life Cycle of Women's/Gender Studies in the 1960s and Beyond	153
	Conclusion	158
	Bibliography	160
7	**Pupils**	163
	Description: Contexts and Biographies	167
	Inside Schools and Classrooms	171
	Climbing the Examination Ladder and Going Down the Snakes	177
	Comprehensive Schooling	184
	Conclusion: Making Connections	186
	Bibliography	187
8	**Students**	189
	Historicising Widening Participation	191
	To Be Educated and Share with My People	197
	Cultural Reproduction in the Historical World of the Ancient University	201
	Changes and Continuities: The Situation after 1940	206
	Conclusion	211
	Bibliography	212

Part III   Teachers and Teaching   215

9   Women in Teaching   217
    Feminisation and the Culture and Politics of Teachers' Work   220
    Pedagogies of Resistance: The Making of Kate Miriam Dice   226
    Education and Democracy: The Making of Florence Key   231
    Gender and Teaching in the Second Half of the Twentieth Century 236
    Conclusion   241
    Bibliography   243

10 Gender Struggles   245
    Women's Liberation: The Breakthrough Generation?   247
    Co-education: The Real Issue?   252
    Inside the Comprehensive Secondary School: Programmes for Boys 257
    Policy Strategies: The Feminist Touch?   261
    Conclusion   267
    Bibliography   268

11 Conclusion: Constancy and Change in the Twenty-First
    Century   273
    Bibliography   284

Appendix: Important and Influential Public Events   287

Index   295

LIST OF FIGURES

Fig. 1.1	UWT/D/37/1 Handbill produced by the NUWT, c.1950. From the Records of the National Union of Women Teachers. UCL Institute of Education Special Collections. (Copyright UCL Special Collections)	12
Fig. 3.1	Upton House Truant School, children cleaning boots in playground, 1904. From the London Picture Archive. (Copyright London Metropolitan Archive, 209340)	68
Fig. 4.1	ABB/A/13/6b Typing lesson, Belper Secondary Modern, c1953. From the Photographic Archive of the Architects and Building Branch, Ministry of Education and its successors. UCL Institute of Education Special Collections. (Crown Copyright)	95
Fig. 4.2	ABB/A/20/16a Boys' woodwork class, Armitage Street School Manchester, c1967. From the Photographic Archive of the Architects and Building Branch, Ministry of Education and its successors. UCL Institute of Education Special Collections. (Crown Copyright)	96
Fig. 6.1	First London School Board showing male and female members attending a meeting, John Whitehead Walton (fl.1831–1885). From the London Picture Archive. (Copyright London Metropolitan Archive, 14317)	139
Fig. 6.2	ABB/B/1/12/1d Girls' domestic science class, Mayfield Comprehensive, Wandsworth (ND). From the Photographic Archive of the Architects and Building Branch, Ministry of Education and its successors. UCL Institute of Education Special Collections. (Crown Copyright)	151
Fig. 7.1	Denmark Hill School housewifery class, 1908. From the London Picture Archive. (Copyright London Metropolitan Archive, 178925)	175
Fig. 9.1	Stockwell College, undated, [c. late nineteenth century]. (Courtesy of Brunel University London Archives)	226

Fig. 9.2   Portrait of Mrs Florence E. Key, Member of the Council 1927–51 and President 1932, UWT/G/1/14, from the records of the National Union of Women Teachers. (Courtesy of UCL Institute of Education Special Collections)   232

Fig. 9.3   UWT/H/10, cover of Emily Phipps 'History of the NUWT,' 1928, from the records of the National Union of Women Teachers. Institute of Education Special Collections. (Copyright UCL Special Collections)   235

LIST OF TEXT BOXES

Text Box 2.1	Pearl Jephcott, Sociologist, Curriculum Vitae	44
Text Box 6.1	Female Members of the London School Board, 1870–1904	140
Text Box 7.1	Life writers by cohort or generation	165
Text Box 9.1	Memorandum Sent by the London Unit of the NUWT on the Employment of Married Women as Teachers	222
Text Box 9.2	The Teaching Career of Kate Dice	227

CHAPTER 1

A Chronological Introduction

> *Education is painful. Few people enjoy much of it, still fewer the whole process. Most of us remember it as a period of captivity, of frustration, of boredom, lit, if we are fortunate, by moments of particular happiness. Others recall it with passionate hatred. 'No power on earth,' said Lord Salisbury who was prime minister in Queen Victoria's reign, when asked to visit Eton, 'would induce me to go back even for a single afternoon to that existence among devils that I remember as a boy.' But he sent his own son to Eton; where else could a Cecil be sent?*
> —Gillian Avery, "Introduction," in *School Remembered*, ed. Gillian Avery (London: Victor Gollancz, 1967), 7

The story of how ideas of gender, culture and power were woven into the fabric of English education is a long and intricate one. Charting that history and, in the process, bringing the past into a critical dialogue with the present are this book's central aims. In looking beyond the 'school' as the only site of educational knowledge production and consumption, the narrative complicates the dominant historical tradition. At each juncture, the account is not just of 'Big History' written from the perspective of the powerful in modern British political history. Oral testimonies, autobiographies and sociological ethnographies sit alongside documentary sources as a way of recalling the everyday worlds of teachers and learners who populated the new and evolving educational settings. The intention being to curate activities, institutions and social movements from the past, to restore people and questions that have been obscured or forgotten and to bring the politics of experience to the fore. Also, to present an interpretation of how new principles and rationales merge with old ones to see what stays the same and what changes.

The impetus behind my writing is a desire to understand and recover not simply my own family history but the histories of generations of people, the life chances of individuals and social groups, and the set of opportunities open to them. Growing up in a twentieth century garden city, I noticed a tendency for boys to leave my state primary school as their parents moved them into private schooling, but I accepted the loss without recognising the structural inequalities based on the intersection of class and gender in spatial terms. Neither did I question it when a female friend at my state-maintained comprehensive secondary school told me her brothers were being educated at one of the leading fee-paying schools in the country. The making of the feminine through single-sex lessons in cookery and needlework, including overt messages about dress, deportment and etiquette, seemed pointless but laughable and while I dreamed of being an architect was dissuaded when told that technical drawing was a 'boy's subject.' As was my mum when she raised the issue at a parent's evening. Few people in a social and cultural landscape with persisting beliefs about what boys/men and girls/women should and should not do thought to challenge the status quo.

In 2019, Caroline Criado Perez's bestseller *Invisible Women* exposed a data gap that is at the root of perpetual, systemic discrimination, and has created a pervasive but invisible bias with a profound effect on people's lives.[1] It is a smart strategy, therefore, to look to the past to develop understandings of gender today, which I define as a social identity originating in the individual, including a deep-seated psychological state, as the result of cultural, social and environmental influences. Judith Butler's *Bodies That Matter*, first published in 1993, showed the power at play in statements expressing the sex–gender distinction in the 'girling' and 'boying' of bodies.[2] 'It's a girl!' or 'It's a boy!' is the first in a set of linguistic practices that define the place of a child within a sexed and gendered culture. Colour-coded baby clothes, packaged toy sets and product lines in stereotypical colours and structures (LEGO is a case in point), computer algorithms and micro-profiling all work to sustain common sense, predicting and moulding our behaviour (if you like that, you'll love this).

The wider sense of context and action that this book explores lies in C. Wright Mills's vision of the 'sociological imagination' that enables us to reflect critically upon the moment at which individual lives and social structures intersect. Using biographical approaches to explore the experience of hidden groups and using the term life history to suggest a deeper contextualisation of time and place than biography, my historical writing brings hitherto marginalised moments and experiences to the fore.[3] In the pages that follow, I refer to different kinds of materials that have been my companion texts in this exploration of school remembered. As an undergraduate, for instance, the first thing that struck me when I read Carol Dyhouse's book *Girls Growing Up in Late-Victorian and Edwardian England* was an awareness that it was the first

---

[1] Caroline Criado Perez, *Invisible Women: Exposing Data Bias in a World Designed for Men* (London: Chatto & Windus, 2019).
[2] Judith Butler, *Bodies That Matter: On The Discursive Limits of 'Sex'* (New York: Routledge, 1993).
[3] C.W. Mills, *The Sociological Imagination* (Oxford: Oxford University Press, 1959).

to offer me a past that I could call my own.[4] Bringing back family stories of my maternal great-grandmother, Agnes Ashman, who cooked and cleaned for an elderly Mary Paley Marshall who was one of the first women to gain a Cambridge education and became the university's first female residential lecturer in economics at Newnham College in 1875.

Context matters. Gendering the story of the ideas and decisions which led to an increasing involvement by the state in the provision of working-class education can only be understood in relation to wider economic, social, cultural and political factors to offer a critical overarching perspective of the relationship between class, gender and schooling and other social institutions, events and processes. To begin to construct an alternate imaginary, I examine periods of history in terms of considerations of gender to put forward a theory of social change in relation to both the parallel aspects of men's and women's history and the institutions and social developments that shape the social order. My movements through time and space disrupt linear narratives of progress in favour of histories of contradiction and ambiguity as I interpret the fractured and uneven forms and content of education for children, used to prepare them (by and large) for different and unequal societal roles productive of class, gender, race and ethnic-based inequalities.

To take account of changes that have taken place in English society over the last 250 years, I start with a necessarily brief overview to see how different lives and different events mesh with each other. My purpose is to map long-term historical trends and patterns to ease temporal interpretation but with no attempt to offer the detail and specificity, that is the hallmark of later chapters. Here I make use of global and historic generalisations, which is good for highlighting some aspects but means I am obliged to leave out much of importance. The narrative is chronological to exhibit patterns of continuity and change over time, and the question of gender provides order and coherence to my vistas. Therefore, the sections that follow are intended to give shape and meaning to the larger history presented in the material of this book. Key themes are 1) Enlightenment, industrial capitalism and the sexual division of labour. 2) Resistance, socio-political movements and universal basic education. 3) Social democracy and the neoliberal crisis.

THEME ONE: ENLIGHTENMENT, INDUSTRIAL CAPITALISM AND THE SEXUAL DIVISION OF LABOUR

My periodisation begins with the European Enlightenment and the French Revolution of 1789. In an intellectual climate dominated by men, London was one of a set of city spaces where a network of contacts clustered as contemporary liberalism was forced to reconsider what ideas like individual freedom, independence and responsibility meant in practice. Although learning in the

---

[4] Carol Dyhouse, *Girls Growing Up In Late Victorian and Edwardian England* (London: Routledge, Kegan and Paul, 1981).

female sex was largely abhorred and the term feminism had not been coined, proto-feminists would extend Enlightenment faith in reason, science and progress to make the case for women's rights, notably Mary Wollstonecraft who turned to teaching and writing in order to make a living as her violent father gradually squandered the family fortune.[5]

Education was central to Wollstonecraft's life and thought. Born in 1759, she had a strong inclination for self-improvement, rooted partly in religious imperatives besides the need for some kind of economic security. Bitter at the lack of formal schooling given her as compared with her brother, she thought this was her one chance of an independent life. In one of the earliest works of feminist philosophy, *A Vindication of The Rights of Woman* published in 1792, Wollstonecraft faced the challenge of making the case for female access to the resources that had allowed men to become socially respected and acknowledged intellectuals:

> I will allow that bodily strength seems to give man a natural superiority over women; and this is the only solid basis on which the superiority of the sex can be built. But I still insist that not only the virtue but the *knowledge* of the two sexes should be the same in nature if not in degree, and that women considered not only as moral but rational creatures, ought to endeavour to acquire human virtues (or perfections) by the *same* means as men, instead of being educated like a fanciful kind of *half* being.[6]

Wollstonecraft's equal rights feminism aimed to extend to women the same rights and privileges as men on the basis that they, too, are rational beings who only appear to be inferior to men because they lack formal education. For her, education was not only a natural right for both sexes but would make women better wives and mothers since it would give them the mental discipline to ensure they were not flighty and frivolous. Viewed through the lens of the time, her tempestuous private life (her affair with a married man, her attempts at sustaining a ménage à trois and giving birth to an illegitimate child) helped ensure her almost complete neglect after her death in childbirth in 1797. Half a century later, the mid-Victorian metropolitan women's movement would reclaim her thought and praxis to show how women whose economic resources were limited could claim intellectual and moral authority and a public voice.

Changes broadly associated with what we now call the First Industrial Revolution were another part of the greater whole affecting the basis and structure of relations between men and women and the connection between

---

[5] See Barbara Taylor, *Mary Wollstonecraft and the Feminist Imagination* (Cambridge: Cambridge University Press, 2003; Lyndall Gordon, *Vindication: A Life of Mary Wollstonecraft* (London: Virago, 2006); Joyce Senders Pedersen, "Women and Agency: the educational legacy of Mary Wollstonecraft," in *Women, Education and Agency*, ed. Jean Spence, Sarah Aiston, Maureen Meikle (London: Routledge, 2010), 27-48.

[6] Mary Wollstonecraft, *A Vindication of the Rights of Women* (London: Vintage, [1792] 2015), 26.

these and social and economic organisation and institutional arrangements. One influential account of English economic growth suggests the interaction of ideology and culture influenced the organisation of production through shaping the economic behaviour of key individuals (artisans, entrepreneurs, inventors and thinkers) and thus influencing the spread of capitalist enterprise.[7] Enlightenment political economist Adam Smith, for instance, proposed that British manufacturing could succeed in expanding markets with the rest of the world through innovations like the increasing division of labour to speed up productivity. Worried about the impact of this change, particularly its potential for producing social instability through forcing workers to repeat boring, mundane tasks as part of a mechanised production process, Smith also argued that governments had a responsibility to provide education.

Early capitalist development in England was agrarian in form, and the process of changing to a mechanised, factory-based economy was long, slow and uneven. In an era of what historians' call 'gentlemanly capitalism' dominated by land and financial services, the effect of the Enclosure Movement—the removal of common property rights to areas of ground that accelerated between 1750 and 1850—was to clear labourers and tenant farmers from the rural landscape. With the passing years, a high-intensity agricultural system based on arable crops displaced a low-intensity agricultural system based on fishing and fowling. As the proportion of agricultural workers fell, the proportion working in industry and services rose, helping make industrial capitalism with its smoking chimneys, iron, coal and steel possible.[8] Artisans lost skills and control over their trade as they fought to retain traditional techniques and customs and to keep out unskilled entrants. The decline of some domestic industries, particularly hand spinning, aggravated the situation as cottage industry gradually ceased to be viable.

Among other things, the socio-economic changes associated with the development of industrial capitalism buttressed a gendered workforce. Many working-class women who wanted to engage in paid work or who had to for financial reasons experienced public forms of patriarchy, that is, of male power and control in their paid work. Strategies of exclusion and segregation based on traditional value systems of male superiority and female inferiority operated as a major cultural precondition for the accommodation of family values and structures with the organisation of economic production. The cheap 'competition' of working women was seen to threaten the job security, wage levels and the status of men, both as skilled workers and husbands and fathers providing for their families. Thus, the characteristic factory employment for women in textile production was that of weaving, which did not become a 'skilled' factory occupation whereas male spinning did. Analyses of the home and the workplace demonstrated class struggle took a highly gendered form

---

[7] Joel Mokyr, *The Enlightened Economy* (Harmondsworth: Penguin, 2009).
[8] Mark Overton, *Agricultural Revolution in England: the Transformation of the Agrarian Economy 1500-1850* (Cambridge: Cambridge University Press, 1996).

linked to the logic of a 'breadwinner wage,' which was substantial enough for a man to keep his wife and young children out of the labour market altogether.[9]

Globally, British industrial capitalism and imperial rule drove the expansion of slavery that led to long and painful regimes of exploitation: metropolitan waged labour, directly owned British Caribbean and Mauritian slavery, and American Deep South slavery.[10] New and contrasting racialised orders of hierarchy and inequality emerged and were entrenched, the legacies of which are present today. In the metropole, this epochal change also helped create one of Europe's most mobile workforces as young girls went to work as servants in richer households. The so-called feminization of service was in evidence from the mid-seventeenth century, and by 1850, approximately 80 per cent of servants in middle-class households were women. Indeed, domestic service remained the largest single female occupation until at least 1945.[11]

By the 1830s, industrialisation had brought significant population growth and migration to areas where trading and manufacturing were creating new jobs. In the first three decades of the nineteenth century, cities like Birmingham, Leeds, Liverpool and Manchester more than doubled in size, bringing insanitary housing and disease in their wake. At the same time, the expansion of trade and manufacture brought an increase in the size, wealth and influence of the urban middle class, accompanied by the demise of the traditional household economy in which all, male or female, played their part. Gender norms positioned gentry and educated middle-ranking women in ways that meant they were socially and culturally responsible for the young. Victorian males were to be active in the world whether as professional, propertied or labouring men. Status as a 'gentleman' followed from the ability to support a dependent wife and children in leisure.

In the pre-industrial period, the dominant form of patriarchy was private patriarchy. Women presided over hearth and home, and at the same time assisted the men of a family or community in the processes of production. Industrialisation disrupted and shattered this. On the one hand, middle-class men increasingly sought to confine their wives to the domestic scene, and it was thought necessary for their self-respect to do so. On the other, in specific localities and circumstances, working-class men might find themselves threatened and displaced by cut-price female factory labour. The results were times of acute social disturbance and turmoil about male and female functions with shifts in the balance between and intensity of patriarchal structures and

---

[9] See, for example, Judy Lown, *Women and Industrialisation: gender at work in nineteenth century England* (Cambridge: Cambridge University Press, 1990); Emma Griffin, *Bread Winner: an Intimate History of the Victorian Economy* (Yale University Press: New Haven and London, 2020), 3.

[10] See, for example, Mark Harvey, "Slavery, Indenture and the Development of British Industrial Capitalism', *History Workshop Journal*, 88 (autumn 2019), 68-88; Eric Williams, *Capitalism and Slavery* (Chapel Hill: University of North Carolina Press, 1994).

[11] Alison Light, *Mrs Woolf and the Servants: An Intimate History of Domestic Life in Bloomsbury* (London: Bloomsbury, 2008), xv.

processes within the household, paid labour, the state and cultural institutions, including education.¹²

In mid-Victorian England, the cult of domesticity that travelled through society began to re-define patriarchy in families and workplaces. If working-class women in places like industrial Lancashire developed a tradition of wage earning this did not generally happen outside of textiles, potteries and paper factories. In daily life, the assumption that men and women were biologically and psychologically different legitimated a trade union ideal of a 'breadwinner wage' and depressed female pay. Social and religious beliefs, medical practice and scientific practice, all posed benevolence, compassion, humility, modesty, morality, patience, sensitivity and tact as among women's 'special' traits. Moreover, it was assumed that a combination of maternal capacity, physical frailty and sexual vulnerability placed women in need of care and protection through the presence of a male who provided the economic foundation of any family unit. Fathers were supposed to be breadwinners, and most mothers received their share in the wealth created by industrialisation through the hands of their husbands and older children. Indeed, the ideology of a male breadwinner-family model closed many avenues for women to earn a living wage for themselves.

THEME TWO: RESISTANCE, SOCIO-POLITICAL MOVEMENTS AND UNIVERSAL BASIC EDUCATION

Industrial capitalism brought class-consciousness to a new level and intensity. Historian Edward Thompson wrote of how articulate, freeborn Englishmen 'came to feel an identity of interests as between themselves, and as against their ruler and employers' in his influential masterpiece *The Making of The English Working Class*, first published in 1963.¹³ In 1824, for example, the repeal of the Combination Laws permitted workers to set up trade-based bodies, which offered limited forms of collective protection. Almost contemporaneously, importing the outlook of Robert Owen, Owenite socialism nourished a radical agenda, advocating a new economic and social order, which stressed co-operation and harmony rather than competition and discord. Owen thought the environment shaped personality and behaviour, and the classless, co-operative community represented the ideal circumstance for the development of happy and moral lives. He argued also that the unequal distribution of property had as its foundation the unequal distribution of knowledge.¹⁴

---

¹²Sylvia Walby, *Theorizing Patriarchy* (Oxford: Oxford University Press, 1992); Meg Gomersall, *Working-Class Girls in Nineteenth Century England: Life, Work and Schooling* (Basingstoke: Macmillan, 1997).

¹³E.P. Thompson, *The Making of the English Working Class* (Harmondsworth: Penguin, 1968), 12.

¹⁴Barbara Taylor, *Eve and the New Jerusalem* (London: Virago, 1983).

Chartism, a movement to gain political rights and influence for the working classes, dominated British domestic politics in the later 1830s and 1840s. Disgust at the provisions of the 1832 Reform Act, a corrupt political establishment and the harshness of the 1834 Poor Law Amendment Act intensified popular unrest. In this period, Chartists and other reformers developed a vigorous and varied educational practice, which included formal provision in secular schools as well as informal schooling through the mechanism of radical culture. Ideas discussed in workplaces, pubs and meetings, often from items read out from the radical working-class press, fostered a specific class sensibility that rejected the imposition of schooling and allied cultural forms judged to have been provided *for* them, by the middle class, and thus in some way alien to the interests of the working-class community. Chartist Halls and Halls of Science were built as meeting places, but much of the organised education took place in Sunday schools re-appropriated by working people. By the 1850s, loss of confidence in the immediate political prospects of the People's Charter led a new generation to demand educational institutions funded by the state rather than by faith groups, notably Anglicans.[15]

The Co-operative Movement was another means by which skilled workers associated with the growing trade union movement and with long-standing attachments to the values of self-organisation and self-reliance sought protection. Originating in the north of England, co-operatives provided goods and services via their shops and thanks to their collective purchasing power and supply chains that included their own factories; they protected their members from price swings and profiteering. Despite re-forged links between socialism and feminism within co-operation, men and women had different experiences. In theory, societies ran on democratic lines, allocating one vote to each member and distributing their trading surplus as a dividend proportional to spending. In practice, women generally shopped at the co-op stores and collected the 'divi,' whereas men held the membership of the society. Yet the Women's Cooperative Guild, established in 1883, grew into a formidable rank-and-file organisation that helped shape a range of social legislation from birth control, child health, divorce reform, employment and equal pay, housing policy, maternity, social security and pensions.

Changes made in the British political system between 1832 and 1884 enfranchised male property-owners while denying the vote to millions of working-class men and all women. Class-conscious activity flared in London's Trafalgar Square in 1886 and 1887 as socialist propagandists helped to organise protest at suffering in the wake of economic depression and harsh weather. In London's East End, successful industrial action by women workers at Bryant and May's match factory triggered further strikes and unionisation among

---

[15] See Richard Johnson, "Really Useful Knowledge: Radical Education and Working Class Culture" in *Working-Class Culture* eds. John Clarke, Chas Critcher and Richard Johnson (London: Hutchinson, 1980), 75-102; Jane Martin, *Mary Bridges Adams and the Fight for Knowledge and Power, 1855-1939* (Manchester: Manchester University Press, 2013).

unskilled workers.[16] Poverty was a provocative question present, for instance, in novels like *Oliver Twist* (1839), *Hard Times* (1854) and *Great Expectations* (1861) by writer and social critic Charles Dickens. Social writings like *The Bitter Cry of Outcast London* by the Congregational minister and author Andrew Mearns, first published in pamphlet form in 1883, expressed a late-Victorian 'moral geography' that understood personal character and physical surroundings to be intimately interlinked. Nowhere was the geographic division between wealth and want as complete as in the metropolis although personal lives and experiences sometimes crossed as intrepid urban explorers and commentators shared lurid and sensational tales of a dark and mysterious underworld.

Outcast London was another country—both in the literature of the 'high imperial' period and in its politics. Communities grew up around particular trades, and labour historians have emphasised the complex pattern of class polarisation and residential segregation in the capital, while the coming of the railway, office building and slum clearance exacerbated overcrowding. Threats to public order haunted the liberal intelligentsia, and the theme of a metropolis at risk became an important part of London's political culture. Just as the treating of non-Western cultures as Other played a crucial role in organising ideas of race and civilisation, so the new representational taxonomy of what can be termed 'domestic colonialism' operated at two interconnected levels: the depiction of impoverished neighbourhoods as 'dark' and 'hostile' places and the representation of sections of the urban poor as 'primitive tribes,' 'savages' or 'races' apart. Although essentially different, this Other was split into two camps: the 'worthy' and the 'unworthy' poor who were deemed feckless, shifty and vice-ridden.

In response, the wealthy Liverpudlian Charles Booth who had made a fortune from his family's shipping firm hired a team of social investigators to produce the first major poverty survey. His assistants included Beatrice Webb (née Potter), co-founder of the London School of Economics (LSE) and Octavia Hill whose philanthropic work was an influential model for social housing projects and open spaces for poor people. Starting in the East End, Booth's investigations built a detailed picture of life in London's poor neighbourhoods. The result was the creation of innovative maps, coloured street by street, to indicate income levels. A critical moment in the birth of applied social science and searching questions about the well-being of the whole society, the revelations reinforced demands from the socialist and anarchist groupings of the 1880s and 1890s. Liberals, radicals, trade unionists and philanthropists lobbying for local change and state action to support the 30 per cent, including wage earners, judged to be living without adequate means for a decent subsistence. The measuring rod for Booth's definition of urban poverty was whether people were in regular employment, how they

---

[16] Louise Raw, *Striking a Light: the Bryant and May Matchwomen and their Place in History* (London: Bloomsbury, 2011).

spent their leisure time and whether their income was enough to buy the items he thought were necessary for a modest life.[17]

Women played an important part in this pressure for change. The voluntary sector and various types of self-help in communities enabled female reformers to gain an understanding of social problems—applying their so-called domestic skills to the task of 'municipal housekeeping.' At the same time, a self-propelled female vanguard sought a wider social and political role once the Municipal Franchise Act of 1869 restored the local vote to women ratepayers (a right they had lost in 1835). From the 1870s, British women served on locally elected school boards, which established and administered elementary schools and the boards of Poor Law unions. Within this context, women of relatively high social status were able to overcome opposition to make substantial changes to the policy and fabric of services for basic needs. Emmeline Pankhurst exemplified this pioneering spirit. Between 1894 and 1898, she campaigned as a member of the Independent Labour Party on the Chorlton Board of Guardians improving conditions in the local workhouse, and in 1900, she was elected to the Manchester School Board. When the Conservatives' 1902 Education Act dissolved the School Boards and assigned control over elementary schools to urban district or county councils that did not yet include women, Pankhurst responded by founding the Women's Social and Political Union (WSPU), with the slogan 'deeds, not words,' to secure women's right to vote.

British writer Edith Ayrton Zangwill crystallised women's bid for new identities, new relationships and demands for political rights in her novel of 1924 *The Call*. The stepdaughter of Hertha Ayrton, most probably the first female professional electrical engineer, she and Hertha were members of the WSPU, and she skirts around aspects of Hertha's life in her story about a pioneering woman scientist—Ursula Winfield—who abandons her research work as she is drawn inexorably and with increasing militancy into the women's movement before the First World War began in 1914. As Ursula puts it to her fiancée in the closing pages, 'I had to fight in the woman's Cause. It seemed a sort of—Call, and I nearly died for it. And you had to fight in the war, that was a Call, too, and you nearly died for it. And now, I suppose, we are called to each other; not to die, but to live.'[18] In a more light-hearted way, journalist Mary Stott recollected the suffragette mother of one childhood acquaintance of hers 'who took a pair of scissors with her on demonstrations and snipped the braces of any policemen who tried to restrain her!'[19]

---

[17] Jane Martin, *Women and the Politics of Schooling in Victorian and Edwardian England* (Leicester: Leicester University Press, 1999), 33-34.

[18] Edith Ayrton Zangwill, *The Call* (London: Persephone Books, 2018), 423.

[19] Mary Stott, *Forgetting's No Excuse: the autobiography of Mary Stott* (London: Virago, 1989), 29.

In 1918, the Representation of the People Act was passed which extended the right to vote to virtually all the adult male population plus women over the age of 30 who met a property qualification. This excluded about two million women who were either lodgers, live-in domestic servants or shop assistants, daughters or sisters living in a parent's or siblings home or mothers living with an adult child.[20] Women had success as candidates in local elections, less so nationally. The first woman to take her seat in Parliament, in 1919, was the Conservative Nancy Astor. The Liberal Margaret Wintringham joined her in 1920, and they both won again in 1922. But it was not until the Equal Franchise Act of 1928 that women over the age of 21 were entitled to vote and women except for British wives of aliens achieved the same voting rights as men. On 30 May 1929, women aged between 21 and 29 voted in a general election for the first time. Mary Stott wore a red dress for the occasion, 'a little disappointed that putting a cross on a bit of paper was so undramatic.'[21]

Often, the apparent birth of social democracy in Britain is associated with the beginnings of a 'welfare state' in the early twentieth century. From 1906, a Liberal government introduced the first state pensions, together with national insurance schemes covering some people in times of sickness and unemployment (on the breadwinner-family model) and a more redistributive taxation system to fund the extension of state action. Introduced by a Labour backbencher, a Bill allowing but not yet obliging local authorities to provide free meals for needy schoolchildren introduced a new principle in social legislation by recognising that parents were not generally culpable for child poverty and that many on low incomes needed help caring for their children. Medical inspection became compulsory in 1907, partly as a result of the social panic about working-class health the Boer War stimulated in 1899. However, even during the Great Depression of the 1930s, only 4 per cent of schoolchildren had free meals, with 15 per cent of schools offering no meals at all.[22]

During the First World War, women found themselves doing work which was comparable to men's as they swept into factory and office work to substitute for men on active service. The need for women's labour meant that ideas of equality came to seem credible. Indeed, equal pay was being claimed as a right by striking women transport workers and unionised women teachers. But when the war ended, the peacetime Liberal government fulfilled wartime pledges to male trade unionists by removing women from better-paid industrial work because the soldiers were returning. By 1921, the proportion of women in the

---

[20] See Pat Thane, *Divided Kingdom: A History of Britain, 1900 to the Present* (Cambridge: Cambridge University Press) for a discussion of the 1920s context.

[21] Pat Thane, "The British Imperial State and the Construction of National Identities," in *Borderlines: Genders and Identities in War and Peace, 1870-1930*, ed. Billie Melman, (New York: Routledge, 1998), 29-45; Mary Stott, *Forgetting's No Excuse*, 30.

[22] Brian Simon, *Education and the Labour Movement, 1870-1920* (London: Lawrence and Wishart, 1980); Chris Renwick, *Bread for All: The Origins of the Welfare State* (London: Allen Lane, 2017), 102.

labour force was the same as it had been in 1911.[23] A growing number of women's trade unions, professional, confessional and single-issue groups promoted women's political awareness, and the 1919 Sex Discrimination (Removal) Act was an early response to women's campaigns. A few largely middle-class women gained access to the professions and the exercise of any public function, but many more were excluded from paid work in the 1920s and 1930s, especially when married and mothers. By now feminists in the National Union of Teachers had had enough. Enraged at the failure to support equal pay, they established an independent body, the National Union of Women Teachers, in 1920 (see Fig. 1.1).

One labour market shift that *did* survive the war was the growing numbers of women entering 'white-collar jobs' as both the business world and the public sector expanded. Over the course of 70 years from 1851 to 1911, the proportion of clerks in the workforce quadrupled, while the number of women in

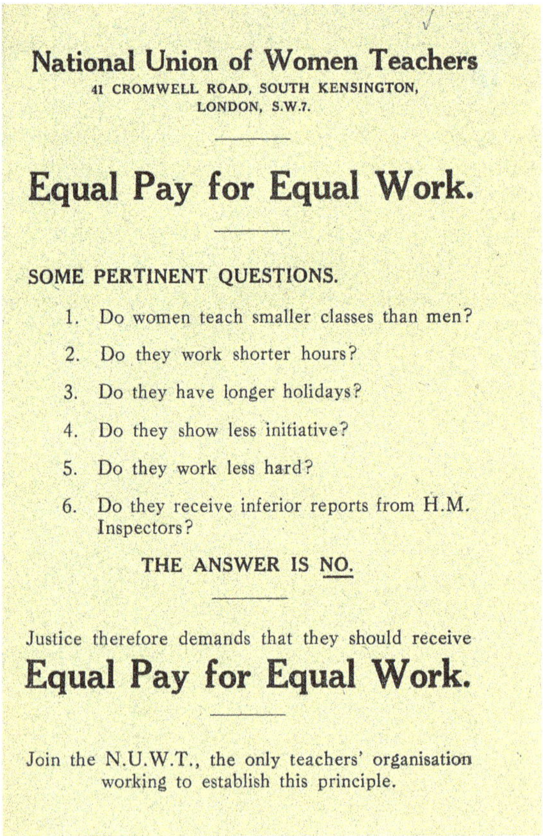

Fig. 1.1 UWT/D/37/1 Handbill produced by the NUWT, c.1950. From the Records of the National Union of Women Teachers. UCL Institute of Education Special Collections. (Copyright UCL Special Collections)

National Union of Women Teachers
41 CROMWELL ROAD, SOUTH KENSINGTON,
LONDON, S.W.7.

Equal Pay for Equal Work.

SOME PERTINENT QUESTIONS.

1. Do women teach smaller classes than men?
2. Do they work shorter hours?
3. Do they have longer holidays?
4. Do they show less initiative?
5. Do they work less hard?
6. Do they receive inferior reports from H.M. Inspectors?

THE ANSWER IS NO.

Justice therefore demands that they should receive

Equal Pay for Equal Work.

Join the N.U.W.T., the only teachers' organisation working to establish this principle.

---

[23] Susan Pedersen, *Eleanor Rathbone and the Politics of Conscience* (New Haven and London: Yale University Press, 2004), 178.

the occupation rocketed from 2 to 20 per cent.²⁴ At the same time, the more highly educated women workers were moving into academia, the civil service and the professions. However, mounting unemployment in the 1920s enabled many private firms, as well as government departments and local authorities to call for the termination of the employment of a woman on her marriage. The BBC and the John Lewis (department store) Partnership were unusual in having no marriage bar and providing equal pay and opportunities, at least in principle. Amid great bitterness at the thought of two incomes going into one home, women workers were frequently presented with domestic service as the sole alternative to unemployment.

In her 1929 novel *Clash*, female MP Ellen Wilkinson would describe contemporary attitudes. It is May 1926 and Joan Craig, a young trade union organiser, is busy mustering support for the General Strike. Bloomsbury writer Anthony Dacre, a married suitor, worries about Joan's assertion of rights and personhood. 'We hear a lot about women's rights these days,' he tells her. Let us talk about the men's side for a bit. A woman cannot have everything. He can understand independent women, like her, hating it 'when getting married was a woman's only hope of a decent status.' He can also understand, 'how when chances opened out, when they were allowed to work and do things, how they must have revelled in it.' However, making a home is not a 'side-line,' something 'any intelligent woman could do in any odd moments, provided she could earn enough to pay a housekeeper and a nurse. It doesn't work, my dear. I *know*. Loving your mate and bearing his children and bringing them up is a whole-time job.'²⁵

Many union men agreed with Dacre and, in redundancy situations, demanded the sacking of married women first. In a context of high unemployment, a 'marriage bar' was widely introduced and almost universally applied, although it was never the subject of central government legislation. There were limits on the hours and type of paid (but not unpaid) work considered suitable for women, and unemployed training programmes included women on very different terms and conditions to men.²⁶ Complaints about being pushed into service were heard at a Trades Union Congress conference of unemployed women in 1922, while Mary Stott learned all about the Means Test as a reporter for the *Bolton Evening News*, which made her sharply critical of how doctors decided what was enough for a single person to maintain health. In her reports, she was aware of 'women who never went to the doctors despite prolapses and cancer fears,' who bought cheap glasses 'and never had their bad teeth attended

---

²⁴ Meta Zimmeck, "Jobs for the Girls: the Expansion of Clerical Work for Women, 150-1914" in *Unequal Opportunities. Women's Employment in England 1800-1918* ed. Angela John (Oxford: Basil Blackwell, 1986), 154.
²⁵ Ellen Wilkinson, *Clash* (London: Virago, 1989 [1929]), 179-80.
²⁶ Celia Briar, *Working for Women? Gendered Work and Welfare Policies in Twentieth-Century Britain* (London: UCL Press, 1997), 54-60.

to because they couldn't afford it. Those were the days of "Love on the Dole" and the hunger marches.'²⁷

Inside Parliament, the 'women's legislation' of the 1920s improved women's access to divorce, the guardianship of children, separation and maintenance allowances from abusive husbands and pensions. The demand for an allowance for mothers became a lifetime's cause for the feminist Eleanor Rathbone whose work on the Liverpool Board of Guardians convinced her that poverty perpetuated problems in working-class families. The guiding spirit of the National Union of Societies for Equal Citizenship, Rathbone's campaign provoked anxiety among some trade unionists, feminist and socialist women who feared it might result in lowered wages by under-cutting the breadwinner wage and that men would vanish and leave mothers to parent alone. The failure of the 1924 minority Labour government to carry out its pledges to extend the franchise to women on the same terms as men and pass bills for mothers' pensions and equal guardianship rights compounded her scepticism about a political alliance with Labour.²⁸ In 1925, the feminist Six Point Group commented that the members of the Labour government 'not only failed to do anything whatsoever to forward it [feminism] when it was in their power to do so easily but have actually gone out of their way to obstruct it.'²⁹

Within the Labour Party, women mounted unsuccessful campaigns for birth control and family allowances. Beyond the national corridors of power, they got through local provisions on housing and social politics in their communities that contributed very greatly to reforms that became the foundation of the welfare state.³⁰ Stott later recalled that she identified with the feminist campaigners of the 1930s and involved herself in Left politics. She read Ray Strachey's history of the women's suffrage movement in her early 20s and found heroines who stayed with her all her life, including Mary Wollstonecraft with her banner line, 'The first object of laudable ambition is obtain a character as a human being, regardless of sex.' Stott's work contacts with Conservative 'ladies' shocked her. 'It is no use giving the working classes council houses; they will keep coal in the bath and gradually turn them into slums. They don't know any better,' they complained.³¹

The visions and struggles of mid-twentieth century socialists and feminists show that class was not outstandingly salient and gender insignificant in the making of the British welfare state. Their social action contributed towards a sea change in the climate of opinion that helped produce the great electoral

---

[27] Mary Stott, *Forgetting's No Excuse*, 31.

[28] Susan Pedersen, *Eleanor Rathbone and the Politics of Conscience* (New Haven and London: Yale University Press, 2004), 186, 201-4.

[29] Pamela Graves, *Labour Women: Women in British Working-Class Politics 1918-1939* (Cambridge: Cambridge University Press, 1994), 121.

[30] Ibid; Pat Thane, "Women in the British Labour Party and the Construction of State Welfare, 1906-1939" in *Mothers of a New World: Maternalist Politics and the Origins of Welfare States* eds. Seth Koven and Sonya Michel (New York: Routledge, 1993), 343-377.

[31] Mary Stott, *Forgetting's No Excuse*, 30, 131.

tide of 1945 which saw Clement Attlee's Labour Party win the faith of the British people 12 weeks after Prime Minister Winston Churchill announced the unconditional surrender of Nazi Germany at the close of the Second World War. In the face of withdrawal of American economic aid, the Attlee governments (1945–51) sought to enact the 1942 Beveridge Report including reforms making the baby boom generation born between 1946 and 1965 the first to grow up taking free secondary education and free health care at the point of delivery for granted. Labour oversaw the creation of a welfare state in an era of optimism over the capacity of a managed economy to secure full (male) employment, decent housing and security for all: meaning that men could count on a family wage, and their wives dedicate themselves to bringing up children and building community spirit.[32]

THEME THREE: FROM SOCIAL DEMOCRACY TO NEOLIBERAL CRISIS

The Village, a 1952 novel by Marghanita Laski, opens on 8 May 1945, Victory in Europe day. With everyone rejoicing and dancing in the streets, Martha Trevor and Edith Wilson show up to their Red Cross post. Edith was Martha's 'charlady' or cleaner before the war, and their conversation is redolent of changing class and gender relations. Martha longs for the old social order and worries for her daughter's future. 'It *was* difficult, Edith could see that. In the ordinary way you'd expect someone like Miss Margaret to stay at home and go to tennis-parties and things until Mr Right came along and she could make a home of her own. But if you couldn't afford to keep a girl at home and there weren't any young men to meet at tennis parties, what *did* you do?' Margaret wants to become a cook, but her mother is hostile. '"Do you realise what you're proposing? You're suggesting that you—my daughter—go and live in somebody else's house as a servant at everyone's beck and call, sleeping in a maid's room, walking out with the butcher's boy mixing with low common"— Her anger; her disgust choked her.'[33]

In common with real places in the Home Counties, Laski's fictional village is in transition. Threatened by creeping suburbanisation, many of the gentry on the hill are less affluent than they were before 1939, although they still snobbishly look down on the residents of the working-class settlement below them. Edith Wilson is thinking of voting Labour and the social change she anticipates will reward those who succeed within the terms of a meritocratic education system in the following decades. In an era of full-male employment, these generations rode the economic and social wave created by the policies adopted to address inequality of condition—the inequality of resources that exists among families from different class backgrounds. Among other things,

---

[32] Dennis W. Dean, "Education for Moral Improvement, Domesticity and Social Cohesion: the Labour Government, 1945-51," *Oxford Review of Education*, 17, 3 (1991), 269-86.

[33] Marghanita Laski, *The Village* (London: Persephone Books, 2004), 13, 59.

the creation of a welfare state provided a very significant opportunity for rising up the social ladder of employment through the expansion of education, health and welfare services. Growth in the public and service sectors expanded the middle class by creating new management-level jobs into which working-class people (mostly men) could move and home ownership started to rise.[34]

University students first shaped the concept of youth culture in the 1920s, and there were urban working-class youth cultures in the 1930s, but it evolved under greater affluence and adolescents, particularly girls, gained a measure of autonomy. By the 1950s, the leisure habits of the affluent teenager had become a source of anxiety, and there was widespread fear over a rise in juvenile delinquency, largely defined as masculine. Researchers based at Birmingham University's Centre for Contemporary Cultural Studies (1964–2002) including Jamaican-born sociologist Stuart Hall pioneered academic studies and beyond the ivory tower, fan worship of the Beatles who emerged in 1963 helped embed the 'new' youth culture in people's minds.[35] In his leader's speech to the Labour Party conference that year, Harold Wilson pointed to the scientific revolution and persistent under-performance of British industry in the face of international competition. 'We simply cannot as a nation afford to neglect the educational development of a single boy or girl. We cannot afford to cut off three-quarters or more of our children from virtually any chance of higher education. The Russians do not, the Germans do not, the Americans do not, and the Japanese do not, and we cannot afford to either.'[36]

A grammar schoolboy who made it to Oxford on his own 'merits,' Wilson believed he embodied his case that Labour was the meritocratic, democratic future, and dismissed the aristocratic Conservatives as yesterday's men. Amid assertions that British society was too class-ridden, he denounced the Establishment for having demeaned Britain's influence in a world of superpowers and new economic groupings. Inefficiency, mismanagement, ignorance of modern business methods raised questions about leadership by men whose only claim was their privileged family connections or the power of inherited wealth or speculative finance. Added to which, labour shortages, technological considerations and a 'baby boom' prompted more wide-ranging considerations embodied in the assumption that 'upskilling' or the need to increase the skills of the workforce was essential to fulfil the talent needs of a rapidly changing economy. In terms of school education, consensus around human capital theory (the belief that expanding opportunities and access promotes growth), combined with forward-looking, technocratic rhetoric set the scene for change.

---

[34] Erzsébet Bukodi and John H. Goldthorpe, *Social Mobility and Education in Britain: Research, Politics and Policy* (Cambridge: Cambridge University Press, 2018); Chris Renwick, *Bread for All*.

[35] David Fowler, *Youth Culture in Modern Britain c. 1920- c. 1970* (Basingstoke: Palgrave Macmillan, 2008); Carol Dyhouse, *Girl Trouble* (London: Zed Books, 2013), 137-174; Stephanie Spencer, *Gender, Work and Education in Britain in the 1950s* (Basingstoke: Palgrave Macmillan, 2005).

[36] Harold Wilson, *The New Britain: Labour's Plan Outlined by Harold Wilson* (Harmondsworth: Penguin, 1964), 9.

Wilson scraped an election success in 1964, overturning a 100-seat Conservative majority to secure a tiny majority that he consolidated 2 years later.

Labour's reform programme included a commitment to comprehensive secondary schools and the abolition of academic selection, the raising of the school-leaving age to 16 and expansion of further and higher education. The 1970 Equal Pay Act and the 1975 Sex Discrimination Act were another layer to the liberal reforms that symbolised the era—on abortion, capital punishment, gay rights and theatre censorship. At the time of his resignation in 1976, Wilson presided over a country greatly more equal than it had been ever before or ever has been since. The 1975 Act purported to outlaw discrimination on the grounds of sex or marriage in employment, education, training, the provisions of goods and services and various other aspects of life. It also set up an Equal Opportunities Commission in Manchester, which was empowered to undertake research, foster public education in 'equality' practices and institute investigations into discrimination by firms or businesses.

Education would take the blame for at least some of the nation's ills as a global oil crisis produced a loop that brought an end to running the economy to ensure unemployment never rose above a particular level and saw the encroachment of neoliberal ideas. The initial response, under Wilson's third term as prime minister (1974–76), was to strengthen the corporate power of the state: controlling wages and prices and introducing regulatory employment policies. By the 1980s, this corporatist approach was giving way to radically different approaches pursued by movements and governments of the New Right following the election of Margaret Thatcher in May 1979.[37] The pulling apart of the social democratic consensus helped create a generation who came to see the welfare state as a cost to be kept down rather than part of an economic and social strategy that aims to deliver security for all and opportunities to obtain more for those who want to.

Thatcher's three terms as Conservative prime minister (1979–91) broke the terms of post-war British politics: with a shift away from the ideals of collective effort, full employment and a managed economy as an objective of all parties and all governments. A series of articles on British education called Black Papers (1969–77) were able to exert considerable influence in the polity with their critique of contemporary development in education, including theories of progressive education, and assertions that more has meant worse. For some, gender equity remained politically contentious despite the changing roles of women in economic and family life.[38] Patrick Jenkin, the Conservative Secretary of State for Social Services, went on record immediately after his appointment in 1979 as saying that: 'If the good Lord had intended us to have equal rights to go out and work, he wouldn't have created man and woman.'[39] Any formal

---

[37] Clyde Chitty, *Towards a New Education System: the Victory of the New Right?* (Lewes: Falmer, 1989).

[38] Miriam E. David, *Parents, Gender and Education Reform* (Cambridge: Polity Press, 1993).

[39] Georgina Ashworth and Lucy Bonnerjea, *The Invisible Decade: UK Women and the UN Decade* (Aldershot: Gower, 1985), 3.

legitimation of women's rights tended to come from UK membership of the European Union (EU 1973–2020) and its judicial authority.

The 1990s were a moment of disjuncture. Women were a closely watched group subjected to uneasy, triumphant attention. They were now deemed to 'have it all' and 'be everywhere' as waged employment altered in its nature and form and, in particular, in its association with masculinity in the wake of labour market restructuring from manufacturing to service sector work.[40] The latter, especially at the bottom end, demands care, deference and docility as key attributes of a desirable workplace identity: characteristics traditionally associated with femininity rather than masculinity. In the new millennium, policy paradigms and perspectives would reconceptualise gender reform's gendered subjects. As the spectre of redundant men and a notion of masculinity in crisis gained traction, young white working-class men were positioned as the new disadvantaged in the wake of a seeming reversal of long-standing relationships between gender and achievement. Against a backdrop of restructured education systems and attention given to the outperformance of boys in examinations, discourses of 'successful girls' versus 'failing boys' were pervasive in media and government discussions across the western world.[41]

Understanding continuity and difference means integrating gender as an organising concept. Historical perspectives show the longevity of many myths about the relative performance of boys and girls in the education system. Gendered vocabularies of practice, for example, can influence the production of facts to 'prove' the mathematical inferiority of girls. As can scientific research to 'prove' that girls and women cannot achieve parity with men because their minds and bodies are not up to it.[42] Intersectional approaches to interacting subjectivities must be the starting point from which we proceed to offer an account of how gendered power works.[43]

Today, the majority of those on zero-hour contracts (with poor pay and working conditions) are women, and the United Nations International Labour Organisation anticipates the COVID-19 economic downturn is likely to hit women hardest with informal female workers under greatest threat. Movement restrictions aimed to reduce the transmission of disease increased women's unpaid care work, made intimate partner violence in homes more frequent, more severe and more dangerous; while middle-aged men from poor backgrounds have been identified as potential 'hidden victims' of the pandemic because they are most at risk from suicide and the least likely to seek help.[44] Questions about gendered pathways from school into early adulthood, and

---

[40] Raewyn Connell, *Masculinities* (Berkeley, Los Angeles: University of California Press, 1995).

[41] Christine Skelton, "Gender and achievement: are girls the 'success stories' of restructured education systems?" *Gender and Education*, 62, no. 2 (2010), 131-142.

[42] Anita Sani, *Inferior* (London: 4th Estate, 2018).

[43] Sara Ahmed, *Living a Feminist Life* (Durham and London: Duke University Press, 2017).

[44] International Labour Organisation, "The COVID-19 response: Getting gender equality right for a better future for women at work, Policy Brief, May 2020; Mark Littleton, "Poorer middle-aged men most at risk from suicide in pandemic, say Samaritans," *Guardian*, 17 May 2020.

the associations between employment, consumption and gendered identities remain salient, as do high levels of sexual abuse, harassment and violence in our culture. Gender/power/politics informs gender/power/knowledge relations in education.

The ideas and arguments that I present are set out in three sections. Part I provides the conceptual and chronological backbone for the whole study. The next chapter has a dual goal. To situate various writings on gender and education that address various aspects of what, in twenty-first century academe, is an established domain of study and sketch out the conceptual terrain across which the analysis moves and introduce some of the key ideas that I draw upon and deploy later. Chapters 3–5 cover politics and policies. Historicising contemporary debates about gender and education, they reveal the psychosocial heritage of the rise and rise of meritocracy since the 1870s. Decades in which the engine of education helped put the seal of approval on the promotion of those judged to have merit of a particular kind according to education's narrow band of values.[45]

The focus of Part II is on learners and learning. Chapter 6 considers the gender dynamics of struggles over curriculum, offering three case studies to explore the contribution of women's educational thought and action based on normative hopes that things can be better. Gender and the experience of compulsory and post-compulsory education is the focus of Chaps. 7 and 8, which draw upon a study of over 100 autobiographies of people whose birth dates span 150 years of state education. Extracting and mining information both from these and sociological studies to develop a 'feel' for the subject and following that to compile a data set on pupil experience and the shaping of subjectivities in the schooling context. Part III examines the gendered culture and politics of teachers' work. Chapter 9 uses documentary and oral testimony to reconstruct the working lives and professional cultures of twentieth century women teachers, while Chap. 10 explores feminist reforms and feminist pedagogies in English classrooms during the 1980s.

To conclude, we look back to look forward. In the present day, many people are able to get ahead as individuals in a way that would have been impossible for previous generations. Many do not. Taking the long view suggests current policy and practice would benefit from a historicised, gender-sensitive and intersectional approach with a dual goal. First, to connect analysis of rhetoric turned on the individual with the social structures, practices, discourses and cultures entangled in the reproduction of a hierarchical society, in which the more fortunate pass on their advantages to later generations. Second, to shed light on the experience of different boys/girls, men/women as they navigate everyday sexism in contexts where anti-discrimination policies are now said to be in place. Knowledge is power. Without this kind of collective memory the on-going struggle for equality, justice and freedom for all will take place with one hand tied behind our backs.

[45] Jo Littler, *Against Meritocracy: Culture, Power and Myths of Mobility* (London: Routledge, 2018).

Bibliography

Primary Sources

Autobiographies, Memoirs, Diaries, Letters

Avery, Gillian. *School Remembered*. London: Victor Gollancz, 1967.
Stott, Mary. *Forgetting's No Excuse: the autobiography of Mary Stott*. London: Virago [1973], 1989.
Stott Mary. *Before I Go*. London: Virago, 1985.

Other Contemporary Books and Pamphlets

Laski, Marghanita. *The Village*. London: Persephone Books, [1952], 2004.
Spender, Dale and Sarah, Elizabeth. *Learning to Lose: Sexism and Education*. London: The Women's Press, 1980.
Stanworth, Michelle. *Gender and Schooling*. London: Hutchinson, 1983.
Wilkinson, Ellen. *Clash*. London: Virago, [1929], 1989.
Wollstonecraft, Mary. *A Vindication of the Rights of Woman*. London: Vintage, [1792], 2015.

Secondary Sources

Ahmed, Sara. *Living a Feminist Life*. Durham and London: Duke University Press, 2017.
Ashworth, Georgina and Bonnerjea, Lucy. *The Invisible Decade: UK Women and the UN Decade*. Aldershot: Gower, 1985.
Briar, Celia. *Working for Women? Gendered Work and Welfare Policies in Twentieth-Century Britain*. London: UCL Press, 1997.
Erzsébet Bukodi and John H. Goldthorpe, *Social Mobility and Education in Britain: Research, Politics and Policy*. Cambridge: Cambridge University Press, 2018.
Butler, Judith. *Bodies That Matter: On the Discursive Limits of 'Sex'*. New York: Routledge, 1993.
Chitty, Clyde. *Towards a New Education System: The Victory of the New Right?* Lewes: Falmer, 1989.
Connell, Raewyn. *Masculinities*. Berkeley, Los Angeles: University of California Press, 1995.
David, Miriam E. *Parents, Gender and Education Reform*. Cambridge: Polity Press, 1993.
Dyhouse, Carol. *Girls Growing Up In Victorian and Edwardian England*. London: Routledge, Kegan and Paul, 1981.
Dyhouse, Carol. *Girl Trouble*. London: Zed Books, 2013.
Fowler, David. *Youth Culture in Modern Britain c.1920-c.1970*. Basingstoke: Palgrave Macmillan, 2008.
Gomersall, Meg. *Working-Class Girls in Nineteenth Century England: Life, Work and Schooling*. Basingstoke: Macmillan, 1997.
Gordon, Lyndall. *Vindication: a Life of Mary Wollstonecraft*. London: Virago, 2006.
Graves, Pamela M. *Labour Women: Women in British Working-Class Politics 1918-1939*. Cambridge: Cambridge University Press, 1994.

Griffin, Emma. *Bread Winner: an Intimate History of the Victorian Economy*. Yale University Press: New Haven and London, 2020.
Harvey, Mark. "Slavery, Indenture and the Development of British Industrial Capitalism.' *History Workshop Journal*, 88 (Autumn, 2019), 68-88.
Johnson, Richard. "Really Useful Knowledge: Radical Education and Working Class Culture." In *Working-Class Culture*, edited by John Clarke, Chas Critcher and Richard Johnson, 75-102. London: Hutchinson, 1980.
Lewis, Jane. *Labour and Love: Women's Experiences of Home and Family 1850-1940*. Oxford: Basil Blackwell, 1986.
Light, Alison. *Mrs. Woolf and the Servants: An Intimate History of Domestic Life in Bloomsbury*. London: Bloomsbury, 2008.
Littler, Jo. *Against Meritocracy: Culture, Power and Myths of Mobility*. London: Routledge, 2018.
Lown, Judy. *Women and Industrialisation: gender at work in nineteenth century England*. Cambridge: Cambridge University Press, 1990.
Martin, Jane. *Women and the Politics of Schooling in Victorian and Edwardian England*. Leicester: Leicester University Press, 1999.
Martin, Jane. *Making Socialists: Mary Bridges Adams and the Fight for Knowledge and Power, 1855-1939*. Manchester: Manchester University Press, 2013.
Mills, C.W. *The Sociological Imagination*. Oxford: Oxford University Press, 1959.
Mokyr, Joel. *The Enlightened Economy*. Harmondsworth: Penguin, 2009.
Overton, Mark. *Agricultural Revolution in England: the transformation of the Agrarian Economy 1500-1850*. Cambridge: Cambridge University Press, 1996.
Pedersen, Joyce Senders. "Women and Agency: the educational legacy of Mary Wollstonecraft." In *Women, Education and Agency*, edited by Jean Spence, Sarah Aiston, Maureen Meikle, 27-48. London: Routledge, 2010.
Pedersen, Susan. *Eleanor Rathbone and the Politics of Conscience*. Yale: Yale University Press, 2004.
Perez, Caroline Criado. *Invisible Women: Exposing Data Bias in a World Designed for Men*. London: Chatto & Windus, 2019.
Raw, Louise. *Striking a Light: the Bryant and May Matchwomen and their Place in History* (London: Bloomsbury, 2011.
Renwick, Chris. *Bread for All: The Origins of the Welfare State*. London: Allen Lane, 2017.
Sani, Anita. *Inferior*. London: 4th Estate, 2018.
Simon, Brian. *Education and the Labour Movement, 1870-1920*. London: Lawrence and Wishart, 1980.
Taylor, Barbara. *Eve and the New Jerusalem*. London: Virago, 1983.
Taylor, Barbara. *Mary Wollstonecraft and the Feminist Imagination*. Cambridge: Cambridge University Press, 2003.
Thane, Pat. "Women in the British Labour Party and the Construction of State Welfare, 1906-1939." In *Mothers of a New World: Maternalist Politics and the Origins of Welfare States*, edited by Seth Koven and Sonya Michel, 343-377. New York: Routledge, 1993.
Thane, Pat. *Divided Kingdom: a History of Britain, 1900 to the Present*. Cambridge: Cambridge University Press, 2018.

Thompson, Edward P. *The Making of the English Working Class*. Harmondsworth: Penguin, 1968.
Walby, Sylvia. *Theorizing Patriarchy*. Oxford: Oxford University Press, 1992.
Williams, Eric. *Capitalism and Slavery*. Chapel Hill: University of North Carolina Press, 1994.
Zimmeck, Meta. "Jobs for the Girls: the Expansion of Clerical Work for Women, 150-1914." In *Unequal Opportunities. Women's Employment in England 1800-1918*, edited by Angela John, 153-177. Oxford: Basil Blackwell, 1986.

PART I

Politics and Policies

CHAPTER 2

Gendering the Educational Landscape

> *My mother was born before women had the vote in parliamentary elections in Britain. She lived to see a female Prime Minister. Whatever her views of Margaret Thatcher, she was pleased that a woman had reached Number 10 and proud to have a stake herself in some of those revolutionary changes of the twentieth century. Unlike generations before her, she was able to have a career and marriage and a child (for her own mother pregnancy necessarily meant the end of her job as a teacher). She was a strikingly effective head of a large primary school in the West Midlands. I am sure that she was the very embodiment of* power *to the generations of girls and boys in her charge. But my mother also knew that it was not all quite so simple, that real equality between women and men was still a thing of the future, and that there were causes for anger as well as for celebration.*
> —Mary Beard, *Women & Power a Manifesto* (London: Profile Books, 2017), ix–x

In 2018, suffragist Millicent Garrett Fawcett became the first woman to be commemorated with a statue in London's Parliament Square, following a campaign and petition by feminist activist Caroline Criado Perez. Speaking at the unveiling, London Mayor Sadiq Khan said that he hoped the statue would be an inspiration to all those fighting for gender equality, adding: 'It's simply not right that this historic square has been a male-only zone for statues, because statues matter. They are a symbol of our values, the demonstration of the importance we place on hard battles won, both in peace and war, and an expression of who and what we choose to celebrate.'[1] The Victorian women's movement viewed education as the first step to equal rights for women. Millicent's sister, Elizabeth, was the first Englishwoman to qualify as a doctor, co-founder of the first hospital staffed by women and the first female mayor. In their

[1] Women and Girls Lead, 24 April 2018. www.womenandgirlslead.org.

lifetime, the Garrett sisters were among the most famous women of their era, seemingly largely deleted from the record because the reservoir of stories that historians use to construct history was, like the heritage of commemoration and the traditional canon of literature, predominantly the domain of dead white European males.

But in the late 1960s, the women's liberation movement surfaced in Western Europe and North America. Within a few years, there were new perspectives on historical writing as scholars mostly writing within the tradition of second-wave feminism showed us that women's experiences cannot be subsumed within conventional narratives centred upon men. In 1976, there appeared a book that in time would be representative of this. *The Rights and Wrongs of Women* edited by Juliet Mitchell, then a lecturer in English literature, and sociologist Ann Oakley offered a powerful corrective to the concepts and analyses of mainstream ('male-stream') history posited on a male paradigm. The publisher had wanted an 'anti-text' to make an impression, to dislodge that *he* that can operate to preclude discussion of the gulf between male and female experiences and a failure to acknowledge its full implications. For Mitchell and Oakley, female exclusion 'did not follow from a sexually egalitarian society but from the reality of a society so deeply unaware of social and economic inequalities between male and female that the possibility of their existence could not be officially acknowledged.'[2]

The educational landscape offers a fertile area within which to explore relationships of gender, culture and power and problems of agency since it was (and is) a public space in which women have achieved a measure of status and social authority. The society in which we live is one in which social relations, including economic relations, are informed by considerations of gender, mediated by cross and inter-class differences and linked to 'race'/ethnicity, which no-one is without. As will be shown, kaleidoscopic intersectional approaches to thinking about the roles of gender and identity in education can help us to understand different aspects of the shifting relationships and assumptions between lives, work and schooling, which were not always consistent with people's lives and behaviours.

I follow in the tradition of education policy sociological analysis that conceives of policy as an ongoing process of enactment in government, institutions, networks and local professional practices including when and where traditional ideas filter through present-day fashionable attitudes. Although not the purpose of a public education system, a shortage of classroom teachers would be solved by the greater involvement of women, and in Jane Miller's view, the legacy of gendered conceptions of culture, hegemony, race and class is a living one.[3] Historical knowledge is essential to present-day understanding

---

[2] Juliet Mitchell and Ann Oakley, *The Rights and Wrongs of Women* (Harmondsworth: Penguin, 1976), 7–8.
[3] Jane Miller, *School for Women* (London: Virago, 1996).

of the educational realm, setting elitist institution building alongside histories of mass provision for those with no wealth, no possessions and no privileges.

My theory and the methodology I call historical ethnography to capture a new imaginary of extending a notion of ethnographic fieldwork into the domains of biography and history, in a similar way to that used by Stephen Ball in his book *The Micropolitics of the School*.[4] Like Ball, I avoid a perspective of struggles in and struggles over schools that takes the rhetoric for granted and use instead historical reconstruction and deepening in the light of documents, oral histories and a review of contemporary positions. With a primary concern with the intersection of gender and social class, this means going beyond the work of historical retrieval involved in seeking to make women visible and recording female voices in terms of their own experience. It means examining the sexual division of labour and the construction of masculinities and sexualities in the mundane, half-forgotten details of everyday life, paying attention to power relations through language and linguistic understanding. It means examining the process of gendering both in the archive we study and in the writing of history as an intellectual enterprise.[5] Therefore, I start with an overview of the history writing on gender and the historian, before moving on to map the conceptual terrain that gives order and coherence to the work, introducing key concepts, questions and theories that I will draw upon later.

Gender and the Politics of Historical Writing

Writing on *The Gender of History* in 1998, Bonnie G. Smith described what happened when the practice of scientific history took root in nineteenth century universities in Western Europe.[6] She suggested that after the Enlightenment, empirically minded men defined themselves and their intellectual products in opposition to an older, more popular amateur history read for moral instruction and entertainment, which they deemed trivial. No longer seen as a branch of literature, a tradition of women's historical scholarship notably as authors of textbooks, biographies and memoirs disappeared because professionalisation and historical science developed at a time when shifting gender relations assumed that a woman's place was in the home. More than this, Judith Bennett argued that these historians enlisted the hidden help of amateur female relatives to do the work of researching, filing, editing and even writing with all credit given to the male breadwinner.[7]

Smith sees gendered foundational claims as fundamental to an appreciation of the development of the terms 'professional' and 'professionalism' as applied

---

[4] Stephen J. Ball, *The Micro-Politics of the School: towards a theory of school organisation* (Abingdon: Routledge, 2012).

[5] Kathleen Weiler, "The Historiography of Gender and Progressive Education in the United States," *Paedagogica Historica*, 42, nos. 1 & 2, (2006), 161–173.

[6] Bonnie G. Smith, *The Gender of History* (Harvard: Harvard University Press, 1998).

[7] Judith M. Bennett, *History Matters: Patriarchy and the Challenge of Feminism* (Manchester: Manchester University Press, 2006).

to academic historians, notably through the historiographical tradition established by German historian Leopold von Ranke. The historian's task, Ranke asserted, comprised the use of contemporary documents to establish a corpus of ascertained facts. Rigorous training in preparation for the practice of archival research enabled the historian to narrate the events of the past as they actually happened based on an objective standard of judgement. Ranke's 'training' and 'practice' conferred the title of professional historian on a 'school' of European men who based their practice on a method and meaning that involved Othering the scholarship, style and preferences of those without the ideological means to achieve disciplinary ascendancy. Therefore, the process of professionalisation involved the crystallisation of certain forms of classed, gendered and racialised power in ways that had not happened when amateurs wrote history.[8]

If a historical method based on the historian's ability to see the past in a detached manner was a nineteenth century invention, there were those who remained more sceptical about the task Ranke proposed. Biographical narrative never disappeared, as Barbara Caine's genealogy of the place of biography within historical writing shows. To illustrate the persistence of a faith in the equation of personal and social history, as opposed to a framework concerned with the underlying structures governing human history, she quotes Cambridge historian and philosopher of history Herbert Butterfield.

> The genesis of historical events lies in human beings. The real birth of ideas takes place in human brains. The reason why this happens is that human beings have vitality. From the historian's point of view, it is this that makes the world go round… Economic factors, financial situations, war, political crises, do not cause anything, do not do anything, and do not exist except as abstract terms and convenient pieces of shorthand… It is men who make history.[9]

Caine and Smith both identified a *genre* of historical writing that depended on the biographical mode, but Caine traces awareness of the need to study the historian to the 1961 observations of Butterfield's Cambridge contemporary, E.H. Carr in *What Is History?*

In one of the most influential books written about historiography, Carr challenged Ranke's belief in an absolute objectivity by arguing that historians decide which facts of the past to turn into history according to their own biases and agendas. On the other hand, in keeping with the dominant ideology which saw women as of no historical consequence, Carr's imaginary historian is male, the function of history to enable '*him* to understand the society of the past and to increase *his mastery* over the society of the present.' Carr also cautions against exaggerating the role of individual too much. Stressing the importance of studying social structures and people in the mass, he thought that any historical resurrection of an obscure figure from the past must rest on a

---

[8] See Philippa Levine, *The Amateur and the Professional: Antiquarians, Historians and Archaeologists in Victorian England, 1838–1886* (Cambridge: Cambridge University Press, 2008).

[9] Barbara Caine, *Biography and History* (New York: Palgrave Macmillan, 2010), 21.

standard of significance by which interpretations could be judged. A point of view that was presented not as male, but as objective.[10]

Encouraged by changing political climates and an intellectual milieu that included the Communist Party historians' group and *New Left Review*, the journal of the English New Left, the notion of history-from-below—constructing a people's history—was underway. Edward Thompson's 1963 work, *The Making of the English Working Class*, influenced a generation of American and British historiography, and he indicated the roots of his practice lay in the collaboration of two previous historians of English labour—Barbara Hammond and her husband, Lawrence, who pioneered British labour history as it emerged at the start of the twentieth century. In *The Making*, Thompson acknowledged the debt he owed the Hammonds' for the way in which they approached the question of what constitutes history and the 'copious quotation and wide reference' in their *Labourer* trilogy. In Thompson's view, these volumes were of lasting importance both as 'source-books' and for their critical understanding of the political context in which industrialisation took place.[11]

Such a clear recognition of a woman historian was atypical, and interpreting partnerships is messy. The Hammonds' biographer, Stewart Weaver, thinks 'Lawrence was the more directed, the more disciplined the more ambitious. He also wielded the readier pen, and for that reason above all Barbara followed his lead to the point of identifying herself equally and essentially with a life project that he, in the main, conceived.'[12] Susan Groag Bell lived with Barbara in the 1950s before attending Stanford University in California where she entertained hopes of postgraduate study. Aged 38, the authorities thought her too old. In response, Bell studied the *Encyclopaedia Americana* and *Encyclopaedia Britannica* to find cases of older people who built a career. Those who did were mostly female, and she found 'the place of women in history depends upon the attitude of the historian…the *Americana* had included many more women than the *Britannica*.' All of which made her 'begin to appreciate how remarkable a man Lawrence Hammond must have been to have shared the title pages and spines of their books with his wife.'[13]

Exploring women writers of history for her book *Gender and the Historian*, Johanna Alberti was struck by a strong sense that many of the ideas which gender historians have put forward in the past 30 years have been expressed by female historians writing and publishing from the 1800s. Alberti cites Alice Clark's *Working Life of Women in the Seventeenth Century* as an example, which sociologist Harriet Bradley used in a chapter on the emergence of new social and sexual divisions of labour for a major new undergraduate textbook of

---

[10] Edward Hallett Carr, *What is History?* (New York: Palgrave Macmillan, 2002), 45, 49, 65.

[11] Edward P. Thompson, *The Making of the English Working Class* (Harmondsworth: Penguin, 1988), 215.

[12] Stewart Weaver, *The Hammonds: A Marriage in History* (Stanford: Stanford University Press, 1997), 70.

[13] Susan Groag Bell, *Between Worlds in Czechoslovakia, England, and America* (New York: Dutton, 1991), 200.

1992, *Formations of Modernity*. Crucially, Clark's assessment of archival material such as judicial, administrative and financial records as well as personal material and prescriptive literature led her to conclude that the introduction of capitalism took place within a system of male domination to which later historians would give the name 'patriarchy' and that the associated changes affected the consciousness of both men and women.[14]

To concentrate briefly on the woman historian as well as the work, for Clark there was a link between her commitment to women's history and campaigns for women's suffrage involving feminist and socialist networks. She completed her research at the LSE through a fellowship the Irish heir and Fabian Charlotte Payne-Townshend Shaw funded. Shaw had friends among the LSE's founders, including Beatrice Webb who described her in her diary:

> She is a socialist and a radical, not because she understands the collectivist standpoint, but because she is by nature a rebel. She has no snobbishness and no convention: she has 'swallowed all formulas' but has not worked out principles of her own. She is fond of men and impatient of most women, bitterly resents her enforced celibacy but thinks she could not tolerate the matter-of-fact side of marriage. Sweet-tempered, sympathetic and genuinely anxious to increase the world's enjoyment and diminish the world's pain.[15]

Between 1906 and 1910, Shaw's studentship went to a man. Frustrated and angry at this turn of events, she stipulated that henceforth it had to go to a woman working on women's history. In 1911, Eileen Power became the first recipient of the award under the new rubric; the final awards went to Clark and Alice Stirling who investigated Anglo-Saxon women.[16]

Lilian Knowles supervised Power, Clark and Stirling. A pioneer in her discipline and the first female professor of economic history in England, Knowles had studied at Girton College, Cambridge, with William Cunningham, a supporter of women's education. Subsequently, she registered as a research student at the LSE where Cunningham was an external lecturer. Power went to Girton on a scholarship in 1907 and then pursued research in Paris and London before returning to Girton to be a History tutor. She claimed she owed her career to Winifred Mercier, Director of Studies in History at Girton between 1909 and 1913.[17] Female students singled Power out as a role model. Social historian Dorothy Marshall later recalled: 'A tutorial in her delightful room in the Tower was never a stilted occasion. Often a chocolate box was at hand, the

---

[14] Johanna Alberti, *Gender and the Historian* (Harlow: Pearson Education, 2002); Harriet Bradley, "Changing Social Structures: Class and Gender". In *Formations of Modernity: Understanding Modern Societies* eds. Stuart Hall and Bram Gieben (Cambridge: Polity Press, 1992), 177–228.

[15] Norman McKenzie and Jeanne McKenzie (eds.), *The Diary of Beatrice Webb Volume Two 1892–1905* (London: Virago, 1986), 100.

[16] LSE Scholarship Files, Shaw studentship.

[17] Linda Grier, *The Life of Winifred Mercier* (Oxford: Oxford University Press, 1937), 81.

substitute of the male don's offering of sherry to his college students and always a friendly smile.'[18]

Appointed a lecturer at the LSE in 1921, Power liked the progressive views prevailing there. She shared a house with an old friend from Girton two doors down from LSE colleague R.H. Tawney and a 20-minute walk to work. Power and Tawney devised the courses of study, which created the discipline of economic and social history. They were prime movers in the foundation of the Economic History Society, but it was Power who drove the new institution forward drawing on her female networks of support to enlist members and raise funds. Consequently, women comprised 20 per cent of the 500 people who joined the newly formed Society in 1927. The field Power entered was a new one, but it was one in which women played a more than proportionate role. For example, Power also founded the *Economic History Review* in 1927, and in 1931, she became the second woman (after Knowles) to be appointed to a chair in Economic History at the LSE. In her 1996 biography of Power, *A Woman in History*, Maxine Berg stressed the neglect of Power's scholarship by the dominant male historical tradition.[19]

Indeed, the idea for the first national women's liberation conference in 1970 came from a group of women historians who rebelled against the domination of the Ruskin history workshops by men who seemed to assume that women had no part in history. Sheila Rowbotham, incensed by a man who stood up during discussion of a paper on women's factory work and supported the logic of the male breadwinner wage, announced a meeting for a group interested in talking about women. Rowbotham and others including Sally Alexander, who Keira Knightley portrayed in the 2020 film *Misbehaviour* about the 1970 flour bomb protests against the Miss World beauty contest, spread the word among the liberation workshops that had begun to proliferate all around London and in some universities. Turnout exceeded their wildest dreams. Rather than the anticipated 200 to 300, about 600 women came together to share 'proposals to lobby for the Sex Discrimination Act; to research into women's history, to campaign for free contraception and abortion on demand; and to study alternatives to the nuclear family and conventional ways of bringing up children.'[20]

Looking back in her 2000 memoir, *Promise of a Dream*, Sheila Rowbotham recollected she began hearing arguments for women's liberation from America and Germany around 1967. Juliet Mitchell was then lecturing in Leeds, in a well-established university department of English literature. Her political involvement centred on *New Left Review*, for which she wrote a path-breaking essay 'Women: The Longest Revolution' prompted by frustration at the failure

---

[18] Dorothy Marshall, *The Making of a Twentieth Century Woman* (London: Blazenbooks, 2003), 57.

[19] Maxine Berg, *A Woman in History: Eileen Power, 1889–1940* (Cambridge: Cambridge University Press, 1996).

[20] See 'Beyond "Misbehaviour": Sally Alexander in conversation,' History Workshop Online: https://www.historyworkshop.org.uk/beyond-misbehaviour, accessed 3 July 2020; Mary Stott, *Before I Go* (London: Virago, 1985), 24.

to acknowledge gender in the Marxist meetings she attended. 'Why this sort of common experience led so many of us to feminism at that particular time, though I can think of many explanations, I do not really know,' she later recalled. Male sociologists were equally dismissive when sexual divisions became the theme of the 1974 annual conference of the British Sociological Association. One going so far as to suggest 'women' were not a sociological category. 'You might as well debate the colour green,' he said.[21]

In Britain, Rowbotham's 1973 book *Hidden from History: 300 Years of Women's Oppression and the Fight Against It* was a formative influence on the development of histories exploring the interplay of class and gender in family and work-based ideology. Research also prompted questions about silences and absences in the memory archive. As Australian feminist Dale Spender put it in her introduction to *Women of Ideas* published in 1982.

> Many of us began to ask whether we were the first generation of women to have felt this way. Some of us were vaguely aware that we did have a past, but even when we had an idea that something like this had happened before, it was usually based on a shadowy impression—from a discussion with one's grandmother, a reference or a quotation in an old book, a comment from one's father about silly and unsexed suffragettes.[22]

By the 1990s, Antoinette Burton noted 'most feminists recognize that history is not simply what happened in the past but, more pointedly, the kinds of *knowledge* about the past that we are *made aware of.*'[23] In their canonical text *Family Fortunes: Men and Women of the English Middle Class, 1780–1850*, for example, Leonore Davidoff and Catherine Hall put women and families into the centre of their analysis of the first industrial revolution and provided a template for the study of the rapidly changing social world of Victorian Britain that connected production and consumption.

The first monograph to explore the nature of men, masculinity and fatherhood, *Family Fortunes* paved the way for analyses of multiple masculinities, codes and behaviours.[24] As Davidoff and Hall showed, the making of the English working class was 'gendered,' class defines gender, and class/gender configurations or codes are not universal but historical phenomena. This had

---

[21] Hilary Rose, *Love, Power and Knowledge: towards a feminist transformation of the sciences* (Cambridge: Polity Press, 1994), 28.

[22] Dale Spender, *Women of Ideas and What Men Have Done to Them* (London: Routledge and Kegan Paul, 1982), 3.

[23] Antoinette Burton, "'History' is Now: feminist theory and the production of historical feminisms," *Women's History Review*, 1, 1 (1992), 26.

[24] Leonore Davidoff and Catherine Hall, *Family Fortunes: Men and Women of the English Middle Class, 1780–1850* (London: Hutchinson, 1987); John Tosh, *A Man's Place: Masculinity and the Middle Class Home in Victorian England* (New Haven: Yale University Press, 1999); Katherine Gleadle. "Re-visiting *Family Fortunes*: reflections on the twentieth anniversary of the publication of L Davidoff and C. Hall (1987) *Family Fortunes: men and women of the English middle class, 1780–1850*," *Women's History Review*, 16, no. 5 (2007), 773–782.

consequences for historical writing. Analyses of how women have been empowered by or seized power in education drew attention to gender relations in theory and practice and the relationship between the two, while opening the door and peering inside everyday life revealed gaps between separate spheres discourse and lived experiences. For example, familial and friendship networks enabled women to develop support systems and new institutions, which did not bifurcate along the lines of social class, gender and ethnicity but were deeply and messily entwined.[25]

American historian Joan Scott argued that scholars should disrupt traditional assumptions about certainty, identity and truth, in this case the subjective and collective meanings of men and women as categories of identity. Her concern was to move beyond what she considered the sterility of binary thinking and philosophical questions about equality vs. difference, indicating the correct opposite of equality is inequality and of difference is sameness.

> Placing equality and difference in antithetical relationship has, then, a double effect. It denies the way in which difference has long figured in political notions of equality and it suggests that sameness is the only ground on which equality can be claimed. It thus puts feminists in an impossible position, for as long as we argue within the terms of a discourse set up by this opposition, we grant the current conservative premise that because women cannot be identical to men in all respects, we cannot expect to be equal to them. The only alternative, it seems to me, is to refuse to oppose equality and difference and insist continually on differences—differences as the condition of individual and collective identities, differences as the constant challenge to the fixing of those identities, history as the repeated illustration of the play of differences, differences as the very meaning of equality itself.[26]

Insisting on a genuine historicisation and continual deconstructive moves, Scott called for a leap in historical writing to provide new perspectives on old questions, redefine old questions in new terms, make women visible as active participants and create analytic distance between the seemingly fixed language of the past and current terminology.

This approach was central to Carolyn Steedman's classic book of 1986, *Landscape for a Good Woman*. Written at the intersections of biography and autobiography, case history and social history, psychoanalysis and oral history, *Landscape* is about lives for whom the central interpretative devices of history

---

[25] Jane Martin, *Women and the Politics of Schooling in Victorian and Edwardian England* (Leicester: Leicester University Press, 1999); Margaret S. Crocco, Petra Munro and Kathleen Weiler, *Pedagogies of Resistance: Women Educator Activists, 1880–1960* (New York: Teachers College Press, 1999); Mary Hilton and Pam Hirsch (eds.) *Practical Visionaries: Women, Education and Social Progress 1790–1930* (London: Longman, 2000); Jane Martin and Joyce Goodman, *Women and Education, 1800–1980* (Basingstoke: Palgrave Macmillan, 2004).

[26] Joan Wallach Scott, "Gender: a useful category of historical analysis," *The American Historical Review*, 91 (December 1986), 1053–75; Joan Wallach Scott, *Gender and the Politics of History* (New York: Columbia University Press, 1988), 46.

and culture do not work because they are posited on a male paradigm. Interweaving fragments of her childhood in South London in the 1950s with those of her mother in 1920s Burnley, Steedman scopes a feminist cultural analysis that draws on the intersecting subjectivities of their lives in ways that help us understand the shifting relationships between different aspects of white, working-class femininity over time and place. Such a perspective has a clear political dimension on women's experiences and life values, invoking the idea of allowing the subaltern to speak. For Steedman, her mother's eyes spoke of longing to get on and get out of the working class, and marriage presented her with the best chance of a home of her own and some kind of economic security. 'From a traditional Labour background' she 'rejected the politics of solidarity and communality, always voted Conservative, for the left could not embody her desire for things to be really fair, for a full skirt that took twenty yards of cloth, for a half-timbered cottage in the country, for the prince who did not come.'[27]

In England, elite white men were (and are) those with access to the material and cultural resources, coupled with public prestige, which allow them to become 'leaders' and wield power.[28] Steedman's mother rages against an unfair world in which she fails to 'catch' her own 'posh boy' despite being just as pretty, just as clever, just as good as American socialite and divorcee Wallis Simpson who caused a constitutional crisis by doing just that in 1938. Low female wages in a small range of jobs with little hope of progression played an active role in keeping women subordinate, and it is unsurprising that some felt disgruntled at the gulf between them and their male counterparts. In common with Steedman, Julia Swindells and Lisa Jardine articulate gendered stresses and strains for women in Left politics and cultural studies. An example came in the response to Juliet Mitchell's article on women from the *New Left Review* editorial board, which suggests the terms of inclusion, insisting that she '*must* situate her discussion of women in the family' and 'that a classic Marxist account had *no room for* discussion of the family at all.'[29]

Dorothy Wedderburn who started life in a working-class family and graduated from Cambridge University helped by school scholarships thought women's silence reflected the norms and values of the time. Wedderburn discussed the issue with Sheila Benson and Lynne Segal in *Out of Apathy: voices of the New Left 30 Years On*. It was not that she was asked and refused to write for the *Review* Wedderburn said, but the journal had much more theoretical interests than her aim to explore poverty, inequality and social purpose and write about her research in an accessible, non-academic way.[30] Benson thought 'it ahistorical

---

[27] Carolyn Steedman, *Landscape for a Good Woman* (London: Virago, 1986), 47.

[28] Robert Verkaik, *Posh Boys: How the English Public Schools Ruin Britain* (London: Oneworld Publications, 2018).

[29] Julia Swindells and Lisa Jardine, *What's Left? Women in Culture and the Labour Movement* (London: Routledge, 1990), 79.

[30] Dorothy Wedderburn, "Activism and the New Left," in *Out of Apathy: Voices of the New Left 30 Years On*, eds. Robin Archer, Diemet Bubeck, Hanjo Glock, Lesley Jacobs, Seth Moglen, Adam Steinhouse, Daniel Weinstock (London: Verso, 1989), 113.

to blame the men of the New Left for failing to understand that the women of the New Left lived and worked within a patriarchal structure of power. We were all prisoners of history, and the women themselves were unaware of the need to challenge the assumption that women had achieved equality with men in post-war welfare state.'[31] Anna Davin, a founder of History Workshop and former student of Edward Thompson, recalls Thompson as historian-teacher at Warwick University. He taught the course on industrialisation, introducing students to the work of Ivy Pinchbeck on women workers, first published in 1930. 'Women were always there in his account, working, singing, rearing children, taking part in bread riots, writing poetry, or—like the early feminist and revolutionary Mary Wollstonecraft—demanding change.'[32]

Wollstonecraft believed that education might empower women, and the persona she projected was that of a 'thinking woman.' As Joyce Senders Pedersen observed, she 'came to view not only her works but also her life as instructive, pointing the way to future generations.'[33] For many feminists, part of Wollstonecraft's imaginative appeal was the sense of the *possibility* of change she engendered consistent with the rise of professional society and the meritocratic claims to social authority to which she broadly subscribed. As a strategy for empowerment, this had mixed implications. To return to the quote with which we started, Mary Beard strikes a cautionary note about female power and agency:

> This offers a very narrow version of what power is, largely correlating it with public prestige (or in some cases public notoriety). It is very "high end" in a very traditional sense, and bound up with the "glass ceiling" image of power, which not only effectively positions women on the outside of power, but also imagines the female pioneer as the already successful superwoman with just a few vestiges of male prejudice keeping her from the top.[34]

Certainly, a focus on 'high end' politics associated with the upper echelons of national and international politics and politicians exacerbates a tendency to exclude anything else which, by default, does not 'count' as politics at all. In order to avoid this, Beard suggests 'thinking collaboratively, about the power of followers, not just of leaders… thinking about power as an attribute or even a verb ('to power'), not as a possession.' The definition she proposes 'is the ability to be effective, to make a difference in the world, and the right to be

---

[31] Sheila Benson, "Experiences in the London New Left," in *Out of Apathy: Voices of the New Left 30 Years On*, eds. Robin Archer, Diemet Bubeck, Hanjo Glock, Lesley Jacobs, Seth Moglen, Adam Steinhouse, Daniel Weinstock (London: Verso, 1989), 110.

[32] Quoted in Cal Winslow, *E.P. Thompson and the Making of the New Left: Essays and Polemics* (London: Lawrence and Wishart, 2014), 308.

[33] Joyce Senders Pedersen, "Women and Agency: the educational legacy of Mary Wollstonecraft," in *Women, Education and Agency*, ed. Jean Spence, Sarah Aiston, Maureen Meikle (London: Routledge, 2010), 27.

[34] Mary Beard, *Women & Power: A Manifesto*, 83–4.

taken seriously. It is power in the sense that many women feel they don't have—and that many want.'[35]

Palestinian-American anthropologist Lila Abu-Lughod inverts the first part of the French philosopher Michel Foucault's proposition 'Where there is power, there is resistance' to read 'Where there is resistance, there is power.'[36] The section that follows draws on this idea to show the possibilities for the writing of histories which threaten the hegemony of the powerful, addressing questions of knowledge, culture and power and a framework for thinking about 'lived experience' by which I mean the way in which an individual makes sense of his or her situation or action. Besides gender and the understanding that sexual difference was historical, three key concepts have come to shape my approach to research and writing—knowledge, language and subjectivity.

GENDERING THE POLITICS OF EXPERIENCE

Ethnographic research in educational settings in 1970s England certainly observed the highly gendered nature of schooling even if it did not always acknowledge or recognise the full implications. Mary Fuller's innovative study of black girls in a London comprehensive school was one of the few early attempts to deal explicitly with the interrelationship of gender, 'race' and class. Employing the concept of subculture, Fuller explained academic achievement for these girls in terms of subcultural resistance. In contrast, Paul Willis regarded white working-class boys' educational performance as the outcome of self-concept and the self-fulfilling prophecy. The 'lads' in his study seemed to invert the mental–manual hierarchy to match the male–female hierarchy in an anti-school culture derived from their families and peer group and therefore acquired gender identities that prepared them indirectly for their future class position.[37]

Whether these approaches result in an unrealistic, 'romantic' appraisal of actions and decisions that diverts attention away from structural issues such as unemployment, miseducation, low pay and dead-end jobs is a matter of ongoing debate. However, in challenging pathological perceptions of outsiders within the education system, they showed the self-awareness of powerless groups and exposed the role of hegemony within culture. Willis's 'lads' are those teachers despaired of as 'undesirable' recognised widely and conventionally in government reports. His privileging of a Marxist frame made a case for the reproduction of class relations, but he was criticised for failing to address the boys' chauvinism. Like Willis, Angela McRobbie was part of the Birmingham Centre for Contemporary Cultural Studies where she helped

---

[35] Op cit, 87.

[36] Lila Abu-Lughod, *Writing Women's Worlds: Bedouin Stories* (Berkeley and Los Angeles: University of California Press, 1993), 42.

[37] Mary Fuller, "Black girls in a London comprehensive school," in *Schooling for Women's Work*, ed. Rosemary Deem (London: Routledge, Kegan and Paul, 1980); Paul Willis, *Learning to Labour* (London: Saxon House, 1977).

start a Women's Studies Group in 1974 with shared concerns about hegemonic masculinist representations and what is given voice to in man-made cultures. 'Socially, but inseparable from our intellectual presence, as one woman put it at the time, we could either strive for a sort of "de-sexualised" intellectual role, or retain femininity either through keeping quiet, or in an uneasy combination with being "one of the lads."'[38]

A decade on, Lynn Davies's *Pupil Power. Deviance and Gender in School* captured much of the current feminist critique of gender blind educational ethnography. Davies found the mental/manual dyad less salient for girls than for boys in the co-educational comprehensive school she studied, but the girls' patterns of resistance including transgression of dress codes and 'silence' in the classroom simply reinforced the stereotypical attitudes of their teachers and the boys in class. She thought it tragic that schools were failing to develop the full potential of their pupils and wanted to bring about a more humane and equitable experience by granting more power to students especially working-class girls.[39]

Philosopher Jane Roland Martin sees a gendered nature/culture split, mind/body dualism and bipolar analysis of society, as part of the deep structure of Western culture's educational thought. In *Education Reconfigured: Culture, Encounter, and Change* (2011), she emphasised the importance of care, concern and connection to others and favoured making violence as learned behaviour an educational issue. Looking to the future, she argued the effects of social change in terms of economic transformations, personal identifications and political action would change the deep structure of thought that she describes, making it harder to marginalise the job of preparing young people of both sexes for life in the world of the private home and family.[40]

The argument for a focus on everyday social relations in research is central to *Feminisms and the Self: The Web of Identity* (1995) by Morwenna Griffiths. Griffiths uses the idea of the 'web' to envision the process of becoming a subject as if analogous to a familiar process (a person spins their own web, but not in circumstances of their own making). In this argument, personal autonomy (the ability to order one's personal life) is the freedom to make the self within specific social and cultural formations. Public autonomy refers to the conditions under which individuals contribute to the ordering of public life. Emphasis on experience confirmed the theoretical value of the individual, autobiographical mode, with various scholars advocating biographical research as a means of

---

[38] Editorial Group, "Women's Studies Group: trying to do feminist intellectual work," in *Women Take Issue*, ed. Women's Studies Group Centre for Contemporary Cultural Studies (London: Hutchinson, 1978), 11–12.

[39] Angela McRobbie, "Settling Accounts With Sub-Cultures: A Feminist Critique," *Screen Education*, no. 34 (Spring 1980), 111–123; Lynn Davies, *Pupil Power: deviance & gender in schools* (Lewes: Falmer Press, 1983).

[40] Jane Roland Martin, *Education Reconfigured: Culture, Encounter, and Change* (London: Routledge, 2011).

grasping the complexity of motivation and experience that make up human history and the search for *subjectivity*.[41]

Produced in and for particular historical moments, as a metaphor subjectivity conveys the constructed quality of memory and experience including the struggle and contest over an unstable, shifting subject constructed through both dominant conceptions and resistance to those conceptions. For Kathleen Weiler, 'The construction of gendered subjectivities through discourse, the contradictions of our various ways of categorizing and understanding what happens in our lives and who we are, naming ourselves, becomes the point of entry for historical analysis.'[42] Likewise, Joan Scott configures the category of 'woman' as a 'site of signification' attending to the historical processes that, through discourse, position subjects and produce their experiences. As historians, this means framing the individual in history as a 'site' on which political and cultural contests are enacted to examine the nature and meaning of individual lives and the cultural network or larger community of which the individual is a part.

Retaining concepts of experience, subjectivity and identity,[43] I adopt Raewyn Connell's concepts to integrate historically situated 'regimes' of gender, entangled with other relational systems of social identity and power, into my research. Thus, the notion of a 'gender order' is used to convey deep cultural structures, a macro-level pattern of gendered power relations within which a particular meso-level 'gender regime' is historically situated. That is, the pattern of practices that constitute various kinds of masculinity and femininity orders them in terms of prestige and power, and constructs a sexual division of labour in space and place that all individuals negotiate as embodied selves. Seen as 'gender projects,' masculinity and femininity refer to aspects of behaviour that can change over time, while the concept of masculinism denotes an ideology that naturalises and justifies men's domination over women. Patriarchy is the structure of unequal power relations and social configurations that disadvantage and devalue the female, sustained through this ideology.

Connell's *Masculinities*, published in 1995, outlined 'hegemonic masculinity.' The impact of which serves to stabilise heterogeneous gendered identities and practices and entrench the dominance of particular norms of 'manly' conduct and behaviour, and taken for granted notions of authority and leadership as masculine domains. In Connell's formulation, 'hegemonic masculinity' draws on Gramscian themes. In his *Prison Notebooks*, Italian Marxist philosopher Antonio Gramsci described common sense as ambiguous, contradictory and multiform, while 'hegemony' refers to the organising principle or worldview diffused through agencies of ideological control and socialisation into

---

[41] Morwenna Griffiths, *Feminisms and the Self: the Web of Identity* (London: Routledge, 1995).

[42] Kathleen Weiler, "The Historiography of Gender and Progressive Education in the United States," *Paedagogica Historica*, 42, 1-2 (2006), 161–173.

[43] See Margaret Wetherell (Editor) *Identity in the 21st Century: New Trends in Changing Times* (Basingstoke: Palgrave Macmillan, 2009).

every area of social life. Central to this idea is the notion that the dominant class lays down the terms and parameters of discussion in society, and in so doing, it tries to define and contain all taste, morality, and customs, religious and political principles. Hegemony is enshrined in the cement of ideology. 'All men are intellectuals,' says Gramsci to appropriate the terms of 'intelligence' such that marginalised social and cultural groups have the capacity to produce a counter-hegemony that might modify, negotiate, resist or overthrow the dominant culture.[44]

In the public sphere, Madeleine Arnot has demonstrated that gender codes play a large part in establishing language and meaning with regard to the role of education as a means of social reproduction. As the historical archive work of Michèle Cohen shows, moral debate presents a hierarchy of intellect based on the premise of a rational, masculine mind and the channelling of irrationality into women. When it came to patterns of male and female educational achievement, boys were positioned as cultivating a habit of 'healthy idleness,' whereas girls were seen to possess an 'unhealthy' tendency to over-exertion. So, male success was attributed to something within such as the nature of their intellect, whereas female success was attributed to something without such as teaching methods, teachers, or learning styles. The opposite was true of male failure which was attributed to something external. Unlike female failure, which was attributed to something within.[45]

To understand the cultural frameworks, ideologies and political preferences that frame experience I have turned to Raymond Williams's expression 'structures of feeling' in the sense of a general or shared culture. Through this concept, configurations of identity are interpretable, in part, as communicative practices about becoming intelligible to oneself and others. A process constituted within every day, practical consciousness in a complex relation with official consciousness or received interpretations that continually shape understandings of society and the world. A particular structure of feeling stands as a mediating term, mapping individual and social history within its telling. Incorporated in its conceptualisation are those almost unconscious, or spontaneous, feelings of 'lived experience' (seen essentially as a process) interacting with the cognitive, or reflexive, dimension (a level of rational, conscious monitoring based on ethical considerations) and in the process reproducing identity and culture.

In Williams's version of culture in *The Long Revolution*, each generation responds in its own ways to the unique world it is inheriting. On the one hand, taking up continuities and reproducing many aspects of the organisation. On

---

[44] Raewyn Connell, *Masculinities*, (Berkeley & Los Angeles: University of California Press, 1995); Antonio Gramsci, *Selections from the Prison Notebooks* ed. Quintin Hoare (London: Lawrence and Wishart, 2005).

[45] Madeleine Arnot, *Reproducing Gender: Essays on educational theory and feminist politics* (London: RoutledgeFalmer, 2002); Michèle Cohen, "'A Habit of Healthy Idleness': boys' underachievement in historical perspective," in *Failing Boys? Issues in Gender and Achievement*, eds. D. Epstein, J. Elwood, V. Hey and J. Maw (Buckingham: Open University Press, 1998), 19–34.

the other, feeling its whole life in certain ways differently, and shaping its creative response into a new 'structure of feeling.' This means yours and my encounter with culture must be *distinct* from Williams's encounter. However, his theory offers a forward thinking for the development of thought and activism, 'not in the name of an individual, but of that *community*—those commonly held values which serve to define a group as socially distinct—in which women and men move together towards a more equal future.'[46]

In exploring the hegemonic processes involved in reproducing gender over time, I deploy the 'thinking tools' of French sociologist Pierre Bourdieu to interpret historical categories of networks, site, subjectivities and socio-cultural reproduction and unpack agency, constraint and power for acting and the fashioning of self.[47] In so doing, I work with a 'social' definition of culture, to consider the meanings and values implicit and explicit in particular ways of life, which express certain meanings and values linked to the production of class and gender difference.

THINKING GENDER AND GENERATION THROUGH APPROPRIATING BOURDIEU

Bourdieu understands the social world as made up of different but overlapping fields of power, which function according to their own set of rules and help explain intergenerational reproduction through historical time. Feel for the game and acceptance as a legitimate player within a specific social field is achieved by the acquisition and deployment of various types of capital—economic, social and cultural.[48] Bourdieu discusses the value of women as repositories of social capital in the marriage strategies of their families in his 1984 book, *Distinction*. Based on the premise that social relationships enable individuals to get on and get ahead, social capital is defined as relational capital or the power and advantage a person rich in symbolic capital may gain from having a network of culturally, economically, or politically useful relations, besides a series of intimate personal relations.[49]

If accepted as legitimate, the different forms of capital take the form of symbolic capital. Social relations and social practice constitute field positions, while

---

[46] Raymond Williams, *The Long Revolution* (Letchworth: Broadview Press, 2001); Julia Swindells and Lisa Jardine *What's Left? Women Culture and the Labour Movement* (London: Routledge, 1990), 152.

[47] Pierre Bourdieu, *Practical Reason: On the Theory of Action* (Cambridge: Polity Press, 1998).

[48] Economic capital refers to income, wealth, financial inheritances and monetary assets. Cultural capital, defined as high culture, can exist in three forms: embodied cultural capital, objectified cultural capital and institutional cultural capital. The last is the product of investment in formal education. Social capital is the product of sociability, which speaks of investment in culturally, economically or politically useful networks and connections.

[49] Pierre Bourdieu, *Distinction: A Social Critique of the Judgement of Taste* (Harvard: Harvard University Press, 1984).

habitus is formed through the process of internalisation of capitals and lived practice. Learned more by experience than by teaching, Bourdieu's notion of habitus relates to the norms or tendencies that guide behaviour or thinking, which offers a way of theorising durable dispositions focused around the connections between public and private lives. It includes cultural, symbolic and economic axes apparent in styles of dress, the way we walk, talk and decorate our living spaces. All of which demonstrate distinctions of disposition, attitude and tastes. Essentially, habitus inscribes the individual with a repertoire of practices, with a history, which are themselves generative of enduring (although not entirely fixed) orientations to action. A radical habitus allows the potentiality of agency and change, a way of interpreting fluid contexts of social power that attend to political and cultural contexts as well as a subject. Some women can offset the social effects of being female, and the English writer Virginia Woolf presents an example.

Born into the liberal intelligentsia in 1882, but denied opportunities given her brothers, servants were part of the furniture for Woolf and her literary circle. Class politics percolated within households associated with an advanced drawing room outlook but whose good fortune depended on 'that division of labour, which made housekeeping a female activity, and housework performed, where possible, by women of the lower classes.'[50] In 1928, when Woolf proposed £400 a year and a private room of one's own as the key to a woman's creative liberation, six million fellow Londoners survived on an annual income of under £200. Driven by anger, Woolf aspired to alter existing culture. In her book-length essay of 1938, *Three Guineas*, she insists war and fascism are the public and international expression of patriarchal power in family life and a masculinist competition for honours and position. She encourages women to break the cycle of subordination by earning their own living and cherishing their position as 'outsiders' so they might behave as moral exemplars, with the status of honourable, detached critic.[51]

The point Woolf makes about being outside the dominant order is akin to standpoint feminism used by Canadian sociologist Dorothy Smith, which looks at the social world from the perspectives of women in their everyday worlds and the ways in which women socially construct their worlds. As Smith puts it when speaking of the control by men of the ideological forms which regulate social relations in this society:

> Men are invested with authority as individuals not because they have as individuals special competencies or expertise but because as men they appear as represen-

---

[50] Alison Light, *Mrs. Woolf and the Servants: An Intimate History of Domestic Life in Bloomsbury* (London: Bloomsbury, 2008), 115; Julia Swindells, *Victorian Writing & Working Women* (Minneapolis: University of Minnesota Press, 1985).

[51] Virginia Woolf, *Three Guineas* (Harmondsworth: Penguin, [1938] 1979).

tative of the power and authority of the institutionalized structures which govern the society. Their authority as *individuals* in actual situations of action is generated by a social organization. They do not appear for themselves alone. They are those whose words count.[52]

Feminists engaging with male theorists is the subject of Toril Moi's essay, 'Appropriating Bourdieu,' first published in 1991. For Moi, Bourdieu's attention to the details of everyday life and approach to theorising subjectivity is the basis of attraction, and she uses her reading of French philosopher Simone de Beauvoir to demonstrate this. Beauvoir's particular utility as a historical subject is to illustrate the significance of gender. As Moi puts it, 'the *only* obvious social stigma from which Beauvoir suffers in the educational and intellectual fields of her day is that of femaleness.'[53]

The final section will model the cultural cartography I use in the rest of the book to help explain the micro-politics of gender, agency and resistance, via small-scale descriptive work, which focuses on the internal operations of educational institutions. Piecing together evidence drawn from a variety of sources (university archives, institutional histories and published autobiographies), my exemplar is the regime of gender within the LSE's Department of Social Administration founded in 1912, whose first head was Edward Johns Urwick, a founding member and vice-president of the Sociological Society.

PEARL JEPHCOTT AND THE GENDERING OF BRITISH SOCIAL SCIENCE IN POST-WAR BRITAIN

Mary Stocks progressed to the LSE as a student in 1910 and revealed unflattering details of how she and other economics students referred to the Social Administration department as 'Urwick's harem.'[54] Sociologist T.H. Marshall said it was 'popularly regarded as a convenient place for wealthy mothers to send their daughters to when disturbed by the dawning of a social conscience.'[55] Until the 1960s, approximately 90 per cent of the students were women, many of whom were residents at the Women's University Settlement in Southwark. They came because the department offered some of the earliest research training and courses for social workers in the country. Courses combined theory and practice through organised placements in charity offices, poor law reception centres, and other social and civic institutions.

---

[52] Dorothy Smith, "An Analysis of Ideological Structures and How Women are Excluded: Considerations for Academic Women," in *Women and Education: a Canadian Perspective*, eds. Jane S. Gaskell and Arlene T. McLaren (eds.) *Women and Education: a Canadian Perspective* (Calgary, Alberta: Detselig Enterprises, 1987), 253.

[53] Toril Moi, *What is a Woman?* (Oxford: Oxford University Press, 1999), 292.

[54] Mary Stocks, *My Commonplace Book* (London: Peter Davies, 1970), 99–100.

[55] Quoted in Ralf Dahrendorf, *A History of the London School of Economics and Political Science 1895–1995.* Oxford: Oxford University Press, 1995), 383.

Carol Dyhouse suggests the LSE offered a research environment that was relatively friendly to women.[56] Within Social Administration, the inverse relation between status level and proportion of women was obvious. Women were concentrated in the position of tutor, while men were lecturers. Appointed lecturer in 1925, Marshall became head of department in 1944, but the person doing the work was Newnham-educated economist Edith Eckhard employed as a tutor in 1919 and denied promotion to lecturer (and hence the promotional ladder leading to professorial rank) because she lacked publications. Her staff file clearly shows how teaching (a technology of the feminine) balanced out with leadership (a technology of the masculine).[57] Richard Titmuss arrived in 1950 as newly appointed professor and departmental head. Ann Oakley has written of the gendered institutional culture fostered by her father, Titmuss, as he transformed the space into a centre of social policy expertise populated mainly by men.[58] At his request, Eckhard postponed her retirement specifically to set up a new degree and generic training in a context of increased demand for social workers in the post-war welfare state.[59] In 1954, Titmuss (who lacked any formal educational qualifications besides commercial bookkeeping) appointed Pearl Jephcott—a gifted female sociologist in her 50s—to investigate the lives of married women workers at the Peek Frean biscuit factory in Bermondsey in south London.

With a professional life in youth work behind her, Jephcott moved to the LSE from a research post at Nottingham University. *Girls Growing Up* published in 1942 formed the bedrock of her academic reputation, followed by *Rising Twenty*, her 1948 study of just over a hundred girls living in three parts of England (a pit village in County Durham, a cluster of decaying and blitzed streets within a mile of London's Piccadilly Circus and a northern industrial town). Through her sociological fieldwork and involvement in the girls' club movement, Jephcott collected a plethora of oral testimony gathered via home visits, meetings in the street, at cafés, cinemas, dance halls, fairs, pubs, shops and youth clubs. In one passage in *Clubs for Girls*, Jephcott comments on the gendering of children's toys, noting how 'when they are small children [girls] have dolls and tea-sets in their Christmas stockings while their brothers are given cranes and aeroplanes.'[60]

---

[56] Carol Dyhouse, *No Distinction of Sex? Women in British universities 1870–1939*. London: UCL Press, 1995).
[57] Edith Eckhard Staff File, archives, LSE.
[58] Ann Oakley, *Father and Daughter: Patriarchy, Gender and Social Sciences* (Bristol: Policy Press, 2014), 118–20.
[59] R.M. Titmuss to Director 21 December 1950, archives, LSE.
[60] Pearl Jephcott, *Clubs for Girls* (London: Faber and Faber, 1943), 59.

Text Box 2.1   Pearl Jephcott, Sociologist, Curriculum Vitae
SECTION 1: Biographical details: education/ qualifications; title and school/ college
Alcester Grammar School, Warwickshire
University College of Wales, Aberystwyth, BA, 1922
MA awarded on publications, 1949
Secretarial Training
SECTION 2: Employment details
1923   Teaching post
1925–27   Fund raiser, Dr Barnardo's Children's Homes
1927–35   Organising secretary, Birmingham Union of Girls Clubs
1935–42   County organiser, Durham Union of Girls Clubs
1942   Temporary national organiser, National Association of Girls Clubs
1943   Publications secretary, National Association of Girls Clubs
1945–46   Barnett Fellowship
1946–48   Political and Economic Planning: research staff
1949–50   Northern Industrial Group: research staff
1950–52   King George's Jubilee Trust (attached to Nottingham University)
1954–60   London School of Economics: senior research officer
1956   Seconded to Colonial Office
1957   Member, Central Advisory Council for Education (England); National Youth Employment Council (Ministry of Labour)
SECTION 3: Publications
Jephcott, Pearl. *Girls Growing Up*. London: Faber and Faber, 1942.
Jephcott, Pearl. *Clubs for Girls*. London: Faber and Faber, 1943.
Jephcott, Pearl. *Rising Twenty*. London: Faber and Faber, 1948.
Jephcott, Pearl. *Some Young People*. London: George Allen and Unwin, 1954.
Jephcott, Pearl. 'Going Out to Work', background paper Duke of Edinburgh's study conference on human problems of industrial communities, 1956a.
Jephcott, Pearl. *Report on the Needs of the Youth of the More Populated Coastal Areas of British Guiana*, 1956b.
Jephcott, Pearl. *Married Women Working*. London: George Allen and Unwin, 1962 (with N. Seear and J. H. Smith).
Jephcott, Pearl. *A Troubled Area*. London: Faber and Faber, 1964.
Jephcott, Pearl. *Homes in High Flats*. Edinburgh: Oliver & Boyd, 1971.

Jephcott and her co-investigators spent five years producing an innovative study of married women's work. Oakley speculates that the genesis of the project lay with Jephcott, and while the evidence for this is inconclusive, the location is significant since strong links had developed between the LSE and Bermondsey's working-class community. Traditionally a district of casual labour and poverty, social work students had been going there for decades: anthropologists had studied kinship, students of economics and sociology had investigated the question of labour turnover. Connections grew up between the local settlement house and LSE social science in the 1900s, and two members of Bermondsey Women's Labour League with links to the Fabian Society represented the area on the London County Council in the 1920s and 1930s.[61]

Married women working was a topical issue in 1950s Britain. Most people thought it wrong for women to combine work and marriage unless it was financially impossible to do otherwise. At a national policy level, the concept of the 'dual job,' of paid work beyond marriage and combined with household responsibilities, had serious consequences but public opinion did not change radically. Men were still encouraged to see themselves as head of households with their main responsibility being as principal wage earner, and it was the era of psychoanalyst John Bowlby's claims about 'maternal deprivation' and the negative effects on infants of working mothers.[62]

In Bermondsey, the tireless Jephcott set up home in the locality and her sustained contact with the working-class community (including two months working as a cleaner in the local hospital) helped build trust among the women employees in the factory study. In a passage whose conclusions are rather remarkable for its time, Jephcott explains the research findings:

> Current fears centre on the possibility of ill effects if the finely balanced relationship between mother and child is disturbed. Society itself has created a dilemma by developing on the one hand a greatly increased concern for children's happiness and health generally, and by extending the provision for deprived children; and on the other, by emphasizing women's freedom as individuals and their right to compete for jobs and status with men…Hemmed between these contradictory forces, it would not be surprising if the wife who works showed some feeling of guilt. Yet little evidence exists which can be said to justify this particular anxiety; and none of these criticisms allow that wives might successfully divide their time between work and home. At least, none seem to grant the working-class wife this ability, for the stereotypes condemning the wife who works invariably concentrate on her.[63]

---

[61] See the discussion in Jane Martin, "Beyond suffrage: feminism, education and the politics of class in the inter-war years," *British Journal of sociology of Education*, 29, No. 4, (2008), 411–423.
[62] Denise Riley, *War in the Nursery* (London: Virago, 1983).
[63] Pearl Jephcott, *Married Women Working* (London: George Allen and Unwin, 1962) (with Nancy Seear and John H. Smith with a Foreword by Richard Titmuss), 22–3.

Yet the project had a troubled passage, congruent with Titmuss being a somewhat elusive supervisor. Added to which, Jephcott's expertise prompted national invitations to report on the needs of young people in British Guiana and the Caribbean and serve on two government inquiries the Central Advisory Council for Education (England) and the Albemarle Committee looking at the Youth Service in England and Wales.

When Titmuss secured additional funding for the Bermondsey study, he approached the LSE's Director about the circumstances of 58-year-old Jephcott's employment. 'From the research she has done and the books she has written she has acquired a national reputation as an authority on the problems of young people ... In view of all this and her academic achievement, I did wonder whether you thought there was any possibility of creating a Readership in the Department for her.'[64] Asked to withdraw the application on the grounds of economy, Titmuss found himself having to negotiate extensions to Jephcott's contract on a shockingly hand-to-mouth basis. One administrator challenged the approach. Reluctant to include the personal position of a retiring staff member when calculating the supplementary pension, s/he was 'particularly hesitant to write to Miss Jephcott to ask her to divulge to us the full nature of her investments so that we can make the calculations you suggest.' Going further, s/he reminded superiors of Marshall's remuneration when he left the School and 'who, on termination of this appointment, was granted a supplementary pension in respect of his employment prior to that last appointment.'[65]

In Jephcott's case, the men in the professional and academic positions of influence closed ranks. Her last temporary contract terminated the day before her 62nd birthday, with no *ex gratia* payment and no supplementary pension. The career, ideas and research of Pearl Jephcott, youth worker and pioneer sociologist, show the evolving opportunities and challenges for women in the post-war years: a graphic illustration of the blocks on female advancement in what could be called a feminized intellectual field if student numbers were the defining criteria.

Conclusion

This chapter has sought to integrate gender as a category of historical analysis into the deep structure of educational thought. Embedded in the field is the way in which the gender of the speaker modifies the message. I refer to *I'm Not Complaining*, a 1938 novel by Ruth Adams and revolving around five teachers in a Nottinghamshire elementary school in the 1930s to show what I mean. The words of unmarried female teacher Marge Brigson have a pungent realism:

> He looked me over and he got the best of it. Though I had a job requiring more brains than his, though the State paid me more for my public value than it did him, though he was only doing the work for which my tax-money paid, I could

[64] Pearl Jephcott Staff File, archives, LSE.
[65] Ibid.

not get even with him. The whole weight of public opinion which believes that there is something comical and humiliating in being an unmarried woman, and something rather dashing and enviable in being an unmarried young man, left me without an answer to crush him. His tone said never so plainly that my own repressed longing for a man of my own made me into a nervy old maid. I felt a hot rush of anger, which mounted up my neck and over my face, and which he could just see under the light of the "daylight" lamps we had just reached. He smiled and looked closely at me, and I would willingly have struck him if I had not been brought up to believe that the tongue is the only legitimate weapon of anger.[66]

The effect is socially constructed, and Dorothy Smith's metaphor of a 'circle' of speakers and hearers relevant to one another remains pertinent in seeing this as an aspect of the social organisation of the ideological formations of education and the wider society. Documenting gendered representations, capitals and recognitions and historicising the institutionalised practices of excluding women from the ideological work of society show the reason why the writing of history was constructed largely from the perspective of men, and largely about men.

Bourdieusian approaches and the 'structures of feeling' examined by Williams provide ways of thinking about and interpreting real-world examples of gender, continuity and difference through time and space. Chapters that follow address the conditionality of the female presence. Taking gender codes and habitus as key concepts, they deploy theories of gender relations to examine the shifting landscape of politics and policy-making in education. A key question being whether to incorporate a select few into a masculinist habitus within narrow meritocratic terms while offering the majority a vocational education intended as preparation for carrying on societies reproductive processes. Moving beyond the making of gendered policy histories, I will be using autobiography, educational ethnography and oral testimony to reconstruct the politics of experience, prioritising the often silenced or marginalised experience of the majority. I will argue that the social relations of schooling play a key role in social and cultural reproduction, and the elite in society is still broadly white and male in terms of access and control of high-status knowledge, educational routes, institutions and employment. To that extent, the educational landscape has proved stubbornly resilient to progressive change.

Bibliography

Primary Sources

Archival Sources

Fabian Society papers, London School of Economics.
Scholarship files: Shaw studentship. London School of Economics.
Staff files: Edith Eckhard, Pearl Jephcott. London School of Economics.

[66] Ruth Adams, *I'm Not Complaining* (London: Virago, [1938], 1983 edition), 233.

AUTOBIOGRAPHIES, MEMOIRS, DIARIES, LETTERS

Bell, Susan Groag. *Between Worlds in Czechoslovakia, England, and America*. New York: Dutton, 1991.
Benson, Sheila. "Experiences in the London New Left." In *Out of Apathy: Voices of the New Left 30 Years On*, edited by Robin Archer, Diemet Bubeck, Hanjo Glock, Lesley Jacobs, Seth Moglen, Adam Steinhouse, Daniel Weinstock, 107–110. London: Verso, 1989.
Marshall, Dorothy. *The Making of a Twentieth Century Woman*. London: Blazenbooks, 2003.
McKenzie, Norman and McKenzie, Jeanne (eds.) *The Diary of Beatrice Webb Volume Two 1892–1905*. London: Virago, 1986.
Rowbotham, Sheila. *Promise of a Dream: Remembering the Sixties*. London: Penguin Press, 2000.
Stocks, Mary. *My Commonplace Book*. London: Peter Davies, 1970.

OTHER CONTEMPORARY BOOKS AND PAMPHLETS

Adam, Ruth. *I'm Not Complaining*. London: Virago, [1938]1983.
Davies, Lynn. *Pupil Power: deviance & gender in schools*. Lewes: Falmer Press, 1983.
Fuller, Mary. "Black girls in a London comprehensive school," in *Schooling for Women's Work*, ed. Rosemary Deem, 52–65. London: Routledge, Kegan and Paul, 1980.
Grier, Linda. *The Life of Winifred Mercier*. Oxford: Oxford University Press, 1937.
Jephcott, Pearl. *Clubs for Girls*. London: Faber and Faber, 1943.
Jephcott, Pearl. *Married Women Working*. London: George Allen and Unwin, 1962 (with Nancy Seear and John H. Smith with a Foreword by Richard Titmuss).
McRobbie, Angela. "Settling Accounts With Sub-Cultures: A Feminist Critique," *Screen Education*, no. 34, Spring 1980.
Mitchell, Juliet and Oakley, Ann, eds. *The Rights and Wrongs of Women*. Harmondsworth: Penguin, 1976.
Mitchell, Juliet. *Women: The Longest Revolution*. Harmondsworth: Penguin, 1984.
Stott, Mary. *Before I Go*. London: Virago, 1985.
Wedderburn, Dorothy. "Activism and the New Left." In *Out of Apathy: Voices of the New Left 30 Years On*, eds. Robin Archer, Diemet Bubeck, Hanjo Glock, Lesley Jacobs, Seth Moglen, Adam Steinhouse, Daniel Weinstock, 111–113. London: Verso, 1989.
Willis, Paul. *Learning to Labour*. London: Saxon House, 1977.
Wilson, Harold. *The New Britain: Labour's Plan Outlined by Harold Wilson*. Harmondsworth: Penguin, 1964.
Woolf, V. *Three Guineas*. Harmondsworth: Penguin, [1938], 1979.

SECONDARY SOURCES

Abu-Lughod, Lila. *Writing Women's Worlds: Bedouin Stories*. Berkeley and Los Angeles: University of California Press, 1993.
Alberti, Johanna. *Gender and the Historian*. Harlow: Pearson Education, 2002.
Arnot, Madeleine. *Reproducing Gender? Essays on educational theory and feminist politics*. London: RoutledgeFalmer, 2002.

Ball, Stephen J. *The Micro-Politics of the School: towards a theory of school organisation.* Abingdon: Routledge, 2012.

Beard, Mary. *Women & Power: a Manifesto.* London: Profile Books, 2017.

Bennett, Judith M. *History Matters: Patriarchy and the Challenge of Feminism,* Manchester: Manchester University Press, 2006.

Berg, Maxine. *A Woman in History: Eileen Power, 1889–1940.* Cambridge: Cambridge University Press, 1996.

Bourdieu, Pierre. *Distinction: A Social Critique of the Judgement of Taste.* Harvard: Harvard University Press, 1984.

Bourdieu, Pierre. *Practical Reason: On the Theory of Action.* Cambridge: Polity Press, 1998.

Bradley, Harriet. "Changing Social Structures: Class and Gender". In *Formations of Modernity: Understanding Modern Societies* edited by Stuart Hall and Bram Gieben, 177–228. Cambridge: Polity Press, 1992.

Burton, Antoinette. "'History' is Now: feminist theory and the production of historical feminisms." *Women's History Review,* 1, no. 1 (1992), 25–38.

Caine, Barbara. *Biography and History.* New York: Palgrave Macmillan, 2010.

Carr, Edward Hallett. *What Is History?* New York: Palgrave Macmillan, 2002.

Connell, Raewyn. *Masculinities.* Cambridge: Policy Press, 1995.

Crocco, Margaret S., Munro, Petro, Weiler, Kathleen. *Pedagogies of Resistance: Women Educator Activists, 1880–1960.* New York: Teachers College Press, 1999.

Dahrendorf, Ralf. *A History of the London School of Economics and Political Science 1895–1995.* Oxford: Oxford University Press, 1995.

Davidoff, Leonore and Hall, Catherine. *Family Fortunes: Men and Women of the English Middle Class, 1780–1850.* London: Hutchinson, 1987.

Dyhouse, Carol. *No Distinction of Sex? Women in British universities 1870–1939.* London: UCL Press, 1995.

Griffiths, Morwenna. *Feminisms and the Self: The Web of Identity.* London: Routledge, 1995.

Hilton, Mary and Hirsch, Pamela, eds. *Practical Visionaries: Women, Education and Social Progress 1790–1930.* London: Longman, 2000.

Levine, Philippa. *The Amateur and the Professional: Antiquarians, Historians and Archaeologists in Victorian England, 1838–1886.* Cambridge: Cambridge University Press, 1986.

Light, Alison. *Mrs. Woolf and the Servants: An Intimate History of Domestic Life in Bloomsbury.* London: Bloomsbury, 2008.

Martin, Jane. *Women and the Politics of Schooling in Victorian and Edwardian England.* Leicester: Leicester University Press, 1999.

Martin, Jane and Goodman, Joyce. *Women and Education, 1800–1980.* Basingstoke: Palgrave Macmillan, 2004.

Martin, Jane. 'Beyond suffrage: feminism, education and the politics of class in the inter-war years', *British Journal of sociology of Education,* 29, no. 2 (2008): 411–423.

Martin, Jane Roland. *Education Reconfigured: Culture, Encounter, and Change.* London: Routledge, 2011.

McKenzie, Norman and McKenzie, Jeanne, eds. *The Diary of Beatrice Webb Volume Two 1892–1905.* London: Virago, 1986.

Miller, Jane. *School for Women.* London: Virago, 1996.

Moi, Toril. *What is a Woman?* Oxford: Oxford University Press, 1999.

Oakley, Ann. *Father and Daughter: Patriarchy, Gender and Social Sciences.* Bristol: Policy Press, 2014.

Riley, Denise. *War in the Nursery.* London: Virago, 1983.

Rose, Hilary. *Lowe, Power and Knowledge: towards a feminist transformation of the sciences,* Cambridge: Polity Press, 1994.

Scott, Joan Wallach. "Gender: a useful category of historical analysis," *The American Historical Review,* 91, December (1986): 1053–75.

Scott, Joan Wallach. *Gender and the Politics of History.* New York: Columbia University Press, 1988.

Rowbotham, Sheila. *Hidden from History: 300 years of women's oppression and the fight against it.* Harmondsworth: Penguin, 1973.

Smith, Dorothy E. "An Analysis of Ideological Structures and How Women are Excluded: Considerations for Academic Women." In *Women and Education: a Canadian Perspective* edited by Jane S. Gaskell and Arlene T. McLaren. Calgary, Alberta: Detselig Enterprises, 1987.

Smith, Bonnie G. *The Gender of History.* Harvard: Harvard University Press, 1998.

Spender, Dale. *Women of Ideas and What Men Have Done to Them.* London: Routledge and Kegan Paul, 1982.

Swindells, Julia. *Victorian Writing & Working Women.* Minneapolis: University of Minnesota Press, 1985.

Swindells, Julia and Jardine, Lisa. *What's Left? Women Culture and the Labour Movement.* London: Routledge, 1990.

Thompson, Edward P. *The Making of the English Working Class.* Harmondsworth: Penguin, 1988.

Tosh, John. *A Man's Place: Masculinity and the Middle Class Home in Victorian England.* New Haven: Yale University Press, 1999.

Verkaik, Robert. *Posh Boys: How the English Public Schools Ruin Britain.* London: Oneworld Publications, 2018.

Weaver, Stewart. *The Hammonds: A Marriage in History.* Stanford: Stanford University Press, 1997.

Wetherell, Margaret. (Editor) *Identity in the 21st Century. New Trends in Changing Times.* Basingstoke: Palgrave Macmillan, 2009.

Williams, Raymond. *The Long Revolution.* Letchworth: Broadview Press, 2001.

Winslow, Cal, ed. *E.P. Thompson and the Making of the New Left: Essays and Polemics.* London: Lawrence and Wishart, 2014.

CHAPTER 3

Childhood, Education and the Family

> *Somewhere about 1880, a little girl might have been seen almost any day in the year looking out of a top-floor window in one of the London squares. She was a lonely little girl; for the Victorian family fell by sheer force of numbers into groups; and the other members of her group, being brothers, were away at school for three-quarters of the year. The schoolroom group led its own life downstairs; so did elder sisters who went to dinner-parties and dances, chaperoned by parents. On the top floor, except in holiday time, the child at the window had the whole of the nursery and its outlook to herself.*
> —Evelyn Sharp, *The London Child* (London: Bodley Head, 1927), 1

These are the words of Evelyn Sharp who spent her life as a professional freelance writer besides being a key figure in the women's suffrage movement. Born in 1869 into a somewhat conventional, comfortable and large middle-class family, Sharp maintained her belief in women's rights into the 1920s alongside a focus on pacifism and socialism. She applied her interest in children in practical relief work and to studies such as in her book *The London Child*, published in 1927. Sharp's reflections summon up the everyday world of urban elite childhood in the late-Victorian period. Like her creator, this little girl is profoundly unconventional and longs to swop places with the boy she watches sweeping a path ahead of people crossing the dirty city street. 'His was a freedom she never would know. He could do what he pleased, untrammelled by manners; he was never crammed into a best suit and sent downstairs to be polite to strangers; he did not look forward to a dreary future filled with dinner-parties and classical concerts and Shakespeare.'[1]

---

[1] Evelyn Sharp, *The London Child* (London: Bodley Head, 1927), 1; Angela V. John, '"Behind the Locked Door": Evelyn Sharp suffragette and rebel journalist', *Women's History Review*, 12, no. 1 (2003): 5-13.

During the eighteenth century, education was regarded as a family decision, but the prosperity of a household was the prerequisite and not the guarantee of a formal schooling. Social class influenced both access to and the duration of education, but in many families, the education of girls had to take second place and cost less than that of boys. One of the housemaids in Jo Baker's novel *Longbourn* retelling Jane Austen's *Pride and Prejudice* from the servants' perspective observes what would have happened if her employer, Mrs Bennett, had had her boy. That child would have been bundled off to school, while his sisters stayed at home. 'Then he'd have been foisted off on one of the Universities, and there he'd have indulged in all the japes, jollies and misdemeanours considered a necessary part of a gentleman's education; he'd have acquired some useful acquaintance, no doubt, and, almost incidentally, a degree. Then he would have lived at leisure, accruing debt, and waiting to inherit.'[2] On the eve of the First World War, militant suffragette leader Emmeline Pankhurst ruminated in her autobiography. 'My parents, especially my father, discussed the question of my brothers' education as a matter of real importance. My education and that of my sister were scarcely discussed at all.'[3]

Most Georgian towns had various educational establishments, but institutional provision was dependent on demand, the personal popularity of the teacher and practical support from the parish, which could make or break a small local school.[4] Owing their existence to public endowments (money, buildings and land), endowed schools offered scholarships, sometimes even free education to the local poor but generally charged fees. Added to which, some did effectively exclude girls by their interpretation of the word 'children' to mean boys alone. Commercial private schools, run for the profit of their teachers, were neither charitable nor endowed foundations. They included dame schools for basic literacy and academies offering classical, scientific or vocational instruction.

Change came in the Victorian age, and this chapter discusses the development of an education system that was decisively divided along the class and gender lines and shaped a wider set of differences in the life opportunities of men and women. Section one examines the education of an elite minority of middle-and-upper class children between the late eighteenth and early twentieth centuries. Section two provides the groundwork for the analysis and presentation of policy in the book, focusing on the emergence of a 'system' of mass elementary schooling for working-class boys and girls first largely run by powerful denominational religious groups and after 1870, in partial fashion, by locally elected school boards.

---

[2] Jo Baker, *Longbourn* (London: Black Swan, 2014), 296.
[3] Emmeline Pankhurst, *My Own Story* (London: Virago, 1979), 5-6.
[4] Margaret Bryant, *The London Experience of Secondary Education* (London: Woburn Press, 1986), 85.

ELITE EDUCATION AND THE GENDER ORDER

Among seventeenth century elites, the ideal of the scholar-courtier set the preference for a pattern of domestic education as an approved practice. Before the 1820s, sons of upper-class families tended to be educated at home at first by women. Later, they had male tutors and went to schools and universities and to travel. Upper-class daughters also received a domestic education first by their mothers and then by governesses. Generally dependent upon the resources of their own homes for their intellectual development, learned women emerged from social backgrounds where some education was accessible within the home, where governesses, books, space and leisure were available. English essayist Vicesimus Knox helped map the discursive terrain on which contemporary debate about home versus school education took place. For Knox, public schooling was the 'natural' site for the development of boys' masculinities, whereas domestic education 'was suitable only for those who would never be men – weaklings, "imbeciles" and, of course, girls.'[5]

Middle-class status was dependent on occupation and gentility, and many middle-class families could not afford to pay expensive school fees for their sons, never mind their daughters. So, the growth of a prosperous urban commercial class brought demands for moderately priced day schools where boys could be educated without having to board away from home. Education helped people to change their inherited rank or status, and commercial day schools mushroomed, particularly in the towns. Tied to the social status of their pupils, educational aims were as much about the making of gentlemen and ladies, as with training the intellect. The new boys' academies were either classical academies kept by clergymen or university graduates, or mercantile and naval academies that offered a more practical education than the standard classical curriculum of the grammar school. Advertisements placed in weekly journals indicate that demand for female schooling was also growing and reflect marketable aspirations if not the quality of education provided. Many were of the type Jane Austen described in *Emma*, her novel of 1815. That is, places where 'girls might be sent to be out of the way and scramble themselves into a little education, without any danger of coming back prodigies.'[6]

The girls' schools were a more dramatic change because for the first time they offered their pupils an alternative to a private education in the home. The mix of subjects like reading, writing and arithmetic with 'accomplishments' such as French, drawing and music ensured their popularity at a time when there was interest in female education and debate about the relative merits of state versus private provision. London, spa towns and fashionable resorts were popular

---

[5] Michèle Cohen, "Gender and the Private/ Public Debate on Education in the Long Eighteenth Century," in *Public or Private Education? Lessons from History*, ed. Richard Aldrich (London: Woburn, 2004), 18-19.

[6] Margaret Bryant, *The London Experience of Secondary Education*, 147; Jane Austen, *Emma* (Harmondsworth: Penguin, [1815] 2012), 20; Christina De Bellaigue, *Educating Women: Schooling and Identity in England and France, 1800-1867* (Oxford: Oxford University Press, 2007).

locations because of the social season, which brought affluent visitors and provided a convenient opportunity for daughters to learn from specialist teachers.[7] Economic and social imperatives both influenced and vindicated change as other education systems and educational approaches and curricula gathered strength.

The boys' public schools in England were established for many reasons and by all sorts of people and organisations. A tiny set of nine schools with the highest status were set up as free schools for the children of the poor. The oldest of which, Eton and Winchester, traced their ancestry from mediaeval collegiate foundations established for the teaching of prayers, Latin and devotion. The others, in order of foundation, were St Paul's, Shrewsbury, Merchant Taylors', Westminster, Rugby, Harrow and Charterhouse. Over several centuries they excluded poor boys from the local community and apart from St Paul's and Merchant Taylors' that remained boys' day schools, turned themselves into boarding schools. In 1818, for instance, Winchester justified its behaviour to government by explaining that its current pupils really were poor—it was only their parents who were rich. This was the context in which the MP Henry Brougham called for a radical shift in public policy. Having identified various abuses where endowments had been taken from free scholars and used to benefit the masters and governors, Brougham urged that 20 per cent of this misused money be endowed in the training of state schoolteachers. Faced with entrenched opposition from those with a vested interest, he gave up efforts to redistribute these assets and concentrated on the education of the poor through the Ragged School Movement instead.[8]

The brutality within this particular model of schooling was notorious also. During the 1820s, the son of the Earl of Suffolk died from injuries sustained at Charterhouse, having been the football in the school's version of the game. Twenty years on, Augustus Hare declared he 'never learnt anything useful' besides 'servility' and 'almost ceaseless' bullying in his time at Harrow boarding school.[9] Shunned by many parents who thought home education more conducive to morality, public school historians credited the influence of reforming head masters in large part for reversing the decline. Notably, Samuel Butler at Shrewsbury, from 1798, and Thomas Arnold at Rugby, from 1828. The emphasis Butler placed on examinations appealed to the emerging middle classes who expected a vocational curriculum that would equip their sons to be doctors, lawyers and civil servants. Whereas the project Arnold had in mind at Rugby was to transform the place from a bear nursery for indolent aristocrats into a rigorous training ground for the construction of masculine virtue focused on male public roles, in the labour force and as citizens.

---

[7] Susan Skedd, "Women teachers and the expansion of girls' schooling in England, c. 1760-1820," in *Gender in Eighteenth-Century England*, ed. Hannah Barker and Elaine Chalus (London: Longman, 1997), 101, 105.

[8] Robert Verkaik, *Posh Boys: How the English Public Schools Ruin Britain* (London: Oneworld Publications, 2018), 29; David Kynaston and Francis Green, *Engines of Privilege: Britain's Private School Problem* (London: Bloomsbury, 2019), 24, 69.

[9] Augustus Hare, "Harrow in the 1840s: servility," in *School Remembered*, ed. Gillian Avery (London: Victor Gollancz, 1967), 79, 85.

As head master from 1827 to 1842, Arnold preserved Rugby for the rich by closing its free lower school so that a boy without access to a private tutor could not learn enough to get into the main school. The hugely popular semi-autobiographical novel *Tom Brown's Schooldays* set in the Rugby of the 1830s portrayed a generation of boys 'who feared the Doctor with all our hearts, and very little besides in heaven or earth; who thought more of our sets in the School than of the Church of Christ, and put the traditions of Rugby and the public opinion of boys in our daily life above the laws of God.'[10] *Tom Brown* helped popularise the 'muscular Christianity,' a brand of Anglicanism equating good health with Christian values of manliness and fortitude, Arnold promoted. From the 1860s onwards, the Arnoldian legacy influenced a developing narrative whereby a 'public' school education became synonymous with a classical curriculum, leadership training and a cult of athleticism. A hierarchy of privilege and power symbolised by a prefect and fagging system, caps, badges, precise gradations of dress and sport to build character and resilience established and diffused the dominance of their products in English society.

One thing on sale was the distance—emotional, intellectual, and spatial—the rich could maintain from the world of factories, mills, cities, poverty, and disease. What parents got for their money was an institutional habitus that clarified to boys the subjective importance of putting and keeping people in their place as well as of knowing one's place in the top tier. But, also, historian J.A. Mangan has described the three sets of values enmeshed in 'the new imperialism' of late Victorian Britain that were central to sturdy public schoolboy masculine identity and heroism. (1) 'Imperial Darwinism – the God-granted right of the white man to rule, civilise and baptise the inferior coloured races.' (2) 'Institutional Darwinism – the cultivation of physical and psychological stamina at school in preparation for the rigours of imperial duty.' (3) 'The gentleman's education – the nurture of leadership qualities for military conquest abroad and political dominance at home.'[11]

Historically, most endowed grammar schools lacked the financial security and patronage of this tiny set of public schools for boys. Prolonged inflation between 1760 and 1815 hurt many as the dividend from the original endowment shrank. This undermined finance leaving the schools with a dilemma. Offering new, more commercial subjects like science and maths for the sons of fee-payers was one way to generate funds. Others excluded free scholars in favour of fee-paying boarders. In effect, becoming Victorian 'public' schools in embryo but failing in the original charitable intention.[12] The institutional history of Uppingham School illustrates the shift.

---

[10] Thomas Hughes, *Tom Brown's School Days. By an Old Boy* (Cambridge: Macmillan and Co., 1857), 126.

[11] J.A. Mangan, *Athleticism in the Victorian and Edwardian Public School: the Emergence and Consolidation of an Educational Ideology* (Cambridge: Cambridge University Press, 1981), 136.

[12] Richard S. Tompson, *Classics or Charity? The Dilemma of the 18th Century Grammar School* (Manchester: Manchester University Press, 1971); Margaret Bryant, *The London Experience of Secondary Education*.

Founded in the East Midlands in 1584, for centuries Uppingham flourished as a local grammar school of 30 to 60 boys who regularly gained entrance to Oxford and Cambridge. Old Etonian Edward Thring became headmaster in 1853 and is usually credited with having initiated the founding of the Headmasters' Conference in 1869, membership of which has come to signify public school status. Thring's desire for 'training for True Life' would lead to major curriculum reform. Rather than cling to 'the classics,' the syllabus was broad, with craft subjects, languages, music and science given equal status to Greek and Latin. Pupils had individual timetables, and boarding houses were staff run (housemasters considered the school as their home), with small dormitories. Uppingham was the first fee-paying school to introduce organised games as a means of character building and the first to possess a gymnasium and swimming pool and the first to set up an educational mission in London's East End.[13]

The mid-Victorian age saw three royal commissions examine the pattern and quality of education by social class. First, the Newcastle Commission (1858–60) looked into elementary education. Second, the Clarendon Commission (1861–64) investigated the state of the top nine 'public' schools in the wake of complaints about the finances, building and administration of Eton College. Third, the Schools Inquiry Commission (Taunton Commission, 1864–67) looked into grammar and endowed schools. Composed of 12 Commissioners chaired by Lord Taunton, the Commission's investigation was vast and thanks to an influential lobby group that included vicar's daughter Emily Davies, it eventually included girls' schools in its agenda. Significance lies in the fact that Taunton was both the first national systematic comparison of boys' and girls' performance on the national scale and the first occasion when a group of educated and eminent men were required to think about gender and achievement in a public discourse.

In making their investigations, the Commissioners heard a complaint from many teachers, repeated well into the twentieth century, that middle-class parents often lavished all they could afford on their son's education but spent hardly anything on that of their daughters. They also uncovered just how few secondary schools there were for girls. At the same time, the Commissioners observed 'mental differences' between boys and girls. Broadly, 'boys were found to have "greater retentiveness" and greater "inductive faculty", they "wrote with vigour and precision" and were "for the most part content to retail information derived from books, or describe the process of some branch of manufacture."'[14] But the gender politics of an unexpected finding that girls could outperform boys soon became sedimented in the national consciousness

---

[13] Donald Leinster-Mackay, *The Educational World of Edward Thring* (Lewes: Falmer, 1987).

[14] Mary Cathcart Borer, *Willingly to School: a History of Women's Education* (Guildford and London: Lutterworth Press, 1976), 277; Michèle Cohen, "Language and meaning in a documentary source: girls' curriculum from the late eighteenth century to the Schools Inquiry Commission, 1868," *History of Education*, 34 no. 1 (2005), 81.

in the need to police the danger of academic overstrain for girls. Some women who fought for an education drew on a notion of equal-but-different to argue their case. Emily Davies was among those who insisted that girls should be educated to match their brothers with access to the same examinations.

Critically, Taunton recommended the establishment of a national system of secondary education with three types of fee-paying school. It was thought obvious that these distinctions should correspond roughly to social class distinctions within society. Thus, *First-grade schools* with a leaving age of 18 or 19 would provide a 'liberal education' to prepare upper and upper-middle-class boys destined for the universities and the older professions. *Second-grade schools* with a leaving age of 16 or 17 would teach two modern languages besides Latin to prepare middle-class boys for the army, the newer professions and departments of the Civil Service. *Third-grade schools* (the cheapest) with a leaving age of 14 or 15 would teach the elements of French and Latin to lower middle-class boys expected to become 'small tenant farmers, small tradesmen, and superior artisans.'[15]

Ultimately the Endowed Schools Act, which a Parliament controlled by public school alumni passed in 1869, paved the way for old, endowed grammar schools, like Uppingham, to claim public school status. In practice, this meant abolishing the *free* education willed by benefactors in the past, as well as the restrictions on curricula. Free places in the remodelled schools were dependent on winning a scholarship through 'merit,' which usually meant proficiency in Greek or Latin, subjects to which the ordinary child was unlikely to be exposed.[16] Despite local protests, the Commissioners also quite ruthlessly confiscated funds from charities providing food and cash for poor families. The outcome was a defence of social and cultural power in political and everyday life. After Clarendon, the Public Schools Act of 1868 gave public schools independence from direct jurisdiction of the Crown, the established church or the government.[17] Over the new few decades, the schools effectively eliminated long established local foundation rights for poor boys living near the schools, besides transferring assets (money, buildings and land), out of the community.[18]

The adaptability of elite schools helped secure their survival. Fast road coaches and the railway age encouraged enrolments. A fall in middle-class infant mortality was also good for recruitment as was demand for such an education from military and colonial families. By the 1870s, the rough and tumble monasticism of boarding school life was accepted as a part of character education that pervaded everything from playing games to the rigours of learning

---

[15] Raymond Williams, *The Long Revolution* (Letchworth: The Broadwater Press, 2001), 159.
[16] Jane Martin, *Making Socialists: Mary Bridges Adams and the Fight for Knowledge and Power* (Manchester: Manchester University Press, 2013), 106.
[17] Robert Verkaik, *Posh Boys*, 51.
[18] David Kynaston and Francis Green, *Engines of Privilege*, 77.

Latin. This was a weak spot for future Prime Minister Winston Churchill. Unable to answer a single question on the Latin paper during his entrance examination for Harrow, he wrote his name at the top of the page, followed by question one. 'After much reflection I put a bracket round it thus "(I)." But thereafter I could not think of anything connected with it that was either relevant or true. Incidentally there arrived from nowhere in particular a blot and several smudges,' he went on in his autobiography. In due course, Churchill was placed in the lowest division of the lowest form. His lowly status communicated through the Harrow custom of 'calling the roll' in which the boys file past a Master in the schoolyard and answer one by one. It was 1887 and Churchill's father was infamous for having resigned his position as Leader of the House of Commons and Chancellor of the Exchequer. Looking back, he recalled how people would gather on the school steps to witness the ritual and express their surprise, 'Why, he's last of all!'[19]

Expensive preparation was essential to win scholarships, and as admissions were cross regional, these elite schools became national not local in their identity. A public-school accent evolved, making received pronunciation one of the foremost indicators of class in England. Alumni helped get each other into jobs, into commissions in the army, the civil service, the judiciary, and the Anglican episcopate, into membership of clubs and into the connections of the privileged. 'There's a blessed equity in the English social system,' Captain Grimes explains to Paul Pennyfeather in Evelyn Waugh's novel of 1928, *Decline and Fall* 'that ensures the public-school man against starvation. One goes through four or five years of perfect hell at an age when life is bound to be hell, anyway, and after that the social system never lets one down.'[20] Circles within circles of patronage, prestige and snobbery that Leonard Woolf described in his childhood memoir. In 1892, his father sent him to an expensive boys' preparatory school in Brighton full of the sons of rich people. Games was of great importance. 'Anyone seen to be good at lessons or rudimentarily intelligent was suspect both to masters and boys; to be a "swot", i.e. to take lessons at all seriously, was entirely despicable.'[21]

Commercial fee-paying schools for girls date back to the seventeenth century.[22] Irish writer Frances Power Cobbe was also sent to Brighton. Later she complained of having exchanged the physical freedom she enjoyed at home for 'parading the esplanade and neighbouring terraces' along with other girls and a governess, whose duty was 'to utilise those brief hours of bodily exercise by hearing us repeat our French, Italian or German verbs, according to our nationality.' On punishment day, miscreants had to sit 'like naughty babies, with their faces to the wall; half of them being quite of marriageable age and all dressed, as was de rigueur with us every day, in full evening attire of silk or muslin, with

[19] Winston Churchill, *My Early Life* (London: Eland, 2012), 14-15.
[20] Evelyn Waugh, *Decline and Fall*, London: Chapman & Hall, [1928] 1949), 34.
[21] Leonard Woolf, *Sowing: an autobiography of the years 1880-1904* (Letchworth: Readers Union, 1962), 51.
[22] Helen M. Jewell, *Education in Early Modern England* (Basingstoke: Palgrave Macmillan, 1998).

gloves and kid slippers.'[23] The life for which their education prepared them was a good marriage and the social setting of the drawing room and parlour as hosts in the social and political networks of their husband and family. Born in 1890 into a middle-class family, Agatha Christie is now remembered as the world's best-selling author of all time. Home schooled until the age of 12, she and her circle contemplated one thing—a happy marriage. 'We were conscious of all the happiness that awaited us; we looked forward to love, to being looked after, cherished and admired, and we intended to get our own way in the things which mattered to us while at the same time putting our husband's life, career and success before our own, as was our proud duty.'[24] Sadly, her first marriage ended in divorce after her husband's infidelity.

There was no expectation on middle-class women to earn, but a growing number faced an uncertain future. In 1851, a question about marital status on the British census sparked concern about a shortage of men in the main marrying age groups. How to ensure a livelihood for these 'surplus' women who failed to marry was becoming an issue and with a quarter of the female population between the ages of 20 and 45 unmarried, there were calls for so-called redundant women to be shipped off to other places in the English-speaking colonial world to improve their chances of marriage. A very small number of feminists and their male supporters had other ideas. Encouraged by the promotion of meritocracy the 1854 Northcote-Trevelyan Report on the Civil Service initiated, the Langham Place Circle who campaigned for women's equality began the fight for access to education and employment and for political rights.

Appropriate occupations seemed hard to find with the result that many indigent middle-class women turned to teaching. Activists, including sympathetic men, pointed out the absurdity of employing ill-educated women teachers who were unprepared and untrained for the task. In 1848, Queen's College opened in London's Harley Street next door to the Governesses' Benevolent Institution that assisted impoverished governesses in case of illness or old age. Queen's was sponsored by a male committee led by Anglican cleric and theologian Frederick Denison Maurice, a professor at King's College, London, who identified with his sister, who was a governess. In 1849, wealthy Unitarian Elizabeth Jesser Reid put up the money to found Bedford College, London, as the first college in Britain for the higher education of women. In this era, the whole idea of women being included on a governing body was a highly radical one. Ultimately, Reid left the college governance in the hands of three female trustees because she wanted it run by as well as for women.[25]

Dorothea Beale and Frances Buss, who were to become England's most famous headmistresses, were two of Queen's College's earliest pupils. Buss had

[23] Frances Power Cobbe, *The Life of Frances Power Cobbe* (London: Swan Sonnenschein, 1904), 54-6, 65.
[24] Agatha Christie, *An Autobiography* (London: Harper Collins, 1993), 153.
[25] Margaret Tuke, *A History of Bedford College for Women, 1949-1937* (Oxford: Oxford University Press, 1939).

left school at 14 and went along to the evening classes, six nights a week, after a day's work teaching. Beale suffered several governesses before briefly attending school and then being left to educate herself, with the help of lessons passed on by her brothers and copious reading. Neither could see any reason for gender distinctions in education. 'The old rubbish about masculine and feminine studies is beginning to be treated as it deserves,' Beale said. 'It cannot be seriously maintained that those studies which tend to make a man nobler or better, have the opposite effect on a woman.'[26] As expert witnesses Beale and Buss steered the findings of the Taunton Commission with help from Emily Davies. Buss was too agitated to speak at first and Davies, 'who had given her evidence and was "being regaled with claret and biscuits" in the Secretary's room, had to be fetched back hurriedly to prop her up.'[27]

Michèle Cohen's analysis of Beale's compilation of the *Reports Issued by the Schools Inquiry Commission on the Education of Girls* makes visible a new construct, 'girls' greater eagerness to learn,' which the Commissioners proffered as an explanation for differences in male–female achievement. Instead of becoming ground for concern about the unstudious male, however, the finding that girls could equal and surpass boys in examinations was seen as potentially damaging for girls. Indeed, some influential physicians considered women physiologically incapable of scholarship, suggesting that if a girl used her brain too much in puberty, she might wear it out and compromise her physical and moral femininity. So, while Taunton recommended the spread of endowments for girls, it also 'helped set up the conditions for the emergence of new constraints and inequalities in girls' education.'[28] Nevertheless, campaigner Maria Grey called it 'The Doomsday Book' for women's education and she responded by helping to set up the Girls' Public Day School Company in 1872, which in 1906 turned into the Girls' Public Day School Trust (GPDST), and helped provide the foundation of sound secondary schooling for middle class girls.[29]

While these new fee-paying high schools were determined to challenge the pervasive frivolity of female education and its emphasis on accomplishment over understanding, gendered teaching styles grew in importance. Thus, whereas 'emulation' or 'the spirit of competition which encourages striving for excellence' became a major pedagogical tool for channelling boys' energies and motivating them to work, competition and rivalry were discouraged for girls. Emily Davies realised the danger vociferous opposition posed in stoking fears

---

[26] Quoted by Felicity Hunt, "Introduction," in *Lessons for Life. The Schooling of Girls and Women 1850–1950*, ed. Felicity Hunt (Oxford: Basil Blackwell, 1987), 7-8.

[27] Carol Dyhouse, "Miss Buss and Miss Beale: Gender and Authority in the History of Education," in *Lessons for Life. The Schooling of Girls and Women 1850–1950*, ed. Felicity Hunt (Oxford: Basil Blackwell, 1987), 28.

[28] Op cit, 93.

[29] Jane E. Sayers, *The Fountain Unsealed: A History of the Notting Hill and Ealing High School* (Welwyn Garden City: Broadwater Press, 1973), 4; David Turner, *The Old Boys: the decline and rise of the public school* (New Haven and London: Yale University Press, 2015), 127, 151-3.

that a girl who used her brain might either mutate into a bluestocking or become a nervous wreck and would sit the prettiest girls in the front row when they sat public examinations, to forestall public opinion caricaturing them as freaks. Legitimated by physicians, concern over emulation as detrimental to female health grew to a crescendo in eugenic anxieties that the strain imposed by too much mental activity in puberty might affect women's capacity for healthy maternity, risking sterility and a drop in the birth rate.[30]

Regardless of the permutations of medico- and socio-biological debates, experienced practitioners like Beale, Buss and their colleagues began with a conviction that women had a special role to play in the world and believed that they could give girls a liberal education, which would fit them for life at home or at work, without compromising their femininity. In practice, this meant teaching a very small number of pupils drawn from a narrow stratum of society that what helped make a man nobler and better would fit a woman for a feminine role of duty and service whether this meant earning a livelihood or not.[31] Contemporaries suggested the prospect of a single future offered an effective incentive to schoolwork, and while paid employment only concerned a minority, the career trajectory of former pupils helped demonstrate the effects of women's education.

Against a backdrop of socialist campaigning against what they called the great educational endowments robbery, Maria Grey displayed the hegemonies of culture and class. She objected to mass schooling funded by local taxation when ratepayers got no help 'in educating their own daughters according to their class in life.' In her view, middle-class parents had little alternative but to use private schools that 'give an education greatly inferior to thoroughness and value as mental training to the elementary schools.'[32] Likewise, Clara Collet, a North London Collegiate-educated civil servant who worked on Charles Booth's survey of the London poor in the late 1880s, backed the need to improve schooling for working-class girls, but she wanted it matched to their domestic and social futures, not unduly academic and focused on areas like child care, hygiene and family economy.[33] Working at the Board of Trade in the 1890s, she advised the middle-class girl required the cultivation of mental culture, whereas 'any system of education for working girls should have as its object their training for the responsibilities of married life.'[34] To

[30] Anna Davin, "Imperialism and Motherhood," *History Workshop*, 5 (Spring 1978), 9-67; Carol Dyhouse, *Girls Growing Up In Victorian and Edwardian England* (London: Routledge, Kegan and Paul, 1981), 91-95.

[31] Felicity Hunt, "Divided Aims: the Educational Implications of Opposing Ideologies in Girls' Secondary Schooling, 1850-1940" in Introduction", in *Lessons for Life. The Schooling of Girls and Women 1850–1950*, ed. Felicity Hunt (Oxford: Basil Blackwell, 1987), 3-21.

[32] Maria Grey, *Journal of the Women's Educational Union*, 15 May 1875, 9-10.

[33] Jane Miller, "Clara Collet's Dissenting Inheritance and the Education of Women," in *Practical Visionaries: Women, Education and Social Progress 1790-1930*, eds. Mary Hilton and Pam Hirsch (London: Longman, 2000), 119.

[34] *British Parliamentary Papers*, Secondary Education, 1895 session, 380.

Elementary Education and the Making of Good Wives and Mothers

In his book *The Enlightened Economy* (2009), Joel Mokyr notes that it is often said Thomas Malthus wrote his highly influential 1798 *Essay on Population* at just about the time it was becoming irrelevant since the rate of income growth was about to exceed the rate of population growth by a larger and larger margin.[35] Nevertheless, for contemporary elites, Malthus's idea that population increase would lead to diminishing returns fed a politics of fearfulness about the obedience of young people and workers. Consequently, some Parliamentary and philanthropic commentators expressed the view that factory production and the emergence of industrial employment for women and children were leading to crisis in the family by removing women from the domestic sphere. For the patriarchal state, universal basic elementary education was a site for creating new forms of social relations as well as policing old ones.

Generally thought of instrumentally, rather than as likely to contribute to the life possibilities of the children themselves, the idea of sending the poor to school gradually took root. Provided schooling included schools established by the Charity School movement which represented the moral rescue as opposed to the moral instruction of the poor.[36] Subscriptions were obtained to establish schools for the purpose of providing the children, both boys and girls, with religion and some secular instruction as would keep them in their place as God-fearing, respectable servants, submissiveness and obedience prevailing. Distinguishable by their function as part of a system of sponsored social mobility for poor scholars, the distinctive uniform of some charity schools effectively 'branded' pupils making them vulnerable to taunts of 'charity brat' in the streets. At the same time, advocates of liberal political economy objected to the schools as dangerous and misconceived acts of benevolence.[37]

Sunday Schools were another intervention. A means of teaching children to read and write without the sacrifice of jobs and wages. The idea of an education to instil the virtues of thrift, temperance and industry, as well as Christian morals, drew considerable support among a group of wealthy, influential evangelical Christians known as the Clapham Sect, prominent in England between 1790 and 1830. Evangelicals produced religious literature in the form of moral tales and ballads with a strong emphasis on children's obedience. It was also necessary that individuals should have personal access to the word of God through reading the Bible, and for this reason, reading and religion became staple elements in the curricula of the early nineteenth century Sunday school.

---

[35] Joel Mokyr, *The Enlightened Economy* (Harmondsworth: Penguin, 2009).
[36] Helen M. Jewell, *Education in Early Modern England*.
[37] See Clyde Chitty, *Eugenics, Race and Intelligence in Education* (London: Continuum, 2007).

As one 1806 publication put it: 'The learning we are to communicate is only intended to enable you to read the scriptures and to see that it is the will of God that that you should be contented with your station in life.'[38]

Leading Evangelical Hannah More learnt Latin and mathematics from her father, although the lessons stopped when he realised how good she was. In adulthood, she used the opportunity the rapidly expanding market in educational works and textbooks offered schoolteachers like herself to push into the public world of writing. A prolific author of conduct books with a significant female readership, she saw women as essentially domestic creatures and yet argued for a rigorous intellectual education for girls, becoming a prominent member of the Bluestocking Society, a literary group run by aristocratic and literary women of the day.[39] More explained gender difference thus. 'Women speak to shine or to please, men to convince or confute – Women admire what is brilliant, men, what is solid… Men refuse to give way to the emotions they actually feel, while women sometimes affect to be transported beyond what the occasion will justify.'[40] The network of charity schools she helped set up in rural Somerset stayed within the evangelical definition of womanhood but her belief 'that if the poor could read the Bible they would learn "habits of industry and piety", due deference and subordination, horrified conservatives.'[41]

Population growth as well as high levels of urbanisation had the effect of making the education of all working-class children an issue. The monitorial system, with ordered routines and set procedures using older children as monitors, or assistants, offered the chance of disciplining the poor. Cheap and easily multiplied, the Quaker Joseph Lancaster and the Anglican Andrew Bell developed the method independently. Lancaster's school in London's Borough Road attracted aristocratic and philanthropic support, building the British and Foreign Schools Society to spread non-sectarian teaching. A group of High Church, middle-class Tories responded by founding the National Society for Promoting the Education of the Poor in the Principles of the Established Church. In Derby, Catholic authorities continued the work of Irish-born Catherine McAuley who founded the Sisters of Mercy, a religious community that pioneered the provision of care and education for poor Catholic girls. Over a thousand Irish adults migrated to Derby between 1840 and 1860 where children received an education using a modified monitorial system with opportunities to become lay teachers in Catholic elementary schools.[42]

---

[38] Quoted in Harold Silver, *The Concept of Popular Education* (London: Routledge, 2007), 43.

[39] See Ruth Watts, *Gender, Power and the Unitarians in England* (Harlow: Longman, 1998), 22, 45; Susan Skedd, "Women teachers and the expansion of girls' schooling in England, c. 1760-1820," 123; Mary Hilton, *Women and the Shaping of the Nation's Young: education and public doctrine in Britain* (Aldershot: Ashgate, 2007).

[40] Quoted in Cohen, "Language and meaning in a documentary source: girls' curriculum from the late eighteenth century to the Schools Inquiry Commission, 1868," 82.

[41] Ruth Watts, *Gender, Power and the Unitarians in England*, 17.

[42] Hilary Minns, H. "Catherine McAuley and the Education or Irish Roman Catholic Children in the Mid-Nineteenth Century," in *Practical Visionaries: Women, Education and Social Progress 1790-1930*, eds. Mary Hilton and Pam Hirsch (London: Longman, 2000), 61-3.

By 1850, the main providers of elementary education were the Anglican, Catholic and Nonconformist school societies supplemented by government grants to contribute to the cost of buildings, heating, lighting and general maintenance besides pupil-teachers, books and equipment. Gordon Cooper's novel *An Hour in the Morning* sets the scene.

> The classroom was long and narrow and was heated by a small iron stove surrounded by a fireguard. There were three windows, but they were set high so that no-one could day-dream by looking out of them. There were no pictures on the walls. The only form of decoration was a large map of the world, with all the parts of the British Empire coloured pink. England itself was only a small country, yet it had many links with the rest of the world, and there were many areas of pink, both large and small on the map. Apart from Miss Crompton's desk set on a low platform, the only other furniture was a tall cupboard where the few books and slates were kept. Miss Crompton would have liked to have more books, but there was not a great deal of money to be spent in a village school, and the school funds were administered by the vicar, who expected a long explanation of why any purchases should be made.[43]

Early providers of elementary schools prioritised basic schooling, which was gendered in nature. Gender codes meant teaching boys and girls different things, differently. For working-class boys, the passing of their schooldays closed down the possibility of following the conventional route to knowledge mapped out for middle-class boys. Working-class girls remained firmly on the fringes since the Victorian ideal of womanhood emphasised their domestic role, with domestic service and needlework seen to be acceptable employment areas whereas the independence of factory work was to be discouraged.

Different gender patterns were being drawn, but school attendance among the children of the working poor was very much dependent on geographical origins. Contemporary educational statistics show that city girls attended school in much lower numbers than boys because of the competitive pull of paid employment or domestic responsibilities. A tendency to establish schools in urban areas undermined female attendance, whereas in agricultural districts, some farmers made the employment of fathers dependent on the availability of their sons for seasonal fieldwork. The operation of gender divisions in the local labour market was a prime determinant of school attendance with evidence of girls' superior access to schooling in the Norfolk and Suffolk countryside, whereas the employment of women and girls in the textile factories of industrial Lancashire reduced attendance.[44] In rural Suffolk, Phyllis Willmott found there were no girls at one National Society's evening school which working children could attend. Most likely, it was not considered safe or desirable for

---

[43] Gordon Cooper, *An Hour in the Morning* (Oxford: Oxford University Press, 1973), 1-2.
[44] Meg Gomersall, *Working Class Girls in 19th Century England: Life, Work and Schooling* (Basingstoke: Palgrave Macmillan, 1997).

young girls to be out in the dark winter evenings, but there were far fewer girls than boys in the locality above the age of 11 since country girls often had to seek work as domestic servants outside their own parish.[45]

At the national policy level, the Liberal government elected in 1868 tried to satisfy two lobby groups. The Birmingham-based National Education League wanted a national system of free, compulsory, secular education and their supporters included dissenters, Liberals, Radicals and trade unionists. Anglican and Conservative supporters of the Manchester-based National Educational Union opposed more government-funded schools and represented the values of the landed aristocracy. Unsurprisingly, the resulting legislative framework was a compromise. The 1870 Education Act resulted in a dual system of universal, basic education. Church schools remained and benefited from extra state aid but where there was a shortage of provision, local school boards could run elementary schools and fund them through a specially raised school rate. Further legislation in the closing decades of the nineteenth century shaped working-class childhoods irrevocably. The Factory Act of 1878 prohibited work before the age of 10 and applied to all trades and the Education Act of 1880 introduced compulsory schooling for 5 to 10-year-olds, with school fees largely abolished 10 years later. Subsequent amendments raised the leaving age to 11 in 1893 and then to 12 in 1899, with dispensations to leave before this age if pupils reached the required standards in reading, writing and arithmetic and if family finances warranted it.

Directly elected and independent of other forms of local government, school boards were responsible for the creation of a system of state-maintained elementary schools for working-class children. Ratepayers of both sexes elected them every three years by secret ballot, and women were similarly eligible to stand in elections. Multiple voting and the possibility of giving all your votes to one candidate favoured the representation of electoral minorities, especially the working classes and women. London had the largest school board with 49 members and nearly 700,000 children (400 schools) under its jurisdiction in the 1870s. It was the first board to impose mandatory attendance in 1871 and played a vital role as a representative of, and in setting the educational standards for, others to follow. Other school boards were restricted to between 5 and 13 members, and many rural boards only had one school under their control.[46]

School board politics seem to have combined just the right degree of adversity and hope to encourage some supporters of independent labour representation and of the women's suffrage movement to make it a main part of their work. Benjamin Lucraft—craftsman chair carver, teetotaller, former Chartist and founder member of the International Working Men's Association—was

---

[45] Phyllis Willmott, *From Rural East Anglia to Suburban London: a century of family history* (London: Institute of Community Studies, 1998), 56.

[46] Jane Martin, *Women and the Politics of Schooling in Late-Victorian and Edwardian England* (Leicester: Leicester University Press, 1999), 2-3, 93; Emma Griffin, *Bread Winner: an Intimate History of the Victorian Economy* (New Haven and London: Yale University Press, 2020), 64.

the sole representative of working-class opinion to be elected to the newly instituted London School Board in 1870 and elected continuously until he retired in 1890. Lucraft supported free education and was a vociferous opponent of the use of corporal punishment and military drill in elementary schools. Above all else, he 'hoped the Board would get rid of all narrow views and strive to give the poor an education which should be on equality with other classes, otherwise the poor would have no opportunity of rising, and things would remain as they are.'[47]

Ostensibly co-educational, purpose built urban board schools segregated older girls from boys socially and academically within the same buildings. Learning and playing together as infants, children aged seven and above had separate entrances, separate playgrounds, separate assemblies and separate departments. From the inception of payment by results in 1862, the performance of working-class children in assisted elementary schools was tested and measured to ensure the state was obtaining value for money. While each pupil earned the school the same amount for successful examination performance, social pressures meant that failing to teach girls needlework was one of the few offences for which a school could lose its government grant. Added to which, the minimum standard of attainment in arithmetic was set lower for girls in recognition of the time they spent sewing. For a little over three decades, the result of a general examination carried out annually by a school inspector and attendance rates determined the size of a school's grant.[48]

Throughout the 1880s and 1890s, the allocation of government grants for Cookery, Domestic Economy and Laundry lessons meant the numbers of girls completing a course of instruction in these subjects spiralled. When the British army found it hard to recruit healthy young men during the Boer War, the movement to expand the teaching of domestic subjects and to introduce lessons in childcare grew, justified on imperialist grounds through the need to improve national efficiency. Public educational discourse centred on three functions for working-class girls: to service their social betters, to be useful citizens and (unlike boys) to be makers of homes. Hence, the forms of femininity upheld were those of the practical housewife and competent domestic servant, with waged domestic service being the largest employer of women in England.

The broad acceptance of natural, inherent, differences between the sexes meant that working-class girls were more involved in unpaid domestic labour, especially childcare. For girls, the family remained the principal site and source for the operation of control. Their school attendance remained lower and more irregular because they were often obliged to help in the home. Acting as surrogate 'wives' and 'little mothers' on washdays, if their mother was ill or having a baby. In the 1880s, plasterer Thomas Smyth explained the relation between home and school to the Cross Commission on Elementary Education. A member of the London Trades Council, Smyth described the hardship families

---

[47] Benjamin Lucraft, *School Board Chronicle*, 1 July 1871, 197.
[48] Jane Martin, *Women and the Politics of Schooling*, 72-3.

incurred 'where the child has to attend school, because it sometimes involved the payment of a nurse in place of the children that would be at home and able to help.' It was common for working-class girls to be put to unpaid domestic work by their families, and they rarely resisted these demands, even when they ran counter to their own wishes.[49]

Then, as now, truancy was a problem. However, the perception of gender differences meant there was a certain tolerance to absentee girls, whereas boys who persistently failed to go to school were more likely to be committed for detention to a truant industrial school. Two School Board women gained notable public exposure for their opposition to the policy attention to male truants and the gendered practice that flowed from it. One was Evangelical churchwoman and author Elizabeth Surr who noted the blatant mouthing of the men.

> I have observed gentlemen rising three or four times in an afternoon only to express with fluent verbosity what has well been said by previous speakers (laughter). Why, gentlemen, if we ladies whose silence has hitherto been golden, and who are supposed to have such a free use of the unruly member, were to follow such an example our debates would be protracted till late in the evening.[50]

The other was the radical socialist feminist Helen Taylor, daughter of the philosopher Harriet Taylor-Mill. Mother and daughter were united by a commitment to women's rights, and Harriet's second marriage to the social critic John Stuart Mill was often lauded as a model of spousal equality. Harriet largely home schooled Helen, giving her the run of her library so that she might 'be encouraged to think for herself, to tackle different concepts which she could not fully grasp.'[51]

Educated, socially aware and with some experience as a political activist, Helen Taylor represented Southwark, one of the poorest borough's in the capital, and she unfailingly, without patronising the poor, championed the rights of the working classes to a liberal, free and secular education. A piece of hate mail found among her personal papers suggests she was struggling against ingrained prejudice against women.

H.T.
Disgusting Creature
Man in Petticoats -
Satan's Masterpiece –
Her end
Destruction.[52]

---

[49] Anna Davin, *Growing Up Poor. Home, School and Street in London 1870–1914* (London: Rivers Oram Press, 1996), 97-111; Jane McDermid, *The Schooling of Girls in Britain and Ireland, 1800-1900* (London: Routledge, 2012); Jane Martin, *Women and the Politics of Schooling*, 93-9.
[50] Elizabeth Surr, *School Board Chronicle*, 13 January 1877, 33-4.
[51] Josephine Kamm, *John Stuart Mill in Love* (London: Gordon and Cremonesi, 1977), 114.
[52] Mill Taylor collection, file 15, no. 100.

Taylor's initial solution to the truancy problem was to propose the establishment of 'Baby Rooms' where younger siblings might be left during school hours, and she convinced the Board to lobby national government for this provision.[53] Subsequently, she and Surr campaigned endlessly to expose the mistreatment when the men running two industrial schools in London, Upton House and St Paul's, were found to have been abusing pupils. Shockingly, St Paul's in Limehouse was an Anglican school to which the Board sent remanded boys, in return for which the school received public money, and it was managed by the chair of the Board's industrial schools committee, ship-owner and leading lay member of the Congregationalist Church, Thomas Scrutton.

The Board's first industrial school, Upton House, opened in Hackney in 1878 (see Fig. 3.1). When Surr and Taylor investigated they found the warders routinely lifted the boys by their ears and refused to allow them to talk. Bedwetting was common, and one 8-year-old was made to march round the parade ground for 10 hours holding his wet bedding aloft on an 8-foot pole. Solitary confinement in darkness was another punishment, while they flogged a recaptured runaway and chained him to a block of wood by his neck. Surr considered this systematic cruelty, but the majority of the Board disagreed.

Fig. 3.1 Upton House Truant School, children cleaning boots in playground, 1904. From the London Picture Archive. (Copyright London Metropolitan Archive, 209340)

---

[53] *School Board Chronicle*, 14 April 1877; 24 February 1881.

They also contested her claim with regard to the illegal use of a penal method known as the silent system, which enforced silence except for 30 minutes per day, during recreation time. Benjamin Lucraft was appalled. He thought 'such treatment was only borne by the children because they were the children of the poor. Members denied cruelty because they belonged to another class. The Board had no right to establish such schools. There ought to be an institution for kindness instead of having an institution for cruelty.'[54]

At St Paul's inmates were kept starving by the governor who stole from the food supplies and failed to provide the boys with proper clothing or footwear. To scare them enough to mend their ways, warders used handcuffs and foot manacles and made half naked, barefoot boys stand on the flagstones in winter resulting in cases of chilblains so severe one boy nearly had to have his toes amputated. Warders locked boys in a bathroom so cold that their cocoa froze. Several died in custody, and when eight inmates set fire to it, the school closed.[55] Tension mounted and tempers flared, with accusations that Surr and Taylor were coaching parents to complain. In reality, the children's parents were powerless since they could do little besides approach the institution directly or go back to the magistrate who had imposed the original custodial sentence. One mother who complained found the authorities were vengeful and simply flogged her son again. In the end, unable to escape the censure of public opinion, Scrutton lost his seat on the Board and Parliament set up a Royal Commission to investigate young offenders' institutions. The Home Secretary wrote and thanked Surr personally for having introduced a basic standard of humanity.[56]

Leaving the question of school attendance aside, increased provision produced increased demand. Because more children were staying on voluntarily, the authorities added a grade to the previous six, prompting the development of 'ex-standard' classes for pupils who had reached a certain level of attainment. Economies of scale enabled some urban boards to draft these older children from several schools into a separate school the first of which opened in Bradford in 1876. Flagship institutions within the elementary-school world, higher grade schools offered a broad curriculum, putting greater emphasis on art and science than the endowed schools, but with a higher level of staffing in terms of academic qualifications and professional competence than the elementary schools. Some were in purpose-built, showpiece buildings that housed all 4-to-19-year-olds, with an additional intake of pupils from other schools into the higher grade departments. Meriel Vlaeminke's historical archive work shows a generous allocation of free places, weekly rather than termly school fees, and a comprehensive curriculum was crucial to their ability to offer an ideal of general education to their working class pupils, including girls.[57]

---

[54] *School Board Chronicle*, 26 July 1979; Minutes of Evidence.
[55] *School Board Chronicle*, 8 and 15 October, 1881.
[56] Op cit, 15 November 1881.
[57] Meriel Vlaeminke, *The English Higher Grade Schools* (London: Woburn Press, 2000).

Higher grade schools were most common in the towns and cities of the West Riding of Yorkshire and parts of Lancashire where they closed the gap on fee-paying secondary schools, preparing pupils for the same examinations and the same occupations. In the case of the London suburb of Tottenham, two higher grade schools, one for boys and another for girls, opened in 1884, but what is significant here is that the lower-middle-class and more prosperous parents of the locality used them and no other schools in the London orbit were as successful at preparing pupils both for the local labour market, pupil-teacher examinations, scholarships, Oxford and Cambridge local examinations and London matriculation.[58] In time, this institutional competition on the borderlines of elementary/secondary education triggered protests from grammar school supporters, and the Bryce Commission reporting on secondary education in 1895 reached the same policy position as Taunton in advocating a hierarchy of school types tagged to particular social classes. Edith Creak, headmistress of King Edward VI Girls' High School in Birmingham, feared class contagion. In her view, secondary school pupils came from cultured homes, and the invasion of too many pupils from the elementary sector would lower the culture of the majority.[59]

Powerful groups in English society supported the conception of an education stratified on class lines, and the 1890s saw the endowed schools mount a vigorous defence of their role. No authority was legally entitled to provide secondary education, and it was hard to decide on the appropriate body to do so. After 1889, county councils could make grants out of the rates to establish classes for technical instruction. They could also provide scholarships offering access to higher than elementary education. As chair of London's Technical Education Board, the Fabian Sidney Webb became an important party in the 1900s debate about national efficiency. Seeking to implement what he regarded as best practice, Webb advocated good basic schooling as being in the national interest.[60] Since public funds were limited, he thought it more efficient to restrict secondary education to fee-paying children from the middle classes, plus 10 per cent of the elementary school population selected because of 'merit.'

The return of a Conservative government in 1895 and again in the 1900 general election reduced the likelihood of the school boards extending their powers to cover all branches of education. Their alleged extravagance had long been the subject of Conservative denunciation, and politicians tied up the administrative question with the problem of the faith schools. The intention being to destroy the school board system and transfer their powers to a committee of the County or County Borough Council that would co-ordinate all

---

[58] Margaret Bryant, *The London Experience*, 423-4.

[59] Andrea Jacobs, "Examinations as Cultural Capital for the Victorian Schoolgirl: 'thinking' with Bourdieu," *Women's History Review*, 16, no. 2 (2007), 258-261.

[60] Geoffrey Russell Searle, *The Quest for National Efficiency: a Study in British Political Thought, 1899-1914* (Oxford: Basil Blackwell, 1971).

public services and subsidise the voluntary schools (most of which were Anglican) out of public funds. In a climate hostile to the political and educational ambitions of the cities, the Education Act of 1902 abolished the school board system, empowering local authorities to found and run fee-paying secondary and technical schools alongside the municipal elementary schools. In London, the County Council became the sole education authority in 1904.

Once again, the fee-paying 'public' school was the defining institution, notably the tiny set of boys' schools that were the Clarendon Commission's main concerns. Forty years on from the post-Taunton adaptation of the endowed grammar schools, public school men associated with the newly formed Board of Education were determined to instil the exclusivity, ethos and characteristics that seemed to them reminiscent of their own education. They measured the new state-maintained secondary schools against the benchmark of their own elite education including the symbiotic relationship between the Clarendon schools and Oxbridge, on the basis that it would facilitate the movement of a select few into the Establishment, and into the capitalist class. Access was through the payment of fees or 'scholarships' for those who passed a competitive examination at the age of 10 and who might still be expected to pay a variety of costs.

Therefore, the educational settlement ushered in after 1902 reaffirmed traditional class, gender and racial identities. Its furtherance involved developing a form of education which was characterised by the assiduous promotion in state-aided secondary schools of the classical/literary curriculum, a sense of high moral purpose and the importance of character formation. Amongst other things, meritocratic success (which could be achieved by only a minority of pupils) became more firmly defined as an induction into a particular culture. Vlaeminke's research shows urban higher grade schools offered choices between subjects and courses 'without glorifying certain areas of study and demeaning others, and by rejecting the notion that children (of both sexes) destined for a particular occupation must be trained in a certain way.'[61] However, social and educational forces led by representatives of established elites recruited from the 'public' schools and Oxbridge overrode the popular protest which greeted the abolition of the directly elected school boards to sanctify an elitist model of secondary education at the expense of the devaluation of technical and scientific-vocational elementary school alternatives. As the battle between various deep-seated conflicting ideas concentrated on the municipal secondary schools, an academic type of education took root based on classed and gendered assumptions that constructed the classical tradition as an ideal to which prestigious schools should aspire.

Everywhere the scholarship ladder was narrow and precarious. Generally, there were more scholarships for boys, meaning the odds against an elementary schoolboy winning a scholarship in the capital, for instance, were 150 to

---

[61] Meriel Vlaeminke, *The Higher Grade Schools*, 40.

one and 500 to one for his female counterpart.[62] Social class, gender and spatiality mattered. As Labour Party support and organisation progressed in the new age of mass democracy, socialist politicians used the power of municipal authority to respond to working-class demand for free secondary education.[63] In places such as Durham, Labour-controlled from 1919, access to secondary schooling depended on test results. In contrast, other authorities prioritized the children of fee-payers over those qualified by 'ability'. Some authorities simply excluded girls and those that did not commonly awarded more scholarships to boys.[64] The practice among lower middle-class families to use the elementary schools as a deliberate way of qualifying for assisted secondary education further disadvantaged working-class girls.[65] Most children attended a free all-age elementary school, leaving at 14 to go into work and therefore unable to sit the public examinations promoted in the secondary schools that led to university and the professions.

Future novelist Walter Greenwood had an impoverished upbringing and left his Salford council school a year early. 'School became a sort of inconvenient necessity, a place which was one forced to attend, an interruption in the earning of a livelihood. Perhaps this explains why I have so little to say about it. All was mean and shabby and without colour. Sooty school, smoky streets, the trudge home.'[66] In the capital, there was gloom in the air at the schools Frances Buss founded. Pupil numbers were down at the North London Collegiate following the head's decision to admit elementary scholarship holders in 1907, and the governors tried unsuccessfully to sell Buss's second foundation, Camden School for Girls, to the capital's education authority. Highlighting the significance of class and location, when Stanley Baldwin's Conservative government required secondary schools in the private sector to choose a single source of grant in 1926, the less socially select Camden joined the state system, whereas the North London became one of the day schools known as direct grants. There, in return for grant-aided support from the state though not at the expense of loss of self-government, up to 25 per cent of places were free to largely middle-class holders of local authority scholarships.[67]

---

[62] Doris Burchell, *Miss Buss' Second School* (London: Frances Mary Buss Foundation, 1971), 63.

[63] Rodney Barker, *Education and Politics 1900-51* (Oxford, Clarendon Press, 1972); Martin Worley, *Labour Inside the Gate: a History of the British Labour Party between the Wars* (London, I.B. Tauris & Co., 2005).

[64] Olive Banks, *Parity and Prestige in English Secondary Education: A Study in Educational Sociology* (London, Routledge and Kegan Paul, 1955), 55.

[65] Jacobs, "Examinations as Cultural Capital for the Victorian Schoolgirl: 'thinking' with Bourdieu," 257-8.

[66] Walter Greenwood, "Langy Road [Langworthy Road Council School Salford," in *The Old School*, ed. Graham Greene (Oxford: Oxford University Press, 1984), 63.

[67] Doris Burchell, *Miss Buss' Second School*, 60-1, 76.

CONCLUSION

This chapter helps to explain how and why the socially dominant paid growing attention to education as a social problem as the nineteenth century ran its course and the great change that took place in people's view of childhood and their treatment of the child. The period from 1870 to 1902 saw the construction of a massive machine of state-organised education, but the destruction of the school boards signalled the triumph of an argument that conserved versions of a national school system sketched in the three major royal commissions of the 1860s. The prospect of an educated, as opposed to a disciplined working-class, had been kicked down the road as particular forms of educational provision remained organised around social class, and the inequalities of the fee-paying system continued. Due to their already existing advantages, children from affluent families continued to have access to education for longer periods whatever their apparent 'potential,' and many elementary boys and girls declined to compete for a secondary school place even when maintenance grants were available.

As policy-makers set about building a 'ladder' for the few, the dissolution of the higher grade school snuffed out the democratic and radical glimmerings of a theory and practice of secondary education for all. Many lost opportunities. Newcastle writer Jack Common expressed a popular sort of insult when describing his schooling in the years leading down to the First World War. In his fictionalised autobiography, *Kiddar's Luck,* he wrote:

> Always the pride that prevailed in this working-class school was that it succeeded in turning out less recruits for the working-class than any other of its kind in the district. That less was still the majority, mind you, a great crowd that stayed on for two or three years after the scholarship culling was over and were then worked upon and encouraged to flash out what talents they had. But the school's official boast was not of them. The names in blue and red displayed on a whole row of rolls-of-honour hanging in the hall were those of educable small fry that had taken kindly to a scholastic bunk-up and been duly dispatched to the sphere of Higher Education.[68]

Ordinary people knew the education offered to them was wretched in many ways. The advocates of eugenics were relentless, and they strongly believed in the importance of the family and especially the mother, which reinforced a surge of concern about the bearing and rearing of children. To return to the quote with which we started, Evelyn Sharp defied the ideology of separate lives and specific roles for males and females in society. She thought it a distortion of educational theory to prioritise the teaching of mothercraft. 'Little boys, who are not required to learn fatherhood at school, are presumably left to conclude that a man has no more concern with family life than to bring home his wages regularly.'[69]

---

[68] Jack Common, Common, *Kiddar's Luck* (Newcastle-Upon-Tyne: Bloodaxe Books, 1990). 84.
[69] Evelyn Sharp, *A London Child*, 81.

Supporters of selective secondary education used the argument that not everyone was educable to the levels hitherto reserved for elite groups, stressing the importance of offering an 'academic' education to a few. The failure of middle-class female education was very much a mid-nineteenth century concern, along with the moral panic surrounding the 'woman question' more generally, but the higher value many still placed on domestic accomplishments in girls' schooling gave little encouragement for effort or achievement in more 'academic' studies. An obvious but overlooked fact inextricably woven into the emergent concept of 'merit.' Besides which the meanings of the language used to describe male-female attainment patterns served to consolidate gender difference. Accomplishments were central to elite female education in late Georgian England, but these were prerogatives of the aristocracy, and anyway the role of the political hostess had changed dramatically by the dawn of the twentieth century.

In the succeeding years, it became common practice for secondary schoolboys to spend more time learning Latin verse and for 'less able' secondary schoolgirls to receive instruction in domestic 'science' as a substitute for lessons in biology and the physical sciences. Those who opposed the traditional orthodoxy regarding the limited availability of intelligence believed education was a right for all. They thought the higher grade school model offered something mirror-image public schools offering classical education to the less affluent did not. The virtues of a common curriculum oriented to arts *and* science *and* practical and craft subjects, and an ethos that emphasised by its very existence that extending one's education was a normal thing for every child—including the girl child—to do.

Bibliography

Primary Sources

Archival Sources

Helen Taylor's papers and letters, Mill-Taylor Collection. LSE archives and special collections.
School Board for London, Minutes, 1870-1904. London Metropolitan Archive.
School Board for London, Minutes of Evidence taken before a Special Committee Regarding Upton House Industrial School. London Metropolitan Archive.

Autobiographies, Memoirs, Diaries, Letters

Churchill, Winston. *My Early Life*. London: Eland, 2012.
Christie, Agatha. *An Autobiography*. London: Harper Collins, 1993.
Cobbe, Frances Power. *The Life of Frances Power Cobbe*. London: Swan Sonnenschein, 1904.
Common, Jack. *Kiddar's Luck* (Newcastle-Upon-Tyne: Bloodaxe Books, 1991).

Greenwood, Walter. "Langy Road [Langworthy Road Council School Salford." In *The Old School*, edited by Graham Greene, 53-64. Oxford: Oxford University Press, 1984.
Hare, Augustus. "Harrow in the 1840s: servility." In *School Remembered*, edited by Gillian Avery, 79-86. London: Victor Gollancz, 1967.
Hughes, Thomas. *Tom Brown's School Days. By an Old Boy.* Cambridge: Macmillan and Co., 1857.
Pankhurst, Emmeline. *My Own Story.* London: Virago, 1979.
Willmott, Phyllis. *From Rural East Anglia to Suburban London: a century of family history.* London: Institute of Community Studies, 1998.
Woolf, Leonard. *Sowing: an autobiography of the years 1880-1904.* Letchworth: Readers Union, 1962.

NEWSPAPERS AND PERIODICALS OF THE PERIOD

Journal of the Women's Educational Union
School Board Chronicle, 1870-1904

OTHER CONTEMPORARY BOOKS AND PAMPHLETS

Austen, Jane. *Emma*. Harmondsworth: Penguin, [1815] 2012.
Banks, Olive. *Parity and Prestige in English Secondary Education: A Study in Educational Sociology.* London: Routledge and Kegan Paul, 1955.
Sayers, Jane E. *The Fountain Unsealed: A History of the Notting Hill and Ealing High School.* Welwyn Garden City: Broadwater Press, 1973.
Sharp, Evelyn. *The London Child.* London: Bodley Head, 1927.
Tuke, Margaret. *A History of Bedford College for Women, 1949-1937.* Oxford: Oxford University Press, 1939.
Waugh, Evelyn. *Decline and Fall.* London: Chapman & Hall, [1928] 1949.

PARLIAMENTARY PAPERS

British Parliamentary Papers Education: Royal Commission on Elementary Education (Cross) 1886-8.
British Parliamentary Papers Education: Royal Commission on Elementary Education (Bryce) 1894-5.

SECONDARY SOURCES

Barker, Rodney. *Education and Politics 1900-51.* Oxford: Clarendon Press, 1972.
Borer, Mary Cathcart. *Willingly to School: a History of Women's Education.* Guildford and London: Lutterworth Press, 1976.
Bryant, Margaret. *The London Experience of Secondary Education.* London: Woburn Press, 1986.
Burchell, Doris. *Miss Buss' Second School.* London, Frances Mary Buss Foundation, 1971.

Cohen, Michèle. "Gender and the Private/Public Debate on Education in the Long Eighteenth Century." In *Public or Private Education? Lessons from History*, edited by Richard Aldrich, 2-24. London: Woburn, 2004.

Cohen, Michèle. "Language and meaning in a documentary source: girls' curriculum from the late eighteenth century to the Schools Inquiry Commission, 1868." *History of Education*, 34, no. 1 (2005), 77-93.

Cooper, Gordon. *An Hour in the Morning*. Oxford: Oxford University Press, 1973.

Davin, Anna. "Imperialism and Motherhood," *History Workshop*, 5 (Spring 1978), 9-67.

Davin, Anna. *Growing Up Poor. Home, School and Street in London 1870–1914*. London: Rivers Oram Press, 1996.

Davies, Nick. *The School Report: Why Britain's Schools Are Failing*. Harmondsworth: Penguin, 2000.

De Bellaigue, Christina. *Educating Women: Schooling and Identity in England and France, 1800-1867*. Oxford: Oxford University Press, 2007.

Dyhouse, Carol. *Girls Growing Up In Victorian and Edwardian England*. London: Routledge, Kegan and Paul, 1981.

Dyhouse, Carol. "Miss Buss and Miss Beale: Gender and Authority in the History of Education." In *Lessons for Life. The Schooling of Girls and Women 1850–1950*, edited by Felicity Hunt, 22-28. Oxford: Basil Blackwell, 1987.

Gomersall, Meg. *Working Class Girls in 19th Century England: Life, Work and Schooling*. Basingstoke: Palgrave Macmillan, 1997.

Griffin, Emma. *Bread Winner: an Intimate History of the Victorian Economy* (New Haven and London: Yale University Press, 2020.

Hunt, Felicity. "Divided Aims: the Educational Implications of Opposing Ideologies in Girls' Secondary Schooling, 1850-1940." In *Lessons for Life. The Schooling of Girls and Women 1850–1950*, edited by Felicity Hunt, 3-21. Oxford: Basil Blackwell, 1987.

Jacobs, Andrea. "Examinations as Cultural Capital for the Victorian Schoolgirl: 'thinking' with Bourdieu," *Women's History Review*, 16, no. 2 (2007): 245-261.

Jewell, Helen M. *Education in Early Modern England*. Basingstoke: Palgrave Macmillan, 1998.

Kamm, Josephine. *John Stuart Mill in Love*. London: Gordon and Cremonesi, 1977.

Kynaston, David and Green, Francis. *Engines of Privilege: Britain's Private School Problem*. London: Bloomsbury, 2019.

Leinster-Mackay, Donald. *The Educational World of Edward Thring*. Lewes: Falmer, 1987.

Mangan, J.A. (Tony) *Athleticism in the Victorian and Edwardian Public School: the Emergence and Consolidation of an Educational Ideology*. Cambridge: Cambridge University Press, 1981.

Martin, Jane. *Women and the Politics of Schooling in Late-Victorian and Edwardian England*. Leicester: Leicester University Press, 1999.

Martin, Jane. *Making Socialists: Mary Bridges Adams and the Fight for Knowledge and Power, 1855-1939*. Manchester: Manchester University Press, 2013.

McDermid, Jane. *The Schooling of Girls in Britain and Ireland, 1800-1900*. London: Routledge, 2012.

Miller, Jane. "Clara Collet's Dissenting Inheritance and the Education of Women," In *Practical Visionaries: Women, Education and Social Progress 1790-1930*, edited by Mary Hilton and Pam Hirsch, 115-128. London: Longman, 2000.

Minns, Hilary. "Catherine McAuley and the Education or Irish Roman Catholic Children in the Mid-Nineteenth Century." In *Practical Visionaries: Women, Education and Social Progress 1790-1930*, edited by Mary Hilton and Pam Hirsch, 52-65. London: Longman, 2000.
Mokyr, Joel. *The Enlightened Economy*. Harmondsworth: Penguin, 2009.
Searle, Geoffrey Russell. *The Quest for National Efficiency: a Study in British Political Thought, 1899-1914*. Oxford: Basil Blackwell, 1971.
Silver, Harold. *The Concept of Popular Education*. London: Routledge, 2007.
Skedd, Susan. "Women teachers and the expansion of girls' schooling in England, c. 1760-1820." In *Gender in Eighteenth-Century England*, edited by Hannah Barker and Elaine Chalus, 101-125. London: Longman, 1997.
Turner, David. *The Old Boys: the Decline and Rise of the Public School*. New Haven and London: Yale University Press, 2015.
Verkaik, Robert. *Posh Boys: How the English Public Schools Ruin Britain*. London: Oneworld Publications, 2018.
Vlaeminke, Meriel. *The English Higher Grade Schools*. London: Woburn Press, 2000.
Worley, Martin. *Labour Inside the Gate: a History of the British Labour Party between the Wars*. London: I.B. Tauris & Co. 2005.

CHAPTER 4

Gender Equity and the 'Ladder of Opportunity'

> *In my year at Nunsthorpe eleven children passed the scholarship. The head, Mr Neil, came specially to the class-room to read out the list of successful candidates. As each name was called out, we were told to stand up. I remember looking down at the blank, despairing face of Audrey, a girl of some intelligence whose name was not on the list.*
> —Brian Cox, *A Great Betrayal* (London: Chapmans Publishers, 1992), 28

Mass secondary education did not exist in 1930s England when Brian Cox was a schoolchild. Born in Grimsby, Lincolnshire, into a frugal, lower middle-class Methodist household, he grew up during the Great Depression. An avid reader thanks to the local public library, his family was confident he had acquired the faculty to demonstrate cognitive intellectual 'ability' via an intelligence test. There was no evidence that girls were less 'able' than boys were, but for those whose parents could not afford to purchase the privilege, there were fewer opportunities for individual girls to win a scholarship giving free education at secondary level. Audrey and Brian were not told this at the time. Neither was a new generation of schoolchildren after the abolition of secondary school fees in the 1944 Education Act. In a society that proclaimed everyone now had a fair chance to go as far as their talent and hard work would allow, they did not know that the pass rate for the examination selecting a new, bigger and better-educated elite was set higher for girls than for boys.

This chapter takes a generally chronological approach to assess gendered educational opportunities and how the policies of various governments and the work of teachers and activists involved in struggle over the gendered power relations within education affected them. Paying attention to the ideological elements that come from the social relations of class and gender in the sense of the Gramscian concept of hegemony, I start with the interwar world before

© The Author(s), under exclusive license to Springer Nature Switzerland AG 2022
J. Martin, *Gender and Education in England since 1770*, Gender and History, https://doi.org/10.1007/978-3-030-79746-1_4

moving on to describe policy and practice in the 1940s and 1950s. In the final sections, I look at the place of gender in rounds of polemic and counter-polemic about the merit of selective secondary education in the 1960s and 1970s, the 1975 Sex Discrimination Act and considerable debate in the schools that followed.

BACKGROUND AND INHERITANCE: THE LANGUAGE OF SCHOLARSHIP SCRIPTS

The Edwardian establishment wanted to provide an education for the masses that was complete, and this left secondary schools with a narrow academic or subject-based curriculum orientated at least in part towards the universities. Before and after 1902, secondary schooling was very much a middle-class enclave, and even a middle-class status symbol with working-class children excluded *en masse* from what was largely the preserve of fee payers. Most children (around 85 per cent) remained in the elementary sector for the whole of their school lives, and very few people commented on the disproportionate number of boys climbing the narrow and precarious scholarship ladder. One of those who favoured common schooling funded by what she saw as the misused educational endowments stolen from the poor was former pupil-teacher Mary Bridges Adams who made a career in teaching and then accessed political power as a socialist member of the London School Board. Adams, who had been raised in comparative comfort in an unusually small working-class home where she was one of two surviving children, demanded 'absolute equality of opportunity for all children, no matter what their poverty, to be helped by education to develop their fullest powers.'[1]

Centralist intervention was a decisive factor in the reshaping of secondary education in England as carried through in cultural, intellectual, professional terms, but also economic and social. The potential to promote 'able' scholars on 'merit' through the deployment of a scholarship ladder was critical to the maintenance of different streams of schooling, segregated from each other and with their sights set on divergent post-school destinations. Four features of curriculum thinking—differentiation, functionality, selection and social advancement—characterised what Simon calls 'the emergent system.'[2] For boys, the intentions were primarily occupational. In terms of gender, this meant the constitution of masculinity and the class cultures embedded in the male preserves of employment. For girls, the intentions were primarily marital through domestic training suitable for their social position. However, the new girls' secondary schools also defined academic objectives predicated upon offering a 'liberal education' as important. For them, pursuit of scholarship was never subservient to the social cachet conferred by attending the school or the

---

[1] Mary Bridges Adams, *School Board Chronicle*, July 1903.
[2] Brian Simon, *The State and Educational Change: Essays in the History of Education and Pedagogy* (London: Lawrence and Wishart, 1994), 42.

task of preparing girls for domesticity, as the decision to undertake the same syllabuses and public examinations as the boys' grammar and 'public' schools showed.

Non-sectarian secondary schools based on the 37 innovative high schools the GPDST (see Chap. 3) maintained helped produce female students for higher education but did not eliminate the reproduction of dominant gender relations. Eleven-year-old Emma Gurney Salter entered the Notting Hill and Ealing High School (part of the GPDST group) in 1886. Emma's father encouraged her to study Classics but feared going to Girton College would ruin her chances of marriage. Emma went, but she never married.[3] In the mid-twentieth century, tensions over marriage and career surfaced in another affluent family willing to pay to educate their daughters. Antonia Pakenham (later Fraser) went to the Godolphin School, a girls' only boarding and day school to get a scholarship in the 1940s. At Godolphin, she encountered girlhood with a capital 'G,' which made her feel like 'Kipling's Mowgli in *The Jungle Book*,' but she followed her mother's example and went to Lady Margaret Hall, Oxford. Still, her father did not even pause when she told him she had failed to get a first-class degree. 'Oh, I'm so glad. Because if you had, you would never have got married,' he said. Years later, she asked her then husband if he would have married her if she had a First, and it turned out he always thought she *did* get the top grade.[4]

Different local policies and circumstances make it hard to assess how far access to secondary education expanded. The number of local authority scholarships increased tenfold between 1895 and 1906 competed for, in the main, by children from parents of a lower middle-class or skilled artisan background who could afford to pay for private tuition.[5] From 1903, there were bursaries for those pledged to teaching, and the 1907 free place system meant the number of children entering from elementary schools grew, though the proportion from the families of unskilled workers remained very low. The 1918 Education Act abolished elementary school fees and raised the school leaving age to 14, but education was targeted for cuts in 1922 and grants for free places in secondary schools and the limited number of state scholarships to university were abolished.[6] Fenland teacher and author Sybil Marshall grew up in rural Cambridgeshire, the second poorest county in England. When she started secondary school as a fee payer in 1924, she had a new bike, a new satchel, a new tennis racquet and a new uniform. Her peers ranged from those who had not

---

[3] Jane E. Sayers, *The Fountain Unsealed: A History of the Notting Hill and Ealing High School*. Welwyn Garden City: Broadwater Press, 1973), 75–6.

[4] Antonia Fraser, *My History: a memoir of growing up* (London: Weidenfeld & Nicolson, 2015), 115, 242–3.

[5] David Reeder, "The reconstruction of secondary education in England, 1869–1920," in *The Rise of the Modern Educational System: Structural Change and Social Reproduction 1870–1920* eds. Detlef K. Müller, Fritz Ringer and Brian Simon (Cambridge: Cambridge University Press, 1989), 142.

[6] Olive Banks, *Parity and Prestige in English Education Parity and Prestige in English Secondary Education: A Study in Educational Sociology* (London: Routledge and Kegan Paul, 1955), 68.

yet learned to read, 'to scholarship boys whose brilliance deserved the university career which the headmaster held up before us as the nearest thing to heaven we could ever hope to attain on earth.'[7]

The central character in Gordon Cooper's 1973 novel *An Hour in the Morning* is Kate Bassett, eldest daughter of a farm labourer growing up in the years leading down to the First World War. Recognising that Kate will pass the Labour Examination and leave school early at the age of 12, her teacher tries unsuccessfully to persuade the vicar to let her become a pupil teacher.

> She lived alone and there was no one to whom she could confide her hopes and disappointments. She had tried to do for Kate Bassett the same thing that a teacher had done for her, Alice Crompton, twenty-five years ago. She had been living at Chaxton, going to the church school near the cathedral close. A teacher there, Miss Huntley, had helped her. She had gone to her home and spoken to her parents, explaining that with her intelligence and ability, Alice could become a teacher… At the vicarage, the vicar finished the letter he was writing to his son. He reminded him of the sacrifices that had been made to enable him to study at Oxford. 'I only ask,' he wrote, 'that your talents be used to the full. I think that one of the greatest sins of all is that of waste—waste of talent and waste of opportunity.[8]

In many cases, boys took precedence over girls. Reginald Farndon, a decorator's son growing up in Ealing and born in 1904, was constantly reminded while at grammar school that he was being educated above the family's station in life. Indeed, his sisters were not given the chance of an extended schooling and had to become domestic servants. Nora Lumb, the daughter of a railway clerk born in 1912, needed to win one of the ten scholarships awarded by her local authority (Sunderland) to get to grammar school in 1923. Her parents would have paid for a boy, but not for a girl.[9]

Prospects for working-class girls declined with the abolition of higher grade schooling because even more than for boys, the skills and qualifications gained at school could mean entrance to a completely different kind of job. A fair proportion of successful higher grade school girls went into teaching, some became clerks, librarians, shop assistants, telephonists or switch-board operators—a wider range of female employment than the early girls' secondary schools could offer as they were constantly aware of the criticism that they put their pupils under too much strain.[10]

Besides a more frequent consignment to the elementary sector, gender divisions touched girls in other ways through the development of co-education

---

[7] Sybil Marshall, *An Experiment in Education* (Cambridge: Cambridge University Press, 1963), 4.

[8] Gordon Cooper, *An Hour in the Morning* (Oxford: Oxford University Press, 1973), 5.

[9] John Burnett, "Education: Introduction," in *Destiny Obscure: Autobiographies of Childhood, Education and the Family* ed. John Burnett (Harmondsworth: London: Routledge, 1984), 163.

[10] Meriel Vlaeminke, *The English Higher Grade Schools* (London: Woburn Press, 2000), 55–62, 157–162.

and the union affiliation (if any) of their teachers. In the early 1920s, the main teachers' union in the elementary sector, the National Union of Teachers (NUT), lost two breakaway factions. One was the National Association of Schoolmasters (NAS) committed to men teachers for boys and the other the first feminist trade union in Britain, the National Union of Women Teachers (NUWT). The NUWT motto proclaimed, 'she who would be free herself must strike the blow,' and it was this ideology which pervaded their critique of girls' schooling, their radical ideals for change and their educational work. Active in their local communities and in the field of practice, they contested 'insidious forms of sex favouritism' including issues relating to the allocation of scholarships and how the curriculum, controlled by the government, was implicated in the construction of gender relations.[11]

At the level of organisational policy concerned with the nature of schooling, officials within the Board of Education developed their own 'line' on the underlying premise for the curricula followed within the elementary sector. At its most overt, the belief that the sexes should have separate but complementary roles found expression in domestic subjects for girls and handicraft for boys. More schools were co-educational, though the sexes did not always mix physically due to the provision of separate departments, classes and playgrounds for older boys and girls within school walls. Where classes were mixed, children would find that the class register was called alphabetically with boys first then girls. Overall, three-quarters of all elementary school teachers were female and the infant or junior department head invariably so. In contrast, the head of the senior department was generally male.

Diversity in the elementary sector was another key element in the evolving status hierarchy of schooling at the local level. From the 1900s, more localities sought to develop special courses for 12–14-year-olds, and types of school proliferated. There were central schools, higher elementary, technical and trade schools and 'senior classes.' London had many of the former as one head teacher explained:

> The County Council has decided to have one school in every district of London where the bright boys and girls can be gathered together for the purpose of giving them a higher education. In these Central Schools it is intended that scholars should have a good general education for a year or so and then be called upon to decide whether they would prefer to earn their living by handling tools, or by doing office work. According to their choice they become Industrials or Commercials, and their education is so arranged as to fit them to do the work they like best.[12]

---

[11] Patricia Owen, "'Who would be free, herself must strike the blow': The National Union of Women Teachers, equal pay, and women within the teaching profession," *History of Education*, 17 no. 1 (1988), 83–99.

[12] *The Monnow*, October 1910, 142.

Central schools were the closest any elementary school came to emulation of the education offered under the secondary school regulations. They recruited at the same age as the municipal secondary schools, and in some places, scholarship winners were able to choose between them. Some authorities developed this type of schooling because it was cheaper and quicker to provide than secondary school accommodation and in London nearly as many children went to central school as attended all the capital's secondary schools combined. Evelyn Sharp, who noted school uniform was fairly common, thought 'it helped to eliminate the class spirit that is based on difference of income.'[13] Unusually for the time, Eve Garnett's children's novel of 1937, *The Family From One End Street*, shows the struggle of a large, small-town, working-class family to support their daughter who wins a central school place and dreams of becoming a farmer when she grows up.[14]

The availability of various sources relating to Monnow Road School in the London borough of Bermondsey makes historical reconstruction in the light of documents possible. Like many urban elementary schools, it was organised on a mixed model, with older boys and girls taught in separate departments under separate heads. Clara Bulcraig, trained teacher and founding headmistress of Monnow Road Girls and Infants School from 1871 to 1911, is acknowledged as instituting the ethos that saw Monnow's evolution into a central school. As the school magazine shows, everyday culture was both organically and integrally connected to configurations of identity, social class and community besides the contemporary gender order. Norms and values made clear in Bulcraig's homily to pioneer female competitors in a swimming gala. 'A boyish girl is even more objectionable than a girlish boy is, and you know what your brothers think of such boys. Do what you do, swimming included, in the very best way, but always let your aim be worthy and upright.'[15]

Reputation was a key factor in Monnow's success. Cultivation of self-improvement, the value of learning, duty and obedience and the ideal of 'service' were among its key features. However, Bulcraig chastised girls to check over-ambition. While she praised the desire to please parents and friends and thought it acceptable to compete in the spirit of friendship, she stressed the benefits of defeat, which teaches empathy 'with the losers in life's race.' Warning of rocks ahead, she continued:

> If you become so bent on winning prizes or championships as to make this the chief end in view, you may lose all proportion and neglect other important duties, to say nothing of injuring your health by too much practice. Again, if you care too much for making a show, you lose refinement and simplicity of character... I want you to retain all the advantages of the present, and yet retain the qualities which go to the building up of a good woman. All the medals and prizes in the

---

[13] Olive Banks, *Parity and Prestige in English Education*, 68; Evelyn Sharp, *The London Child* (London: John Lane Bodley Head, 1927), 75.
[14] Eve Garnett, *The Family From One End Street*, (London: Puffin, [1937] 2014).
[15] *The Monnow*, October 1911, 137.

world can never compensate for them, if you gain those rewards at the expense of the qualities which matter most.[16]

Her judgements are clear, to be aggressively competitive acquires a negative charge, and she reaffirms and stabilises familial gender roles in her assumption that her female pupils need to help at home. 'Let the urgent duty be cheerfully and readily performed, and I am quite sure Mother will allow you to play as often as circumstances permit.'[17]

Monnow School subscribed to the culture of reform in Bermondsey, supporting the local Settlement House established in 1898, in which middle-class volunteers lived, sharing their knowledge and culture through educational and social work, campaigning, politics and research. Staff and pupils organised fundraising activities to support the work of Grace Kimmins, a local pioneer in the field of care and training for young people with disabilities.[18] Bulcraig's successor, Catherine Agutter, articulated altruistic beliefs.

> Begin at good work, and you will succeed at it if you are worth anything, but begin at anything just because the money is good, and that is all you care about, then you will not succeed in making for yourself a good position, but will just be "one of a crowd." Just try to picture for yourself what the word "crowd" means, and I am sure you will not want to be part of one.'[19]

Knowledge is power girls are told. Waiting for change during the First World War, Agutter asserted 'it must be "girls and boys are equals" in the future.' Her writing illustrates the part school played in the construction of a gendered national identity. The idea of patriotic imperialist citizens was part of a wider rhetorical convention, 'both must be honourable, unselfish, healthy and noble, both must be treated with the same respect and with the same justice and deserts if this England of ours is to keep its place as foremost among the nations of the Earth.'[20]

In 1929, a biographical feature in *Bermondsey Labour Magazine* described the teaching life of Robert Jones who had been head of Monnow Central School for Boys since 1916. Trained and certificated, with a part-time degree and doctorate, under Jones's leadership Monnow earned a reputation for citizenship education, music and drama to release, foster and protect children's potential. 'In every little thing you do that you think worthy of a Monnovian in all such things as these, no less than in your actual lessons (indeed far more) you build up our Monnow, brick by brick, into a University of Bermondsey that shall send out boys and girls fit to be citizens of no mean city,' he declared. Monnow made history as the first English school to broadcast over the radio

---

[16] Ibid.
[17] *The Monnow*, November 1911, 153.
[18] *The Monnow*, August 1912, 68.
[19] *The Monnow*, July 1912, 105.
[20] *The Monnow*, May 1915, 74.

from Europe, while Jones pioneered school journeys and exchange programmes with Eton College. He was proud when Monnovian cricketers beat the Etonians despite having to practice with a soft ball and an asphalt wicket. Well respected in the locality, Monnow became famous in education circles and attracted many visitors. Jones never caned a boy, and the press dubbed Monnow the 'school that boys did not wish to leave' when he retired in 1932.[21]

Sir Henry Hadow, Vice-Chancellor of Sheffield University, chaired a Board of Education committee for six reports between 1923 and 1933. In 1926, the committee recommended raising the school leaving age to 15 and the reorganisation of secondary schooling. Test results would determine whether children attend an academic, technical or new type of 'modern' school, in which 'the courses of instruction though not merely vocational or utilitarian should be used to connect the school work with interests arising from the social and industrial environment of the pupils.' In large part, this reflected the fact that the country's leading educational psychologist, Cyril Burt, thought it possible to say what a child's future accomplishments might be on the basis of tests applied at the age of 10 or 11. The committee believed girls 'should also be shown that on efficient care and management of the home depend the health, happiness and prosperity of the nation.'[22]

Selection and the theory of children falling naturally into distinct 'types' was educational orthodoxy from at least the 1930s when belief in the efficacy of intelligence tests made streaming as a 'system,' a practically universal method of internal school organisation to achieve a homogenous 'ability' grouping. Although girls' secondary schools were much less amenable to central directives to stream pupils by 'ability' than boys' schools, the NUWT was exceptional in challenging the 1938 Spens Report for failing to consider gender in discussing the merits of technical education.[23]

During the war the development of reforms that were to culminate in the Education Act of 1944 received a hiccup when female MPs successfully introduced an amendment granting equal pay to teachers. The next day the man leading the wartime coalition government, Winston Churchill, designated it a matter of confidence and the House capitulated. Churchill, under pressure, appointed a Royal Commission on Equal Pay and approved the ending of the marriage bar. Fees were finally prohibited in state secondary schooling, there were increased grants to universities and students, provision of free school meals and milk, school transport and clothing grants. However, claims made in

[21] Robert Jones, *Bermondsey Labour Magazine*, July 1919, 60; *The Star*, 20 May 1932.
[22] *Report of the Consultative Committee of the Board of Education on the Education of the Adolescent*, 1927.
[23] Brian Simon, "Streaming and Unstreaming in the Secondary School" in *Education for Democracy* eds. David Rubinstein and Colin Stoneman (Harmondsworth: Penguin, 1970), p. 143; Sarah King, "Feminists in Teaching: the National Union of Women Teachers: 1920–1945," in *Women Who Taught: Perspectives on the History of Women and Teaching* eds. Alison Prentice and Marjorie R. Theobald (Toronto: University of Toronto Press, 1991), 195.

the 1943 report of the Norwood Committee that it was possible to identify three types of children with three types of mind—the academic, the technical and the practical—supported the separation of pupils into three sorts of secondary school—grammar, technical and secondary modern. The grammar schools would offer a curriculum that emphasised PE, 'character' and the English language as opposed to anything more technical or modern.

SECONDARY EDUCATION FOR ALL?

When the Labour Party gained sole power in May 1945, education policy continued to unfold on selective lines. Technical schools never accounted for more than 5 per cent of children, and scientific belief in the validity of intelligence testing would provide a justification for who went to grammar school and who went to a secondary modern.[24] As newly elected Prime Minister, Labour's Clement Attlee appointed Ellen Wilkinson as the first woman Minister of Education in Britain. The new secondary moderns, Wilkinson assured her party conference in June 1946, 'were to be modern in aim as well as name and in no sense dumping grounds,' and she foresaw the danger of labelling non-academic children as failures. As she put it, 'the higher IQs will become intolerable little wretches if they are stamped from the age of 11 as superior beings.'[25] Though she did prevent further postponement to the raising of the school leaving age to 15 in 1947, she was dead less than a month after.

Nevertheless, meritocratic arguments cut no ice with Cambridge-educated Shena Simon, a progressive leading figure for many years on Manchester's education committee. 'Will not a school which alone leads eventually—if only for the few—to the highest educational institutions in the land, and for the many, to secure white-collar occupations, not carry a prestige higher than the school which leads to manual work, although skilled, and one which leads to nowhere in particular,' she asked in *Three Schools or One?*[26] Tellingly, the word 'modern' was pejorative in eighteenth and nineteenth century educational discourses and both here and in the French *collèges modernes* a euphemism for less clever.[27] In most towns or cities, there was considerable prestige attached to the grammar schools. Tradition and long-established links with the middle and upper classes gave strength to the endowed variety, and those whose pretensions were more brittle could still offer their pupils a sense of distinction, of having been

---

[24] Brian Simon, *Intelligence Testing and the Comprehensive School* (London: Lawrence and Wishart, 1953); Brian Simon, *Education and the Social Order, 1940–90* (London: Lawrence and Wishart, 2010).

[25] David Kynaston, *Austerity Britain*, 150; Olive Banks, *Parity and Prestige*, 141–2; Denis W. Dean, "Planning for a Postwar Generation: Ellen Wilkinson and George Tomlinson at the Ministry of Education, 1945–51," *History of Education* 15, no. 2 (1986), 108.

[26] Shena Simon, *Three Schools or One* (London: Frederick Muller, 1947), 43.

[27] Michèle Cohen, "A Little Learning? The Curriculum and the Construction of Gender in the Long Eighteenth Century," *Journal for British Eighteenth Century Studies*, 29 (2006), 321–335; Anthony Sampson, *Anatomy of Britain* (London, Hodder and Stoughton, 1962), 143.

'chosen' for 'better' things. Historian David Kynaston notes 'almost all their pupils were deeply imbued with a guilt-free sense of belonging to the present and future elite' and perhaps more than any other institution the grammar school 'set the moral as well as the intellectual standards of the community.'[28]

Post-war governments put strong pressure on women to become mothers and homemakers. Patriarchal social policy for the reconstruction and rehabilitation of social harmony and cohesiveness under Attlee's Labour governments (1945–51) supported this, and as wartime nurseries closed, working women made way for returning soldiers who also had priority access to education and training. A 1952 World Health Organisation monograph *Maternal Care and Mental Health* by psychoanalyst John Bowlby proved particularly popular, and his name became synonymous with 'Bowlbyism,' the message that any separation of young children from their mothers results in emotional damage. This 'was fastened on as a sort of proof that all babies needed the round-the-clock care of their natural mothers and that there was a sort of mystical tie between mother and child.'[29] Conservative retrenchment under Winston Churchill after 1951 left technical and vocational education in short supply and largely male. At Birmingham, for instance, three-fifths of the provision was for boys. Wallasey Education Committee ran two single-sex technical schools teaching adult gender roles. Building and engineering were male-only. Art, commercial pre-nursing or domestic training were female only.[30]

By the 1950s, research largely based on boys confirmed that selection advantaged the children of middle-class parents, concluding that grammar schools served to widen existing divisions of power and prestige in the social structure. Coaching and intensive tuition used by the middle classes improved test scores. Middle-class offspring dominated grammar intakes owing to advantages imbued by family background, and social class remained a major influence on educational attainment.[31] From 1946, secondary moderns and the bottom streams of grammar schools were full of working-class children who often had a negative experience.[32] A 1954 government report on early school leaving noted that working-class children were more likely to leave school at 15 to go to work, whatever type of school they attended, and the Crowther Report of

---

[28] David Kynaston, *Austerity Britain*, 567.

[29] Dennis W. Dean, "Education for Moral Improvement, Domesticity and Social Cohesion: the Labour Government, 1945–1951," *Oxford Review of Education* 17, no. 3 (1991), 269–86; Denise Riley, *War In the Nursery* (London: Virago, 1983); Mary Stott, *Forgetting's No Excuse: the autobiography of Mary Stott* (London: Virago, 1989), 138–9.

[30] Brian Simon, *Education and the Social Order, 1940–1990* (London: Lawrence and Wishart, 2010), 135; Olive Banks, *Parity and Prestige*, 158.

[31] Alice Heim, *The Appraisal of Intelligence* (London: Tavistock, 1954); Banks, *Parity and Prestige*; Jean E. Floud, Albert Henry Halsey, F.M. Martin, *Social Class and Educational Opportunity* (London: Greenwood Press, 1956).

[32] Brian Jackson and Dennis Marsden, *Education and the Working Classes* (Harmondsworth: Penguin, 1962); Brian Jackson *Streaming: An Education System in Miniature* (London: Routledge, 1964).

1959 drew attention to a 'wastage of talent' among working-class leavers, male and female.

Opposition to the divided education system came from the experience of teachers, children and parents aware that educational selection rested on spurious educational thinking that made it acceptable for many, if not most, children to fail. It was certainly evident that lower-funded secondary moderns run by academically less well-qualified teachers did not enjoy equivalence with the traditionally elite, middle-class grammar schools as McCulloch's research testifies.[33]

Only obliquely acknowledged was female disadvantage. Therefore, generations of girls had to outperform boys to succeed within the terms of an equal opportunities discourse. Buried in an appendix of Brian Jackson and Dennis Marsden's analysis of adults from working-class families who attended Huddersfield grammar schools in the 1940s and 1950s is a reflection on a finding they did not anticipate:

> Small details give some sense of the discrepancies between the education of boys and the education of girls. Between 1955 and 1960, Huddersfield maintained its very prominent place in English education by winning 100 state scholarships to universities from its four grammar schools. Of these 83 per cent were awarded to boys and only 18 to girls. It seems that this kind of detail can be repeated again and again, locally and nationally.[34]

In fact, there was a clear gender bias in educational selection. Girls frequently had better raw test results but lost out in the annual competition to boys with lower scores. A legacy of more limited provision for girls led some authorities to use separate gender norms either through a policy of marking girls' down or adding new tests to ensure an equal allocation of grammar school places.

Despite the language of meritocracy, advocates of separate gender norms argued that the relative early superiority of girls over boys diminishes or is reversed by 16, making it necessary to tilt the balance in favour of the late-developing 'maturity' of boys. Common sense and social observation suggested the difference 'is not real because it does not last, it is not a phenomenon produced by the test, it is a phenomenon produced by "nature".'[35] There were, however, a number of flaws in the reasoning. For one thing, the idea of 'maturity' was borrowed from physical maturity (relating to differences in terms of bone density and size), and measures for intellectual maturity were not available.

---

[33] Clyde Chitty, *Eugenics, Race and Intelligence in Education* (London: Continuum, 2009); Gary McCulloch, *Failing the Ordinary Child? The Theory and Practice of Working-Class Secondary Education* (Buckingham: Open University Press, 1998).

[34] Brian Jackson and Dennis Marsden, *Education and the Working Classes*, 251–2.

[35] Deborah Thom, "'Better a teacher than a hairdresser? A mad passion for equality' or, keeping Molly and Betty down' in *Lessons for Life. The Schooling of Girls and Women 1850–1950* ed. Felicity Hunt (Oxford: Basil Blackwell, 1987), 141.

For another, boys did not catch up in verbal and non-reasoning tests, often the main tests used in selection. Indeed, subsequent performance was an unreliable guide since it was influenced by the selection itself. Whenever selection occurs, someone else is left behind and no choice is purely 'educational' set outside of a socio-cultural context. 'Cultural assumptions and expectations, organizational constraints and explicit ideologies all play a part in the measurement of achievement, and in inferring individual potential.'[36]

Feminist teachers argued vehemently against such a policy and thought schooling should give boys *and* girls the potential to enter a wide range of employment and to achieve economic independence and stability. In the era of 'Bowlbyism,' the female version of the grammar school was rooted in the gender aspirations in which higher education and a career took second place to a good marriage. Alison Hennegan, whose mother was a primary school teacher, passed her 11-plus in 1959. At grammar school in Epsom, she 'watched the dreary procession of girls who left school either before "O" levels or in the middle of "A" levels. Blinded by the dazzle of their engagement rings, they rushed to submerge themselves in marriages with men they'd outgrown half a decade later.' The women Stephanie Spencer talked to in the 1990s spoke of failure, early leaving and low expectation with memories of having being pulled out of school by their parents and fear of a single life. Careers advice attenuated this, while the media ran endless debates about whether a university education was a waste of money for daughters. Educating girls for housework was mighty convenient for men, as the provost of King's College, London, let out in a speech at Keele University reported in July 1969. 'It was time, he said, that we stopped educating women like men and producing "second-class males", because it was "getting too difficult to get anyone willing to do domestic chores".'[37]

It was different for Jane Thompson, who grew up on a white, working-class council estate in East Hull. In September 1958, her mother folded her starched white blouse, black pencil skirt, white frilly apron into a Woolworth's carrier bag and rode with Jane on the bus, into town, on to another bus, and out to the leafy suburbs. It was her daughter's first day at grammar school, and she was juggling part-time work in a pub, but she did not want the girls at Jane's new school to know what her mother did for a living. She saw grammar schooling as her daughter's escape route, and when Jane started to rebel, she marched her straight to the new supermarket where girls she had known at junior school,

---

[36] Harvey Goldstein, "Gender bias and test norms in educational selection," in *Gender and the Politics of Schooling*, ed. Madeleine Arnot and Gaby Weiner (London: Hutchinson, 1987), 122–126.

[37] Alison Hennegan, "And Battles Long Ago" in *Truth, Dare or Promise: Girls Growing Up in the Fifties*, ed. Liz Heron (London: Virago, 1985), 148; Stephanie Spencer, "Reflections on the 'site of struggle': girls' experience of secondary education in the late 1950s," *History of Education*, 33, no. 4 (2004), 437–449; Carol Dyhouse, *Students: a gendered history* (London: Routledge, 2006); quoted in Mary Stott, *Forgetting's No Excuse: the autobiography of Mary Stott* (London: Virago, 1985), 142.

who failed their 11-plus, were already *in situ*. 'If you don't get down and do your homework—it'll be stacking shelves in Frank Dees for the rest of your life,' became her mother's most constant challenge during her remaining years at school.[38]

The rules at Thompson's single-sex grammar school were remorseless. Pupils had to walk down the right-hand side of the corridor only. They could not talk in any of the lobbies. They had to stand when a teacher either entered or left the room. They could not eat sweets or remove their berets in public places. Uniform meant not wearing stockings until they were 17, shoes with laces and flat heels and no talking to boys. They could not smoke, dye or backcomb their hair (current fashion), wear jewellery or make up. 'Skirts, when kneeling, had to be precisely one inch from the floor. Hockey boots had to be polished. Gym shoes whitened.' Homework was immediately handed-in, parttime jobs forbidden. Among this welter of disapproval, 'the influence of men was in the very fabric of the place.' The history they learned was all about men, the French and English literature they read was written by men and the mental arithmetic they had to practise in their heads 'was about men on train journeys doing miles that had to be calculated, and men laying carpets which had to be added together in square yards. Latin was all about Caesar and the Gallic Wars. Geography was about sheep farmers in Australia. Dog eared texts, smelling of formaldehyde, showed men in white coats doing experiments.'[39]

Michael Young intended his 1958 book *The Rise of the Meritocracy* to warn against an imagined future society in which individual 'merit,' based on a narrow understanding of intelligence, determines social station. This would produce a community bound together by the belief that those at the top deserve their power and their fortunes because of innate 'ability.'

> The educational ladder was also a social ladder—the scruffy, ill-mannered boy who started at five years old at the bottom had to be metamorphosed, rung by rung, into a more presentable, more polished, and more confident as well as a more knowledgeable lad at the top. He had to acquire a new accent—the most indelible mark of class in England—and to any but the most determined man, that was well-nigh impossible unless he started young. When he finished his climb, he could then stand comparison with others who had begun their ascent from a much higher level.[40]

In Young's book, women and 'populists' emerge as critics of this new social order designed to lend the illusion of social mobility, to give credibility to the classless nature of a so-called meritocracy while producing new inequalities of power and social stratification. A world in which white, middle-class men were still the prime beneficiaries such that the small number of largely middle class

---

[38] Jane Thompson, *Women, Class and Education* (London: Routledge, 2000), 17.
[39] Op cit, 21–2.
[40] Michael Young, *The Rise of the Meritocracy* (Harmondsworth: Penguin, 1958), 53–4.

and largely white young women who were beginning to emerge through the education system did not yet attract wide public attention.

With feminists lacking the political and economic advantage to influence the reassertion of the breadwinner norm in social inquiry, politics and policy-making, domestic training enjoyed a surge in popularity after the introduction of sex education in schools in 1956. The Crowther Report articulated an ideology of gender difference based on heredity, which assumed that all women would want marriage and motherhood, as well as whatever paid work they could do. Values that especially influenced the female curriculum in secondary modern schools. 'It is plain, that if it is sound educational policy to take account of natural interests… [the direct interest of a girl] in dress, personal appearance and in problems of human relations [these] should be given a central part in the education.'[41] The NUWT objected. 'If the Crowther Report felt that education for marriage was so important,' a delegate inquired at annual conference, 'why was it not advocated for boys as well as for girls? Was the role of father so insignificant that it could be ignored?'[42]

Ideological emphases on women's place in the home remained strong. In his foreword to the 1963 Newsom Report on 'average' and 'below average' children, Conservative Education Minister Edward Boyle said all 'should have an equal opportunity of acquiring intelligence, and of developing their talents and abilities to the full.' Except for women. An education system committed to formal equality was seen by the Report as a weakness from the standpoint of girls.

> We try to educate girls into becoming imitation men and as a result we are wasting and frustrating their qualities of womanhood at great expense to the community… In addition to their needs as individuals our girls should be educated in terms of their main social function—which is to make for themselves, their children and their husbands a secure and suitable home and to be mothers.[43]

All did not pursue the same curriculum goals, and degrees of emphasis were gendered. Put another way, the girl may respond to the science lesson with a 'less eager curiosity' than the boy who 'experiences a sense of wonder and power. The growth of wheat, the birth of a lamb, the movement of clouds, put him in awe of nature, the locomotive he sees as man's response: the switch and the throttle are his magic wands.'[44] Similar numbers of boys and girls achieved academic qualifications, but girls tended to leave school earlier as did children growing up in northern England, where the proportion of 16-year-olds in state schools was 15.3 per cent, compared with 28.6

---

[41] Sue Sharpe, *Just Like a Girl* (Harmondsworth: Penguin, 1976), 20.

[42] *The Woman Teacher*, April 1960, 229.

[43] Quoted in Sue Lees, *Sugar and Spice: Sexuality and Adolescent Girls* (Harmondsworth: Penguin, 1993), 154.

[44] Rosemary Deem, "State policy and ideology in the education of women, 1944–1980," *British Journal of Sociology of Education*, 2, no. 2 (1981), 135.

per cent in the south.⁴⁵ Maureen O'Connor taught at a West Country girls' secondary modern school in the 1960s. Her pupils were fatalistic. 'You don't need to bother about us, Miss,' they assured her. 'All the bright ones have gone up the road to the grammar school.'⁴⁶

Some did bother. In 1956, Labour politician Anthony Crosland described British education as 'the most divisive, unjust, and wasteful of all aspects of social equality.'⁴⁷ Most children left school at 15 and went straight into full-time employment, though older teenage boys faced 18 months to 2 years of National Service in the armed forces until 1960. Youth unemployment was rare, but over seven out of ten school leavers had no educational qualifications, and for most girls, education and training took place before joining the paid workforce.⁴⁸ Crosland wanted to establish a national network of comprehensive schools that would deal equally with all children. By the 1960s, a new emphasis on human capital theory, combined with forward-looking, technocratic rhetoric, set the scene for change. Labour leader Harold Wilson's vision of a New Britain captured the mood of the time. To mobilise the female vote in the 1964 general election, Labour strategists appealed to married women as mothers, offering a 'new deal for the family' focused on education, housing, improving pensions and provision for widows. Although women were still treated as marginal reserves in the labour market, there were promises to introduce equal pay and to improve nursery facilities for working mothers.⁴⁹ In office, the Wilson administration issued a Circular, 10/65, requesting the reorganisation of secondary schooling along comprehensive lines.

The canvas was not completely blank. After 1944, some powerful authorities such as Coventry, London and the West Riding established the right to experiment with comprehensive education. Different types of secondary school co-existed in the capital, and despite an acrimonious quarrel with the local grammar, Britain's first purpose-built comprehensive was Kidbrooke, a school for 2000 girls in southeast London.⁵⁰ Founded in 1954, Kidbrooke became an educational sensation, and organised tours were booked to capacity. Set among vast playing fields, playgrounds, lawns and gardens, its architecture expressed the idealism and the size of the concepts. While *Labour Woman* presented it as 'London's pride,' the right-wing magazine *Time and Tide* said its motto should be 'All Equal and All Stupid.'⁵¹ Mary Green, Kidbrooke's founding head, was proud local people called her pupils Smarties, thinking it a reflection on their

---

⁴⁵ Brian Simon, *Education and the Social Order*, 215.

⁴⁶ Maureen O'Connor, *Secondary Education* (London: Cassell, 1990), 1.

⁴⁷ Anthony Crosland, *The Future of Socialism* (London: Constable & Robinson, 2006 edition), 216, 231.

⁴⁸ Hilary Land, "We Sat Down at the Table of Privilege and Complained about the Food," *The Rise and Rise of Meritocracy* ed. Geoff Dench (Oxford: Blackwell Publishing, 2006), 48.

⁴⁹ Stephen Fielding, *The Labour Governments 1964–1970 volume 1 Labour and cultural change* (Manchester: Manchester University Press, 2003), 78.

⁵⁰ I.G. Fenwick, *The Comprehensive School 1944–1970* (London, Methuen & Co. Ltd, 1976), 45.

⁵¹ Quoted in Hunter Davies, *The Creighton Report* (London, Hamish Hamilton, 1978), 25.

intelligence. The girls knew the nickname came from the berets they had to wear—a colour for each of the eight houses.⁵²

A year later, Margaret Miles led the transformation of Putney County Secondary School, a girls' grammar, to Mayfield, a girls' comprehensive. She expressed exasperation at the representation of secondary modern girls as the pathological 'other' who would not wear uniform or do homework. Mayfield girls did both. For Miles, comprehensive education was an idea whose time had come. 'It is not murder, but cultivation, to bring a school up to date and to remodel it to meet modern needs,' she said.⁵³ While many worried about the scale of comprehensives, pioneer teachers like Green and Miles were unflappable.⁵⁴

Outside Whitehall, those who were dissatisfied with Labour's approach launched the Comprehensive Schools Committee (CSC) in the autumn of 1965. Information Officer Caroline Benn bore the brunt of the writing and data analysis for the first report on the British comprehensive reform, *Half Way There*, first published in 1970. Co-authored with Brian Simon, she wrote 13 of the 21 chapters, including the line 'A comprehensive school is *not* a social experiment; it is an educational reform.'⁵⁵ Overall, a shift from 11-plus testing benefitted some, predominantly middle-class girls. A comprehensive curriculum would have aided inclusivity. At the mixed grammar school future social scientist Hilary Land went to in the 1950s, there was a Latin stream and science stream. Few science stream girls learned chemistry and physics. Timetabled against these classes was domestic science, and girls were expected to take this, along with biology.⁵⁶ In practice, Benn and Simon found that very few pioneer comprehensive schools offered a common curriculum. Childcare, domestic science and typing were female-only, and metalwork, technical drawing and woodwork still for boys (see Figs. 4.1 and 4.2). Links between the distribution of educational knowledge and the characteristic pattern of men and women of different classes distributing themselves into different sectors of the economy continued.

In 1969, Jane Thompson returned to Hull from university to teach in a new purpose-built comprehensive school. Hull's David Lister High School was the focus of a 1967 film *Education for the Future* made to answer critics who feared a lowering of academic standards. Headteacher Albert Rowe said his school had a cooperative and community ethic and avoided rigid classification, making the full range of opportunities available to all. Media interest enthused the local community, as did the appearance on a derelict bombsite of a futuristic, modernist building large enough to amalgamate three secondary moderns housed in former board schools. Looking back over more than 30 years, Thompson

⁵² Roy Hattersley, "Dame Mary Green obituary", *Guardian*, 23 April 2004.
⁵³ Margaret Miles, *And Gladly Teach* (London: Carousel, 1973), 93.
⁵⁴ Lottie Hoare, "Margaret Miles: the educational journey of a comprehensive school campaigner," *FORUM: for promoting 3–19 comprehensive education*, 54, no. 1 (2012): 91–102.
⁵⁵ Caroline Benn and Brian Simon *Half Way There* (Harmondsworth: Penguin, 1972), 110.
⁵⁶ Hilary Land, "We Sat Down at the Table of Privilege and Complained about the Food," 51.

Fig. 4.1 ABB/A/13/6b Typing lesson, Belper Secondary Modern, c1953. From the Photographic Archive of the Architects and Building Branch, Ministry of Education and its successors. UCL Institute of Education Special Collections. (Crown Copyright)

said, 'The motivation and commitment of the teaching staff was strong. It was an optimistic time when many of us—ourselves the beneficiaries of decent council houses, grammar school places and redbrick universities influenced by the politics of the New Left—set out to change the world for the class we had come from through comprehensive education.'[57]

Two-fifths of married women were in paid employment in this era, but generally schooling led boys towards a wider and better choice of work than girls. In terms of training schemes either immediately before or during the early years of work, young men tended to get day-release for craft and technical subjects at a junior level, and for professional qualifications when older. In 1977, 2 out of 5 male school leavers took up apprenticeships, whereas 1 in 16 girls did. Three-quarters of these female apprenticeships were in hairdressing—a traditionally female and badly paid occupation. Advertisements could be blatantly sexist:

> Before every new Hertz girl meets her public, she has to learn to always say Yes to a customer. It's easy when you work for Hertz because there's no limit to what

---

[57] Jane Thompson, *Women, Class and Education*, 26; BFI (2010) 'Education for the Future (1967)', *Shadows of Progress; Documentary Film in Post-war Britain 1951–1977*, Disc Four: Today in Britain.

96   J. MARTIN

Fig. 4.2 ABB/A/20/16a Boys' woodwork class, Armitage Street School Manchester, c1967. From the Photographic Archive of the Architects and Building Branch, Ministry of Education and its successors. UCL Institute of Education Special Collections. (Crown Copyright)

>   Hertz has to offer. In fact, it takes us six weeks to fill her pretty head with all the facts and figures. We start off with the easy ones… What we don't spell out in the book, we know a Hertz girl can handle naturally. We choose her because she's the kind of girl who enjoys solving all the little things that don't seem so little at the time. Yes, I'll phone your wife to tell her you'll be late. Yes, I'll find the briefcase you left in the car. Yes, I'll sew the button on your coat. The next time you want to rent a car, ask a Hertz girl. You'll see how well she's learned her lessons.[58]

The National Council for Civil Liberties was unequivocal in its condemnation of the status quo in a 1973 pamphlet on *Women's Rights*. 'Poor job opportunities, low pay and discrimination at work both cause and reflect discrimination at school… The education system is, we believe, creating discriminatory attitudes and low expectations in new generations of children.'

[58] Advertisement in *The Times*, 12 October 1972, quoted in Carol Adams and Rosalind Laurikietis, *The Gender Trap Book 1: Education and Work* (London: Virago, 1980, 73–4).

Labour's Sex Discrimination Act of 1975 indicated change in policy awareness and policy climate, though exceptions included indirect discrimination within the curriculum, private and single-sex schools. As a consequence, there was an abundance of studies exploring gender inequalities in classroom, written in an accessible, non-academic, way for teachers and parents. Many showing the power relations embedded in constructions of masculinity and femininity, which underpin the idea of rationality central not only to the process of schooling but to a gendered division of labour in the wider society also. Often the approach taken traversed disciplines, uncovering ideas and practices inimical to the full development of potential.[59]

FAILING GIRLS?

Generally, men ran the schools, dominating the administrative and policy-making side of education, whereas women stayed in the classroom. Female heads of department in secondary schools were usually in low status knowledge spaces like home economics and girls' physical education. Women dominated primary schooling. New inquiries drew attention to gender dynamics within schools, to shed light on the practices of pupils and teachers, which reproduce a hierarchical system of gender divisions in and through schooling. Sociologist Michelle Stanworth, for example, explored gender differentiation in a sixth form college where she found that boys received a disproportionate amount of attention from teachers, which was deleterious for girls' self-esteem. This gave boys an overall advantage, and one girl experienced this in such negative terms that she described herself as a 'wallpaper person.'[60]

Among other things, teachers readily used stereotypical binaries. Boys were lively, adventurous, boisterous, self-confident, independent, energetic, couldn't-care-less, loyal and aggressive. Girls were obedient, tidy, neat, conscientious, orderly, fussy, catty, bitchy and gossipy. The samples of staffroom talk quoted by Kathleen Clarricoates in an early study of the hidden curriculum in primary schools show the conditioned response to sex-role stereotypes.

> Michael, much to the concern of his teachers and to the contempt of his peer group, loved to play with dolls. He liked to bake, and constantly sought the company of girls, despite their insults. He was constantly admonished by his teacher 'to try to behave properly'. But to no avail. During a conversation in the staffroom about his particular behaviour: 'Ah, yes,' said one teacher, 'bionic woman'. 'Don't be unkind,' laughed another. A well-meaning teacher added, 'His brother

---

[59] See Rosemary Deem, "Series Editor's Introduction", in *Just a Bunch of Girls*, ed. Gaby Weiner (Milton Keynes: Open University Press), vii-ix.

[60] Pat Mahony, *Schools for the Boys? Co-education Reassessed* (London: Hutchinson, 1985); Dale Spender and Elizabeth Sarah (eds.) *Learning to Lose: Sexism and Education* (London: The Women's Press, 1980); Michelle Stanworth, *Gender and Schooling* (London: Hutchinson, 1983).

is really a nice little boy and quite normal.' 'Perhaps when he grows up, he'll get straightened out.'[61]

Using the language of Madeleine Arnot from her analysis of the reproduction of class and gender relations, we see how schooling transmits a specific gender code whereby children are discouraged, by their peers and adults, from participating in activities considered unsuitable for their sex. Michael, who does not 'fit' conventional notions of masculinity, does not come out equally through the recontextualisation at school of gender codes learned within the home.[62]

Discipline and control of male youth received a lot of attention in research and policy circles following the removal of unskilled labouring jobs which were the forms of entry for young men of the lower working class into the labour force. These were the 'lads' described in Paul Willis's study *Learning to Labour* written in the 1970s, which talked of boys' relations to girls as 'Exploitative and hypocritical. Girls are pursued, sometimes roughly for their sexual favours, often dropped and labelled as "loose" when they give in.'[63] To meet the challenges of a system that privileged the academic, the 'lads' created a counter-culture that valued practical knowledge, life experience and 'street wisdom' over mental qualities, which are for most people what education is self-evidently about. To retain some sense of dignity, they block teaching because the culture and community of hard manual labour enables them to sustain their inversion of the mental-manual distinction their teachers operate.

Willis's influence was extensive. His analysis concentrated on forms of cultural production, arguing that the 'lads' colluded in their own continued subordination in the workplace as a direct outcome of their adherence to their youth sub-culture. The affordances and limitations for boys' agency were also evident in Phillip Corrigan's research in two single-sex Sunderland schools in the early 1970s, with almost exclusively working-class intakes. Put simply, Corrigan argued the 'lads' disliked school, examining truancy, 'messing about in class,' street trouble, involvement in football and pop music, he provides a compelling picture of male youth engaged in a social 'guerrilla struggle' against the 'occupying army' of teachers who would control and shape them. A capacity for quick repartee and the ability to outsmart, a deep resistance to those in authority, sticking together and 'having a laff' all offer a way of earning 'respect.'[64]

Most ethnographic studies of delinquency, education and youth subculture were male oriented. Audrey Lambart joined the Department of Social

---

[61] Kathleen Clarricoates, "The importance of being Ernest, Emma, Tom, Jane. The perception and categorization of gender conformity and gender deviation in primary schools," *Schooling for Women's Work*, ed. Rosemary Deem (London: Routledge, 1980), 35.

[62] Madeleine Arnot, *Reproducing Gender?* (London: Routledge, 2002).

[63] Paul Willis, *Learning to Labour: How Working-Class Kids Get Working-Class Jobs* (London: Saxon House, 1977), 67.

[64] Phillip Corrigan, *Schooling the Smash Street Kids* (London: Macmillan, 1979).

Anthropology and Sociology at Manchester in 1963 to work on the first government-financed project in the sociology of education. Her study of a girls' grammar school remained in the shadows, although the studies of boys' schools (one grammar, one secondary modern) became widely known. Adolescent girls tended to appear fleetingly and often through the eyes of the 'lad's' in the literature, which was something sociologist Angela McRobbie sought to address. Hence, McRobbie focused on female samples 'to map out that which they experienced and make sense of the social institutions which they inhabited, and to consider in some detail their interpersonal relationships.' She found female resistance to be largely 'invisible' either because they just skipped school or used humour and femininity to create a sense of dignity inside the classroom. In common with alienated boys, many of these girls could not wait to leave school and get a job, though the possibility of girls achieving in the public sphere was not taken very seriously.[65]

In terms of the curriculum, what emerged in a 1975 survey of gender differences was anxiety over an absence of reading materials appealing to boys, girls disadvantaged by a lack of mechanical and spatial experience, and stereotypical teacher behaviour. Christine Griffin analysed a group of Birmingham girls in 1979.

> Male students who took 'girls' subjects' were assumed to be learning a skill for future use in the labour market. They were taken more seriously than their female peers in the same classes, to whom such skills were supposed to come naturally for use in their future roles as wives and mothers [...] Female students who took 'boys' subjects' were either presumed to be interested solely in flirting with the boys or discounted as unique exceptions.[66]

Griffin presents empirical material suggesting nobody took girls' attending non-traditional subjects seriously. The mass of girls was sitting examinations in a narrow cluster of subjects seen as supporting 'natural' female interests, needs and choices with respect to personal/domestic life. Gillian Plummer's research corroborated this, showing working-class girls directed towards a curriculum for domestic, factory and office work.[67]

In sum, school ethnographies showed schooling played a large part in convincing girls that their education was unimportant, their training was unimportant, their jobs were inessential and their husbands were financially responsible for them. In mixed schools, boys and girls were still listed

---

[65] Audrey Lambart, "Mereside: a grammar school for girls in the 1960s," *Gender and Education*, 9, no. 4 (1997), 441–456; Angela McRobbie, "Working-class girls and the culture of femininity," in *Women Take Issue: aspects of women's subordination*, ed. Women's Studies Group Centre for Contemporary Cultural Studies (London: Hutchinson, 1978), 96; Lynn Davies, *Pupil Power: deviance & gender in schools* (Lewes: Falmer Press, 1983).

[66] Christine Griffin, *Typical Girls? Young Women From School to the Job Market* (London: Routledge, Kegan and Paul, 1985), 78–9.

[67] Gillian Plummer, *Failing Working-Class Girls?* (Stoke-on-Trent: Trentham, 2000).

separately, with the boys first; boys dominated playground space, with girls standing in small groups around the edges, and children being told to line up according to sex. In assemblies, girls sometimes sat, while boys stood. Uniform meant a skirt for female pupils, and many authorities discouraged women teachers from wearing trousers. Boys were the target of rules on hair length.

Sociologist Sara Delamont claimed that schools were more conservative than the wider society. Classroom observations in the secondary sector revealed the seating arrangements might well follow the segregated pattern of class registers—boys first, followed by girls. Male-first allocation of space in practical lessons meant it often proved impossible to accommodate all the girls, who had to start each lesson by trying to find a seat. In assembly:

> Pupils are told they will soon be given a form to take home—school wants the phone number of where mother works. Mrs Marks says that if they are ill or have an accident, school tries to get mother. The school try not to bother father, because he is the head of the family, his wage keeps the family while mother's is only for luxuries, so try to contact mother... If no-one at home—mum, granny or auntie—put to bed at school.[68]

The literature on girls in schools focussed increasingly on their reported experiences, particularly in relation to boys, with some work claiming boys' behaviour to be a cause of the apparent failure of girls. For Arnot, the comprehensive reform 'did not represent... a challenge to the reproduction of dominant gender relations but rather a modification of the *form* of its transmission.'[69]

Jane Miller began teaching at Holland Park mixed comprehensive school in London in the late 1960s. Women teachers often found themselves made responsible for the failure of boys, and Miller sees the gender script of 'discipline man' as implicit in the Othering of mixed comprehensives as 'bad' and single-sex education in grammar schools as 'good.'

> The control of working-class boys was understood to be the principal problem for schools like mine, and, of course, a particular problem for their women teachers. And we did worry about boys: about the large number of them who failed to read and write, about their truancy and their disruptive behaviour in class. When the English department decided to take over and teach 'remedial reading' required by a good number of children, it was boys who appeared in our classes, hardly ever girls.[70]

[68] Sara Delamont, *Sex Roles and the School* (London: Routledge, 1980), 50.

[69] Madeleine Arnot, "A cloud over co-education: an analysis of the forms of transmission of class and gender relations," in *Gender, Class & Education*, eds. Stephen Walker and Len Barton (Lewes: Falmer, 1983), 71.

[70] Jane Miller, *More Has Meant Women: The Feminisation of Schooling* (London: Institute of Education, 1992), 9.

As a pupil at Bedales, a progressive, mixed boarding school in the private sector, Miller outswam and outfought her male peers, and assumptions that she might find it difficult to teach boys surprised her, although she admits she found it hard to teach the early leavers 'with their cropped hair, cropped jeans, large boots and braces.' Boys who 'looked forward eagerly to their fifteenth birthdays and the end of school' when they anticipated earning more than she did as a teacher. Nonetheless, teachers dedicated their efforts to the boys rather than the 'quiet' girls who behaved well in class and did well in their schoolwork.[71]

Alice Sullivan examined the link between gender, school contexts and self-concept for a child cohort born in 1958 who experienced a system that was in transition from selective to non-selective admissions in secondary schools. Even controlling for prior test scores, Sullivan found a large gender difference. Boys had higher self-concepts in subjects perceived as 'masculine' such as mathematics and the sciences, and girls in 'feminine' subjects such as English. Single-sex schooling reduced the gender gap, but selective schooling was linked to lower academic self-concept overall. Research from the 1980s suggested girls did better in single-sex schools where the emphasis was on intellectual development rather than the attempt to produce the domesticated girl. Sue Lees found the girls attending such schools were on the whole far more work-oriented and positive in their approach to teachers than those in the co-educational schools.[72]

In terms of attainment, there were fewer female entries for public examinations at 16 and 18 and gender differentiated subject choice. More males than females attended part-time further education after leaving school, and of the group that went on to full-time higher education, more young women attended teacher-training colleges than universities or polytechnics. In short, men dominated the most prestigious spaces. Most elite universities accepted fewer women than men, but the new polytechnics appealed to women with their broad curricula, particularly in the arts.[73] Founded in 1969, the Open University (OU) had the highest proportion of female students, including many women teachers in search of a degree. Open-access and flexible distance learning allowed women previously denied higher education to combine study with domestic and/or work roles.

However, change occurred at precisely the point when, for the first time since 1945, there was a growing problem of youth unemployment. A decline in vocational apprenticeships and industrial jobs with release for college training affected working-class males leaving school. Consequently, two Black male pupils of a London comprehensive school AnnMarie Wolpe interviewed in 1976 thought girls stood a better chance to get work, and all the boys were

---

[71] Ibid.
[72] Alice Sullivan, "Academic self-concept, gender and single-sex schooling," *British Educational Research Journal*, 35, no. 2 (2009), 259–288; Sue Lees, *Sugar and Spice*, 161.
[73] Carol Dyhouse, *Students: a Gendered History*, 102.

fully aware that girls were likely to have to work even if they married.[74] The reorganisation of teacher training, which saw the absorption of many colleges into polytechnics and huge competition for university places in the arts, reduced opportunities for some young women who were less likely than young men to achieve the qualifications that gave access to higher education. Drastic cuts in teacher training also helped 'bump' women into other forms of training and graduate employment such as commerce.

Women's full-time employment remained steady in the 1970s and 1980s at 5.5 million, but there was a significant increase in part-time female employment from 2.8 million to 4.4 million as a post-war trend of married women with families taking jobs that fitted around home life and unpaid domestic duties intensified. The characteristic pattern of men and women distributing themselves in different sectors of the economy saw women clustered in clerical jobs, teaching and welfare work, while part-time women workers dominated the service sector (e.g. catering, cleaning and hairdressing) and distribution (shops). By the 1980s, it was observed that the radical Right's educational agenda, with its commitment to 'family values,' might conflict with liberal feminist moves that could improve career prospects for girls.[75]

Conclusion

Evidence assembled here shows the odds were stacked against a working-class girl climbing the English 'ladder of opportunity' because the male breadwinner remained a historical reality and the prevailing discourse of merit and social mobility was gender blind. Nevertheless, the few girls, initially from independent and grammar schools who did well academically, helped change perceptions that educating girls was a 'waste.' Grocer's daughter Margaret Thatcher was one female beneficiary—winning state scholarships to fund her secondary schooling and a place at Somerville College in 1943—when there was a special dispensation for girls from grammar schools to take their Oxford Entrance early. Twenty years on, when future sociologist Valerie Walkerdine passed the 11-plus, it was presented as a ticket to the high life, a way out of the post-war respectable working class. 'Come, they told me. It is yours. You are chosen. They didn't tell me, however, that for years I would no longer feel any sense of belonging nor any sense of safety. That I didn't belong in the new place, any more than I belonged in the old.'[76]

It is my view that the NUWT made the most notable contribution to contexts of class and gender inequalities in this era, focusing attention on the overt and covert influences in the formal and the hidden curriculum and enduring

---

[74] Ann-Marie Wolpe, *Within School Walls: The Role of Discipline, Sexuality and the Curriculum* (London: Routledge, 1988), 75.

[75] Miriam E. David, "Thatcherism is anti-feminism,"' *Trouble and Strife*, 1 (Winter 1983), 44–48.

[76] Valerie Walkerdine, "Dreams from an Ordinary Childhood," in *Truth, Dare or Promise: Girls Growing Up in the Fifties*, ed. Liz Heron (London: Virago, 1985), 74.

backlash and harassment from anti-feminist colleagues. When the union disbanded in 1961, members said they left the future of feminism in teacher trade unionism to younger women. As women teachers, they recognised the need to consider education from the perspective of gender, developing intersectional analyses and forming support systems. Unearthing the girls who were marked down in intelligence tests suggests some of the biggest losers in this era. Caroline Benn opposed selection for the few, which means discarding or underestimating those left behind. That was why she campaigned for legislation to realise the learning community explicit in the comprehensive ideal. 'Only a system which gives each boy and girl the same high-quality education all along the line, so that each can show his or her individual intelligence and develop his or her individual gifts, can ever be sure to do equal justice,' she said.[77]

Harold Wilson's 'New Britain' rhetoric changed the focus of female education somewhat because it recognised that girls were likely to go into paid employment. Added to which, changes in the climate of opinion about women's role and a wave of equality legislation were highly influential in bringing gender codes into educational policy and practice, and a feminist critique of gender relations in a patriarchal society helped articulate this. The comprehensive secondary school placed all pupils in one school and theoretically encouraged more young people to succeed within the terms of a meritocratic education system, but the women who did so quickly confronted structural inequalities in the labour market. Those young people who lacked educational credentials and who did not get on-the-job training generally ended up in the worst jobs. Unpleasant, monotonous and badly paid. Whether sitting at a factory assembly line, in an office or supermarket, unskilled women workers had the lowest pay, and somewhere, generally, there was a man above them all.

Bibliography

Primary Sources

Archival Sources

Bermondsey Labour Magazine, Southwark Local History Library and Archive.
The Monnow School Magazine, 1909–1930, Southwark Local History Library and Archive.

Autobiographies, Memoirs, Diaries, Letters, Obituaries

Burnett, John. "Education: Introduction." In *Destiny Obscure: Autobiographies of Childhood, Education and the Family* edited by John Burnett, 135–170. Harmondsworth: London: Routledge, 1984.

---

[77] Caroline Benn, "Elites versus Equals: The Political Background to the Comprehensive Reform" in D. Rubinstein (ed.) *Education & Equality* ed. David Rubinstein (Harmondsworth: Penguin, 1979), 205.

Cox, Brian *A Great Betrayal*. London: Chapmans Publishers, 1992.
Fraser, Antonia. *My History: A Memoir of Growing Up*. London: Weidenfeld & Nicolson, 2015.
Hattersley, Roy. "Dame Mary Green obituary," *Guardian*, 23 April 2004.
Hennegan, Alison. "And Battles Long Ago." In *Truth, Dare or Promise: Girls Growing Up in the Fifties* edited by Liz Heron. London: Virago, 1985.
Lumb Nora. In *Destiny Obscure: Autobiographies of Childhood, Education and the Family* edited by John Burnett. London: Routledge, 1994.
Marshall, Sybil. *An Experiment in Education*. Cambridge: Cambridge University Press, 1963.
Miles, Margaret. *And Gladly Teach*. London: Carousel, 1973.
Stott, Mary. *Forgetting's No Excuse: the autobiography of Mary Stott*. London: Virago, 1989.
Walkerdine, Valerie. "Dreams from an Ordinary Childhood." In *Truth, Dare or Promise: Girls Growing Up in the Fifties* edited by Liz Heron. London: Virago, 1985.

NEWSPAPERS AND PERIODICALS OF THE PERIOD

School Board Chronicle, 1870–1904
The Woman Teacher, 1919–1960

OTHER CONTEMPORARY BOOKS AND PAMPHLETS

Banks, Olive. *Parity and Prestige in English Secondary Education: A Study in Educational Sociology*. London: Routledge and Kegan Paul, 1955.
Benn, Caroline. "Elites versus Equals: The Political Background to the Comprehensive Reform." In *Education & Equality*, edited by David Rubinstein, 191–206. Harmondsworth: Penguin, 1979.
Clarricoates, Kathleen. "The importance of being Ernest, Emma, Tom, Jane. The perception and categorization of gender conformity and gender deviation in primary schools." In *Schooling for Women's Work*, edited by Rosemary Deem, 26–41. London: Routledge, 1980.
Cooper, Gordon. *An Hour in the Morning*. Oxford: Oxford University Press, 1973.
Corrigan, Phillip. *Schooling the Smash Street Kids*. London: Macmillan, 1979.
David, Miriam E. "Thatcherism is anti-feminism,'" *Trouble and Strife*, 1 (Winter 1983): 44–48.
Davies, Hunter. *The Creighton Report*. London: Hamish Hamilton, 1978.
Floud, Jean. E.; Halsey, Albert Henry, Martin, F. M. *Social Class and Educational Opportunity*, London, Greenwood Press, 1956.
Garnett, Eve. *The Family from One End Street*. London: Puffin, [1937] 2014.
Heim, Alice. *The Appraisal of Intelligence*. London: Tavistock, 1954.
Jackson, Brian. *Streaming: an education system in miniature*. London: Routledge, 1964.
Jackson, Brian and Marsden, Dennis. *Education and the Working Classes*. Harmondsworth, Penguin, [1962], 1969.
Lees, Sue. *Sugar and Spice: Sexuality and Adolescent Girls*. Harmondsworth: Penguin, 1993.
Griffin, Christine. *Typical Girls? Young Women From School to the Job Market*. London: Routledge, Kegan and Paul, 1985.

McRobbie, Angela. "Working-class girls and the culture of femininity." In *Women Take Issue: aspects of women's subordination*, edited by Women's Studies Group Centre for Contemporary Cultural Studies, 96–108. London: Hutchinson, 1978.
Sampson, Anthony. *Anatomy of Britain*. London: Hodder and Stoughton, 1962.
Sayers, Jane E. *The Fountain Unsealed: A History of the Notting Hill and Ealing High School*. Welwyn Garden City: Broadwater Press, 1973.
Sharp, Evelyn. *The London Child*. London: John Lane Bodley Head, 1927.
Simon, Brian. *Intelligence Testing and the Comprehensive School*. London: Lawrence and Wishart, 1953.
Simon, Brian. "Streaming and Unstreaming in the Secondary School." In *Education for Democracy* edited by David Rubinstein and Colin Stoneman, 142–150. Harmondsworth: Penguin, 1970.
Simon, Shena. *Three Schools or One?* London: Frederick Muller, 1947.
Spencer, Stephanie. "Reflections on the 'site of struggle': girls' experience of secondary education in the late 1950s," *History of Education*, 33, no. 4 (2004): 437–449.
Spender, Dale and Sarah, Elizabeth (eds.) *Learning to Lose: Sexism and Education*. London: The Women's Press, 1980.
Stanworth, Michelle. *Gender and Schooling*. London: Hutchinson, 1983.
Wolpe, Ann-Marie. *Within School Walls: The Role of Discipline, Sexuality and the Curriculum*. (London: Routledge, 1988).

PARLIAMENTARY PAPERS

Report of the Consultative Committee of the Board of Education on the Education of the Adolescent, 1927.

SECONDARY SOURCES

Arnot, Madeleine. "A cloud over co-education: an analysis of the forms of transmission of class and gender relations." In *Gender, Class & Education*, edited by Stephen Walker. Lewes: Falmer, 1983.
Arnot, Madeleine. *Reproducing Gender?* London: Routledge, 2002.
Chitty, Clyde. *Eugenics, Race and Intelligence in Education*. London: Continuum, 2009.
Michèle Cohen, "A Little Learning? The Curriculum and the Construction of Gender in the Long Eighteenth Century," *Journal for British Eighteenth Century Studies*, 29 (2006): 321–335.
Dean, Dennis W. "Planning for a Postwar Generation: Ellen Wilkinson and George Tomlinson at the Ministry of Education, 1945–51," *History of Education* 15, no. 2 (1986): 95–117.
Dean, Dennis W. "Education for Moral Improvement, Domesticity and Social Cohesion: The Labour Government, 1945–1951," *Oxford Review of Education* 17, no. 3 (1991): 269–86.
Deem, Rosemary. "State policy and ideology in the education of women, 1944–1980,'" *British Journal of Sociology of Education*, 2, no. 2 (1981): 131–43.
Delamont, Sara. *Sex Roles and the School*. London: Routledge, 1980.
Dyhouse, Carol. *Students: A Gendered History*. London: Routledge, 2006.
Fenwick, I.G.K. *The Comprehensive School 1944–1970*. London: Methuen & Co., 1976.

Fielding, Stephen. *The Labour Governments 1964–1970 volume 1 Labour and cultural change*. Manchester: Manchester University Press, 2003.

Goldstein, Harvey. "Gender bias and test norms in educational selection." In *Gender and the Politics of Schooling*, edited by Madeleine Arnot and Gaby Weiner, 122–126. London: Hutchinson, 1987.

Kynaston, David. *Austerity Britain 1945–51*. London: Bloomsbury, 2008.

Lambart, Audrey. "Mereside: a grammar school for girls in the 1960s," *Gender and Education*, 9, no. 4 (1997): 441–456.

McCulloch, Gary. *Failing the Ordinary Child? The Theory and Practice of Working-Class Secondary Education*. Buckingham: Open University Press, 1998.

Mahony, Pat. *Schools for the Boys? Co-education Reassessed*. London: Hutchinson, 1985.

Owen, Patricia. "'Who would be free, herself must strike the blow': The National Union of Women Teachers, equal pay, and women within the teaching profession,'" *History of Education*, 17 no. 1, (1988): 83–99.

Plummer, Gillian. *Failing Working-Class Girls?* Stoke-on-Trent: Trentham, 2000.

Reeder, David. "The reconstruction of secondary education in England, 1869–1920." In *The Rise of the Modern Educational System: Structural Change and Social Reproduction 1870–1920* edited by Detlef K. Müller, Fritz Ringer and Brian Simon, 135–150. Cambridge: Cambridge University Press, 1989.

Riley, Denise. *War in the Nursery*. London: Virago, 1983.

Sharpe, Sue. *Just Like a Girl*. Harmondsworth: Penguin, 1976.

Simon, Brian. *The State and Educational Change: Essays in the History of Education and Pedagogy*. London: Lawrence and Wishart, 1994.

Simon, Brian. *Education and the Social Order 1940–1990*. London: Lawrence and Wishart, 2010.

Sullivan, Alice. "Academic self-concept, gender and single-sex schooling," *British Educational Research Journal*, 35, no. 2, (2009): 259–288.

Thom, Deborah. "Better a teacher than a hairdresser? 'A mad passion for equality' or, keeping Molly and Betty down". In *Lessons for Life. The Schooling of Girls and Women 1850–1950* edited by Felicity Hunt, 124–45. Oxford, Basil Blackwell, 1987.

Thompson, Jane. *Women, Class and Education*. London: Routledge, 2000.

Vlaeminke, Meriel. *The English Higher Grade Schools*. London: Woburn Press, 2000.

Young, Michael, F.D. *The Rise of the Meritocracy*. Harmondsworth: Penguin, 1958.

CHAPTER 5

Perspectives and Debates Since the 1970s

> *Apart from one or two women teachers, no one at Cato Park thought it was odd that 'hard men' like Dave felt more at home than nice, quiet girls like Carol Lamb. Elsewhere, educationists were beginning to recognize that girls' experiences of education are different from boys, and that strange distinctions, based on gender, are common in all types of school from Siberia to Surrey, but the news had not yet filtered down to Morriston teachers, who brushed aside gender in the same way as race, by claiming to treat all pupils alike. They did not entirely convince the parents that everyone was equal, for some of them muttered about 'class distinction', or clever lads 'getting the lion's share'. Some families thought lads like Dave had problems largely because they were in the lower band.*
> —Julia Stanley, *Marks on the Memory: Experiencing School*, 1989, 58

Marks on the Memory is an ethnographic representation of Cato Park, a co-educational Midlands comprehensive school in the conservative town of 'Morriston.' Most of the material concentrates on the responses of six teenagers, two boys and four girls who frequently described themselves as 'ordinary people,' as they worked towards examinations between 1984 and 1986. Unlike many earlier studies of youth culture, Julia Stanley's work was unusual in the attention paid to discrepant cases that work against normative understandings of the relationship between social class, gender and schooling. Few of Cato Park's pupils were seriously delinquent, but the legacy of its single-sex secondary modern past conditioned staff attitudes. This was a school run by men with boys in mind. Discrimination was subtle. The social norm against 'pushiness' in women led teachers to describe forthright lads and lasses as either 'a bit of a character' or 'a difficult person,' and the difference was made by whether they were male or female. Troubled and troubling youth paid a price for their rebellion seen in the construction of unequal educational trajectories and labour market outcomes in late-modern society.

Quiet girls dismissed as of no account by boys, and by some teachers, feature in Stanley's study as do conversations very like those in Paul Willis's study of working-class 'resistance' in an English secondary school. Dave Callaghan, a lower band boy, posed as an anti-school rebel but was less 'macho' and hostile than Willis's 'lads.' Times had changed. The decline of unskilled manufacturing work with relatively good rates of pay and some prospect of security was conspicuous in the UK, and insecurity about jobs was especially marked in the Midlands. Not surprising when the capital of the region, Birmingham, had an unemployment rate approaching 20 per cent. Lower band male pupils at Cato Park had fewer rigid ideas about women's work than the lads Willis observed, and their families generally agreed. For instance, Callaghan held a grudge against teachers who had not allowed him to take cookery for the exam course. 'You've got more of a chance of getting a job with something like catering, 'cos everyone needs food. And not everyone needs chunks of metal.'[1] With industrial jobs drying up and the growth of a new service-sector working class, the traditional transition from school to labour market was changing, especially for working-class young men.

I examine three questions and concerns here. First, I investigate transference from concerns about the learning, social outcomes, and schooling experiences of girls, to discourses of male disadvantage in a context of competition for pupil credentials and qualifications and the effects of a focus on standards. This means analysing what changed not in an all-embracing and parochial way, but asking which boys, which girls and addressing outcomes, including gender differentials in vocational education and in the labour market. Moving on, ethnographic detail from research is used to illustrate various ways in which boys and girls went about constructing identities in this era, including confusions and contradictions in their gendered experiences and discussion of the way in which gender identity is intersected by other variables such as sexuality, ethnicity, culture and social class. Third, I bring together arguments articulated in terms of a 'crisis of masculinity' and 'boys' underachievement' to explore long-standing issues and debate about sex and gender in society. Theoretical analysis of power relations and material evidence shows the persistence of gender differences in adult behaviour and achievement and what lies behind it.

From Equal Opportunities to Identity Politics in a Competition State: Setting the Context

When Tessa Blackstone produced a survey of the evidence on the impact of gendered schooling in the mid-1970s, she noted 'control over one's destiny, and one's access to power and prestige will vary according to whether one is male or female.' She thought it just as important 'to educate boys to be fathers

[1] Julia Stanley, *Marks on the Memory: Experiencing School*, 1989, 56.

and husbands as well as workers, as it is to educate girls to be workers as well as wives and mothers,' adding that only when men can escape dominant constructions of masculinity 'will more flexible and less segregated role playing occur within the family.'

Current statistics showed greater female participation in post-compulsory education taking courses like shorthand and typing. Boys sat a greater range of O-level subjects (the final certification for secondary school) and despite a lower pass rate, dominated higher education. Men made up 70 per cent of undergraduates (a decrease of 5 per cent over a decade), 84 per cent of postgraduates, 91 per cent of university teachers and 99 per cent of professors. The number of men and women graduating with a first-class or upper second-class honours degree was virtually the same, but women gained half as many firsts. One explanation being that female-dominated arts and humanities subjects award fewer firsts than male-dominated pure and applied sciences.[2]

In compulsory schooling, gender difference showed itself when boys played football, and were taught woodwork, metalwork and technical drawing, while girls played netball and were taught to cook, sew and type. It showed itself in the use of corporal punishment to maintain order and discipline (until 1986). In Morriston, Stanley cites the specific importance of the disciplining of bodies to gender and education discourses. One long-standing Cato Park teacher claimed lower band boys ran a league table for canings, with the greatest prestige going to the one with the most beatings in his school career: '"taking your punishment" was all bound up with being manly, and in the eyes of unsuccessful scholars it was an alternative way of getting status.'[3] A violent discipline system inviting competition in machismo to see who could get caned the most.

Manufacturing began to decline as a major part of the British economy from the 1960s. This sector was a source of good jobs (usually for men) with specific entry points, meaning they could get a job (often with few qualifications), acquire skills and training and progress on to more senior roles. A global economic crisis exacerbated this decline, leading to the abandonment of policies committed to full male employment. With complaints from industrialists that schools were not adequately preparing children for the world of work, the predominant focus of commentary, explanation and various government initiatives aimed at solving the problem of youth unemployment focused on young people and implicitly working-class young people and their failings.

In terms of accessing training and skills, courses developed by the Manpower Services Commission (MSC) created by Edward Heath's Conservative government in 1974 and abolished by another Conservative administration in 1988 propelled more boys into training workshops, whereas girls mostly went into community work experience schemes. That said, the MSC identified sex stereotyping as an obstacle to educational progress and increasingly repositioned

---

[2] Tessa Blackstone, "The Education of Girls Today," in *The Rights and Wrongs of Women*, ed. Juliet Mitchell and Ann Oakley (Harmondsworth: Penguin, 1976), 200, 216, 204–207.

[3] Julia Stanley, *Marks on the Memory*, 58.

skill 'as a way of organizing activity' involving communication, numeracy and practical aspects, 'together with social and life skills, attitudes to work and a knowledge of working life.'[4] By the 1980s, the Technical and Vocational Educational Initiative (TVEI) aimed to steer schools towards a more vocationally orientated curriculum with a funding regime that required care be taken to avoid gendered and racialised discrimination. But the gendering of 'craft skills, which represents a way in which groups of workers gained control of an area of knowledge and competence to create and preserve their own space and then elevate its status,' still largely went under the radar.[5]

After 1979, governments favoured controlling inflation at the expense of jobs, leading to millions becoming unemployed. In a series of articles written in the 1980s, Willis speculated on the consequences for the traditional sense of 'working-class masculinity' and considered two possibilities. First, that traditional male working-class identity might be softened when the link with wage labour and the dignity and sacrifice of manual work was broken. Second, that the loss of the wage might lead young males to a 'gender crisis' to which one solution 'might be an assertion of masculinity and masculine style for its own sake.'[6]

Within the family, some teenagers seemed to reject the stereotype. Jerry, who did the washing-up when asked and sometimes cooked a family barbecue, said his dad taught him everything he knew. 'Everything my mum can make, I can make. I do the Hoovering and some housework. My sister used to do it, but she's gone now. I never leave it all to my mum, never. I spend about three to four hours on housework a week.' Mike didn't agree with acting 'macho.' 'Not all boys try and act macho and tough. I mean, I try not to go around looking like a macho man, girls think it's daft. If you go around trying to look really tough another tough boy might come up to you and start trying to look tougher and start a fight. Personally, I think it looks daft.'[7]

In June 1987, Margaret Thatcher's Conservative Party was elected for a third term pledged to the introduction of a common curriculum the assessment of which would allow national comparisons to be drawn between schools. Kenneth Baker was running the Department of Education, and Thatcher had warned him previously that she wanted the system fundamentally reformed.[8] The content Baker introduced following the Education Act of 1988 was largely

---

[4] Richard O'Brien, "The Rise and Fall of the Manpower Services Commission," *Journal of Policy Studies*, 9, no. 2 (1988), 3–8; Anne Wickham, "The state and training programmes for women," in *The Changing Experience of Women*, ed. Elizabeth Whitelegg, Madeleine Arnot, Else Bartels, Veronica Beechey, Lynda Birke, Mary Anne Speakman, Susan Himmelweit, Diana Leonard, Sonja Ruehl (Oxford: Basil Blackwell, 1982), 157.

[5] Cynthia Cockburn, *Two Track Training* (Basingstoke: Macmillan, 1987).

[6] John Clarke and Paul Willis, "Introduction" in Ian Bates, John Clarke, Phil Cohen, Dan Finn, Robert Moore and Paul Willis, *Schooling for the Dole?* (Basingstoke: Macmillan, 1984); Paul Willis, 1984, in *New Society*, 29 March, 5 April, 12 April 1984.

[7] Sue Lees, *Sugar and Spice: Sexuality and Adolescent Girls* (Harmondsworth: Penguin, 1993), 159–160, 177.

[8] Nick Davies, *The School Report* (London: Vintage, 2000), 39.

based on a version of the nineteenth century public school curriculum and clung to the 1904 *Regulations for Secondary Schools*, with English, Mathematics and Science taking most of the timetable in primary schools and 30 to 40 per cent in secondary schools.

The national goal was quality. The method of working towards it a National Curriculum the assessment of which would allow comparisons between schools after the publication of test results and help to shore up traditional values and social boundaries. Any focus on equality of outcome was shunned. 'The pursuit of egalitarianism' is over, Baker triumphantly declared.[9] Thatcher mocked current social, political and educational intentions:

> Too often, our children don't get the education they need—the education they deserve. And in the inner cities—where youngsters must have a decent education if they are to have a better future—that opportunity is all too often snatched from them by hard left education authorities and extremist teachers. And children who need to be able to count and multiply are learning anti-racist mathematics—whatever that may be. Children who need to be able to express themselves in clear English are being taught political slogans. Children who need to be taught to respect traditional moral values are being taught that they have an inalienable right to be gay. I believe that government must take the primary responsibility for setting standards for the education of our children. Of course—in the country as a whole—there are plenty of excellent teachers and successful schools. And in every good school, and every good teacher, is a reminder of what too many young people are denied. I believe that government must take the primary responsibility for setting standards for the education of our children. And that's why we are establishing a national curriculum for basic subjects. It is vital that children master essential skills: reading, writing, spelling, grammar, arithmetic; and that they understand basic science and technology.[10]

Right-wing bodies and individuals tried to control and influence the working groups appointed to devise the programmes of study and attainment targets, and Thatcher interfered to steer the subject in a more nationalistic direction when the history working group delivered its report. Peter Watkins was deputy chief executive of the National Curriculum Council, and he supported a common curriculum to which all children were entitled with 'fewer signs of the gender bias whose effect was usually to discriminate against girls.'[11]

Others expressed reservations. Feminists supported the notion of a common curriculum experience but recognised that formal equality serves to reinforce myths of neutrality. Meg Gomersall, for example, noted the reform did little to challenge the gendered division of labour both in the workplace and in the family: 'while girls must be educated in the skills and attitudes to achieve

---

[9] Quoted in Madeleine Arnot, "Consultation or legitimation? Race and gender politics and the making of the national curriculum," *Critical Social Policy*, 29, (1989/90), 21.

[10] Margaret Thatcher, http://www.britishpoliticalspeech.org/speech-archive.htm.

[11] Peter Watkins, "The National Curriculum—An Agenda for the Nineties," in *Education Answers Back: Critical Responses to Government Policy*, ed. Clyde Chitty and Brian Simon (London: Lawrence and Wishart, 1993), 72.

an academic equality with boys—and to challenge inequalities within the labour market—the education of boys in the skills and attitudes to address their equal responsibilities within the family are of equal if not greater importance.'[12]

Throughout the 1980s, a neoconservative emphasis on direct management and neoliberal emphasis on competition and market principles characterised education reform.[13] The state bestowed additional financial aid on the private sector through the 1981 Assisted Places Scheme, whereby eligible children won free or subsidised places in fee-charging schools as part of the renewed emphasis on parental choice. Other policies such as compulsory competitive tendering (requiring local authorities to contract services to the lowest bidder and transferring work to private providers), and local management of schools (giving schools control of their budgets with a freedom to make spending decisions), positioned schools as 'buyers' of services and began to displace local authority provision. Differentiation was reasserted through the creation of City Technical Colleges independent of local authority control and the offer of grant-maintained status to state schools (following a parental ballet to 'opt-out'), with differential funding from central government.

New nomenclatures of performance standards and application of school effectiveness rhetoric saw the promotion of a concept of 'excellence' that began to shape and suffuse discourses of gender and education through the dynamic of 'success' and 'failure.' In 1990, the election of a new Conservative leader, John Major, brought with it a reconstituted inspection regime, the Office for Standards in Education (OFSTED) to monitor standards in state-funded schools by regular inspections and producing published reports. This was the educational climate in which the then Equal Opportunities Commission (EOC) commissioned Madeleine Arnot, Miriam David and Gaby Weiner to study the consequences of recent reform, notably the introduction of a new national qualification taken at age 16, the General Certificate of Secondary Education (GCSE, 1988). GCSEs replaced previous qualifications to allow more students access to the full range of grades in individual subjects. Generally, the qualification combined examinations with assessed coursework, although the regulations, the content and the grading changed considerably over time.

Studying historical exam records for England and Wales between 1985 and 1994, Arnot, David and Weiner used a statistical construct of a 'gender gap' to compare male-female performance rates. At GCSE level, there were two key findings. On the one hand, more girls were entered for examinations and were more successful in terms of the proportion of top grades gained. On the other,

[12] Meg Gomersall, "Education for domesticity? A nineteenth century perspective on girls' schooling and domesticity," *Gender and Education*, 6, no. 3 (1994), 246.

[13] Stephen J. Ball, *The Education Debate* (Bristol: Policy Press, 2010), 75–83; Brian Simon, *Education and the Social Order, 1940–1990* (London: Lawrence and Wishart, 2010), 500–517.

more boys chose to study chemistry, computer studies and economics, with a more balanced entry pattern for English and mathematics. However, the relation between gender and subject choice was more dramatic post-16. Many more young men took 'A' levels in STEM subjects (science, technology, engineering and mathematics). Young women taking vocational qualifications clustered in beauty, commerce and hairdressing.

However, the EOC report offered no insight into the outcomes at this time for minority ethnic pupils in general nor for black girls in particular. No centralised data existed, but researchers used local authority data to show differential achievement with white girls outperforming all groups except Chinese girls and black African and Caribbean girls performing better than their male counterparts. The data also showed diversity between the performance of girls of different racial identity and ethnicity relative to each other.[14]

In their 2001 study *Growing Up Girl*, Valerie Walkerdine, Helen Lucey and June Melody drew on studies spanning nearly 20 years to provide an account of gendered educational outcomes as a 'class related phenomenon.' None of the educationally successful working-class young women among their research participants trod a linear academic path, whereas only one of their middle-class counterparts did not go from school to university. The experience of Patsy (working class) and Julie (middle class), who attended the same nursery, infant and junior schools, and whose parents did all the 'right things,' is illuminating. At ten, both girls were failing at junior school, but whereas teachers read Patsy's results as lack of ability, the explanation for Julie's lay in a problem of motivation. Neither did at all well in national examinations at 16, but whereas Patsy (whose mother had been involved in work with teachers to help raise her performance) left school and later worked part-time as an escort on local authority buses for the disabled, Julie stayed in education. 'In spite of the parallel educational histories up until GCSE level they eventually conformed to their class-specific educational stereotype: at 21 Julie was back on track and was likely to become a graduate professional, while Patsy, painfully aware of her lack of qualifications, was equally likely to remain in relatively poorly paid, low-status work.'[15]

Similarly, Stephen Ball and Sharon Gewirtz showed the significance attached to 'successful' middle-class girls positioned as a valuable and sought-after resource in the education marketplace because 'their presence in school

---

[14] Madeleine Arnot, Miriam David and Gaby Weiner, *Educational Reforms and Gender Equality* (Manchester: Equal Opportunities Commission, 1996); David Gillborn and Caroline Gipps, *Recent Research on the Achievement of Ethnic Minority Pupils Office for Standards in Education* (Institute of Education, London: HMSO, 1996); Marina Foster, "A Black perspective", in *Whatever Happened to Equal Opportunities? Gender Equality Initiatives in Education*, ed. Kate Myers (Buckingham: Open University Press, 2000), 189–200.

[15] Valerie Walkerdine, Helen Lucey and June Melody, *Growing Up Girl: Psychosocial Explorations of Gender and Class* (Basingstoke: Palgrave, 2001), 125–126.

normally conveys positive impressions to parents about ethos and discipline.'[16] The research of others continued to point to the many nuances and complexities and connections between gender and education across time and space. Sue Lees, for example, concluded that 'academic' girls now expected careers, whereas 'nonacademic' girls anticipated the need to combine unskilled and part-time work with housework and child-rearing but that girls from backgrounds that are of 'low socio-economic status' were most likely to be in the latter group.

Heidi Safia Mirza's study of African Caribbean girls in London showed how participants adopted strategies to succeed in their run-down, poorly staffed, chaotic schools: working at the back of the class on their own and at home in crowded rooms. As they moved into the labour market, they would accept the 'realistic' careers they were guided towards as carers, nurses and office workers, because it meant a system of 'backdoor entry' into further and higher education. Above all else, like the mature women students Gillian Pascall and Roger Cox interviewed, they believed education offered an escape route out of domesticity and into more rewarding forms of paid work. Indeed, when it came to girls' experiences of exclusion and inclusion in this era, Audrey Osler and Kerry Vincent found girls were still more likely than boys to be drawn into domestic duties and caring responsibilities, sometimes because their education was seen as less important than that of their brothers.[17]

During the 1990s, Máirtín Mac an Ghaill investigated the social construction and regulation of masculinities in Parnell School, a predominantly working-class co-educational state comprehensive in a Midlands inner-city industrial locality. Class, ethnicity and sexuality all played a part, as did the remasculinisation of Parnell's vocational curriculum and the practice of setting pupils. Mac an Ghaill reports four ethnically diverse male peer groups who responded in different ways—'academic achievers, 'macho lads,' 'new enterprisers' and a group of white, middle-class boys, the 'real Englishmen.'[18]

'Academic achievers' prioritised learning and sought to avoid trouble at all costs. Surviving everyday life in school meant distancing themselves from top set boys who could 'think for themselves' but were less 'into the subjects, like history and English' than they were and steering clear of bottom set 'macho lads.' A hallmark of how streaming and 'failure' in school populations alienates some, remaking learner identities around combative social practices that run counter to the values that school instils. 'They can't think for themselves, so they go round being hard and causing trouble all the time. They'll just end up on the dole' (regional male unemployment was double the national average at

---

[16] Stephen J. Ball and Sharon Gewirtz, "Girls in the education market: Choice, competition and complexity," *Gender and Education*, 9, no. 2 (1997), 214.

[17] Sue Lees, *Sugar and Spice*; Heidi Safia Mirza *Young, Female and Black* (London: Routledge, 1992); Gillian Pascall and Roger Cox, *Women Returning to Higher Education* (Buckingham: Open University Press, 1993); Audrey Osler and Kerry Vincent, *Girls and Exclusion: Rethinking the Agenda* (London: RoutledgeFalmer, 2003), 139, 146.

[18] Máirtín Mac an Ghaill, *The Making of Men* (Buckingham: Open University Press, 1994).

about 24 per cent). 'New enterprisers' studying new school subjects like business and technology and trying to negotiate status struggles around knowledge thought it important to permanently exclude 'macho lads' who 'just give us all a bad name.' In contrast, 'real Englishmen' felt ambivalent towards the academic curriculum and refused to accept the legitimacy of the teachers' authority. 'Teaching is a low-skill job,' said one. 'They're mostly technicists, not into ideas. They've no idea how patronizing they are to us. They don't like us because we're cleverer than them.'[19]

At Parnell School, a group of working-class girls named themselves the Posse. For Linda, belonging meant 'People can't just boss you around like they could if you are on your own. They won't mess with us. And it's just good because school is so boring. It's something to do and you look after each other. If I have any problems, I'd talk about them with my mates.'[20] Posse members challenged the way male staff verbally abused boys by humiliating them for being 'beaten by a girl' and directed low-set female pupils towards domestic subjects. As Kerry said:

> When he [teacher] asked me what I had learnt, I told him, "I've learnt that you are trying to make us housewives". He went mad, saying that we were learning lots of new skills. That's rubbish, it's just common sense; to us anyway. They should be teaching us things that will help us to get a real job. But once they've taught you how to read and write, that's it, isn't it really?[21]

While Kerry and her friends rejected attempts to demonise macho lads, suggesting 'tough' middle-class male teachers helped to produce 'tough' working-class boys, they protested continuing discrimination in favour of boys when it came to grasping opportunities for training and work. I give Linda the last word. 'Nearly everyone we know round here has been unemployed sometime… It's just terrible, if that's all you've got to look forward to. You can see it with a lot of the boys' round here. They've just got no future and it's not their fault. But the teachers are wrong, it's not the girls' fault either.'[22]

Linda captures an important strain in the defining spirit of the era. The slow death of British industry accelerated during her childhood, as Britain lost its manufacturing capacity and jobs flooded out, mainly to the Far East. Alongside the diminishing youth labour market, the increasing dominance of service sector employment and the re-emergence of the City of London as a global finance capital were recognised as significant in the new labour market formations which were emerging.[23] At the lower end, service sector jobs typically demand care, deference and docility as key attributes of a desirable workplace

---

[19] Op cit, 63, 64, 67.
[20] Op cit, 114.
[21] Op cit, 119.
[22] Op cit, 141.
[23] Linda McDowell, *Redundant Masculinities? Employment Change and White Working Class Youth* (Oxford: Basil Blackwell, 2003).

identity—stereotypical characteristics more commonly identified as feminine qualities. Simultaneously, traditional middle-class male management and professional career structures were vulnerable to both restructuring and 'downsizing' and new practices arising from privatisation and marketisation with growth in companies by acquisition and financial engineering rather than through organic development and building on products and markets.[24]

With waged work altered in its nature and form, a story about gender told in media and policy arenas began to reach fever pitch. A narrative of boys in terminal decline ran alongside concern about perceived threats to the roles of men in economic and family life and an increase in problematic and antisocial behaviour, crime and deviance, stemming in part from an increasing number of women in paid work. The challenge to working-class men was economic, but public analyses of gender gaps in examination performance seemed to give added legitimacy to rising anxiety in popular discourse about a 'crisis of masculinity' and the 'problem of boys.' Girls were not only purportedly outstripping boys in the academic rat race, but deemed guilty of outstripping their male peers in the race to find work in a diminishing youth labour market. The BBC current affairs programme Panorama, for example, was unequivocal in its invocation of young men 'losing out' to young women, who were 'fighting back' against patriarchal discrimination.[25]

Couched within the slow-burning processes of economic and social change, threats to male bread winning became a reference point for popular and policy discussions about the relationships between gender and schooling. Much of the debate couched in such a way as to give the impression that no issues remain about girls' education while insinuating females, including women teachers, were the cause of boys' alleged failure. A narrative that ignored the research of others on the feminisation of teaching, which showed the male exodus, coincided with the introduction of payment by results in 1862. A pattern repeated after the 1988 Education Act, when the percentage of full-time male teachers in early years and primary schools fell from 25 to 16 per cent.[26] With girls' academic achievements turned on their head and presented in the media and in popular discourse as a widespread problem of failure among boys, studies suggested that newly qualified teachers had greater sympathy for work to address inequalities of poverty, class and ethnicity than those associated with girls' education.[27]

---

[24] Brown, P. (1995) 'Cultural capital and social exclusion: Some observations on recent trends in education, employment and the labour market', *Work, Employment and Society*, 9 (1), 29–51.

[25] 'The Future is Female', 24 October 1994; 'Men aren't Working', 16 October 1995.

[26] Department for Education and Skills, *Gender and Education: The Evidence on Pupils in England* (Nottingham: DfES Publications, 2007), 122.

[27] Arnot, M. (1996) 'The return of the egalitarian agenda? The paradoxical effects of recent educational reforms', *NUT Education Review*, 10 (1), 9–14.

The Academically Underachieving Male: The New Disadvantaged?

In 1996, the narrative of male disadvantage received official legitimation when Chris Woodhead, then Chief Inspector of Schools for England, described the apparent failure of white working-class boys as 'one of the most disturbing problems we face within the whole education system.'[28] The timing was perfect when Panorama screened 'Missing Mum' (3 February 1997) to ask if working mothers were bad for their children, specifically sons needing to knuckle down to their homework. Concern about the dynamic of educational success and failure as played through a gender binary led Tony Blair's New Labour administration (elected in May 1997) to intervene. In a speech at the 11th International Conference for School Effectiveness and Improvement, then Schools Standards Minister Stephen Byers argued that the 'laddish, anti-learning culture' was impeding boys' achievement. Henceforth, each authority was required to address the 'problem with boys' in its Education Development Plan.[29]

However, the consequences of this strategy and action ran against official policy statements dominated by a progressive discourse that men and women are equally capable of working with children and recruiting a more gender-equal workforce will affect the cultural environment. In contrast, 'male role model' rhetoric urging men to consider teaching drew on assumptions that gender roles are relatively fixed and healthy child development requires distinctive and complementary male and female influences. Other 'solutions' seemed to reach for a masculinisation of teaching styles, both by using curriculum content thought to be more interesting to boys and by adopting teaching styles likely to favour boys particularly in secondary schools. In the case of literacy, however, the assertion that giving boys' adventure stories and factual books to read could address male underachievement ran counter to evidence that boys have a more positive attitude to reading when all pupils are encouraged to read as wide a range of books as possible.[30]

Boys/men negotiate and take up a variety of masculinities, and some of these confer power and prestige, while others are stigmatised and subordinate. Social constructions of gender encourage boys to be competitive. However, such constructions also involve a dislike and/or fear of 'losing.' Given there can only be a few 'winners' in competitive educational practices, those failing

---

[28] Quoted in the *Times Educational Supplement*, 26 April 1996.
[29] *The Guardian*, 6 January 1998.
[30] Lynn Raphael Reed, "'Zero tolerance': Gender performance and school failure," in *Failing Boys? Issues in Gender and Achievement*, ed. Debbie Epstein, Raphael Reed, Lynn. "'Zero tolerance': Gender performance and school failure," in *Failing Boys? Issues in Gender and Achievement*, edited by Debbie Epstein, Jannette Elwood, Valerie Hey and Janet Maw (Buckingham: Open University Press, 1998), 56–76; Molly Warrington and Mike Younger with Ros McLellan, *Raising Boys' Achievement in Secondary Schools: Issues, Dilemmas and Opportunities* (Buckingham: Open University Press, 2005).

to 'win' academically may disengage or find alternative ways of 'winning' by becoming disruptive. Young boys positioned as slow learners, poor at sport and lacking physical strength and skill may resort to overtly challenging behaviour that makes them vulnerable to classification as having special needs. Indeed, black working-class boys dominated 'less acceptable' categories of emotional and behavioural difficulties and moderate learning difficulties, and white middle-class boys dominated the non-stigmatised category of specific learning difficulties.[31]

In a climate of public policy discourses about school improvement and effectiveness incorporating neoliberal tenets of educational achievement as the means of addressing issues of social exclusion, Stephen Ball, Meg Maguire and Sheila Macrae undertook a study of the transition to post-compulsory education and training within the dynamics of an education market setting. In their 2000 book *Choices, Pathways and Transitions post-16*, they address concerns about discourses of 'individualism' and 'individualization' that had achieved cultural hegemony.[32] For the urban millennials these authors studied, qualities of reinvention, adaptation and flexibility have a central place in a discourse of success, as does the ability to invent and reinvent oneself. Lucy, White, middle class, articulates a process of self-construction and reconstruction as part of a lifetime biographical project.

> Life's different now. You don't have to go from school to college to university and then into a job for thirty or forty years and you don't have to wait until you're forty or something to reach the top, to be a manager... I got a university place but I'm not going just yet. I've got a job, I've got responsibility and I work hard. I'm going to make lots of money and spend it having loads of laughs and loads of experiences and that. You just go for it, grab it while you can, enjoy it, whatever it is, use it, add it to your CV and move on to something else. There's loads of opportunities and I'm just taking them while I can. My mum and dad didn't have these opportunities. Just go for it, I say.[33]

Luke's story is told for its 'ordinariness.'[34] A 'respectable,' law-abiding, conformist young man, Luke is interested in family, heterosexual relationships and

---

[31] Shereen Benjamin, "Gender and special educational needs," in *Boys and Girls in the Primary Classroom*, ed. Christine Skelton and Becky Francis (Maidenhead: Open University Press, 2003), 98–112.

[32] Stephen J. Ball, Meg Maguire and Sheila Macrae, *Choice, Pathways and Transitions Post-16: New Youth, New Economies in the Global City* (London: RoutledgeFalmer, 2000). Ball, Maguire and Macrae discuss the impact of individualism and individuation as presented in hugely influential books by Anthony Giddens, *Modernism and Self-Identity: Self and Society in the Late Modern Age* (Cambridge: Polity, 1991) and Ulrich Beck, *Risk Society: Towards a New Modernity* (London: Sage, 1992).

[33] Stephen J. Ball, Meg Maguire and Sheila Macrae, *Choice, Pathways and Transitions Post-16*, 151.

[34] Ball, Maguire and Macrae discuss a tendency for the study of youth, masculinity and schooling to focus on those constructed as having the 'wrong' kinds of attitudes and behaviours. Tony Sewell, *Black Masculinity and Schooling: How Black Boys Survive Modern Schooling* (Stoke-on-Trent: Trentham Press, 1997); Paul Willis, Learning to Labour (London: Saxon House, 1977).

getting on. He sees his girlfriend as a good influence in this respect, helping him focus and steer through the education market, playing safe by staying at school and going to a local university in order to maximise his security.

One consistent research finding in this era was a tendency for young people to reiterate a concept of individual freedom and 'blame' themselves if they did not do well, rather than see themselves as classed or gendered members of an unequal society. Born as Thatcher won power and growing up in a sociopolitical climate in which neoliberal ideas of choice and competitive individualism were sedimented in the national consciousness, this generation were more likely to see themselves as individuals in a meritocratic setting when questioned on their aspirations and future possible selves. To explain educational 'success' or 'failure' in terms of hard work and sheer determination or lack of it, rather than class differences and family connections as some Cato Park families muttered. These sociological explorations show the discourses of economic individualism and individualisation, working together, in a social world in which problems read as individual rather than structural failings that constrain the choices made. Along similar lines, a growing political and academic concern with boys' underachievement led some scholars to refocus on gender in education.

Coterminous with the work of Ball, Maguire and Macrae, fieldwork carried out in an inner-city primary school over the academic year 1997–98 identified the importance of power and of seeing femininity and masculinity as relational phenomena. Diane Reay found children in a class of predominantly working-class children readily named a hierarchical peer group—hard-working 'nice girls,' 'girlies' who did the gender work of maintaining conventional heterosexual relationships, 'spice girls' and 'tomboys' who shunned all things female. To be a 'nice girl' had derogatory connotations, while boys described the 'girlies' as 'stupid' and 'dumb' even though they were educationally productive, and their attainment was generally higher than their male counterparts. The 'spice girls' belief in 'girl power' allowed them to make bids for social power involving assertive behaviour, which tended to be viewed more negatively than similar behaviour in boys. Jodie shunned all things feminine and loved playing football. She was not a girl, but a 'tomboy' she said, and managed to persuade two boys to confirm her male status as she struggled to assume a male subject positioning. Indeed, Reay found 16 examples of Jodie saying 'boys are better than girls' in her field notes. Most commonly, for most of the children, gender operated as opposition and hierarchy simultaneously, weaving difference through the developmental system.[35]

---

[35] Diane Reay, "'Spice Girls', 'Nice Girls', 'Girlies', and 'Tomboys': Gender discourses, girls' cultures and femininities in the primary classroom," *Gender and Education*, 13, no. 2 (2001), 153–166.

Despite girls being heralded as educational 'success stories,' classroom research continued to find girls were less confident than boys. Plus male domination of school space, teacher time and attention.[36] Other studies drew particular attention to gender interacting with other factors. Here the talk of two 15/16-year-old boys of Caribbean heritage draws upon a notion of professional identities as being incompatible with black masculinity.

RICHARD: All right Steven, do you think you is going to be a manager? How many black managers do you know?
STEVEN: [pause] Not much.
RICHARD: How many black headmasters do you know?
STEVEN: But—but.
RICHARD: I'm not asking that. How much do you know?
STEVEN: Me? None.
RICHARD: Yes, so who is giving you the jobs then?
STEVEN: A white man, innit.
RICHARD: Yes, so you think he'd give you a job yeah of being a schoolteacher when he could make you sweep the floors instead?[37]

Richard and Steven spoke about a tension between getting on and getting out, 'leaving' and 'holding on to' gendered, classed identities as 'bad boys.' In contrast to the inner-city youth Ball, Maguire and Macrae focused on, theirs is not the language of structured individualism. Richard explains multiple inequalities in terms of structural and material continuities through which racism operates.

If girls in school settings were the success story of the 1990s, drilling down into the metrics used complicates the narrative. Researchers noted a tendency for policy and media discourses oriented towards tracking testing results at the GCSE level (in terms of girls and boys performance) to confuse percentages and percentage points in ways that construct a 'gender gap' that is only statistically evidenced at the higher level of assessment and 'simply does not exist' in any generalisable form.[38] The Leverhulme Numeracy Research Programme, a study of teaching and learning in English primary schools between 1997 and 2002, showed girls did not match boys' performance in mathematics. The gap was small, but there were more female entries into the lower tier for GCSE Maths with a top grade C. This mattered since only pupils with higher tier

---

[36] Christine Skelton, "Gender and achievement: Are girls the 'success stories' of restructured education systems?", *Educational Review*, 62, no. 2 (2010), 131–142.

[37] Christine Skelton, "Gender and achievement: Are girls the 'success stories' of restructured education systems?", *Educational Review*, 62, no. 2 (2010), 131–142; Farzana Shain, "Refusing to integrate? Asian girls, achievement and the experience of schooling," in *Girls and Education 3-16: Continuing Concerns, New Agendas*, ed. Carolyn Jackson, Carrie Paechter and Emma Renold (Maidenhead: Open University Press, 2010), 62–74.

[38] Louise Archer and Hiromi Yamashita, "Theorising Inner-City Masculinities: 'Race', class, gender and education," *Gender and Education*, 15, no. 2 (2003), 125.

passes at grade A or B were eligible to continue learning maths and physics post-16.[39] When 2009 figures showed a higher percentage of boys gained A*-C grades in GCSE mathematics, media hype speculated a trend of girls 'increasingly outperforming boys could begin to reverse because coursework is now due to be scrapped for nearly all subjects following the move with maths this year.'[40]

There has been a lot of what David Gillborn calls 'Gap Talk' in the last 25 years.[41] Qualifications, content and delivery have social consequences. Arguments about gender and achievement are played out in children's experiences of schooling through cultural misconceptions that are significant in shaping understandings of which group has a certain advantage when it comes to assessment types. Among these are the common perception that coursework is a major determinant of male 'under-achievement' when the influence of coursework was less than that of examination performance as a determinant of GCSE grades. Schools in which all pupils achieve, for example, have high expectations of everyone and in English encourage wide reading, offer plenty of choice and plan to engage children's interests.[42]

Much of the 'under-achieving' boys discourse failed to deal adequately with racialised power or to see femininity and masculinity as relational phenomena, ignoring differences in social class and ethnic origin and the ways in which elite white males maintained their social advantage and held on to their social power. The development of a deficit model for boys predicated on the need to engage specific pathologized masculinities pandered to a compensatory culture of aggressive laddism that neither addressed gender stereotypes nor remembered that boys are all individuals. Separate to this, growing criticism of the notion of a 'reproduction of roles' in relation to social class and/or gender was addressed through studies showing the self is not simply a passive recipient of socialisation, but actively constructs and impacts upon the world.

SCHOOLING AND ITS IMPACT ON GENDER RELATIONS IN NEW TIMES

To address the question of 'successful girls', Jessica Ringrose analysed media coverage to explore the truth claims being made about contemporary educational equality and girls educational victories in the new millennium. She

---

[39] Jannette Elwood, "Gender and achievement: What have exams got to do with it?" *Oxford Review of Education*, 31, no. 3(2005), 373–393.

[40] *Daily Mail*, 28 August 2009.

[41] David Gillborn, "Coincidence or conspiracy? Whiteness, policy and the persistence of the Black/White achievement gap," *Educational Review*, 60, no. 3 (2008), 229–248.

[42] Jannette Elwood, "Exploring girls' relationship to and with achievement: Linking assessment, learning, mind and gender," in *Girls and Education 3-16: Continuing Concerns, New Agendas*, ed. Carolyn Jackson, Carrie Paechter and Emma Renold (Maidenhead: Open University Press, 2010), 38–49.

describes a social and cultural landscape which she called post-feminist, and by that term, she meant a situation (temporal, political and theoretical) where backlash against the seeming gains made by feminist activities in the 1970s and 1980s and moves both to destabilise and deconstruct gender occur. Ringrose suggests 'the idea of post-feminism is a useful *conceptual tool* that helps in tracing the complex *effects of and implications* of various forms of feminism (like liberal and neoliberal feminism) over time in popular culture and beyond.' As shown in the previous section, the rhetoric and policy to promote assessment as a primary mode of improving institutional, group and individual standards and effectiveness in schooling played out through a gender binary and a 'victim/victor' cycle took hold.[43]

In putting the 'sex-war' mentality into context, Ringrose suggests a close correlation between liberal feminism and the development of what Madeleine Arnot, Miriam David and Gaby Weiner call post-war 'education feminisms.'[44] For her, an emphasis on the 'individualism' of classical liberalism was key to the articulation of feminist demands from the nineteenth century onwards, with identifications forged around policies designed to guarantee equal opportunities at a formal, or legal, level. Significantly, liberal feminism did not (and does not) posit the same challenges to educational processes as those of radical, socialist or Black feminism with increasing awareness of issues of social class, disability, ethnicity and race. Reviewing the research on gendered test results in 2007, the Department for Education and Skills (responsible for the education system and children's services in England between 2001 and 2007) showed the limitations of gender-only analyses. At GCSE level, for example, the effect of free school meal status (FSM used as a proxy for poverty) was most pronounced on the attainment of female pupils, and the gender gap was greatest for Black Caribbean pupils. Overall, Black Caribbean FSM boys and White British FSM children had an attainment level below the national average.[45]

The 2006 Equality Act placed a statutory duty on public bodies to promote gender equality, which came into force the following year. A key report from the Brown Government (2007–10), produced by a committee chaired by Alan Milburn, on fair access to the professions (July 2009) outlined the limits on gendered social mobility through higher education, and professional development in higher education. The committee noted that there remained a glass ceiling for women in the professions and across all major professional groups. Harriet Harman, inaugural Minister for Women and Equality (2007–10),

---

[43] Jessica Ringrose, "Successful girls? Complicating post-feminist, neoliberal discourses of educational achievement and gender equality," *Gender and Education*, 19, no. 4 (2007), 477.

[44] Madeleine Arnot, Miriam David and Gaby Weiner, *Closing the gender gap: Post-war education and social change* (Cambridge: Polity Press, 1999).

[45] Christine Skelton, "Gender and achievement: Are girls the 'success stories' of restructured education systems?", 133.

fought for further legislation to promote equality, fight discrimination and introduce transparency into the workplace to tackle the gender pay gap. However, Harman's Bill went through Parliament on the eve of a general election and the Conservative-led Coalition government under David Cameron (2010–15) failed to implement key provisions. As Prime Minister, Cameron offered four cabinet jobs to women (14 per cent of the total) rather than the third he previously promised.[46]

Michael Gove, Conservative Education Secretary between 2010 and 2014, asked economist Alison Wolf to investigate how to improve practical education. Addressing the problem of what to do about non-academic pupils, Wolf noted that a large proportion of 16- to 19-year-olds were on vocational courses that failed to promote progression into either employment or further education. She also pointed to the long-term disadvantages of being a NEET that is Not in Employment, Education or Training, a term Labour politician Ed Balls (Secretary of State for Children, Schools and Families, 2007–10) used to describe 14 to 19-year-old disadvantaged and working-class boys. Concern about systematic failure of 'NEETs' goes back at least to the late 1950s, with the Newsom Report of 1963 commissioned to investigate education for 13-to-16-year-olds of average or less-than-average ability. By 2011, the Wolf Report neglected the gender dimensions of the transitions to employment, and Lord David Willetts, Conservative Minister of State for Universities and Science, blamed the entry of women into the workplace and universities for the lack of progress of working men. Feminism, he said, had trumped egalitarianism.[47] Willetts' assertions and simplistic representations helped feed a growing discourse making the 'f' word (in this case feminism) toxic.

Even a cursory look at the evidence mapping inequality suggests Willetts risked misunderstanding the standing of males and females in society. Indeed, in other circles, the financial crisis and subsequent austerity policy reawakened debate on the gender impact of the economic cycle. The Fawcett Society, the TUC and the Women's Budget Group all suggested women would be disproportionately affected, one factor being that 40 per cent of women work in public sector jobs compared to less than 20 per cent of men. A TUC report *Women and the Recession—One Year On* (2010) showed that female unemployment had increased faster than male and anticipated this would escalate. So, too, would poverty levels among female 'baby boomers' due to an increase in the pace of the rise in state pension age for women, who previously had a retirement age of 60 as opposed to 65 for men. Statistical research by the Resolution Foundation, *Low Pay Britain 2013*, showed that 25 per cent of women and 15 per cent of men earned less than the living wage in 2012, up from 18 per cent and 11 per cent in 2009.

The Labour Party published a *Manifesto for Women* in the 2015 general election. Chief policies included doubling the amount of paid paternity leave

[46] *Guardian*, 12, 14 May 2010.
[47] *Telegraph*, 1 April 2011.

fathers can take, appointing a new commissioner to enforce national standards on tackling domestic and sexual abuse, and introducing age appropriate compulsory sex and relationship education in schools.[48] Labour lost the election, and this manifesto, hinting at using schooling as a means of preventing violence against women and girls, disappeared. However, in November 2016, the parliamentary women and equalities committee reported 'shocking levels' of sexual harassment in English schools amid reports that over 40 per cent of teenage girls felt pressured to have sex and some had been raped.[49] Following this, Conservative politician Justine Greening (Education Secretary and Minister for Equalities, 2016–18) announced her intention to put Relationships and Sex Education on a statutory basis, making the subject (including internet porn and sexting) mandatory in all schools, though parents would have the right to remove their children.[50]

Meanwhile, a 2015 analysis focussing mainly on GCSEs taken in England using data from the National Pupil Database reported that boys formed the greater proportion of examination entry in nearly all STEM subjects in both 2005 and 2014, whereas nearly 70 per cent of the entry for Psychology and Sociology was from girls. The biggest gender difference in the proportion of the entry was in the Applied and Expressive category where Design and Technology (D&T) Electronic Products and D&T Engineering comprised nearly 90 per cent boys, whereas D&T Textiles and Health and Social Care comprised nearly 90 per cent girls.[51] Overall, gender differences in subject choice were greater than gender differences in achievement and seemingly 'the average boy-girl difference in GCSE outcomes is notably larger than the average difference between those born in the first six months of the academic year and those born in the last six months of the academic year.' Alongside commentary on the average boy-girl difference in GCSE outcomes,[52] there were continued predictions that the gender gap in attainment could narrow because of England's new linear GCSEs in maths and English, with new subject content and assessment structure for examinations in 2017.[53] What happened next?

With the public discourse focused on a refrain of gendered competition, GCSE result tables showed girls gained two-thirds of the top grades awarded for English Language, English Literature and Mathematics. Girls outperformed boys in most subjects including construction and engineering, and the gender gap in English actually widened. However, boys did pull further ahead of their female peers in maths, making it the only subject in which boys received a higher proportion of top grades than girls. Boys outnumbered girls by two to

[48] UK Labour Party 2015, 3.
[49] *The Guardian*, 8 March 2017.
[50] http://www.gov.uk/government/news/schools-to-teach-21st-century-relationships-and-sex-education.
[51] Tom Bramley, Carmen Vidal Rodeiro and Sylvia Vitello, *Gender Differences in GCSE. Cambridge Assessment Research Report* (Cambridge, UK: Cambridge Assessment, 2015), 36.
[52] Op cit, 38.
[53] *The Guardian*, 25 August 2016.

one at GCSE design and technology and almost ten to one at A-level.[54] At A-level, boys took the lead in top grades overall for the first time in 17 years, but this appeared to be a result of female grades falling, rather than a spike in male performance.[55]

In 2018, a new grading system numbered from nine to one replaced the letter grades in all subjects at GCSE. The previous top grades, A*-A, split into three grades with grade four and above matching those of C and above under the previous scheme. Simultaneously, media analysis implied too many girls doing well were a problem solved by changing the assessment modes. The following headlines are drawn from a selection of national daily newspapers:

'GCSE results: Pass rate RISES as boys close the gap on girls despite tougher exams' (*Daily Mirror*, 23 August 2018)
'GCSEs: boys' close gap on girls after exams overhaul' (*Guardian*, 23 August 2018)
'New "tougher" exams favour boys as gender gap narrowest in five years' (*Telegraph*, 23 August 2018)[56]

Examination scores showed boys had 'more significant improvements' in biology, chemistry, history and physics where the proportion gaining a seven or above went up, whereas the proportion of girls went down. The inferences were clear. 'Under the reforms the exams have also been made more testing, with subjects such as chemistry including a higher proportion of questions involving maths. The amount of assessed coursework has also been greatly reduced in many courses, making grades depend on final exam performance.'[57]

On GCSE results day in 2019, the proportion of the age cohort achieving grade seven or above was the highest since 2015. The subject of computing where female entries increased to 21.4 percent of the total student numbers and females outperformed males provides an interesting case. Under David Cameron, the Conservatives scrapped GCSE and A-level information communication technology (ICT) qualifications in 2015 as part of a package of assessment reforms aimed at 'more academically challenging and knowledge based' qualifications, with new syllabuses for teaching from 2017. Intended to develop the computational thinking skills needed for today's economy, the reformed computer science GCSEs saw a 32 per cent drop in the number of combined entries for ICT and computing compared with computing students. While the overall number of computer entries rose by 7.6 per cent on the 2018 figure, the uptake among girls accelerated more, which mirrored results at A-level.

---

[54] *The Guardian*, 24 August 2017.
[55] *The Independent*, 17 August 2017.
[56] *Daily Mirror*, 23 August 2018; *The Guardian*, 23 August 2018; *Daily Telegraph*, 23 August 2018.
[57] *The Guardian*, 23 August 2018.

Females also continued to outperform males in the subject, with more girls scoring top grades.

Now it seemed more rigorous courses benefitted girls, including in 'masculine' domains such as physics and mathematics, where girls narrowed the gap in results previously enjoyed by boys at 16. At A-level, however, top grades saw their biggest drop since records began as the proportion of A*/A grades fell to the lowest in over a decade. Entries for English Language plummeted by over 20 per cent, prompting calls for an inquiry into the decline, while girls sitting science subjects overtook boys for the first time following another major drive to encourage girls to take STEM subjects. Chemistry saw the biggest rise for girls since 2011, with the number of female students taking the subject increasing by 28.4 per cent in the past 8 years. Although biology was traditionally more popular for girls than boys, it, too, saw an increase in female entries (19.4 per cent) over the same period. Males continued to dominate in physics, making up 77% of all entries in England in 2019. Female entries scored slightly more top grades, but boys retained their lead in gaining more A* grades alone—8.2 per cent of boys getting the highest result, compared with 7.5 per cent of girls.[58]

Embedded in discourses relating to gender and assessment is power. Research positions that consider socio-cultural perspectives on learning and situated views of mind highlight the significance of the social, cultural and historical experiences that participants bring to the spaces where formal learning takes place. 'Assessment within this view becomes a cultural artifact that only has meaning in relationship with, and between, the teacher and the students and/or peer and the context in which it occurs.'[59] Thus, for example, gender norms ensured 1950s grammar schools were not female-dominated. Putting assessment in the public domain has had an electrifying effect today, but it is important to sustain a more nuanced analysis of attainment than the competitive pitching of a 'sex-war' permits.[60]

At the macro level of structure and the micro level of interpersonal relations, the gender order, codes and regime change according to space and time. Nevertheless, there is a remarkable consistency embedded in the public discourse of male failure within the educational system, which has important consequences educationally, politically and socially. Arguably, the implication of girls' faring better than boys is portrayed as upsetting the safe parameters of natural social order, put down to dogged hard work and conformism rather than 'ability.' In contrast, the appeal of pseudo-scientific discourse as an

[58] *The Guardian* 15 August 2019; 22 August 2019.

[59] Jannette Elwood, "Exploring girls' relationship to and with achievement: Linking assessment, learning, mind and gender," 45.

[60] Heidi Safia Mirza and Veena Meetoo, "Empowering Muslim girls? Post-feminism, multiculturalism and the production of the 'model' Muslim female student in British schools," *British Journal of Sociology of Education*, 39, no. 2 (2018), 227–241; Helen Fisher, "'White British girls on free school meals': Power, resistance and resilience at secondary school transition," *Gender and Education*, 29, no. 7 (2017), 907–925.

explanation for differential performance between the sexes in mathematics and the sciences is strong, sometimes seen as being either genetic, or at least so deep-seated that it is unlikely to be amenable to intervention. A construction that serves to legitimate what Sara Ahmed sees as gender fatalism.[61]

As outlined by Cordelia Fine, evolutionary biologists and psychologists promulgate the fable of hormones like testosterone as the essence of masculinity even though there is plenty of evidence to show that when hormones affect the brain, they do so in interaction with the effects of the social world. Debunking the myth of 'testosterone rex' the name she gives that familiar, pervasive story telling us inequality of the sexes is natural, not cultural and that hormones make the man or woman, Fine explains how nature works in concert with relationship structures. 'It's the genitalia—and the gender socialisation this kicks off—that provides the most obvious indirect developmental system by which biological sex affects human brains.' To present gender gaps in fields in further and higher education as natural, for instance, as testosterone rex does, is a powerful fiction and one that in no way deserves to be enthroned as king in our understanding of our possible selves.[62]

Understanding boys and girls as real as opposed to understanding boys and girls as discourses tells us different identity assemblages could be attempted, potentially challenging and changing the learning spaces in which they were created. Recent research on girls' identities and science learning shows the tensions of navigating performances of both femininity and being academically successful, especially for girls from racialised minorities. In this case, Amber (a Black-African, working-class girl) who belonged to her urban school's science club struggled to engage with tasks in her male-dominated group, where she is put in an impossible position through the boys dominating behaviour:

> No one is interested to join Amber in the group task, so she does it by herself. Amber is keen on science and goes to the science club, which she told me proudly. It seemed that she did not get along with the boys in her group. For example, when they were asked to give her feedback about her presentation, all started shouting "louder" (about 10 times in total!) and teased her that she never speaks at all.[63]

The boys silence Amber, who does not purposefully avoid science-learning but adopts a strategy whereby she insulates herself and operates under the radar of teachers whose attention is commandeered by boys. Studies of girls' identity performances in science museum visits suggest ways of 'doing science' and

---

[61] Heidi Safia Mirza, "Race, Gender and IQ: The social consequence of a pseudo-scientific discourse," *Race, Ethnicity and Education*, 1, no. 1 (1998), 109–126; Sara Ahmed, *Living a Feminist Life* (Durham and London: Duke University Press, 2017).

[62] Cordelia Fine, *Testosterone Rex* (London: Ircon, 2016), 91–93, 136–141.

[63] Emily Dawson, Louise Archer, Amy Seakins, Spela Godec, Jennifer DeWitt, Heather King, Ada Maur and Effrosyni Nomikou, "Selfies at the science museum: Exploring girls' identity performances in a science learning space," *Gender and Education*, 32, no. 5 (2020), 673.

'doing girl' were rarely straightforward or neatly separated and might better be understood as 'kaleidoscopic'—that is differing in influence and overlap at different moments and in different spaces. While kaleidoscopic performances of masculinity and 'race'/ethnicity seemed to support some girls' participation in science learning, it is argued requiring girls to 'do boy' in order to 'do science' is no solution to long-standing gender inequalities in science education.

Deconstructing dichotomised gender stereotypes by means of studying gendered subjectivities and intersecting axes of experience and identity in school shows the fallacy of truth claims shored up through a proliferation of post-feminist stories, images and representations of unambiguous winners and losers in the education game. Intersectional approaches that pull 'doing boy' or 'doing girl' into view can help us understand this, when thinking about gender performances as situated practices marked by structural inequalities rooted in space and time. Discussions of gender located within classroom studies can 'speak' to teachers and policy-makers to realize the learning community explicit in the comprehensive ideal.

Many people invest in their education in the expectation that they will get a better job, and that their salary will rise more rapidly. It remains the case that this is less true for women than for men. Each year the Fawcett Society marks Equal Pay Day as the point when women stop earning relative to men. In 2019, this fell on 14 November. That autumn, a male full-time worker earned 13.1 per cent more than his female counterpart. The difference was 16.2 per cent for part-time workers with the largest pay gaps experienced by black and minority ethnic women.[64] On 24 March 2020, just before the April deadline, the Government Equalities Office and the Equality and Human Rights Commission said it would not be taking action against employers that fail to submit their pay gap data, effectively suspending the reporting requirement for 2019–20 because of the coronavirus pandemic. It was feared the crisis could lead to a widening of the pay gap, making reporting especially important, while others warned the crisis would have a disproportionate impact on female jobs as women took on a greater share of childcare and home schooling during national lockdowns.[65]

---

[64] https://www.fawcettsociety.org.uk/news/the-fawcett-society-announces-date-of-equal-pay-day-2019.

[65] https://www.gov.uk/government/news/employers-do-not-have-to-report-gender-pay-gaps; UN Secretary General's Policy Brief: the impact of COVID-19 on women, https://www.unwomen.org/en/digital-library/publications/2020/04/policy-brief-the-impact-of-covid-19-on-women.

Conclusion

To return to the quote with which we started, the culturally exalted form of masculinity at Cato Park was grounded *outside* the education context in the local area. Parents did not use the phrase Victorian values but the emphasis on thrift, respect for authority and self-reliance was much in vogue in the 1980s, having been revived by Conservative governments to help justify a shift from a culture of commitment to a welfare to the competition state and the 'freedoms' offered by market egalitarianism. Arguably, Cato Park, Parnell School and the schools studied by other educational researchers that form the material for this chapter were schools run by men with boys in mind. Studies raised questions about the ethos of state schools whereby 'noisy, demanding boys got the lion's share of good equipment and teacher time, while the better-mannered, more considerate, or less confident girls hung back.'[66]

At the same time, changes in school culture together with the raising of the school leaving age to 16 (in 1972), comprehensive education, equal opportunities and the National Curriculum made a difference as more children began, for the first time, to have access to learning experiences previously denied to them. Added to which, the decline of large manufacturing industries bringing the emasculation of traditional working-class men, the growth in the service industry and increased female employment challenged the parameters of gender difference. Simplistic male–female binaries are unhelpful because not all girls are academically successful and not all boys are academically unsuccessful, but for some girls, doing 'well' at school was a positive response to an opening of educational and career choices to girls and women that contributed to late twentieth century change in the gender order. Subsequently, a perception that males who face significant disempowerment in terms of the extent of their resources and the range of available choices had become the new victims of the competitive nature of schooling produced a dominant educational narrative that contributed to the cultivation of a 'sex-war' mentality.

Looking back over changes since the 1970s, it is arguable that more 'girl winners' was an unintended consequence of a human capitalist belief in skilled labour to ensure national competitiveness in a global marketplace and the continued promotion of meritocratic assessment as a primary mode of improving standards and effectiveness in schooling. We see this in the diffusion of individualising discourses in terms of male-female test results as trying to score, to make points, to dominate. Gendered language and meaning put to work in the service of an ideology that anyone can get on provided they are academically 'able' and work hard. An educational sorting mechanism privileged by those paying homage to the social and cultural trope of meritocracy and the idea of potential for movement up a social ladder. Nevertheless, fixed 'ability' thinking, subject boundaries and curriculum categories like the science-humanities division, the academic-vocational split, interact with culture and power to produce gendered and racialised ideologies of 'merit' overcut with social class.

---

[66] Julia Stanley, *Marks on the Memory*, 68.

Bibliography

Primary Sources

Contemporary Books and Pamphlets

Archer, Louise, and Yamashita, Hiromi. "Theorising Inner-City Masculinities: 'Race', Class, Gender and Education." *Gender and Education*, 15, no. 2 (2003): 115–132.

Arnot, Madeleine. "The Return of the Egalitarian Agenda? The Paradoxical Effects of Recent Educational Reforms." *NUT Education Review*, 10, no. 1 (1996): 9–14.

Ball, Stephen, Maguire, Meg and Macrae, Sheila. *Choice, Pathways and Transitions Post-16: New Youth, New Economies in the Global City*. London: RoutledgeFalmer, 2000.

Ghaill, Máirtín Mac an. *The Making of Men*. Buckingham: Open University Press, 1994.

Reay, Diane. "'Spice Girls', 'Nice Girls', 'Girlies', and 'Tomboys': Gender Discourses, Girls' Cultures and Femininities in the Primary Classroom." *Gender and Education*, 13, no. 2 (2001): 153–166.

Stanley, Julia. *Marks on the Memory: Experiencing School*. Milton Keynes: Open University Press, 1989.

Walkerdine, Valerie, Lucey, Helen and Melody, June. *Growing Up Girl: Psychosocial Explorations of Gender and Class*. Basingstoke: Palgrave, 2001.

Willis, Paul. *Learning to Labour*. London: Saxon House, 1977.

Published Reports

Arnot, Madeleine, David, Miriam and Weiner, Gaby. *Educational Reforms and Gender Equality*. Manchester: Equal Opportunities Commission, 1996.

Bramley, Tom, Rodeiro, Carmen Vidal and Vitello, Sylvia. *Gender Differences in GCSE*. Cambridge Assessment Research Report. Cambridge, UK: Cambridge Assessment, 2015.

Department for Education and Skills. *Gender and Education: the Evidence on Pupils in England*. Nottingham: DfES Publications, 2007.

UN Secretary General's Policy Brief: The Impact of COVID-19 on Women, https://www.unwomen.org/en/digital-library/publications/2020/04/policy-brief-the-impact-of-covid-19-on-women

Published Speeches

Margaret Thatcher, http://www.britishpoliticalspeech.org/speech-archive.htm

Secondary Sources

Arnot, Madeleine. "Consultation or Legitimation? Race and Gender Politics and the Making of the National Curriculum." *Critical Social Policy*, 29 (1989/90): 20–38.

Arnot, Madeleine. *Reproducing Gender?* London: Routledge, 2002.

Arnot, Madeleine, David, Miriam and Weiner, Gaby. *Closing the Gender Gap: Post-war Education and Social Change*. Cambridge: Polity Press, 1999.

Ball, Stephen J. and Gewirtz, Sharon. "Girls in the Education Market: Choice, Competition and Complexity." *Gender and Education*, 9, no. 2 (1997): 207–222.

Beck, Ulrich. *Risk Society: Towards a New Modernity*. London: Sage, 1992.
Benjamin, Shereen. "Gender and Special Educational Needs." In *Boys and Girls in the Primary Classroom*, edited by Christine Skelton and Becky Francis, 98–112. Maidenhead: Open University Press, 2003.
Brown, Phillip. "Cultural Capital and Social Exclusion: Some Observations on Recent Trends in Education, Employment and the Labour Market." *Work, Employment and Society*, 9, no. 1 (1995): 29–51.
Clarke, John and Willis, Paul. "Introduction." In *Schooling for the Dole?* edited by Ian Bates, John Clarke, Phil Cohen, Dan Finn, Robert Moore and Paul Willis, Basingstoke: Macmillan, 1984.
Cockburn, Cynthia. *Two Track Training*. Basingstoke: Macmillan, 1987.
Davies, Nick. *The School Report*. London: Vintage, 2000.
Dawson, Emily, Archer, Louise, Seakins, Amy, Godec, Spela, DeWitt, Jennifer, King, Heather, Maur, Ada and Nomikou, Effrosyni. "Selfies at the Science Museum: Exploring Girls' Identity Performances in a Science Learning Space." *Gender and Education*, 32, no. 5 (2020): 664–681.
Elwood, Jannette. "Gender and Achievement: What have Exams Got to Do with It?" *Oxford Review of Education*, 31, no. 3 (2005): 373–393.
Fine, Cordelia. *Testosterone Rex*. London: Ircon, 2018.
Fisher, Helen. "'White British Girls on Free School Meals': Power, Resistance and Resilience at Secondary School Transition." *Gender and Education*, 29, no. 2 (2017): 907–925.
Foster, Marina. "A Black Perspective." In *Whatever Happened to Equal Opportunities in Schools? Gender Equality Initiatives in Education*, edited by Kate Myers, 189–200. Buckingham: Open University Press, 2000.
Giddens, Anthony. *Modernism and Self-Identity: Self and Society in the Late Modern Age*. Cambridge: Polity, 1991.
Gillborn, David. "Coincidence or Conspiracy? Whiteness, Policy and the Persistence of the Black/White Achievement Gap." *Educational Review*, 60, no. 3 (2008): 229–248.
Gillborn, David and Gipps, Caroline. *Recent Research on the Achievement of Ethnic Minority Pupils Office for Standards in Education*. Institute of Education, London: HMSO, 1996.
Gomersall, Meg. "Education for Domesticity? A Nineteenth Century Perspective on Girls' Schooling and Domesticity." *Gender and Education*, 6, no. 3 (1994): 235–247.
Gorard, Stephen, Rees, Gareth and Salisbury, Jane. "Reappraising the Apparent Underachievement of Boys at School." *Gender and Education*, 11, no. 4 (1999): 441–454.
Lees, Sue. *Sugar and Spice: Sexuality and Adolescent Girls*. Harmondsworth: Penguin, 1993.
McDowell, Linda. *Redundant Masculinities? Employment Change and White Working Class Youth*. Oxford: Basil Blackwell, 2003.
Mirza, Heidi Safia. "Race, Gender and IQ: The Social Consequence of a Pseudo-Scientific Discourse." *Race, Ethnicity and Education*, 1, no. 1 (1998): 109–126.
Mirza, Heidi Safia and Meetoo, Veena. "Empowering Muslim Girls? Post-feminism, Multiculturalism and the Production of the 'Model' Muslim Female Student in British Schools." *British Journal of Sociology of Education*, 39, no. 2 (2018): 227–241.
O'Brien, Richard. "The Rise and Fall of the Manpower Services Commission," *Journal of Policy Studies*, 9, no. 2 (1988): 3–8.

Osler, Audrey and Vincent, Kerry. *Girls and Exclusion: Rethinking the Agenda*. London: RoutledgeFalmer, 2003.

Raphael Reed, Lynn. "'Zero Tolerance': Gender Performance and School Failure." In *Failing Boys? Issues in Gender and Achievement*, edited by Debbie Epstein, Jannette Elwood, Valerie Hey and Janet Maw, 56–76. Buckingham: Open University Press 1998.

Ringrose, Jessica. "Successful Girls? Complicating Post-feminist, Neoliberal Discourses of Educational Achievement and Gender Equality." *Gender and Education*, 19, no. 4 (2007): 471–489.

Sewell, Tony. *Black Masculinity and Schooling: How Black Boys Survive Modern Schooling*. Stoke-on-Trent: Trentham Press, 1997.

Shain, Farzana. "Refusing to Integrate? Asian Girls, Achievement and the Experience of Schooling." In *Girls and Education 3-16: Continuing Concerns, New Agendas*, edited by Carolyn Jackson, Carrie Paechter and Emma Renold, 62–74. Maidenhead: Open University Press, 2010.

Simon, Brian. *Education and the Social Order, 1940–1990*. London: Lawrence and Wishart, 2010.

Skelton, Christine. "Gender and Achievement: Are Girls the 'Success Stories' of Restructured Education Systems?" *Educational Review*, 62, no. 2 (2010): 131–142.

Warrington, Molly and Younger, Mike with McLellan, Ros. *Raising Boys' Achievement in Secondary Schools: Issues, Dilemmas and Opportunities*. Buckingham: Open University Press, 2005.

Watkins, P. R. "The National Curriculum—An Agenda for the Nineties." In *Education Answers Back: Critical Responses to Government Policy*, ed. Clyde Chitty and Brian Simon. London: Lawrence and Wishart, 1993.

Wickham, Anne. "The State and Training Programmes for Women." In *The Changing Experience of Women*, edited by Elizabeth Whitelegg, Madeleine Arnot, Else Bartels, Veronica Beechey, Lynda Birke, Mary Anne Speakman, Susan Himmelweit, Diana Leonard, and Sonja Ruehl, 146–163. Oxford: Basil Blackwell, 1982.

PART II

Learners and Learning

CHAPTER 6

Culture and Curriculum

The education of girls is beset by problems and difficulties, from which that of boys is happily free; for the boys have so far had it all their own way. Not only has the educational process until quite a recent date been thought of exclusively in terms of their needs—and ordered—as indeed it still is, mainly with their interests in view; but there is, in the nature of things, neither uncertainty nor division of aim in the education of boys; since their training as citizens and workers is not held to unfit them automatically for exercising the functions of husband and father. To give a girl an education suited to her capacities—should she happen to have any out of the ordinary— is still widely held to be at best a folly, at worst a crime, if matrimony and motherhood are in view
—Mary Gavin Clarke, "Feminine Challenge in Education" in
The Headmistress Speaks (London: Kegan Paul, Trench, Trubner & Co., 1937), 59

Mary Gavin Clarke spoke to the educational world with an authoritative voice. Head teacher of Manchester High School, one of the leading girls' secondary schools in England, her social and cultural capital included an education at Girton College, Cambridge, and strong familial connections to the world of nineteenth century feminism through her maternal aunts, the pioneering Garrett sisters. Writing in an era when it was fashionable to criticise the elite secondary sector minority for failing to allow for gender difference and ignoring a crude domestic definition of social function for girls, she was very much opposed to teaching or examining designed particularly 'for women.' Her message in *The Head Mistress Speaks*, an edited collection the Association of Head Mistresses produced in the late 1930s, is clear. She and her school stood for the idea that academic scholarship as defined by the Board of Education, the examining boards and the universities, could serve independent women taking their places within a new female professional class as well as those destined for marriage and motherhood.

In this chapter, I argue that the theoretical foundations and cultural practices on which current curriculum orthodoxies are based need situating in the context of former contestation and struggle between powerful individuals and social groups. In focusing on the politics of curriculum, I deconstruct an inside/outside dichotomy in relation to links between educational knowledge and social and cultural power. Gaby Weiner observes four notions that began to infiltrate western curriculum thinking after the Enlightenment—that curricula should be represented as a *selection* from available knowledge, that there should be *differentiated* curricula for different social groups, that *functionality* or usefulness is important, as well as the aim of promoting upward *social mobility*.[1] Thus, the selection of subjects considered appropriate, the form and content of curriculum provision is achieved in space and time on the basis of certain social and political priorities. We see this in the roles of class-and-gender-specific curricula as Michèle Cohen shows in the case of elite masculine identities and classical learning. Therefore, whereas middle-and-upper-class boys received a diet of Latin in order to train the minds of future imperial leaders, the acquisition of conversational French was conceived as an ornamental, feminine accomplishment rejected as superficial continental learning in the ideological context of anti-Jacobinism after the French Revolution.[2]

Those levering the claims of Victorian women to self-development operated in this climate and Dorothea Beale's leadership of the highly select Cheltenham Ladies College illustrates the intertwining of female class relations. Her school offered classics, logic and mathematics, but Beale worried about her pupils taking the newly created examinations for the middle classes. 'The brothers of our pupils go to the universities,' she said in her evidence to the Taunton commission. 'Now generally speaking, those who go in for the local examinations occupy a much lower position in the social scale, and our pupils would not like to be classed as equal with them but regarded as equal in rank to those who pass at the university.'[3]

Working in the day-school environment of the fee-charging North London Collegiate School and an enthusiastic supporter of girls' ability to surmount successfully the same problems as boys, Frances Buss paid lip service to domestic ideology. Molly Hughes breezed through the school's entrance examination in the late 1870s, but the request to make a buttonhole floored her. Sent

---

[1] Gaby Weiner *Feminisms in Education* (Buckingham: Open University Press, 1994), 32-38.

[2] Michèle Cohen, "A Little Learning? The Curriculum and the Construction of Gender in the Long Eighteenth Century," *Journal for British Eighteenth Century Studies*, 29 (2006), 321-335. Latin was the most important subject in the West Riding Grammar school that Miriam David attended in the 1950s and 1960s. She was streamed in to 2L, 3L 4L and 5L as the top stream in her four-stream school whereby L stood for Latin, and G the next down was for German and then 2 parallel streams that did neither. Personal communication with the author April 2020.

[3] Cited in John Roach, *Public Examinations in England 1850-1900* (Cambridge: Cambridge University Press, 1971), 115.

home and asked to return in a week's time, her mother taught her in five minutes. 'It seemed absurd to take the railway journey just for that, but it was a rule of the school that no girl should enter who couldn't make a buttonhole.' In the justification for her curriculum thinking, Buss queried of Molly's elder brother 'Why did the Lord create Messrs. Huntley & Palmer to make cakes for us, if not to give our clever girls a chance to do something better?'[4]

Reconfigurations of social class and gender were manifest in the systematisation of secondary education in England. Male civil servants who attended a tiny set of elite schools never let go of the structure of feeling they associated with those beginnings, and this model of schooling had a substantial influence over the structures, rituals and heraldry of the municipal secondary schools set up after 1902—for example, houses, prefects, school uniforms and school crests with Latin mottoes. Rejecting the higher grade elementary model of a 'good' secondary schooling, the essential features testify to a desire to reproduce class-based ideas about the role of particular groups in society and the economy, which served to create and re-create expectations and opportunities for children. This was in stark contrast to England's higher grade school prototype, where a willingness to innovate and fuse general and vocational education into a purposeful whole sought to avoid glorifying certain subjects and demeaning others, by rejecting the notion that young people destined for particular work must be educated in a certain way. Indeed, some higher grade schools were resisting the cult of domesticity in dominating and channelling education for girls—trying out subjects like hygiene and physiology, besides offering chemistry and mathematics. Meriel Vlaeminke thinks it 'likely that in relative terms more girls studied science and mathematics on an equal footing with boys—and not infrequently outshone them in competitive examinations and awards.'[5]

Nevertheless, the power of social and cultural capital meant a tiny set of boys' 'public schools' and endowed grammar schools became what Hilary Steedman calls 'defining institutions.' Instead of having to change their selection of subjects and teaching style to meet what some well-known scientists and industrial leaders saw as the needs of the twentieth century, the classics were elevated to a position of unprecedented status and influence—part of the tight nexus that existed between elite education and the ancient universities of Cambridge and Oxford who associated masculinist classics with accomplishment and cultivation. Strictly separated from 'the modern,' to reject science was a statement of hegemonic masculinity that addressed not only 'the general anxiety that secondary would be subordinated to technical education' but a conception of the female mind as fundamentally different from the male mind.[6]

---

[4] Molly Hughes, *A London Girl Growing Up in the 1880s* (Oxford: Oxford University Press, 1979), 11, 81.

[5] Meriel Vlaeminke, *The English Higher Grade Schools: a lost opportunity* (London: Woburn Press, 1999), 61.

[6] Hilary Steedman, "Defining institutions: the endowed grammar schools and the systematisation of English secondary education," *The Rise of the Modern Educational System: Structural Change and Social Reproduction 1870-1920*, ed. Detlef K. Müller, Fritz Ringer and Brian Simon

Curriculum design often shelters behind notions of common sense, but classed cultural and patriarchal power set the parameters. The ongoing effects of industrialisation and urbanisation, questions of social and political identification and solidarity surface in curriculum histories from the Education Act in 1870 down to the outbreak of the First World War and what Raymond Williams calls the 'selective tradition' recognises this.

> It is not only that the way in which education is organized can be seen to express, consciously and unconsciously, the wider organization of a culture and a society, so that what has been thought of as simple distribution is in fact an active shaping to particular social ends. It is also that the content of education, which is subject to great historical variation, again expresses, again both consciously and unconsciously, certain basic elements in the culture, what is thought of as 'an education' being in fact a particular selection, a particular set of emphases and omissions.[7]

Following Williams, I take the idea of a 'selective tradition' to map relations between the development of a gendered hierarchy of mental differences and the content of education thought to be appropriate for males and females. Williams identifies three groups and ideologies that emerged most clearly in the nineteenth century. 'Industrial Trainers' who supported utilitarian, objectives-driven curricula, based on economic goals and future adult work. 'Public Educators' who called for expansionist education policies and 'Old Humanists' who thought a man's (sic) spiritual health depended on education of a kind variously defined as 'liberal,' or 'humane' or 'cultural.'

This chapter offers four cases of gendered power/knowledge relations. Section one analyses debate over 'schooling for role' in the elementary school system within what was at the time the world's largest educational Parliament, the London School Board (Fig. 6.1). It focuses, therefore, on the ways in which prevailing values and social judgements shape curricular patterns—what becomes school knowledge, what knowledge is made available to which pupils, who supplies the knowledge and how.

It is against the background of Victorian debate about curriculum and schooling for gendered roles that I open the door to discussion of new problems in the twentieth century. A close and careful reading of pioneer headteacher Mary O'Brien Harris's 1923 book *Towards Freedom*, educationist John Newsom's 1948 book *The Education of Girls* and mathematician and politician Kathleen Ollerenshaw's *Education for Girls* published in 1961 forms the basis of the arguments that follow.[8] Finally, I come full circle to review movements

---

(Cambridge: Cambridge University Press, 1989), 111-134; Olive Banks, *Parity and Prestige in English Secondary Education: A Study in Educational Sociology* (London: Routledge and Kegan Paul, 1955), 41.

[7] Raymond Williams, *The Long Revolution* (Letchworth: Broadview Press, 2001), 151.

[8] John Newsom, *The Education of Girls* (London: Faber and Faber, 1948); Kathleen Ollerenshaw, *Education for Girls* (London: Faber and Faber, 1961).

Fig. 6.1 First London School Board showing male and female members attending a meeting, John Whitehead Walton (fl.1831–1885). From the London Picture Archive. (Copyright London Metropolitan Archive, 14317)

to counter the marginalisation of both women's experiences and gender relations through an account of the life cycle of women's studies courses in England between 1970 and 2010 grounded in a wider set of assumptions about a masculine bias within particular disciplinary fields and pedagogical spaces.

Viewing Elementary Curriculum Formulations Historically

Most standard histories of Victorian and Edwardian politics make fleeting references to the involvement of women because they tend to treat local and national government dichotomously. A more complete understanding involves greater emphasis on the former where women made a substantial contribution.[9] In the case of politics and policy-making in elementary education, London not only set the example for other school boards to follow and but was the place where white, middle-class, Liberal women's political advancement was swift. For instance, female representation rose from 4 per cent in 1870 to 18 per cent in 1879, though it stagnated after.

---

[9] Patricia Hollis *Ladies Elect* (Oxford: Clarendon Press, 1989); Jane Martin, *Women and the Politics of Schooling in Victorian and Edwardian England* (Leicester: Leicester University Press, 1999).

Text Box 6.1 Female Members of the London School Board, 1870–1904

Board	Female Members (birth/death dates in brackets when first named)
1870–1873	Emily Davies (1830–1921), Elizabeth Garrett Anderson (1836–1917).
1873–1876	Jane Chessar (1835–1880), Alice Cowell (1842–1925).
1876–1879	Florence Fenwick Miller (1854–1935), Elizabeth Surr (1825–1901), Helen Taylor (1831–1907), Julia Augusta Webster (1837–1894), Alice Westlake (1842–1923).
1879–1882	Rosamond Davenport-Hill (1825–1902), Florence Fenwick Miller (1854–1935), Henrietta Müller (1846–1906), Mary Richardson (1848–1937), Edith Simcox (1844–1901), Elizabeth Surr, Helen Taylor, Julia Augusta Webster, Alice Westlake.
1882–1885	Rosamond Davenport-Hill, Frances Hastings (1824–1913), Florence Fenwick Miller, Henrietta Müller, Mary Richardson, Helen Taylor, Julia Augusta Webster, Alice Westlake.
1885–1888	Rosamond Davenport-Hill, Julia Augusta Webster, Alice Westlake.
1888–1891	Annie Besant (1847–1933), Rosamond Davenport Hill, Margaret Mary Dilke/Cooke (1857–1914), Frances Hastings, Ruth Homan (1850–1938), Emma Maitland (1844–1923).
1891–1894	Rosamond Davenport Hill, Margaret Eve (1844–1917), Ruth Homan, Emma Maitland, Alice Mary Wright (1855–1896).
1894–1897	Rosamond Davenport Hill, Margaret Eve, Ruth Homan, Emma Maitland.
1897–1900	Mary Bridges Adams (1855–1939), Rosamond Davenport Hill, Eugenie Dibdin (1864–1925), Constance Elder (1858–1940), Margaret Eve, Ruth Homan, Emma Maitland, Ellen McKee (1844–1933), Honnor Morten (1861–1913).
1900–1904	Mary Bridges Adams, Margaret Eve, Edith Glover (1860–1943), Ruth Homan, Maude Lawrence (1864–1933), Susan Lawrence (1871–1947), Hilda Miall-Smith (1861–1943), Emma Maitland, Ellen McKee (1844–1933).

The first women members, Emily Davies and Elizabeth Garrett Anderson, belonged to the Langham Place group which began to develop a cautious Liberal feminist politics in the 1850s. Out of these initiatives came the first women's network in Britain, which served as a conduit for political patronage in Anderson's division of Marylebone where her sister Alice Cowell and teacher Jane Chessar, a protégé of Frances Buss and friend of Mary Richardson, succeeded her. When Chessar retired, Alice Westlake stepped in. Westlake canvassed for Garrett in 1870 and held office until 1888 when Emma Maitland replaced her. Did these pioneer female politicians challenge a domestic emphasis in girls' schooling?

In 1871, the Board appointed Thomas Huxley principal of the South London Working Men's College and elected representative for Marylebone, to chair a special committee to devise the programmes of study. Members included Greenwich representative Emily Davies. Transcripts of debate at public Board meetings reproduced in the *School Board Chronicle*, a weekly publication directed at an audience of elementary teachers, show the impact of the three ideologies Williams' identifies.

Coal merchant William Green was an industrial trainer who proposed working-class girls be prepared for their employment destinations in domestic service, which included the classic domestic servant who boarded with her employers, but also encompassed a wide range of daily service jobs in private homes. On the question of whether to teach them freehand drawing, he thought 'the only drawing such girls would require to know would be the "drawing" of geese and other things for the table.'

In contrast, Huxley was a public educator who argued that 'men had a natural right to be educated and that any good society depended on governments accepting this principle.' He said art was for all, suggesting lessons might aid girls' rational understanding. Based on the drawings he had just seen on display in the office of a fashion journal, he wondered 'if women in general had a little more knowledge of art their attire would be more in accordance with aesthetic principles than at present: but he would defer to the judgment of the ladies who were members of the Board.'[10]

Socially and politically conservative, Emily Davies urged equal opportunities in ways that invited the support of like-minded men. She muted the strictly self-serving aspects of women's intellectual emancipation and granted that generally men and women were destined for different roles and responsibilities. However, she regarded family life and public life as interdependent. Speaking after Green, her words were judicious:

> They would all agree with the last speaker that it was undesirable to make the education of girls such that it would discourage them from taking an interest in the daily duties of life; but she could hardly think that the way to make them take an interest in such matters was to make them entirely ignorant of everything else… what was wanted was to make the girls intelligent and capable of making their homes and their husbands comfortable, and of improving the present state of things which so often led the husbands to the public house. She thought education for girls should be a little wider and more interesting than it was at present.[11]

This time Anderson, Davies and Huxley helped ensure the capital's working-class girls had drawing lessons. In 1886, policy changed. Drawing became compulsory in boys' schools, seen as a necessary skill because it included geometry, useful for builders, carpenters or engineers. Girls' schools took it up again in the 1890s after new national regulations dropped the geometry requirements in the drawing examination.

Co-founder of the first hospital staffed by women and the first woman in Britain appointed to a medical post, Anderson's medical qualifications conferred symbolic capital. She dismissed Green's enthusiasm for utilitarian classes in cooking and washing for older girls as a waste of time and money and

---

[10] Raymond Williams, *The Long Revolution*, 162; *School Board Chronicle*, 1 July 1871.
[11] *School Board Chronicle*, 1 July 1871.

thought the idea that people would send in their laundry for washing as fantastically unrealistic in an era when working-class families had few clothes. The situation for Kathleen Dayus in Hockley, inner Birmingham, illustrates this. One lunchtime, hardship and poor conditions drove her and her friends to eat what they thought was chocolate inside the packets of 'Ex-lax' they spotted on their neighbour's doorsteps but they got into trouble after. Refused permission to go to the toilet and locked in the classroom for punishment they soiled themselves. Next morning every child had to stay at home in bed because they lacked clothes until their wet ones dried. In public debate, Anderson proposed all elementary schoolchildren, boys and girls, be taught the importance of fresh air, cleanliness and hygiene. Although her suggestion was unsuccessful, she and Davies played a leading role in stalling consideration of a motion calling for the promotion of basic domestic training as part of the female curriculum in elementary schools.[12]

An analysis of School Board voting records in the 1870s and 1880s shows some members tried to prevent domestic subjects teaching becoming part of official school knowledge. Between 1879 and 1882, a caucus of two working-class men, Benjamin Lucraft and trade unionist George Potter, and five middle-class women Frances Hastings, Florence Fenwick Miller, Henrietta Müller, Elizabeth Surr and Helen Taylor opposed utilitarian justifications. Potter stressed the gulf between the practical cookery lessons and the materiality of working-class lives. For him, the use of gas cookers suggested 'the girls must be intended for service' since that kind of 'knowledge would not be of much use to them in an artisan's home.' Fenwick Miller accused the Board of double standards. 'While the women of the upper classes are claiming equal intellectual opportunities with their brothers for themselves, are the women of the artisan classes to be permanently relegated to a position of female inferiority of educational advantages and if so, why?'[13]

After 1882, changes in government policy and the influence of Social Darwinist thinking put opponents on the defensive, and they struggled to make an impression with their ideas. In this context, Hastings supported Taylor's unsuccessful attempt to reduce girls' exposure to cookery lessons. Hastings also attacked the amount of time girls spent sewing in school. Infant departments used it to teach hand-eye co-ordination, but older girls spent between five and seven hours a week learning needlework, which she thought unnecessary. Teachers reported that it was damaging the girls' eyesight, and Hastings appealed to the liberal ideal, arguing they should receive 'a foundation of general knowledge' instead. Müller criticised the demanding standards and secured a reduction in the recommended number of stitches per inch for

---

[12] Kathleen Dayus, *Her People* (London: Virago, 1982), 54-58; *School Board Chronicle*, 1 July 1871.
[13] *School Board Chronicle*, 30 March 1878; *The Governess*, 5 May 1884.

seaming and stitching which, she evidenced, were 'higher than that featured in work sold in the best London shops.'[14]

Rosamond Davenport Hill, possibly the Board's most enthusiastic supporter of domestic subjects teaching, was also the longest serving female member (18 years). Born into a family of social reformers, her father and his four brothers were all active administrators and social reformers, sharing an interest in various issues including mass schooling, penal reform and the temperance movement. As chair of the School Board's Domestic Subjects Subcommittee, Davenport Hill oversaw the founding of 140 cookery centres and 50 centres for laundry work and gave evidence on the subject to the Cross Commission. She was all in favour of the making of good domestic servants. As she argued in *Macmillan Magazine*, the knowledge gained: 'will enable these poor children to command somewhat higher wages than otherwise, as mere drudges, they could hope to obtain and is of greater value to them than even a competent knowledge of the 3R's.' Henrietta Müller thought her biased and 'not a friend of woman.' Some mothers were inclined to agree and complained bitterly at the encroachment that practical skills best learnt at home made into girls' education.[15]

In 1897, Ruth Homan succeeded Davenport Hill as chair of the Domestic Subjects subcommittee. The widowed daughter of a former Lord Mayor of London, as a young woman she took classes at the South Kensington School of Cookery and underwent basic nurse training at St. Bartholomew's Hospital, London. As a mature woman, social and cultural capital empowered her to earn a reputation as a conscientious and able public representative.

> Few homes are so well organised as that over which she presides at Kensington. Every morning at half-past eight she arranges the duties for the day of her servant, breakfast having been served half-an-hour earlier. At half-past-nine she is free to take her share of the work of the Board, whether she happens to be visiting any of the fifteen schools in Tower Hamlets under her supervision, answering letters sent by teachers, attending committee meetings, or visiting some industrial of housewifery centre.[16]

Likewise, her daughter was a voluntary welfare worker, helping the Children's Country Holiday Fund associated with Toynbee Hall social settlement house. In the 1890s, Homan produced educational plans to teach cookery to boys at Bow Creek School in Poplar where she was a school manager.

---

[14] *School Board Chronicle*, 12 March 1885; *The Governess*, 17 November 1883; *The Times*, 17 January 1906.

[15] Deborah Gorham, "Victorian reform as a family business: the Hill family," in *The Victorian Family*, ed. A.S. Wohl (London: Croom Helm, 1978), 119-147; Rosamond Davenport-Hill, *Macmillans Magazine*, June1884; *Women's Penny Paper*, 24 November 1888; Carol Dyhouse, *Girls Growing Up In Victorian and Edwardian England* (London: Routledge, Kegan and Paul, 1981), 90.

[16] Morrison, M. "Ladies on the London School Board," 1897, *Newscuttings*, "School Boards."

Subsequently, the Board of Education issued a special dispensation allowing boys living in seaport towns to attend cookery classes in the elementary schools.[17]

First elected in 1876, English artist and engraver Alice Westlake served on the London School Board election committee and helped other women to win seats. Westlake believed schooling played a role in preparing girls for their role as wives and mothers and was a strong supporter of girls' physical education. Having witnessed an activity called 'desk drill' during school visits—when girls were required to stand on benches and do arm movements—she urged the teaching of calisthenics or educational gymnastics. It was made clear the emphasis was on grace and deportment due to fears the effort of physical activity might prove injurious to female health. In fact, Westlake and her networks ensured greater sporting opportunities for working-class girls but without the emphasis on the competition and rivalry that were major pedagogical tools for boys. Histories of school drill illustrate this.[18]

Initially the only form of school exercise, drill was a defining feature of the elementary curriculum taught to boys by ex-army sergeants. Advocates focused on its role in disciplining bodies, promoting its place on the curriculum as a means of securing social order. This was a model intended to teach habits of obedience as a preparation for manual labour and/or military service and forge a sense of collective identity and a strong, competitive nation. Benjamin Lucraft challenged this thinking. A founder member and for nine years chair of the Workmen's Peace Association, Lucraft secured the abolition of the Board's 'Summer Manoeuvres' when boys' schools formed into companies at word of command to compete for an embroidered banner. Adamant the working classes had no desire to see their sons turned into soldiers, he advocated teaching gymnastics instead. Lobbying intensified after the humiliations of the Boer War when supporters argued the malformation of working-class bodies posed a threat to the nation as a whole. The case presented for school meals and sport, including the use of ropes, dumbbells and wooden clubs swung in patterns, was to address body failings and malnutrition.[19]

Gender was fundamental to the construction of what counted as school knowledge within the elementary sector. Male handicraft teaching involving workshop instruction, woodwork or manual work expanded after 1890, but boys did not receive practical instruction equivalent to the girls' and were usually doing extra mathematics while girls sewed. Few girls learned science

---

[17] *School Board Chronicle*, 3 March 1900.

[18] Sheila Fletcher, *Women First: The Female Tradition in English Physical Education, 1880-1980* (London: Continuum, 1984); Sheila Scraton, *Shaping Up To Womanhood: Gender and Girls' Physical Education* (Buckingham: Open University Press, 1992); Carrie Paechter, *Changing School Subjects: power, gender and curriculum* (Buckingham: Open University Press, 2000), 105.

[19] John Hurt, "Drill, discipline and the elementary school ethos," in *Popular Education and Socialisation in the Nineteenth Century* (London: Methuen and Company, 1977), 167-91; George Dyer, "Benjamin Lucraft," in *Six Men of the People: Biographical Sketches with Portraits*, ed. William Catchpole and George Dyer (London: Dyer Brothers, 1882), 10-12.

subjects nor algebra, mechanics and mensuration. In the 1900s, concern about 'national efficiency' served to legitimate a policy response from the Infant Welfare Movement promoting domestic subjects teaching as a solution to the social problem of 'ignorance' and 'negligence' among working-class mothers. In the 1920s, East Ender Dorothy Scannell spent a fifth of her time on domestic subjects. 'The teacher was a motherly type of woman; we all knew she wasn't a real teacher, and she would train us how to be good wives, from a financial point of view, of course, to a working man.' Dorothy's goal was to get a good housewifery certificate she could show to 'Mr Right.'[20]

A Carlisle child of the 1900s, Lily Hinds was one of 16 elementary school children in her age cohort to win a scholarship to the city's higher grade school. Lily's daughter, the novelist Margaret Forster, was convinced she would have been better off as a boy.

> Boys were taught fractions and equations while girls had to be content with multiplication and division; boys learned Physics, girls Physiology; boys had Chemistry lessons while Girls had Botany. But at least both boys and girls took commercial classes. These were very popular because, as was well known, knowledge of everything to do with commerce led to office jobs and everyone wanted those, even the brilliant Lily who certainly didn't think an office job too lowly for her academic talents. Ask her what she was going to do when she left school and she'd say, get a job in an office *if she could*. She had no other ambition. Nobody mentioned university or college, an outlandish notion for a working-class girl, and she never thought of it herself. She hoped to get a good job, then eventually marry and have children. It was what girls did.[21]

Many employment opportunities for working-class boys could be grasped with a few years of elementary schooling, but this was not the case for their female counterparts. Teaching and clerical work were hard to access, and working-class girls largely joined the workforce in domestic service, dressmaking, manufacturing (covering the relatively well-paid textile machines operators of Cheshire, Lancashire and Yorkshire at one end to the poorly paid women working either in small workshops or in the home), offices and shops. In every sector, the divergence between male–female earning potential was huge.

Nevertheless, few questioned the idea that there should be different curricula for different social groups reflective of classed and gendered notions of pupil competencies. Traditional views about women's role ran deep. As an adult, Molly Hughes took issue with her former head teacher:

> To be deeply pleasing to a husband, and widely pleasing to other men, seems to me as good an ideal as a woman can have. But instead of facing squarely the real needs of future wives and mothers, as the vast majority of girls were to be, Miss

---

[20] Dorothy Scannell, *Mother Knew Best: Memoir of a London Girlhood* (New York: Pantheon Books, 1974), 136.
[21] Margaret Forster, *Hidden Lives: a family memoir* (London: Penguin Books, 1995), 4-5.

Buss seized the tempting instrument at her hand—the stimulus to mental ambition afforded by the outside examinations.[22]

Despite the prevailing ideology of domesticity, however, waged domestic service was in long-term decline as an employer of female labour. Mary Smith (a pseudonym), who wrote her education biography for Pearl Jephcott in the 1930s, was a former elementary pupil who resisted becoming a domestic servant. Unemployment was at its peak, and her parents needed her wage, but believed a position in service to be a 'last resort.' The camaraderie found in retail or factory work with greater independence and sense of identity was preferable to the subordinate atmosphere of life 'below stairs.'[23]

One of the limits of Williams's 'selective tradition' is that it ignores the impact of patriarchal relations on organisational policy and by implication deals with the actions of men in thinking about the struggle for subject definition which is understood almost exclusively in terms of social class. A focus that ignores cultural emphases about woman's nature as outside of rationality and woman's minds as incapable of reason. It follows that femininity is inscribed as antithetical to dominant scientific discourses that discursively produce science and technology as a branch of male culture. As witness to the power of these cultural codes, we have pupil testimony in late-twentieth century ethnographic studies showing the damaging results of sexist assumptions including the fear of effeminacy.[24]

More recent investigations of masculinities in mathematics suggest the ways children position themselves in binaries such as fast/slow, competitive/collaborative, independent/dependent, active/passive, naturally able/hardworking and reason/ calculation are critical to identifying as being/doing 'good at maths' and that, in turn, shapes subject choice.[25] So, how did we get here? What happened after the abolition of the School Board system? We start with a personal account of pedagogy in London's East End in the 1920s.

---

[22] Molly Hughes, *A London Girl Growing Up in the 1880s*, 35.

[23] Mary Smith, "An Ordinary Girl," in Pearl Jephcott, *Girls Growing Up* (London: Faber, 1942), 19.

[24] Christine Griffin, *Typical Girls? Young Women From School to the Job Market* (London: Routledge, Kegan and Paul, 1985); Annmarie Wolpe, *Within School Walls: The Role of Discipline, Sexuality and the Curriculum* (London: Routledge, 1988); Julia Stanley, *Marks on the Memory: experiencing school* (Milton Keynes: Open University Press, 1989); Sue Lees, *Sugar and Spice: Sexuality and Adolescent Girls*. Harmondsworth: Penguin, 1993; Máirtín Mac an Ghaill, *The Making of Men* (Buckingham: Open University Press, 1994).

[25] Heather Mendick, *Masculinities in Mathematics* (London: McGraw-Hill, 2006).

Viewing Secondary Curriculum Formulations Historically

The principle of a general education on liberal lines was at the heart of curriculum design in the secondary sector before the passing of the 1944 Education Act. Debate over content surfaced in the deliberations of the Consultative Committee of the Board of Education including the 1923 report on the *Differentiation of Curricula for Boys and Girls in Secondary Schools*. Perspectives had more than a backward glance to the views of Victorian school inspector Matthew Arnold on the role of culture in the transformation of the middle class, especially the importance of nurturing the aesthetic faculties, which was seen as particularly important for girls, given their 'double function' and 'natural destiny as makers of homes.' The examination system did not value all subjects equally, and the fundamental principles that prevailed echo the workings of Bourdieu's 'cultural arbitrary' with judgements based on taste acting as a means of social distinction allied to the reproduction and realignment of gendered class practices founded on meritocratic discourses of equal opportunities.[26] Related to this were the problems of needing to accommodate individuals of mixed experience and prior knowledge in core subjects on entry, the examination syllabus and the demands of matriculation.

In 1917, the Board of Education appointed the School Schools Examination Council to co-ordinate examinations including the School Certificate for 16-year-olds, a precursor of today's GCSEs. There were four examination groups, and individuals had to pass in at least five subjects from groups I to III to gain a Certificate. Group IV subjects (such as bookkeeping, drawing, economics, housecraft, hygiene, map work, mensuration and music, needlework, shorthand and surveying) did not count towards a Certificate. Women teachers led the calls for greater flexibility amid speculation that if the headmistresses proposed Group IV parity for girls, change would follow. Nevertheless, a dominant epistemology in English education which ranks knowledge hierarchically and distributes it selectively lived on. Group IV subjects were not taken seriously at Wolverhampton grammar school when Derek Davies went there in the 1930s, and Group I subjects like geography 'rapidly disappeared from the timetables of academically able boys… Maths was respectable, but Science was modestly provided for, and English, History and Modern Languages were heavily overshadowed by Classics.'[27]

Born in 1865, Quaker socialist Mary O'Brien Harris was one teacher who adopted a radical position on curriculum design in a municipal secondary

---

[26] Andrea Jacobs and Joyce Goodman, "Music in the 'Common' Life of the School: Towards an Aesthetic Education for All in English Girls' Secondary Schools in the Interwar Period," *History of Education*, 35 no. 6 (2006), 670-5.

[27] Felicity Hunt, *Gender & Policy in English Education 1902–1944* (London: Harvester Wheatsheaf, 1991), 84; David Davies, *Breakthrough: autobiographical accounts of the education of some socially disadvantaged children*, ed. Ronald Goldman (London: Routledge & Kegan Paul, 1968), 34.

school launched under the 1902 Act. She graduated from the University College of Aberystwyth in Wales before becoming one of the first people in the University of London to be awarded a PhD. After a spell in a London elementary school, she was appointed as a lecturer at Southwark's Centre for Girls, one of 12 day pupil-teacher centres established to offer pupil teachers half-time instruction in central classes held during normal school hours. When the Centre closed, she became founding head of Clapton County Secondary School for Girls, a school ministering to the daughters of the working poor living in overcrowded homes and tenement blocks in Hackney, in London's East End.

Headmistress of Clapton from 1906 to 1928, Harris took the ideas of progressive education and tried to put them into practice. She thought education should encourage self-discovery and self-expression in a non-competitive, egalitarian atmosphere and explained her pedagogy, which she called the Howard Plan of Individual Timetables, in her 1923 book *Towards Freedom*. For her, the problem was 'what to do under *existing* conditions, so as to get the best out of the *present* curriculum.' Learning and teaching was organised on the basis of vertical classification into 'Houses' rather than the horizontal class or form, and she placed a strong emphasis on auto-education by which she meant putting the pupil in charge of his/her intellectual work (what she called his/her 'soul').

Teachers' control and supervision was essential. Her starting point was a core curriculum of creative work to solve the problem of differing rates of progress among groups of children. Running alongside these practical subjects, pupils designed their own timetables in accordance with needs and interests. As she put it in the school magazine:

> 'The School as University' is how I sometimes speak of our organisation. Let a pupil fitted for such training be educated chiefly for Handwork, without debarring him from first rate teaching in language or science, for he may in due course be ready for them. Do not let the academic pupil be cut off from handicrafts; and above all, let him not be encouraged by segregation to think himself superior. Let no-one who is to become one of the citizens of tomorrow be prevented by difference of taste or ability from sharing with as many as possible of his fellows the Art and the Music, the Acting and the other Games, and the other interests of everyday life which are common to all. We do not want at the age of adolescence separate schools for clerks and for dressmakers, one for future nurses and doctors, and others for housekeepers and shop assistants respectively. A common social life and as much common teaching as possible should be shared by diverse pupils so that all types may mix together as they do in the University, and as they should afterwards mix in the world, all with the common aim of our school motto: 'To do good work whether we live or die.'[28]

This was a move towards freeing children to develop as autonomous learners, learning by doing. While preserving the standard academic curriculum, the

---

[28] *School Magazine*, 1927.

constraint of lesson times disappeared as pupils worked at their own pace in each subject, studied in termly or half-yearly blocks, with a large proportion of time spent working through individualised learning cards, using the school library for reference. Home-school learning agreements were set up, and pupils built up personal records of achievement.[29]

Life stories offer a glimpse into the daily life of the school and the professional practice of a progressive headmistress who regularly invited groups of her older students to her home for 'Shaw teas.' The teas, which consisted of brown bread with raw carrots, were provided by her husband who did all the shopping and housework. These events were a highpoint in the childhood of scholarship winner Minnie Nirenstein who went to Clapton School in 1920. Nirenstein, whose experience at school was a happy one, described Harris as a severe, 'principled person,' who set 'high standards' but was 'very kind at heart.' The school day began with secular readings, and since half the pupils were Jewish, they sang 'hymns that didn't mention Jesus, so that the Jewish girls could join in' or we were 'told to omit the verses with Jesus's name.' Whereas other local schools had French as their first language, Clapton taught German 'so we shouldn't be enemies of the German people.' Visitors came 'from all over the world… We were like a little university—you could drop subjects to concentrate on those you liked.' Weather permitting, study periods were in the fresh air and 'the gym was, by the standards of the day, liberated.' 'We used to take our gym-slips off and do gym in our jersey and knickers.'[30]

Against the grain of powerful forces, Harris argued manual training at the right age was the shortest route to 'true intellectual education,' and the value of games greatly exaggerated. Challenging contemporary education practices, she envisioned pedagogy as the integration of living and learning, a form of community sharing. For her, the social and cultural life of the school modelled the good society. A place where each person endeavoured to help the other for the common good. Although the school was successful and Clapton's examination rates leapt, inspectors criticised her for lacking 'brightness' and a 'sense of humour' and castigated individual timetables as unsuitable for an academic secondary school—saying this to her employer while she was kept outside the room, unable to defend herself. On the other hand, the first principal of the London Institute of Education praised 'her remarkable gifts of organisation, her exceptional insight into junior human nature and her skill in managing young people.'[31]

In most secondary schools, working-class scholarship winners experienced the classed and gendered meanings of their academic education through the new subjects they studied and the cultural reproduction of the mode of behaviour expected of and by the professional middle-class boy or girl. The school

---

[29] Mary O'Brien Harris, *Towards Freedom* (London: University of London Press, 1923), 18, 21.
[30] Raphael Samuel, *The Lost World of British Communism* (London: Verso, 2006), 64-5.
[31] Hilda Kean, *Challenging the State? The Socialist and Feminist Educational Experience, 1900-1930* (London: Falmer Press, 1990), 11; Mary O'Brien Harris, *Towards Freedom*, x.

that Harris built was unusual in offering gardening, spinning with weaving and woodwork to girls, alongside the conventional art, cookery, music and needlework. Her cousin and fellow member of the Headmistresses' Association, head of Bishop Auckland County School for Girls, summed the Howard Plan up. 'The essence of that creed is that, given material and encouragement, children, through their natural curiosity and intellectual activity, will be stimulated to a willing self-education far more valuable than an education imposed on them by outside pressure or authority.'[32]

By the 1930s, the formal strictures of education followed the thinking of the Hadow Reports, which were advocating the primary/secondary split at age 11 and recommended a triple track streaming system for large elementary schools. In wartime, the 1942 Beveridge Report endorsed eugenic thinking about women's role, which carried the message that schooling is not a serious undertaking for girls:

> The attitude of the housewife to gainful employment outside the home is not and should not be the same as the single woman. She has other duties… Taken as a whole, the plan for Social Security puts a premium on marriage in place of penalizing it… In the next thirty years housewives as mothers have vital work to do in ensuring the adequate continuance of the British race and of British ideals in the world.[33]

Scrutiny of mothers intensified after 1945 as the desire for social construction through a consolidation of the family meant that women as mothers, or potential mothers, were the target of post-war social philosophy.[34] The thinking of John Newsom at that time Director of Education for Hertfordshire exemplifies this.

Newsom endorsed gender stereotypes without question. The Victorians would have easily recognised the family he had in mind. In his view, education for motherhood was important for women of all class and educational levels, and he criticised those leading the single-sex girls' grammar schools for their insistence that their pupils required the same curriculum as their brothers arguing 'this mad passion for equality has masked the fact that men and women are different.' He explained that:

> No woman in this age of equality of opportunity, of careers open to all, of equal education and political rights is compelled to get married and to accept the degradations involved. Yet she chooses it deliberately as her main occupation and a

---

[32] *The Friend*, 6 May 1938.

[33] Quoted in Sue Sharpe, *'Just Like a Girl': How Girls Learn to be Women* (Harmondsworth: Penguin, 1976), 37.

[34] Denise Riley, *War in the Nursery* (London: Virago, 1983); Angela Davis, "'Oh no, nothing, we didn't learn anything': sex education and the preparation of girls for motherhood, c. 1930-1970,'" *History of Education*, 37 no. 5 (2008), 661-677.

Fig. 6.2 ABB/B/1/12/1d Girls' domestic science class, Mayfield Comprehensive, Wandsworth (ND). From the Photographic Archive of the Architects and Building Branch, Ministry of Education and its successors. UCL Institute of Education Special Collections. (Crown Copyright)

great part of her early womanhood is spent trying by one artifice or another to get entangled in the domestic toils.[35]

Despite Newsom's concerns, the effect of government policy was such that educational choice for girls was largely a fiction. The same was true for most boys but the educational hierarchy postulated gender differences that did nothing to challenge the idea that the economic function of all women was both temporary and insignificant (Fig. 6.2). NUWT calls for a more equal preparation for future home life went unheeded, along with those for the giving of instruction to boys in domestic subjects and to girls in light woodwork. Girls' secondary schools remained rooted in minor professional and moderate gender aspirations in which higher education and a career took second place to a good marriage.[36]

---

[35] Deborah Thom, "Better a teacher than a hairdresser? 'A mad passion for equality' or, keeping Molly and Betty down," in *Lessons for Life. The Schooling of Girls and Women 1850–1950*, ed. Felicity Hunt

(Oxford: Basil Blackwell, 1987), 110-111; John Newsom, *Education of Girls* (London: Faber and Faber, 1948), 25.

[36] Felicity Hunt, *Gender and Policy-Making*, 103; Penny Summerfield, "Cultural Reproduction in the Education of Girls: a Study of Girls' Secondary Schooling in Two Lancashire Towns,

Unlike Newsom, Kathleen Ollerenshaw thought girls should learn about homemaking from their mothers. The 1950s saw the Scientific Manpower Committee forecast a severe shortage of scientists and technologists serving the new 'high technology' industries, and as demographic change took effect, she noted universal and near youthful marriage had displaced the Victorian discourse of 'surplus women.' For her, this altered the terms of debate from the standpoint of educating girls. The questions she pursued here relate to whether it is right to 'take account in school of a girl's future vocational work' and not whether 'schools should acknowledge that many schoolgirls take a serious interest in boys, but to what extent we should and can contrive to exploit this to girl's educational advantage?'[37]

Going beyond statements of policy and intent to investigate the realities of young people's educational experiences, Ollerenshaw quotes essays by 14-year-olds on the question 'Why educate girls?' Secondary modern girls show a blend of sense and sensibility in recognising the relevance of specific subjects. 'Arithmetic is a very good subject to learn as it will help both the housewife and the career girl when they come to spend their money,' says one. 'Science teaches you how to mend plugs, wire and fuses, and the facts of life which is very important to a girl'; 'History is a waste of time, why learn about dead people and the Stone Age which I don't think we'll go back to.' A male counterpart suggests English should command curriculum time for future office workers, should a secretary need to correct 'her boss's phraseology'; another thinks women are capable of doing much of the work that men do, and can't see why they shouldn't be educated. A third claims, 'A woman can stand up to more torment than the average man' with the result that 'many scientists believe that the first space man will be a woman.'[38]

Grammar girls shared a sense that change was possible. 'Education for girls is a must. Menfolk have made a pretty mess of governing the world so why not let women try?' 'There will come a time in the near future when women will rule the world and so prove the worthwhileness of their education.' Subjects like domestic science and electricity were valued for their relevance to everyday life but some doubted 'whether a secondary school equips a girl for getting married' and questioned the need for geometry and music. Cookery and needlework lessons seemed pointless when it took a year to make one blouse and a whole lesson to make blancmange. In wrestling with the kind of society we want to create, Ollerenshaw spoke of the next generation of girls and women bearing 'a special responsibility' and warned of a serious loss if we either fail to make them appreciate this or 'if women default in fulfilling their responsibilities.'[39]

The United Nations (UN) designated 1968 Human Rights Year and the period 1975 to 1985 the UN Decade for Women. In Britain, the Women's National Commission in 1969 and the Equal Opportunities Commission in

---

1900-50," in *Lessons for Life. The Schooling of Girls and Women 1850–1950*, ed. Felicity Hunt (Oxford: Basil Blackwell, 1987), 149-170.

[37] Kathleen Ollerenshaw, *Education for Girls* (London: Faber and Faber, 1961), 16.
[38] Op cit, 23-4.
[39] Op cit, 18.

1975 had the advantage of government funding for the first time. Leafing through a prospectus for local evening classes, the novelist Margaret Drabble noted 'with amusement' that 'one had to bring along one's own ingredients' for every cookery class except the one called 'Mainly-for-Men Cookery' where the tutor provided the ingredients. 'Men may learn to cook, but of course they are far too busy (unlike most working wives) to do the shopping too.'[40] Not everyone was laughing. Some thought a domestic curriculum had kept girls' education inferior and their expectations low.[41] Others went further. Challenging the idea that a woman's place was in the home, they argued a woman's place was on the syllabus as the emergence of feminist women's/gender studies shows.

The Life Cycle of Women's/Gender Studies in the 1960s and Beyond

In 1960, Sociology graduate Hannah Gavron found it hard to win approval for a doctoral study investigating the conflicts of housebound mothers at the all-women's Bedford College on the edge of Regent's Park, London. Reconstructing his mother's life, her son, Jeremy, thinks it safe to assume that 'for all her privileges of class and money, her choice of subject was in part a response to her own experiences, the stresses of balancing her studies with being a wife, a mother, a woman, an individual.' In 1965, Hannah Gavron took her own life. A year later her thesis was published as *The Captive Wife*. It became set reading on a course Miriam David taught as part of London University's Diploma in Sociology.[42]

The academic field of women's studies came out of feminist politics. In 1969, Juliet Mitchell ran what may have been the first course in England and Audrey Battersby went along with a friend. Betty Friedan's *The Feminine Mystique* had appeared in 1963 and her dissection of the frustrations of the educated, middle-class housewife chafing against gender-confining stereotypes made a strong impact. Battersby read Friedan as a student. 'Then the bells rang and there was that feeling of militancy that I'd never experienced before despite involvement in several left-wing groups. I was no longer alone, but part of a movement which was primarily political but could be personal to me.' It was the same for Newnham graduate Jessica Mann who remembered being wildly relieved to know she 'wasn't a freak.' At the University of London, Sally Alexander wanted to research the industrial revolution from the female perspective for her History dissertation. But her tutor, who had seen her television appearance before the 1970 Miss World contest when she and other feminist activists dramatically flour bombed

---

[40] Extract in *Half the Sky: an introduction to women's studies*, ed. Bristol Women's Studies Group (London: Virago, 1979), 68-69.

[41] Dena Attar, *Wasting Girls' Time: the history and politics of home economics* (London: Virago, 1990), 127-8.

[42] Jeremy Gavron, *A Woman on the Edge of Time* (London: Scribe, 2015), 129; Miriam E. David, *Personal and Political: feminisms, sociology and family lives* (Stoke-on-Trent: Trentham Books, 2003), 35.

the stage, advised a re-think. 'Interesting stuff but don't let it draw you into a cul-de-sac academically speaking, your subject needs to have genuine relevance. Best to steer clear of minority interests.' Alexander, who hadn't wanted to bring down the male establishment but had hoped for a seat at the table, felt as if she'd been offered a high chair.[43]

When Miriam David started out as an undergraduate, reading Sociology at the University of Leeds in the early 1960s, she did so in the company of more than 50 other young women and about half a dozen young men mainly middle class and all white. She assumed women of her generation chose Sociology because it was not a school subject and/or because of its possible links with a career in social work or the social services. Rosemary Deem, in the Sociology department at the University of Leicester from 1967, began to include feminist research in reaction to an essay title from a male tutor 'Why women don't want to work.'

> The essay, as with most of my written work, was returned after many weeks marked only with a brief comment, in this case, 'V. good and v. comprehensive: B+'. I felt that this understated feedback was itself a kind of exposition on female knowledge and male power, as well as an indication that in those days concern about the quality of teaching and assessment were not always at the forefront of higher education.[44]

She explained a gendered tripartism built into the organisation of sociological knowledge at Leicester. 'The tiers were theoretical sociology (regarded as high status, difficult and a masculine preserve), empirical sociology (of medium status and difficulty, with no particular gendered appeal) and applied sociology, which was generally regarded as being of somewhat lower status, although essential for would-be social workers and female-dominated.' Distinctions that show a fit between curricula, inculcation of social attitudes and employment opportunities in keeping with the priorities Gaby Weiner identifies.[45]

If the Leicester Sociology department in which Deem studied bore similarities to the institutional habitus in which Pearl Jephcott worked in the 1950s, the Women's Caucus of the British Sociological Association (BSA) was determined to change things. Inspired by Sheila Allen and Diana Leonard in 1974, the BSA gave over the annual conference to the topic of sexual divisions and society. Allen, who started her working life at the University of Birmingham and was the University of Bradford's first woman professor of Sociology, became the first woman president for the BSA a year later.[46] An Equality of the Sexes committee was set up, and Deem describes a feminist network with career connections to the Women's Caucus and the University of York where

---

[43] Maggie Humm, *Feminisms: a reader* (London: Routledge, 1992), xvi; Anna Coote and Beatrix Campbell, *Sweet Freedom: The Struggle for Women' Liberation* (Oxford: Basil Blackwell, 1982), 17; Jessica Mann, *The Fifties Mystique* (Sheffield: The Cornovia Press, 2012), 178; *Misbehaviour* (2020).

[44] Rosemary Deem, "Border Territories: a journey through sociology, education and women's studies," *British Journal of Sociology of Education*, 17, no. 1 (1996), 8.

[45] Op cit, 7; Gaby Weiner, *Feminisms in Education*.

[46] BSA *Network*, 1975.

she held a temporary post and become friends with another sociologist, Mary Maynard, who subsequently founded the York Centre for Women's Studies. Meanwhile, feminist scholarship found a home in new independent publishing houses such as Pluto Press (1969) and Virago Press (1973) and Anglo-American journals like *Women's Studies International Quarterly* (later *Forum*, 1978).

Virago published the first UK reader in the field in 1979. Compiled by the Bristol Women's Studies Group, *Half the Sky* helped produce a corpus of literature, which became core reading.[47] In varied institutional cultures, women were challenging existing understanding of society, the role and construction of sex/gender within this and the ways in which this understanding is achieved and transmitted. As Australian feminist Dale Spender put it:

> We no longer wish to give substance to patriarchal order and its integral component, the superiority of the male. We have started to formulate different rules for classifying the world, rules that are not based on the assumption that the proper human being is a male one and that female is a negative category. We have begun to codify the meaning that woman is an autonomous category and we are beginning to make this version of the world come true. We are gathering our own evidence which disproves male superiority, and which unmasks the many mechanisms which have helped to sustain this unfortunate and inappropriate reality.[48]

Hence, the initial imprint of women's studies in English higher education had both academic and political roots. Sociologist AnnMarie Wolpe, for example, was an anti-apartheid activist who found herself exiled in England having helped her husband escape from a South African jail. In 1969, Wolpe obtained a post in the development of women's studies courses at what is now Middlesex University where she co-edited the landmark collection *Feminism and Materialism* (1978) with Annette Kuhn and became a founding member of the journal *Feminist Review* that started in 1979.[49]

Pioneers had to fight for institutional recognition. 'It was the Division of Continuing Education, and they let me put that course on and about 50 or 60 students turned up on the first night, so they realised there was a market for it, and there were some individuals who were prepared to back me and take a chance.' There was resistance, too.

> One of my colleagues he was just sitting there and he was sort of going purple in the meeting when I was just talking in a very academic way about how many women writers we would cover and it would all be historically accurate and how we would relate it to other movements. He just sat there then he suddenly said, 'I've been kicked around by women all my life and now what they want to do is

---

[47] The Bristol Women's Studies Group, *Half The Sky: an Introduction to Women's Studies* (London: Virago, 1979).
[48] Dale Spender, *Man Made Language* (London: Routledge & Kegan Paul, 1980), 2.
[49] AnnMarie Wolpe, *The Long Way Home* (London: Virago, 1994).

run courses on it'. I remember just sitting there shaking at the violence of it all and thinking I don't know if I can take this.[50]

Popularity counted in an increasingly marketised higher education system and the subject grew, but participants had to guard against everyday sexism. Like the male librarian who 'just looked at your legs' in planning meetings and the male academic who exclaimed 'whatever next, Budgerigar Studies.' Curriculum innovation crystallised into opposing ideas which lingered obstinately on: that a politics course on feminism lacked 'seriousness,' was 'women's stuff' and 'people cannot teach about their biases.' In many places, intertwining feminist perspectives with an exploration of sex and gender roles on an optional course for Sociology undergraduates was a more acceptable format.[51]

Feisty individuals found it a slow and contested process to develop a curriculum and a pedagogy that involved personal experiences and sought to challenge traditional academic notions about the disciplines. The University of Kent was the first UK institution to offer a named women's studies degree programme (an MA, founded by Mary Evans, Janet Sayers and Clare Ungerson in 1980) and established the first Chair in the field. Some welcomed the innovation at Kent, seeing it as part of an attempt to modernise the institution. Something that seemed less important at the University of Sussex with its schools of study as opposed to traditional academic faculties where Jenny Shaw started the first MA in Gender and Education in the 1990s.[52]

Women's/gender studies teachers and researchers recognised with critical pedagogy scholars that the curriculum is an *official* selection that structures content in ways that privilege a particular construction of knowledge and the history of knowledge. With roots in the liberation theories of adult learning and small group work used for consciousness sharing, feminist pedagogy focused on enabling parity of participation. Some sympathetic males saw themselves as fellow travellers, with interests in the field and supportive of participative learning and non-traditional assessment based on coursework rather than examinations. Course content enabled participants to situate personal experience in a sociological and historical context, offering spaces and resources for studying voices excluded from the traditional canon. New curricula opened up a dialogue over the desirability of women-only spaces, whether men can be

---

[50] Elizabeth Bird, "The academic arm of the Women's Liberation Movement Women's Studies 1969-1999 in North American and the United Kingdom," *Women's Studies International Forum*, 25 no. 10 (2002), 142, 144.

[51] Elizabeth Bird, "The sexual politics of introducing women's studies: memories and reflections from North America and the United Kingdom," *Gender and Education*, 16, no. 1 (2004), 55; Gill Kirkup and Elizabeth Whitelegg, "The legacy and impact of Open University women's/ gender studies: 30 years on," *Gender and Education*, 25, no.1 (2012), 7; Kelly Coate, "The History of Women's Studies as an Academic Subject Area in Higher Education in the UK" (PhD thesis, University of London, 1999), 151.

[52] Coate, "The History of Women's Studies", 8, 151.

feminists, whether the goal should be women's studies and/or gender studies to include men and masculinity and possibly run the risk of becoming men's studies modified.[53]

Best known for her work on the way rape victims were treated by the police and the legal system and the extent to which men appeared to be getting away with it, Sue Lees was involved in setting up the Women's Studies Network (UK) Association. In her late teens, she attended Queen's College for girls in London's Harley Street before taking a social policy diploma at Edinburgh University, where she won the prestigious Radzinowicz Prize in criminology. In 1976, she went to the then Polytechnic of North London (PNL now London Metropolitan University) where she co-founded the first undergraduate degree in women's studies in the country and later set up a local authority-funded women's studies unit. As PNL developed a modular degree structure, foundation courses for women the institution would otherwise not reach were one of the unit's first projects. Lees was also, for four years, a co-opted member of the women's committee on Islington council.[54] When Chris Kitch arrived at PNL in the late 1980s, having been expelled from grammar school in the 1950s, the support she received from Sue Lees and the other women's studies lecturers helped her climb out of drug addiction and homelessness. When Kitch graduated in 1993, she fulfilled a childhood dream. 'As I walked on to the red carpet it was a tremendous moment. I felt so powerful. I knew the meaning of self-esteem.'[55]

Diana Leonard first articulated the objectives of women's studies in 1973. She felt they involved 'increased awareness, knowledge and new (feminist) understanding of the relationships between the sexes in society with special concentration on the position of women, and, insofar as we find the situation in our own society to be unsatisfactory, to seek ways to change it.'[56] Over three decades later, Gabriele Griffin tried to explain what made women's/ gender studies distinctive. In part difference lay in its having grown out of a social movement as opposed to being set up by elites. Added to which it was a female-dominated political discipline targeted at gender transformation within

---

[53] Paulo Freire, *Pedagogy of the Oppressed* (Harmondsworth: Penguin, 2017); bell hooks, *Teaching to Transgress: Education as the Practice of Freedom* (Abingdon: Routledge, 1994); Penny Jane Burke, "Re/Imagining Higher Education Pedagogies: Gender, Emotion and Difference," *Teaching in Higher Education*, 20, no. 4 (2015), 388-401.

[54] Coate, "The History of Women's Studies", 140.

[55] Melissa Benn, 'Sue Lees: feminist who changed the rules for rape victims in court', *Guardian*, 24 September 2002; Miriam David, "Sue Lees: An Appreciation", *Gender and Education*, 15, no. 1 (2003): 3-4; Chris Kitch, *Pavement for My Pillow* (London: Orion, 1996), 188. In 1999 Sue Lees made a cameo appearance on the 11 o'clock show at Channel 4 for an interview on feminism with Ali G. See https://youtu.be/oftOCN1jkNo.

[56] Quoted in Kelly Coate, "The History of Women's Studies", 10.

masculinist cultures and institutions. Last of all, it used a woman-centred and interdisciplinary approach that recognised the value of personal experience and the skills and awareness that we accumulate through the politics of everyday life, in the context of epistemic cultures that privilege abstract bodies of knowledge.[57]

In 1980, Leonard was seconded to the Open University to develop its first women's studies course, which ran between 1983 and 1991. Looking back, former students shared with other women students the sense that a university education was more than the sum of its parts.

> Imagine my delight when a young student came to work with me during the summer of 2007, who… told me about the current 'third-wave- feminism which I had been entirely ignorant of! We are still friends and she is now studying for a PhD in Women's Studies at the University of York. Only last year when she was feeling a little discouraged by some of her experiences in the academic world, I 'told her about the excitement of taking U221 in its very first year, when Women's Studies was a totally new field. And now, here she was, taking a PhD. That's surely progress.[58]

Campus feminists had brought female experiences and feminist knowledge production into the academic world, although the number of full-time, single or combined honours degree programmes in women's studies in England was always relatively small. Student demand kept it alive. Jo Winrow-Jones came to Ruskin College, Oxford, after 18 years as a firefighter. She took an MA in the subject because the public perception of her occupation made her want to learn more. 'We make flippant remarks about women being "primary carers" but don't ask why that is,' she said.[59]

CONCLUSION

To return to the quote with which we started, Mary Gavin Clarke expressed an unease at the heart of which was an underlying theme of gender difference in education that organisational policy promulgated. This chapter has reconstructed women's involvement in curriculum contestation and critique, bringing together Williams's 'selective tradition' with an analysis of gender as an integral aspect of class practices. From the 1870s onwards, England's educational apartheid reinforced status hierarchies within academic fields modelled on formulations of what counts as a well-rounded liberal education of a White

---

[57] Gabriele Griffin, "The 'Ins' and 'Outs' of Women's/ Gender studies: a response to reports of its demise in 2008', *Women's History Review*, 18, no. 3 (2009): 485-496.

[58] Gill Kirkup and Whitehead, "The legacy and impact of Open University women's/ gender studies: 30 years on," *Gender and Education*, 25, no. 1 (2013): 16, 19.

[59] Chris Green, "Women's studies are alive and well," *The Independent*, 23 October 2011, https://www.independent.co.uk/news/education/higher/women-s-studies-are-alive-and-well-810050.html.

'gentleman.' Working-class scholarship winners and 11-plus 'successes' experienced the classed and gendered meanings of their academic education through the new subjects they studied and the cultural reproduction of the mode of behaviour expected of and by the White, professional middle-class boy or girl, and by the way in which homework curtailed their leisure time. Teachers also knew the amount of time girls spent on housework to the detriment of their schoolwork and that they were not joined in this work by their brothers.

Studying women as curriculum architects shows the rise of domestic subjects and women's studies was not painless, with each being a political and educational project in an overtly gendered field. The first embracing a role-oriented education for girls, focused around elements of traditionally female service to others with an emphasis on a femininity that is part of teachers and pupils/students' identity as well as that of their subject. The second tracing thought inside the feminist academy highlighting inequality in the position of women, locally and globally, based on new perceptions of experience, with new input into methods and practices, while making off-campus connections with peace movements, women's aid and rape crisis centres. In both cases, their marginality within the larger educational field serves to highlight how gender/power/knowledge intersect.

Debate about the gendering of knowledge and the question of education for liberation or for subordination continues. It extends both to current perceptions of 'gender-appropriate' subjects and the power/knowledge relations exposed by the 'hidden' curriculum with its own special subjects such as the state of feeling bored and the capacity to endure it. Within and without the formal organisation of the school and the university campus, there are ongoing struggles to decolonise the selective tradition, challenging long-standing biases and omissions that limit how we understand politics and society.[60] Making use of scattered traces of women's history shows the scope and possibility for recovering lost histories of radical educational practice and challenges to the status quo. It shows the possibility of fostering interest and talents through content that is relevant and meaningful for all not to threaten but to develop their potentialities.

---

[60] Kehinde Andrews, "The Black Studies Movement in Britain: Becoming an Institution not Institutionalised," in *Dismantling Race in Higher Education: Racism, Whiteness and Decolonising the Academy*, ed. Jason Arday and Heidi Safia Mirza (Cham: Palgrave Macmillan, 2018), 271-288; Michael Andrew Peters, "Why Is My Curriculum White? A Brief Genealogy of Resistance," in *Dismantling Race in Higher Education: Racism, Whiteness and Decolonising the Academy*, ed. by Jason Arday and Heidi Safia Mirza, (Cham: Palgrave Macmillan, 2018), 253-270.

Bibliography

Primary Sources

Archival Sources

Morrison, M. "Ladies on the London School Board," 1897, Newscuttings, "School Boards," LSE archive and special collections.
The Friend, Library of the Society of Friends, Friends House, London.

Autobiographies, Memoirs, Diaries, Letters, Obituaries

Benn, Melissa. "Sue Lees: Feminist who Changed the Rules for Rape Victims in Court", *The Guardian*, 24 September 2002.
David, Miriam, E. *Personal and Political: feminisms, sociology and family lives*. Stoke-on-Trent: Trentham Books, 2003a.
David, Miriam E. "Sue Lees: An Appreciation", *Gender and Education*, 15, no. 1 (2003b): 3-4
Davies, David. *Breakthrough: autobiographical accounts of the education of some socially disadvantaged children*, edited by Ronald Goldman. London: Routledge & Kegan Paul, 1968.
Dayus, Kathleen. *Her People*. London: Virago, 1982.
Deem, Rosemary. "Border Territories: a journey through sociology, education and women's studies," *British Journal of Sociology of Education*, 17, no. 1 (1996): 5-19.
Forster, Margaret. *Hidden Lives: a family memoir*. London: Penguin Books, 1995.
Hughes, Molly. *A London Girl Growing Up in the 1880s*. Oxford: Oxford University Press, 1979.
Kitch, Chris. *Pavement for My Pillow*. London: Orion, 1996.
Mann, Jessica. *The Fifties Mystique*. Sheffield: The Cornovia Press, 2012.
Scannell, Dorothy. *Mother Knew Best: Memoir of a London Girlhood*. New York: Pantheon Books, 1974.
Wolpe, AnnMarie. *The Long Way Home*. London: Virago, 1994.

Newspapers and Periodicals of the Period

The Governess
Macmillans Magazine
School Board Chronicle
The Times
Women's Penny Paper

Other Contemporary Books and Pamphlets

Banks, Olive. *Parity and Prestige in English Secondary Education: A Study in Educational Sociology*. London: Routledge and Kegan Paul, 1955.
Bristol Women's Studies Group. *Half the Sky: an introduction to women's studies*. London: Virago, 1979.
Clarke, Mary Gavin. "Feminine Challenge in Education." In *The Headmistress Speaks*, 59-77. London: Kegan Paul, Trench, Trubner & Co., 1937.

Dyer, George. "Benjamin Lucraft," in *Six Men of the People: Biographical Sketches with Portraits*, edited by William Catchpole and George Dyer, 10-12. London: Dyer Brothers, 1882.
Griffin, Christine. *Typical Girls? Young Women From School to the Job Market*. London: Routledge, Kegan and Paul, 1985.
Harris, Mary O'Brien. *Towards Freedom*. London: University of London Press, 1923.
Lees, Sue. *Sugar and Spice: Sexuality and Adolescent Girls*. Harmondsworth: Penguin, 1993.
Newsom, John. *The Education of Girls*. London: Faber and Faber, 1948.
Ollerenshaw, Kathleen. *Education for Girls*. London: Faber and Faber, 1961.
Samuel, Raphael. *The Lost World of British Communism*. London: Verso, 2006.
Stanley, Julia. *Marks on the Memory: experiencing school*. Milton Keynes: Open University Press, 1989.
Wolpe, Annmarie. *Within School Walls: The Role of Discipline, Sexuality and the Curriculum*. London: Routledge, 1988.

SECONDARY SOURCES

Andrews, Kehinde. "The Black Studies Movement in Britain: Becoming an Institution not Institutionalised." In *Dismantling Race in Higher Education: Racism, Whiteness and Decolonising the Academy*, edited by Jason Arday and Heidi Safia Mirza, 271-288. Cham: Palgrave Macmillan, 2018.
Attar, Dena. *Wasting Girls' Time: the history and politics of home economics*. London: Virago, 1990.
Bird, Elizabeth. "The academic arm of the Women's Liberation Movement Women's Studies 1969-1999 in North American and the United Kingdom," *Women's Studies International Forum*, 25, no. 10 (2002): 139-148.
Bird, Elizabeth. "The sexual politics of introducing women's studies: memories and reflections from North America and the United Kingdom," *Gender and Education*, 16 no. 1, (2004): 51-63.
Burke, Penny Jane. "Re/Imagining Higher Education Pedagogies: Gender, Emotion and Difference," *Teaching in Higher Education*, 20, no. 4 (2015): 388-401.
Coate, Kelly. "The History of Women's Studies as an Academic Subject Area in Higher Education in the UK: 1970-1995." PhD thesis, University of London, 1999.
Cohen, Michèle. "A Little Learning? The Curriculum and the Construction of Gender in the Long Eighteenth Century," *Journal for British Eighteenth Century Studies*, no. 29 (2006): 321-335.
Coote, Anna and Beatrix Campbell, Beatrix. *Sweet Freedom: The Struggle for Women' Liberation*. Oxford: Basil Blackwell, 1982.
Davis, Angela. "'Oh no, nothing, we didn't learn anything': sex education and the preparation of girls for motherhood, c. 1930-1970,'" *History of Education*, 37, no. 5 (2008): 661-677.
Dyhouse, Carol. *Girls Growing Up In Victorian and Edwardian England*. London: Routledge, Kegan and Paul, 1981.
Fletcher, Sheila. *Women First: The Female Tradition in English Physical Education, 1880-1980*. London: Continuum, 1984.
Gavron, Jeremy. *A Woman on the Edge of Time*. London: Scribe, 2015.
Gorham, Deborah. "Victorian reform as a family business: the Hill family." In *The Victorian Family*, edited by Anthony S. Wohl, 119-47. London: Croom Helm, 1978.

Griffin, Gabriele. "The 'Ins' and 'Outs' of Women's/ Gender studies: a response to reports of its demise in 2008', *Women's History Review*, 18, no. 3 (2009): 485-496.

Hollis, Patricia. *Ladies Elect*. Oxford: Clarendon Press, 1989.

Humm, Maggie. *Feminisms: a reader*. London: Routledge, 1992.

Hunt, Felicity. *Gender & Policy in English Education 1902–1944*. London: Harvester Wheatsheaf, 1991.

Hurt, John. "Drill, discipline and the elementary school ethos." In *Popular Education and Socialisation in the Nineteenth Century*, edited by Phillip McCann, 167-9. London: Methuen and Company, 1977.

Jacobs, Andrea and Goodman, Joyce. "Music in the 'Common' Life of the School: Towards an Aesthetic Education for All in English Girls' Secondary Schools in the Interwar Period," *History of Education*, 35, no. 6 (2006): 669-687.

Kean, Hilda. *Challenging the State? The Socialist and Feminist Educational Experience, 1900-1930*. London: Falmer Press, 1990.

Kirkup, Gill and Whitelegg, Elizabeth. "The legacy and impact of Open University women's/ gender studies: 30 years on," *Gender and Education*, 25, no. 1 (2013): 6-22.

Martin, Jane. *Women and the Politics of Schooling in Victorian and Edwardian England*. Leicester: Leicester University Press, 1999.

Mendick, Heather. *Masculinities in Mathematics*. London: McGraw-Hill, 2006.

Paechter, Carrie. *Changing School Subjects: power, gender and curriculum*. Buckingham: Open University Press, 2000.

Peters, Michael Andrew. "Why Is My Curriculum White? A Brief Genealogy of Resistance." In *Dismantling Race in Higher Education: Racism, Whiteness and Decolonising the Academy* edited by Jason Arday and Heidi Safia Mirza, 253-270. Cham: Palgrave Macmillan, 2018.

Riley, Denise. *War in the Nursery*. London: Virago, 1983.

Roach, John, *Public Examinations in England 1850-1900*. Cambridge: Cambridge University Press, 1971.

Scraton, Sheila. *Shaping Up To Womanhood: Gender and Girls' Physical Education*. Buckingham: Open University Press, 1992.

Spender, Dale. *Man Made Language*. London: Routledge and Kegan Paul, 1980.

Steedman, Hilary. "Defining institutions: the endowed grammar schools and the systematisation of English secondary education." In *The Rise of the Modern Educational System: Structural Change and Social Reproduction 1870-1920*, edited by Detlef K. Müller, Fritz Ringer and Brian Simon, 111-134. Cambridge: Cambridge University Press, 1989.

Summerfield, Penny. "Cultural Reproduction in the Education of Girls: a Study of Girls' Secondary Schooling in Two Lancashire Towns, 1900-50." In *Lessons for Life. The Schooling of Girls and Women 1850–1950*, edited by Felicity Hunt, 149-170. Oxford: Basil Blackwell, 1987.

Thom, Deborah. "Better a teacher than a hairdresser? 'A mad passion for equality' or, keeping Molly and Betty down." In *Lessons for Life. The Schooling of Girls and Women 1850–1950*, edited by Felicity Hunt, 124-146. Oxford: Basil Blackwell, 1987.

Vlaeminke, Meriel. *The English Higher Grade Schools: a lost opportunity*. London: Woburn Press, 1999.

Weiner, Gaby. *Feminisms in Education*. Buckingham: Open University Press, 1994.

Williams, Raymond. *The Long Revolution*. Letchworth: Broadview Press, 2001.

CHAPTER 7

Pupils

> *Started school again. Good to see all the old mugs again. New secretary. Good face and figure. Old Girl. Miss Haigh started at once nagging "<u>Do</u> be <u>sensible</u>," her warcry. School dinners murder as usual and there were a lot of dirty remarks flying about them! M. and I nearly died in physics at Red Nose antics! We got our experiment right and exchanged gossip with everyone. Everyone howled at my new year resolutions! Miss Wynne very bright and cheery! (!) Got a good seat in form room.*
> —Margaret Forster, *Diary of An Ordinary Girl* (London: Chatto & Windus, 2017), 4

My epigraph is the diary entry of future novelist and biographer Margaret Forster for the day she went back to school after the Christmas holidays. A period piece used to evoke the approach this chapter adopts. Margaret's version of a working-class childhood was not particularly unusual save for the fact that she passed the eleven-plus and was educated in a grammar school. In common with most young girls, she chronicles the work she did around the home. The catalogue of her activities the morning her mother returned after a short break captures the density and texture of everyday life. 'Got up at 7.30 & had all the housework done by 9.30. Started baking at 10 and made a chocolate cake, some buns & scones (fairly successfully!) Also did flowers, scrubbed floors, iced cakes & generally got everything in apple pie order.'[1] Pupils have seldom had a voice in history. Here the voices of those for whom compulsory schooling was intended take their place as part of the essential fabric of our educational landscape.

The bulk of the narrative draws upon an exhaustive study of over 100 autobiographies and memoirs. A close and careful reading of these life histories produced a sample of 50 published books of 100 or more pages. Elite boarding

---

[1] Margaret Forster, *Diary of An Ordinary Girl* (London: Chatto & Windus, 2017), 102.

school voices have tended to dominate histories of English schooling; therefore, most of my chosen texts (42) convey the experiences of pupils in maintained schools who constituted the biggest group of children. Beyond making pupil voices heard, my purpose is to write about 'typical' schooldays in contexts, offering a practical example of how to bring to life what a teenage participant in Julia Stanley's study called the 'worm's eye view.'[2] Individually and collectively, the accounts show the ways in which schools became an important factor in reinforcing lessons in gender relations and patterns of authority between men and women. The lives include those of academics, actors, footballers, film and television producers, musicians, singer-songwriters, reality-television personalities, politicians, trade unionists and writers.

For the historian, autobiography has the merit of being the direct, personal testimony of the person concerned and may bring together several strands of thought relating to one's home background, to one's sex, to other pupils and to the curriculum. English children's author Leila Berg offers a good example. Her 1998 autobiography *Flickerbook* uses a series of sequential word-pictures, one after the other. 'Today we had a photograph. We had to come very clean, in our best clothes. Some girls had white pinnies, but I didn't. White pinnies are Christian. Mammy made me a pale blue one, and a mauve one. I sat on the ground in the front row and Miss Reilly leaned the notice against me. It said, "Grecian Street School, Class 6". That's the first class.'[3] In common with *Flickerbook*, this chapter uses slices of personal accounts, and quotes are given verbatim in a r*eportage* form, to provide a v*ersion* of the past to complement the policy histories in previous chapters.

Throughout the chapter, the main unit of analysis is cohort or generation, based on year of birth. German sociologist Karl Mannheim offers a theory first published in 1927, showing generations as age cohorts shaped by their experience of influential public events in their youth. Different historical periods have mutually agreed-upon, perceptions of the world that reflect the codes of an established generational culture. This is analogous to Raymond Williams's concept of 'structures of feeling' which he defined as being 'the culture of a period' to signify unconscious or spontaneous feelings of 'lived experience' in reciprocal action with the cognitive, or reflexive, dimension and in the process reproducing identity and culture. This is important because it allows for the placing of memory in a wider political and cultural milieu.[4]

The five age cohorts start with the first generation to experience universal basic education. It includes pioneering women like Hannah Mitchell, a working-class suffragette, and Edith Morley, believed to be the first woman awarded the title of professor at a British university-level institution. Four of this cohort went

---

[2] Julia Stanley, *Marks on the Memory: Experiencing School* (Buckingham: Open University Press, 1989).

[3] Leila Berg, *Flickerbook* (London: Granta, 1998), 17.

[4] Karl Mannheim, "The problem of generations," in *Studying aging and social change*, ed. Melissa Hardy (London: Sage Publications, 1997), 22–65; Raymond Williams, *The Long Revolution* (Letchworth: Broadview Press, 2001).

Text Box 7.1 Life writers by cohort or generation

Cohort 1 Born < 1900	Cohort II 1900–1918	Cohort III 1919–1944	Cohort IV 1945–1964	Cohort V 1965–1985
Vera Brittain Born 1893	Grace Foakes Born 1901	Valerie Avery Born 1940	Viv Albertine Born 1954	Andrea Ashworth Born 1969
Charlie Chaplin Born 1889	Cecil Rolph Hewitt Born 1901	Nina Bawden Born 1925	Danny Baker Born 1957	Victoria Beckham Born 1974
Katharine Chorley Born 1897	Laurie Lee Born 1914	Trevor Baylis Born 1937	Paul Dash Born 1946	Karren Brady Born 1969
Richard Church Born 1893	Margaret McCarthy Born 1907	Maureen Duffy Born 1933	David Essex Born 1947	Russell Brand Born 1976
Matthew Davenport Hill Born 1872	Margaret Powell Born 1907	Tony Garnett Born 1936	Alan Johnson Born 1950	Andrew Collins Born 1965
Hannah Mitchell Born 1871	Angela Rodaway Born 1918	Roy Hattersley Born 1932	Annette Kuhn Born 1945	John-Paul Flintoff Born 1972
Edith Morley Born 1875	Robert Roberts Born 1905	Louis Heren Born 1919	Robert Lindsay Born 1949	Jade Goody Born 1981
Harry Patch Born 1898	Alfred Rowse Born 1906	Evelyn Haythorne Born 1927	Hilary Mantel Born 1952	Stephen Gerrard Born 1980
Walter Southgate Born 1890	Stephen Spender Born 1909	Michael Parkinson Born 1935	Janet Street-Porter Born 1946	Lynsey Hanley Born 1976
Flora Thompson Born 1876	Dorothy Scannell Born 1911	Katharine Whitehorn Born 1928	Ann Widdecombe Born 1947	Ledley King Born 1980

to private schools (Brittain, Chorley, Hill and Morley). Richard Church won a scholarship to art school. His father was a sorter for the Post Office, his mother an elementary teacher, but she died when he was a youth and his father became increasingly abusive so he left school and started evening classes to prepare for the boy clerks' examination, which he passed in 1909.

War and the economic problems of the Depression influenced the youth of birth cohorts II and III. Growing up in an impoverished South Yorkshire mining village in the 1930s, Evelyn Haythorne remembered her mother saying of an old lady who had no family to look after her and was taken into the workhouse, 'Poor old sod, they'll suck the soul out of her.'[5] Eight of the 20 (40 per cent) had opportunities to share in education after the age of 14 (from 1918).

---

[5] Evelyn Haythorne, *On Earth To Make the Numbers Up* (Castleford: Yorkshire Arts Circus, 1991), 30.

In chronological order, Cecil Rolph Hewitt, Laurie Lee and Louis Heren attended central schools. Angela Rodaway, Alfred Rowse, Nina Bawden, Maureen Duffy and Roy Hattersley were scholarship winners, and all except Rodaway went from municipal secondary school to university.

Cohort IV is the baby boom generation, beneficiaries of the post-war welfare state and free secondary education for all. Danny Baker, Paul Dash, David Essex and Robert Lindsay attended single-sex secondary modern schools. Annette Kuhn, Hilary Mantel and Janet Street-Porter sat and passed the 11-plus, as did Alan Johnson. Ann Widdecombe failed. Australian-born former guitarist for the English punk group *The Slits*, Viv Albertine, went to a north London comprehensive school. Excluding Albertine and Dash, who is a Barbados-born artist, the rest were born in England. Members of Cohort V grew up after comprehensive secondary education became national policy. Karren Brady is the only person who went to private school, the rest attended comprehensive schools. The grandparents of former Tottenham footballer Ledley King belonged to the Windrush generation of people arriving in the UK between 1948 and 1971. Caribbean migrants who travelled to Britain to help fill labour shortages in the post-war years.

The decline of older manufacturing industries led to rising rates of unemployment among young men in the 1980s. This, combined with a trend to increasing female employment, undermined the sexual division of labour in which men worked for a 'family wage,' while women managed the home and reared the children. In Manchester, Andrea Ashworth started truanting. Her grandmother urged her not to, and she stopped. Others in her peer group did drop out despite the raising of the school-leaving age to 16 (in 1972). Crime reduced the number of boys, pregnancy the number of girls. 'Getting O levels, everyone agreed, was a bit poncy but fair enough if you had it in you; plodding on after that was a sheer waste of time.'[6] As younger members of Cohort V moved through primary school into their secondary education, the impact of authoritarian populism and the New Right, of neo-liberal policies and the deregulation of capital, formed the background to changes in education. The 1988 Education Act introduced a national curriculum meaning schools were compelled to provide both sexes with core content and an increasing proportion of girls chose not to leave school early. In 1992 for the first time in the UK, more young women than young men entered university.

Although it is only possible to draw on a few accounts in detail, they all inform the argument. Writers address themes that, by inference, they regard as of significance: examinations, teachers and punishment, the curriculum, uniform and friends. Some remember school as dull and monotonous. In the words of former Liverpool footballer Stephen Gerrard: 'My journey through the Merseyside school system was straightforward and undistinguished. I looked on schools as fantastic playing fields with boring buildings attached.'[7]

---

[6] Andrea Ashworth, *Once In A House of Fire* (London: Picador, 1998), 262.
[7] Stephen Gerrard, *Gerrard: My Autobiography* (London: Bantam Press, 2006), 28.

We start with some sequential word-pictures to manifest the background characteristics of this pupil group. The object is to illuminate individual lives and show that time, space and place matter. I am not presenting these voices as somehow representative of a specific period; they are here to bring to life the experience of policies and practices, showing how boys and girls from each cohort learned the lessons of gender and power.

Description: Contexts and Biographies

Hannah Mitchell's early years on a remote Derbyshire farm during the 1870s were blighted by having to do the work of the home, and her only formal education was two weeks at elementary school.[8] Labourer's daughter Flora Thompson grew up in rural Oxfordshire where most village girls had little choice but to go into domestic service, though boys were not encouraged out into the world in quite the same way. As soon as the school-leaving age allowed a girl 'was made to feel herself one too many in the overcrowded home; while her brothers, when they left school and began to bring home a few shillings were treated with a new consideration and made much of.'[9]

Vera Brittain, Katharine Chorley and Edith Morley provide evidence of middle-class girlhoods in late Victorian and Edwardian England. Vera began her education at home, but the family relocated so she and her brother might attend 'good' local day schools. An anecdote records the stigma attached to being seen talking to her brother outside his school. 'At tea-time a heavy and to me inexplicable atmosphere of disapproval hung over the table; shortly afterwards the storm exploded, and I was severely reprimanded for my naughtiness in thus publicly conversing with Edward's companions.'[10] At boarding school, Vera's passion for learning surprised and pleased the other girls. 'Many of them were fashionable young women to whom universities represented a quite unnecessary prolongation of useless and distasteful studies, and they looked upon my efforts to reach the top of a form, and my naïve anxiety to remain there, as satisfactorily exonerating them from the troublesome endeavour to win that position for themselves.'[11]

Morley shared happy memories of a much loved nurse, annual seaside holidays and trips to the theatre, and has quite a lot to say about the nature of gender and femininity. Her account makes it clear that she found it hard to bear the stigma of having to wear a 'thick woollen veil' to protect her complexion and to adhere to a ban on sliding down bannisters and doing gymnastics. She describes her love of swimming and her feelings of indignation when she overheard her brother being told that only girls cheated at games or cried when they were hurt. Her father, a surgeon-dentist, wanted her to receive home schooling but

---

[8] Hannah Mitchell, *The Hard Way Up* (London: Virago, 1977), 52–3.
[9] Flora Thompson, *Lark Rise to Candleford* (London: Penguin, 1973), 155.
[10] Vera Brittain, *Testament to Youth* (London: Virago, 1986), 28.
[11] Op cit, 33.

yielded to her desire to go to school. This meant a local kindergarten and a select private school, to prevent social mixing with 'tradesmen's daughters.'[12]

The daughter of an engineer who went on to become a Conservative MP, Katharine Chorley objected to an education designed to groom her for the marriage market. She looks back on a scene of early twentieth century English life in a large house with servants in the prosperous suburb of Alderley Edge, near Manchester. Daily the men travelled into work on commuter trains leaving the women to play their part in the social ritual of noblesse oblige. 'My schooling should lead up to a few years of life at home before, if all went well, I got suitably married, my days being filled by golf, and tennis with other social activities, some philanthropy—that was important—and some reading and perhaps a little art.' Her parents had an aversion to girls' high schools due to the potential for contact with people 'whose suitability they would not be able to control.' So, they chose a boarding school in Folkestone for their daughter where an anti-suffragist headmistress had evolved an educational model guaranteed to produce socially suitable female material. That is, high-minded and cultured homemakers.[13]

Katharine Whitehorn's father was a housemaster at various public schools; her mother came from a family of Christian Socialists. They already had a son and longed for a daughter. Consequently, Katharine felt she 'was born luckier in one respect than about half the world's female babies, who are greeted as an unfortunate second-best.' It never occurred to her parents to give her a worse education than her brother, and only later did she realise they were ahead of their time. 'My aunt Margaret, ten years younger than my mother, went to Cambridge in the thirties and didn't think it odd, because her own aunts had gone before the First World War.'[14] In contrast, Ann Widdecombe's parents did differentiate between the educational needs of sons and daughters. Whereas her brother attended private schools, she was expected to pass the 11-plus examination and 'go through grammar school.'[15] Things did not turn out that way. Ann failed and her parents used their wealth to bypass the local secondary modern. What happened to those from Cohorts I and II with fewer material resources in the era before state welfare?

Margaret Powell grew up in Hove, on the Sussex coast, the second child of a family of seven. Her father was a painter and decorator, and her mother worked as a cleaner. As a schoolgirl, she would give her siblings their breakfast, take the two youngest to nursery, get the dinner on and do the washing up at midday (there were no school meals), collect the children from nursery, take them home, do the housework and make the beds. Although she won a scholarship, Margaret left school to become a wage earner. She wanted to become a teacher, but when her parents found out there was no pay until she turned 18

[12] Edith Morley, *Before and After* (Reading: Two Rivers Press, 2016), 9.
[13] Katharine Chorley, *Manchester Made Them* (London: Faber and Faber Ltd, 1950), 186–7.
[14] Katharine Whitehorn, *Selective Memory* (London: Virago, 2007), 11.
[15] Ann Widdecombe, *Strictly Ann* (London: Orion Publishing, 2014), 36.

and that they would have to keep her and buy her books and clothes, they just couldn't do it. 'I never used to feel that I was suffering in any sense from ill-usage. It was just the thing. When you were the eldest girl in a working-class family, it was expected of you.'[16]

Hilary Mantel shows how the behaviour of one generation tended to become the blueprint for the next. Teachers denied her mother the chance to compete for a scholarship, but it didn't matter she told her daughter, since her parents wouldn't have let her go to secondary school. It would have been just as it was for her father, who pounded the cobbled streets of his mill town *circa* 1905, shouting, 'I've passed, I've passed. But there was no money for uniform; anyway, it just wasn't what you did, go to the grammar school. You accepted your place in life.'[17] Hilary was not the only person to feel grief. The teacher who tricked her mother into believing she was too old to sit for the scholarship angered future trade unionist and politician Margaret McCarthy who longed to attend secondary school but had to make a swift start at the local textile mill as soon as the law allowed. The barriers in the way of women politicised her. 'I compelled myself harder and further than the boys to prove to these indifferent creatures that I myself and my sex in general were as good as, and if need be better than, they in creative capacity and ability, endurance and persistence.'[18]

The chance of winning a scholarship was one in 400 at Walter Southgate's elementary school. The youngest child of a quill pen maker, he liked school and was never late nor absent but found it hard to persuade his teacher to enter him for the London County Council's Merit Certificate. Despite working a 40-hour week as a milk boy and no quiet space to do his homework, he secured distinctions in geography, history, drawing and English composition. Armed with this qualification, the future political activist and co-founder of the National Museum of Labour History began work as a clerk.[19] A girl in Dorothy Scannell's class was less fortunate. Caught swinging on the blackboard, her punishment was to be denied the chance to compete for a scholarship.[20]

Alone of the boys in the Cornish community he was part of, historian Alfred Rowse won a scholarship. First impressions of secondary school were of smells: the odour of carbolic soap, new paper, pencils, rubbers and exercise books. Unlike at elementary school, he had his own desk and text books courtesy of the local education authority, and there was 'space: empty classrooms unused, wide corridors, a staircase which we thought magnificent, an upper story with windows giving on to the football field and looking out across to the bay.'[21] He made friends among the girls who were his competitors for the top spot since they worked harder, and did their homework. On the other hand, Stephen

---

[16] Margaret Powell, *Below Stairs* (London: Pan Books, 2011), 6.
[17] Hilary Mantel, *Giving Up the Ghost* (London: Fourth Estate, 2013), 50.
[18] Margaret McCarthy, *Generation in Revolt* (London: William Heinemann, 1953), 42.
[19] Walter Southgate, *That's The Way It Was: A Working-Class Autobiography 1890-1950* (Surrey: New Clarion Books, 1982), 53.
[20] Dorothy Scannell, *Mother Knew Best: Memoir of a London Girlhood* (New York: Pantheon Book, 1974), 77.
[21] Alfred L. Rowse, *A Cornish Childhood* (Truro: Dyllansow Truran, 1998), 167.

Spender had miserable memories of ranking by ability at Gresham's boarding school in Norfolk. In 1918, he chose to follow his elder brother there but said sibling excelled to the same extent as he failed. A general knowledge exam sat by the entire school was the nadir of his Gresham career. 'At the top of a chart denoting the results there came the name of Spender Major with 90 per cent correct answers, at the bottom was Spender Minor with 0.5 per cent.'[22]

Laurie Lee was one of eight siblings growing up in a fatherless household in the 1920s. He described his two-room Cotswolds village school in his childhood memoir, *To Cider with Rosie*. Here is part of his commentary on the ranking and grading of pupils.

> My brother Jack, who was with me in the Infants, was too clever to stay there long. Indeed he was so bright he made us uncomfortable, and we were all of us glad to get rid of him. Sitting pale in his pinafore, gravely studying, commanding the teacher to bring him fresh books, or to sharpen his pencils, or to make less noise, he was an Infant Freak from the start. So he was promoted to the Big Room with unprecedented promptness, given a desk and a dozen atlases to sit on, from which he continued to bully the teachers.[23]

One pupil was goaded mercilessly. Spadge Hopkins was nearly 14, 'thick-legged, red-fisted, bursting with flesh, designed for the great out-doors… physically out of scale—at least so far as our school was concerned. The sight of him squeezed into his tiny desk was worse than a bullock in ballet-shoes.' Usually, he struggled with his schoolwork, and the teacher took pleasure in making him read out loud or asking him sudden unintelligible questions in front of the class. One day he snapped, lifted the teacher on top of the store cupboard and walked out. He never came back.[24]

In London's East End, shopkeeper's son Louis Heren passed the examination to go to central school, St George's in the East. He counted himself lucky. His English teacher, a woman who loved Shakespeare and Wordsworth, fired his imagination. The maths teacher politicised him. 'About once a week he would cut a lesson short and talk about economics and comment on the Depression and unemployment. I can't remember him talking about communism as such, or party politics, but that was unnecessary. His talks amounted to an indictment against the capitalist system, and most of us were willing converts.'[25] Other teachers took them on trips to the zoo and the People's Palace at Mile End after it re-opened in 1936 and in an era when it was one of London's top entertainment venues. Louis thought sport betrayed the English social system more than accents. 'After all, we did not know that we spoke cockney. For us it was the King's English. But the working class played soccer although we did not know it by that name. It was simply football.'[26]

---

[22] Stephen Spender, *World Within World* (New York: St Martin's Press, 1994), 327.
[23] Laurie Lee, *Cider With Rosie* (Harmondsworth: Penguin, 1973), 47–8.
[24] Op cit, 50–1.
[25] Louis Heren, *Growing Up Poor in London* (London: Orion Books, 1973), 74.
[26] Op cit, 60–61.

Evelyn Haythorne was less fortunate. She won a place at a grammar school that restricted the supply of uniform to one retailer through an exclusive contract making it very expensive. It saddened her father, but her mother refused to accept charity.

> If you think I'm going begging to give her high falutin ways you're wrong and anyway what sort of life do you think she'd have at her posh school if they knew we'd had to beg for her to get there? No! It's not as though it was one of the lads that had passed. She's a lass and she'd no sooner get through school than she'd be married; then where's her education gone, down the bloody washtub with the mucky nappies.[27]

Evelyn never contemplated leaving elementary school, but she was demotivated and resentful, and misbehaved in housewifery lessons. She clearly saw herself as a classed and gendered member of an unequal society. 'I couldn't help but feel that if I had been a boy a little more effort would have been made.' Turning 14 in wartime, she got what was normally a boy's job loading lorries and railway wagons.[28]

The next section shows how the early twentieth century reproduced discrimination characteristic of Victorian schooling. Academic competition did not take place on a level playing field and the trappings of the old elementary schools lived on in some 1950s secondary moderns.

INSIDE SCHOOLS AND CLASSROOMS

Victorian and Edwardian school architecture embodied normative understandings of the relation between gender, class and schooling. A wall segregating boys and girls, and rules against approaching the frontier divided mixed elementary school playgrounds. Urban elementary schools usually had two entrances with GIRLS AND INFANTS over one doorway, BOYS over the other. In the country, a curtain to accommodate two classes could divide schoolrooms. Oldest children could be 14 after 1918; a few 11-year-olds might leave to take up secondary school scholarships, and some schools streamed senior classes by age and graded 'ability' into sub-groups of standards.

Grace Foakes was a Londoner who sat down in her 70s to write her memoirs. Her elementary school was in a narrow street opposite a soap factory and surrounded on three sides by high tenement buildings.[29] The building had two storeys with an attic above, where the caretaker lived. The girls' department was on the upper floor. The infants' school, which was on the ground floor, accepted toddlers from the age of two-and-a-half, not always fully toilet trained. Teacher or elder sister, if they had one in the school, cleaned up after any accidents. Cecil Hewitt was first a policeman and then a writer using the pseud-

---

[27] Evelyn Haythorne, *On Earth To Make The Numbers Up*, 52.
[28] Ibid.
[29] Grace Foakes, *Four Places for Fourpence* (London: Virago, 2011), 133.

onym C.H. Rolph. He recalled seeing a child having their legs sponged down on his first day at school and asking the teacher why she was crying. It turned out, it was a little boy, 'Not a little girl; and he had had an accident.'[30] It was a long time before he learned that little boys wore dresses not because their mothers were grieving that they hadn't turned out to be girls, but because no one had yet invented disposable nappies.

Fifty years on, four-year-old Viv Albertine was too scared to ask to be excused to go to the lavatory during class. 'The choice between raising my hand and my voice whilst the teacher was talking or quietly soiling myself was not an easy one, but I chose the option I could bear. I was such a baby that I didn't think anyone would notice.'[31] Hilary Mantel's family shared an outside toilet at home, 'but excuse me, *this*? I had to go to what was called "the babies' lavatory", which was half-size. The trouble with the babies was, they were so very approximate in their arrangements; they didn't know the lavatory bowl from the floor.' Bladder control is her first lesson for life at infant school.[32]

Harry Patch grew up in Somerset where he attended a mixed Anglican elementary school. The boys sat in one block of desks, the girls in another. 'As well as learning the three Rs, there was woodwork and clay modelling for the boys while the girls did housewifery.'[33] When it suited, the headmaster marched the children to his allotment. In the name of science, they would turn over and weed his garden, besides planting vegetables. In History, they learned about such dead white Englishmen as Admiral Horatio Nelson, the Duke of Wellington and Robert Scott of the Antarctic.

The pupils at Robert Roberts's Salford elementary school loved it when the inspectors called, although the staff were frightened. Physical punishments stopped for the duration of the inspection, and children felt that in school at least, they were the ones who mattered. Debates were part of a progressive new regime intended to increase verbal flow and self-assurance, which was what the inspectors were after. 'Children should go to school until they are 15' was the first motion, and Roberts's teacher dragooned a terrified girl to make the opposing case. 'Her words were few but explosive. "I think," she said, "we should gerrout to work at fourteen and fetch some money in for us parents." Then she stepped off the box to a thunderclap of applause, cheering and clog-stamping that rocked the school.'[34]

Teachers developed an elaborate system of reward and punishment to achieve control. Grace Foakes thoroughly understood the euphemism 'traditional discipline.' At her school, it meant slapping and caning. Grace did not remember there ever being an open day, or anything like a parents-teacher association. Parents (usually mothers) were only consulted if a school nurse said their child had head lice.

---

[30] C.H. Rolph, *London Particulars* (Oxford: Oxford University Press, 1980), 26.

[31] Viv Albertine, *Clothes, Clothes, Clothes, Music, Music, Music, Boys, Boys, Boys* (London: Faber & Faber, 2016), 26.

[32] Hilary Mantel, *Giving Up The Ghost*, 64.

[33] Harry Patch, *The Last Fighting Tommy* (London: Bloomsbury, 2014), 29.

[34] Robert Roberts, *A Ragged Schooling* (Manchester: Manchester University Press, 1976), 172.

If the head had vermin, then you were given a card which warned that if this was not clean by the nurse's next visit you would be sent to the cleansing station, where all your hair was cut very short. This was a disgrace, for all who saw you with your hair cut this way knew you were dirty and shamed you until your hair grew long again.[35]

A shortage of money because her father was out of work brought suffering at higher grade school. 'One day at Assembly, the Headmaster asked who needed a dinner ticket. Imagine my dismay when I saw I was the only person to put up a hand. I had to walk to the front of the whole school to receive this ticket, which enabled me to have dinner at a centre for poor children.' Grace's acute sense of shame about free food dampened her hunger, and she walked the streets rather than collect the meal. Bullied for her oversized school uniform (to allow room for growth) and dubbed 'Polly Long Frock,' she failed her exams and begged to return to her old elementary school after a teacher called her a 'big-eyed goon.'[36]

In the 1880s, local politician Helen Taylor opposed physical punishment and criticised elite male policy-makers 'who had had punishment in their own youth, and intend now to give it to the young, declaring that they had it themselves and it did them much good.'[37] Eton used a wooden birching block, and new boy Matthew Davenport Hill never forgot being made to hold a fellow pupil's shirt up after the offender took his trousers and underwear down for a thrashing.[38] Girls' punishment may have been less severe. Dorothy Scannell thought her teachers were stern and strict, but the men who taught the boys were harsh. She saw one stamp on a boy's foot in temper. The boy was barefoot, 'not an uncommon sight, even in winter.'[39]

Richard Church saw one terrified boy throw an inkpot at the headmaster as he waited for a beating. As the culprit was carried face downwards out of the hall, Richard looked along the queue. One boy wet himself; the rest stood there, toes to the white line in front of the head's desk awaiting his return.

> Even the spot of ink on his trousers, and another on one of the fawn spats, did not compromise his dignity. His eyes behind the pince-nez gleamed, and his large mouth was set firmly. Picking up the cane from the desk where he had dropped it, he replaced it in the chest *and closed the lid*! Turning, still in slow motion, he faced us, looking at each boy individually. Then the oracle spoke. "Let that be a lesson to all of you," he said. "Dismiss!"[40]

---

[35] Grace Foakes, *Four Meals for Fourpence*, 140.
[36] Op cit, 145.
[37] Mill-Taylor Special Collection, Newscuttings, 28 November 1877.
[38] Matthew Davenport-Hill, *Eton and Elsewhere* (London: John Murray, 1928), 38–9.
[39] Dorothy Scannell, *Mother Knew Best*, 74.
[40] Richard Church, *Over the Bridge* (London: The Reprint Society, 1956), 151.

Church's rebel did not reappear. Rumours circulated. People said inspectors had been to see his parents. There were stories of dreadful punishments, nakedness and flogging. Some said he had gone to prison and that his father had lost his job at the insistence of the police. Quickly, they forgot him.

Known all over the world for his on-screen character 'the tramp,' film icon Charlie Chaplin is acknowledged as one of the great comic creators of the twentieth century. But his early years were blighted by domestic crises, poverty and hardship. Twice his mother took the decision to enter her and her two sons into the workhouse where female paupers bathed Charlie: 'having to submit to the ignominy of a young girl of fourteen manipulating a facecloth all over my person was my first conscious embarrassment.'[41] Friday floggings in the gymnasium were traumatic events when the boys marched in and lined up forming three sides of a square.

> On the right and in front of the desk was an easel with wrist-straps dangling, and from the frame a birch hung ominously. For minor offences, a boy was laid across the long desk, face downwards, feet strapped and held by a sergeant, then another sergeant pulled the boy's shirt out of his trousers and over his head, then pulled his trousers tight. Captain Hindrum, a retired Navy man weighing about two hundred pounds, with one hand behind him, the other holding a cane as thick as a man's thumb and about four feet long, stood poised measuring it across the boy's bottom. The spectacle was terrifying and invariably a boy would fall out of rank in a faint.[42]

On Thursdays, a bugle sounded in the playground and the boys stood to attention to hear the punishment rota announced through a megaphone. One day, Charlie heard his name called for setting fire to the lavatory. Nervous, he admitted guilt, and received three strokes. His brother, who witnessed it, wept with rage.

Sometimes the hitting of a child could trigger protest. The first nation-wide children's strike occurred during 1889, against a background of widespread industrial unrest. In 1911, there were strikes at elementary schools in various parts of the country, the pupils demanding an extra half-day holiday a week and the abolition of caning, again at a time of labour upheaval. A *Daily Graphic* cartoonist depicted a crowd of boys holding aloft homemade banners saying DOWN WITH SKOOL. Alfred Rowse described what happened when boys at his Cornish elementary school refused to obey a male teacher who was over fond of caning. Social relations deteriorated when the teacher started punching them, some hit him back and school closed early. As the teacher ran home, 'he was pelted with turfs and stones and cut about the face.'[43]

Resistance comes in many forms. Grace Foakes loved it when she was sent to a housewifery centre in the 1900s (see Fig. 7.1) but not for the reasons the

---

[41] Charlie Chaplin, *Charlie Chaplin: My Autobiography* (London: Penguin, 2003), 29.
[42] Op cit, 30.
[43] Alfred Rowse, *A Cornish Childhood*, 112.

Fig. 7.1 Denmark Hill School housewifery class, 1908. From the London Picture Archive. (Copyright London Metropolitan Archive, 178925)

authorities might have wished. With only one teacher in charge, she and her classmates were quick to take advantage when she went to inspect some other part of the house where the lessons took place. 'We jumped on the bed, threw pillows, drowned the doll and swept dirt under the mats. This was the highlight of the week, the one lesson that we never minded going to.'[44] Viv Albertine is another 'bad' girl who mucks about in class, plays truant and does so little homework her teachers refuse to enter her for 'O' levels. The school expels her when she admits to having taken drugs. 'My mother goes up to the school and insists that the headmaster put it in writing that I've smoked hash

---

[44] Foakes, *Four Meals for Fourpence*, 139–40.

once, and that's why he's expelling me. He doesn't want to do that so I'm allowed to stay.'[45]

Most school playgrounds were congested. Walter Southgate says boys stood like statues when the whistle blew. At a second blast, they 'fell into pre-ordered lines and marched upstairs.'[46] Louis Heren befriended the son of the school caretaker and went to play at his house after tea. 'The asphalt playgrounds were deserted. Being able to play in an area of about 300 by 200 feet without a mob of kids was sheer heaven. I suppose it was my first experience of space and at times, we would run about like young puppies.'[47] Nina Bawden recalls a bully who pushed her to the ground, grabbed bunches of her hair and thudded her head up and down on the concrete. 'Pride prevented complaint, or even explanation, but one morning at break, when we had drunk our milk, I cracked the neck of my empty bottle on the step and threatened to jab it into her hateful piggy face.'[48]

In an era of co-education, the future Labour MP Alan Johnson describes the gender play at his 1950s inner-city primary school, 'a thick painted red line separated the boys from the girls. Flick Cards was for the boys. The girls' sporting seasons consisted of skipping in the winter and in the summer the game of Two Balls, which involved bouncing rubber balls off a wall with a level of skill far greater than was required for anything the boys attempted.'[49] Johnson's contemporary, Hilary Mantel, shuns girl's toys because she wants to be a boy. She is at ease with male attributes but forced to acknowledge her female status. Therefore, boys become what she has to fight at school. Her grandfather teaches her how. 'If you can't join them, beat them,' she says. 'Tears spring from the eyes of the big boy. He reels, clutching his diaphragm, away from the railings. "Oh Miss, she hit me, she hit me!" I am amazed: less by my performance, than by his; his alarming wails, his bawls.'[50]

Twenty years later, the future singer and designer Victoria Beckham dreaded break time. 'At least in class, even if no one wanted to sit next to me, I could get on with my work. But out in the playground with everyone else rushing around, it was like hell.'[51] During summer holidays, the sight of Back to School posters made her feel sick. Like Beckham, the upcoming comedian and writer Russell Brand was a social outcast. Unlike Beckham, this was not because of his pristine uniform, the family Rolls Royce, telling tales on other teenagers or having spots. No, it was because he was hopeless at football and fighting—the currency that mattered among the young boys at the primary school he attended in the 1980s.[52] In Elstree, future businesswoman Karren Brady joined

---

[45] Viv Albertine, *Clothes, Clothes, Clothes, Music, Music, Music, Boys, Boys, Boys*, 33.
[46] Walter Southgate, *That's The Way It Was*, 54.
[47] Louis Heren, *Growing Up Poor in London*, 60.
[48] Nina Bawden, *In My Own Time: Almost an Autobiography* (London: Virago, 1997), 18.
[49] Alan Johnson, *This Boy* (London: Corgi, 2013), 62.
[50] Hilary Mantel, *Giving Up The Ghost*, 73.
[51] Victoria Beckham, *Learning to Fly: The Autobiography* (London: Penguin, 2001), 34.
[52] Russell Brand, *My Booky Wook* (London: Hodder & Stoughton, 2008), 47.

the newly co-educational sixth form of a fee-paying boys' boarding school. She did not think she was academic, but the experience helped her recognise her qualities: 'pride, a relentless drive, the capacity to make the best of difficult situations and self-reliance.' Mainly, she learned how to behave around men, including 'when not to be one of the lads. There was a real culture among some of the girls of matching the boys' pint for pint, and that wasn't me at all.'[53]

This section addressed the question of gender and power inside schools and classrooms. In so doing, it took stock of the formal and informal curriculum, using moments of endurance and rebellion to reflect agency and resistance, creating understanding of the role of education in the mediation of intersectional relationships within the social complex. However, what does the *longue durée* show of the psychic processes and the making of classed and racialised masculinities and femininities in a selective education system?

CLIMBING THE EXAMINATION LADDER AND GOING DOWN THE SNAKES

British academic Richard Hoggart was born into a working-class home in Hunslett in south Leeds. The 'structure of feeling' of his 1957 text, *The Uses of Literacy*, portrayed the way the self-motivated, self-improving lad with ambition had to cut himself off from family and friends.

> At his "elementary" school, from as early as the age of eight, he is likely to be in some degree set apart... He is similarly likely to be separated from the boys' groups outside the home, is no longer a full member of the gang which clusters round the lamp-posts in the evenings; there is homework to be done. But these are the male groups among which others in his generation grow up, and his detachment from them is emotionally linked with one more aspect of his home situation—that he now tends to be closer to the women of the house than to the men. This is true, even if his father is not the kind who dismissed books and reading as 'a woman's game'. The boy spends a large part of his time at the physical centre of the home, where the women's spirit rules, quietly getting on with his work whilst his mother gets on with her jobs—the father not yet back from work or out for a drink with his mates. The man and the boy's brothers are outside, in the world of men; the boy sits in the women's world.[54]

In describing the discourses of masculinity the scholarship boy has to 'leave' in order to 'get on,' Hoggart shows how gender performances are constructed in practice in specific educational contexts. He finds comfort in domesticity, while taking it for granted that he bears no responsibility for household chores. At university, he studies English not normally the reserve of boys ('a woman's game').

---

[53] Karren Brady, *Strong Woman: The Truth About Getting to the Top* (London: Collins, 2012), 31–3.
[54] Richard Hoggart, *The Uses of Literacy* (Harmondsworth: Penguin [1957] 1971), 295.

Angela Rodaway was Hoggart's contemporary, growing up in North London. Her mother thought a clerical job was the measure of a good life—nice, clean, with comparatively high pay and comparatively low hours. That meant higher than elementary education.

> If I did not get the scholarship I should have to work in a factory. Sometimes, going home with my mother, after dark, on a Saturday night, I would see girls of fourteen or fifteen sauntering along, eating chips from greasy newspaper. They were always laughing loudly and shouting and pushing each other off the kerb. I was frightened of them and my mother said that they were factory girls and, if I did not get a scholarship, then I should become like them and have similar people as my constant companions.[55]

After passing the examination, Rodaway's proudest moments were the hours she spent wheeling her twin sisters' pram up and down the street wearing her new school hat. Old women told her how clever she was to have won a scholarship and what a 'good girl' to look after the babies.

The working-class concept of 'respectability,' a symbol of the way one behaved, impelled Rodaway towards secondary school. As it did Nina Bawden. Nevertheless, whereas it did not occur to Rodaway to challenge the homogenised factory girl script as a term of opprobrium, it did Bawden. She had classmates whose parents and siblings worked on the factory floor for Ford, in Dagenham, and 'seemed to lead perfectly bearable, indeed often enviable, lives. Some of the fathers had cars. Even some of the mothers drove. They all went to the cinema and away on holiday more often than my family, and they stayed in hotels or boarding houses, not as we did, with Aunt Peg.'[56] Her mother, a trained teacher, disagreed with her daughter's observations. She coached Bawden, who passed the scholarship examination and later Oxford entrance.

Former Labour politician, journalist and author Roy Hattersley was born in Sheffield. The only child of a Catholic priest who left the church to set up home with his mother, who was already married, his story contains themes that resonate with other autobiographical material from Cohort III.

> Thanks to caps and scarves the difference between 'passing' and 'failing' was visible to every neighbour. Green, maroon and navy blazers were the raiment of success. Second-hand jackets handed down from elder brothers and sweaters hastily knitted by grandma were the apparel of defeat. The lucky parents regarded the weeks of outfitting as a period of public rejoicing. They announced the dates of their visits to the recommended outfitters as if they were invites in the social calendar. Close relatives were invited to attend the scene of the actual purchase as if it were a wedding or christening.[57]

---

[55] Angela Rodaway, *A London Childhood* (London: Virago, 1985), 67.
[56] Nina Bawden, *In My Own Time*, 28.
[57] Roy Hattersley, *A Yorkshire Boyhood* (London: Abacus, 2008), 143.

Roy won a grammar school place but denounced his teachers for their treatment of two under-nourished boys who 'proclaimed their poverty even to insensitive twelve-year-olds. Both wore the cheap blazers which were supplied to sons of the unemployed, and both lacked the extra items of equipment which, though not compulsory, were essential to grammar school life.'[58] Regularly shamed and punished, these two boys grew to dislike and hate school. Teachers went to great lengths to minimise contact between boys and girls. 'We were taught in mixed classes, with boys on one side of the room and girls on the other. But the register was marked, milk money collected, dinners eaten and leisure time spent in rigid segregation.'[59]

Maureen Duffy's mother was determined her daughter would never know the kind of poverty she had experienced and goaded her through the scholarship examination to a place at secondary school. Racked with tuberculosis, she made Maureen's uniform and satchel. This last made from canvas. 'Secretly I was a bit ashamed of it—it was so different from the glossy leather ones, like new conkers, that the others had but it was the only one I ever had.'[60] For Maureen, the cost of not jumping each hurdle as it presented itself was clear. 'I was just a girl and life offered only things I despised, houses, children, security, housework.'[61]

It pleased journalist and media personality Janet Street-Porter's father no end when she won a grammar school place in the late-1950s. 'He had grown up seeing this snobby girls' school every day as he attended an extremely working-class elementary school around the corner in New King's Road. He loved the look of the young ladies in their formal uniform of panama hats, gingham dresses and striped red and black blazers in summer, hexagonal berets in winter.'[62] Future sociologist Annette Kuhn's impression of all this was that a school*girl's* uniform meant trivial things like fashion would not obstruct the grammar school syllabus and would hold in check the unruly side of her individuality. 'In this context, order is equated with a specific model of femininity. The rules for behaviour when wearing uniform outside the school—you were supposed to comport yourself with ladylike decorum—have everything to do with presuppositions about the proper conduct in public of young women of a certain class.'[63]

When it came to his turn, future film and television producer Tony Garnett didn't know the meaning of the 11-plus. He passed. His best friend didn't. They played in the playground and in the park together. They were inseparable. At first, Tony refused to go to a different school but had to relent. 'I still lived in the same road as Barry, but we were now in different worlds. After a

---

[58] Op cit, 155.
[59] Op cit, 156.
[60] Maureen Duffy, *That's How It Was* (London: Virago, 2002), 103.
[61] Op cit, 99.
[62] Janet Street-Porter, *A Baggage: My Childhood* (London: Headline Books, 2004), 122.
[63] Annette Kuhn, *Family Secrets: Acts of Memory* (London: Verso, 1995), 93.

few months we hardly saw each other and when we did, there was nothing to talk about,' he wrote.⁶⁴ Still there was school to survive.

> On arrival, big older boys would take you into the loos and ask if you wanted to see the goldfish. Not understanding, but apprehensive, you would nod. They then tipped you up, stuck your head down the loo and pulled the chain. Or they would ask if you knew what the 'black hole of Calcutta' was. Not waiting for an answer, they would throw you into the corner of a wall, pushing and squeezing until you screamed. But the scariest thing they did was to hold you by your braces and hang you out of the second-floor window.⁶⁵

Small for his age and a child who wore glasses, Tony ran the school library, edited the school magazine and acted in school plays. To avoid the label 'geek' and potential bullying, he learned a specialist 'forward' position as a rugby hooker, which offered macho cover. His reflexes were quick. 'Whether this was enough for me to win a regular place in the first fifteen or whether I was picked because, especially on the coach to away matches, I could entertain everyone with lurid stories of lascivious Germans in the war, ravishing pretty women—all improvised on the spot—I don't know.'⁶⁶

Yorkshire miner's son Michael Parkinson went to Barnsley Grammar School. He disliked the culture, which he thought did for his education what myxomatosis did for the rabbit.

> Now I was in an all-male world, instructed by short-tempered brutes who, when all else failed would try to beat information into you. The specialist at this form of teaching was our German master, Goodman, an angry-looking man whose favoured form of instruction was to emphasise a point by drilling his knuckle into the top of a boy's head. Alternatively, he would raise you to your feet by hoisting you up by your hair. If he considered a boy to be particularly stupid, he would make him stand by the blackboard and belittle him by asking questions he knew he couldn't answer.⁶⁷

Days before he was due to sit his examinations, the head caned him on the hand saying that unless he 'bucked up' he would never amount to much. The caning left him unable to write for several days, and Michael sat his exams without caring and without doing any work. He passed Art and English and left school to become a junior reporter on the *South Yorkshire Times*. Years later, when invited to be guest of honour at a dinner to pay tribute to his old head, he declined.⁶⁸

---

[64] Tony Garnett, *The Day the Music Died: A Life Lived Behind the Lens* (London: Constable, 2016), 50.
[65] Op cit, 52.
[66] Ibid.
[67] Michael Parkinson, *Parky* (London: Hodder & Stoughton, 2009), 31.
[68] Op cit, 36–7.

Hoggart's way of examining culture and class spoke to subsequent generations of working-class children who got some kind of selective schooling and were trying to make sense of their own experience of social mobility. But his script was gendered. It expressed the conventional view that boys would have major familial responsibilities as adults, and this affected the way they should work at school, as Annette Kuhn notes.

> There is no place at this table, though, for the scholarship girl, least of all for the London girl of the 'you've never had it so good' era whose mother, after long hours of work in a café, seldom goes near her own kitchen. Here, a grown daughter surrounded by school books would be nothing short of provocation. The only young women in Hoggart's account are the undifferentiated, briefly flowering girls in flimsy frocks and bright lipstick, the scholarship boy's flighty, factory-working sisters, giggling together on their way to the cinema or the dance hall. The scholarship girl does not belong with them, either. If she wants a role in this story, the scholarship girl must, it seems, create it for herself.[69]

In her classic 1986 text, *Landscape for a Good Woman*, Carolyn Steedman explored Hoggart's work as related to becoming an upwardly mobile man, which meant negotiating class transition by projecting backwards a nostalgic image of working-class community. As a social mechanism, he acknowledges yet glosses over gender. For Steedman, becoming a feminist helped her to make sense of a 1950s girlhood in the early years of the British welfare state, based on the principle of universality but at odds with the workings of a gendered meritocracy.[70]

The father of the novelist Andrea Levy sailed to England on the Empire Windrush ship in 1948. Her mother joined him six months later. Levy's semi-autobiographical novel *Every Light in the House Burnin'* tells the story of a Jamaican family living in North London in the 1960s and includes a short description of her single-sex state grammar school staffed by single women. Pupils romanticised over the secret sadness of the teaching staff and their personal lives as they sought to institutionalise them through education. 'They made up rules, new ones every day, with a rigidity the Foreign Legion would have been proud of. We stood up when they entered a room and said good morning or good afternoon no matter how often they came in and out.'[71] Her parents thought the school wonderful because 'it reminded them of schools in Jamaica.'[72]

In 1960s Notting Hill, Alan Johnson's mother hastened her premature death by taking on an extra cleaning job to pay for his grammar school uniform. There was, in fact, another local alternative—the purpose-built Holland Park Comprehensive School, which opened in 1958. The school buildings,

---

[69] Kuhn, *Family Secrets*, 102.
[70] Carolyn Steedman, *Landscape For A Good Woman* (London: Virago, 1986).
[71] Andrea Levy, *Every Light In The House Burnin'* (London: Headline Books, 1995), 180.
[72] Ibid.

including a swimming pool, were large, glass-plated, with open staircases, designed by the London County Council's chief architect, Leslie Martin, who had planned the Royal Festival Hall on London's south bank. 'But for working-class Lily, there was no point in passing the Eleven-Plus if it didn't lead to grammar school which she saw as her children's escape route from the kind of life to which she'd been condemned.'[73] What about those left behind?

Future inventor Trevor Baylis, musician, singer-songwriter and actor David Essex and actor Robert Lindsay were among the 75 per cent or so allocated to secondary modern schools. Trevor remembered sucking his pencil during his test as everyone else was writing feverishly and thinking he 'might just as well pack up and go home,' while suspecting his friends were in the same boat. 'The following September, 1948, that select band, whose lips moved when we were doing silent reading, all met up again in the playground of the secondary modern.'[74] He regretted not learning Latin, playing rugby and wearing a blazer and cap. What he learned was woodwork, metalwork and dexterity with tools and machines.

David Essex wanted to play football for West Ham. He knew grammar boys played rugby and flunked the test in order to play school football. Sad to leave primary school, he was even sadder when he found what awaited him at his single-sex secondary modern. 'Forget about getting an education—you were happy just to get through the day in one piece. Shipman County didn't have a uniform, unless you count the jeans, leather jackets and steel-toe-capped boots that all the boys wore.'[75] Being tough was vital to survive. When the father of one victim turned up to confront the bullies, they simply kicked him to the ground and beat him up in front of his crying son. The science teacher was an amateur beekeeper. Trouble ensued when he brought his bees in to show the class. 'As he headed towards the blackboard, a couple of the boys inserted the rubber tube from a nearby Bunsen burner into the hole, fastened it in place with chewing gum, and turned on the gas.'[76] On seeing his lifeless bees, he started smashing desks and test tubes. Pupils ran for cover, some crying, while one boy set fire to a broken chair.

Born in Ilkeston, an East Midlands town clustered around the huge iron-works that employed most of his family, Robert Lindsay's mother worked variously in the Raleigh and the Players factories in Nottingham when he was a child. He was in the top stream at primary school and expected to pass his 11-plus. There are commonalities with Essex's account in his description of power relations and the performance of masculinity at secondary level. There was no uniform besides 'an unofficial dress code of leather jacket and bike chain,' and the school had a terrible image. 'Everyone knew and dreaded what happened to all the new boys who entered Gladstone. As part of your initiation

---

[73] Alan Johnson, *This Boy*, 214.
[74] Trevor Baylis, *Clock This: My Life As An Inventor* (London: Headline Books, 1999), 38.
[75] David Essex, *Over The Moon* (London: Random House Books, 2012), 18–19.
[76] Op cit, 23–4.

you were put inside a dustbin. It was then shut, chained up and thrown down the school steps.'[77] Robert managed to avoid this and aged 13 got the opportunity to go to Nottingham High School, but his parents could not afford it. However, the art teacher at Gladstone Boys' formed a drama group that united the school and proved to be Robert's salvation.

Danny Baker rejected a grammar school place to go with his friends. His docker father was sanguine. '"Boy," he said, "if going to a top school made you clever then the Houses of Parliament would be full of fucking geniuses. But it ain't, so you do what you like."'[78] Like Trevor Baylis and David Essex, he found working with your hands dominated the curriculum at his boys' secondary modern school, to forget your protective cloth apron was a major crime. The teaching context was rarely conducive to academic learning. Once boys in the bottom class smashed a crystal radio set their teacher, a strict disciplinarian heading for retirement, brought in to show them. Another disciplinarian was put into a coma from which he never recovered, 'Having brooded over a perceived slight from the old boy, the kid heaved a shot put at his head.'[79]

Paul Dash learned about English schooling the hard way. In 1957, he rejoined his parents who had migrated from the Caribbean and settled in the Oxford industrial suburb of Cowley. Without sitting a single test, he found himself in the 'B' stream of a small, all-boys secondary modern. He knew his education was a sub-standard shutting down of potential and that he was the victim of racism. His form teacher slapped, punched and kicked him for dropping his ruler; the PE teacher threw a heavy medicine ball on his head.[80] The science teacher expressed the views of many staff when he referred to Paul's class as 'dead-end kids,' fit only for 'working in the local factory.'[81] Paul often walked to school with grammar boys and 'desperately wanted to be treated like someone special, as they were, to wear a uniform like theirs, to carry a satchel fat with books, to be respected and admired for being the schoolboy success that I wasn't.'[82] Eventually, he played cricket for Oxfordshire at the schools' county level, and the experience of walking on to the close-cropped grass of Magdalen College sports ground stayed with him.

Alan Johnson remembered feeling sorry for one boy whose parents refused a grammar school place because they could not afford the uniform. The lad wore glasses and Alan worried about the bullying he would experience as 'four-eyes' at an all-boys' secondary modern.[83] Valerie Avery wants to make her mother proud through passing, but her grandmother offers reassurance: 'Well, this is a big day for you, love, but don't you worry. I never was a believer in

---

[77] Robert Lindsay, *Letting Go* (London: Thorogood, 2009), 39.
[78] Danny Baker, *Going To Sea In A Sieve: The Autobiography* (London: Phoenix, 2013), 52.
[79] Op cit, 58–9.
[80] Paul Dash, *Foreday Morning* (London: BlackAmber Books, 2002), 133, 141.
[81] Op cit, 132.
[82] Op cit, 140.
[83] Alan Johnson, *This Boy*, 123.

education, especially for girls.'[84] Scored as a border-line case, worthy of a second chance, Valerie's mother learns of another way her daughter might belong to a good place within schooling, a school with a uniform, where some go onto college and become teachers: 'apparently it's what they call a Con-Comprehensive School.' Valerie liked the uniform, and since it was a mixed school, she thought it 'bound to be more fun.'[85]

COMPREHENSIVE SCHOOLING

Attending one of London's first experimental co-educational comprehensive schools made Valerie's an exceptional experience. Outside of London, the only English comprehensive school was in the Lake District where from 1945 the former Windermere grammar school was non-selective. Personal accounts from Cohort V capture the comprehensive moment and the move from single sex to co-educational secondary schooling. Autobiographical evidence shows that while power relations vary from school to school, there were commonalities in the tapestry of gender. Communities of masculinity and femininity practice show this, with teenagers taking on compliant, oppositional and other stances in relation both to discrimination and to the demands of schooling.

Andrew Collins grew up in 1970s Northampton. He found the 'hardos' at his comprehensive secondary school disparaged neat and tidy, 'academic' boys. For them, carrying a briefcase was tantamount to 'an admission of homosexuality,' and being clever was 'uncool.'[86] Jockeying for position in relation to the performance of masculinity and to the demands of schooling, he adopts a new football team, Leeds United (supported by the male ringleaders), wears trainers for lessons, pretends to be anti-school and becomes a punk rocker. All of which is a rude awakening after his previous state school where he was part of the second male intake. Because of its former life as a St Trinian's-style girls' school, he wrote, the school boasted excellent facilities in the 'lady sciences' (cookery and needlework). 'It was a triumph for women's lib: girls did woodwork, while the boys learned how to thread a bobbin and flour a rolling pin.'[87]

Middle-class John-Paul Flintoff went to Holland Park between 1979 and 1986. Teachers seat him next to a girl in class, who apparently takes it badly because of his sex and resents the disruptive behaviour of the boys around her. John-Paul tries to construct a masculinity focused around physical toughness, changing his accent and swearing. The choice for a boy, he says, is stark—behave badly or you get 'killed.' Best friends, two girls from his primary school talk 'posh,' and one has an unconventional dress code (velvet shirts, with big dungarees and chunky shoes). To ingratiate himself with a rebel lad who

---

[84] Valerie Avery, *London Morning* (London: Pergamon, 1969), 101.
[85] Op cit, 112.
[86] Andrew Collins, *Where Did It All Go Right? Growing Up Normal In The 70s* (London: Ebury Press, 2003), 202.
[87] Op cit, 75.

publicly refuses to comply with teachers' requirements, he starts a rumour about their sexuality. This boy called 'them lesbians for weeks. One day they both run out of the classroom crying, Melissa first, and Rosalind soon after. Melissa stubbed her toes on a desk as she was running out but didn't stop. They never even knew I started it.'[88]

The journalist Lynsey Hanley grew up on a Birmingham council estate and went to her neighbourhood comprehensive school. Constructed for the purpose of telling of the psychological cost of becoming middle class, her narrative recalls how she recognised the anti-school group but unlike Collins and Flintoff, had no wish to join them. Of the rebels' stubborn obstinacy, she wrote: 'They knew they were throwing their lives away, and yet they refused to acknowledge that that was what they were doing. The cost of one of them saying, "*Come on lads, we can have a laff outside of school, we're here to learn so we don't have to do jobs we hate later on,*" would have been too much for any of them to stand.'[89] At the same time, she rejected the cultural reference point of popular girls who modelled their talk on the right time 'to get engaged, whether before leaving school or waiting till just after. They would be aware that once they had said yes to marriage they might never be able to say no to anything again.'[90]

Perception of order could be important to parents. Ledley King grew up in a lone mother family in London's East End. When he moved to secondary school, his mother sought high standards and discipline. She chose a streamed, single-sex Catholic school. For a time, Ledley played the cello in the school orchestra and got good grades but soon found he had more in common with boys who played football and 'had a laugh.' Moved down a class after 18 months, he recognises the academic basis of the merit system he describes. 'At first, I was a little bit embarrassed, but once I was there, I felt quite happy. But I was very sure that I never wanted to be in the bottom two classes, Loyola or Clitheroe. The kids in those classes were seen as no-hopers even by the twelve-year-olds, winding each other up and cussing, as we'd say.'[91]

Jade Goody's narrative provides a different example of home-school relations. A former 21-year-old dental nurse from Bermondsey who entered the world of reality television, her father suffered from drug addictions and she often missed school for domestic reasons. As she grew up, she said that if pupils weren't afraid of her, they were afraid of her mother. Her father was of dual ethnic heritage, and she suffered racist abuse both at school and in her local community. 'My mum got into fights with a lot of women who lived in our block because she thought they were prejudiced,' she said, and her mother took her out of school for similar reasons. Teachers said she talked too much, never concentrated and was dominating, which she interpreted as code for

---

[88] Jean-Paul Flintoff, *Comp* (London: Victor Gollancz, 1998), 87.
[89] Lynsey Hanley, *Respectable: Crossing the Class Divide* (London: Penguin, 2016), 17.
[90] Op cit, 15.
[91] Ledley King, *King: Ledley King My Autobiography* (London: Quercus, 2013), 25.

being a bully, which she denied. She fought with a boy on her second day in secondary school and lost interest in qualifications, though she got one top grade in her GCSEs, for drama.[92]

Individual stories reveal educational 'performers' and 'underperformers' as 'typical' children who grow up and fit in with the social world. Collectively we can use them to reveal how masculinities and femininities are developed and understood by children and young people in family, school and locality. To show the persistence of structural inequalities and the difference parents and teachers, 'good' and 'bad,' can make. Through listening to the voices from the margin, we see alternative sets of gender relations, and elements of continuity and difference within the gender order across the decades.

Conclusion: Making Connections

Surviving autobiographies complement ethnographic representations of boys and girls within the context of schooling. Individually and collectively, they reveal a balancing act between academic success, social acceptability and the development of tangled gender identities in the local settings of everyday lives. Autobiographical examples show boys and girls are a multiplicity of subjectivities, and an individual's position is not uniquely determined by being male or female. Some girls wanted to escape working-class jobs and the backbreaking domesticity of their mother's lives, like Duffy and Rodaway, others seemed more accepting like Powell and Scannell. For some, like Lindsay, an English teacher made the difference that set him on the journey from secondary modern school to the Royal Academy of Dramatic Art (RADA).

Viewed as local and everyday resistances, we can read the commonality of refusal to ask to go to the toilet as bringing to light power relations inside and outside schools such as, historically, the child's retention of physical dependence as a way of regulating mothers.[93] The masculinising and feminising process of schooling restricted pupils, but 'tomboy' behaviour related to violence and aggression allowed some girls to become space invaders. Therefore, the young Hilary Mantel fought rough, tough boys while clinging to the prospects of a man's life that seems to guarantee power and status. In primary school, she persuades another girl to play the 'Game of Men' but feels crushed when her peer role-plays her father who 'never does anything manly. The whole excitement is confined to "Walter comes home for his tea."'[94]

To return to our starting point, Margaret Forster's diary gives personal expressions of key points in a pupil's life. She has examinations hanging over her, and her concerns with where she is in the class, her hair, weight and clothes

---

[92] Jade Goody, *How It All Began: My First Book* (London: John Blake Publishing, 2006), 41, 58–60, 69–70.
[93] Valerie Walkerdine and Helen Lucey, *Democracy In The Kitchen: Regulating Mothers and Socialising Daughters* (London: Virago, 1989).
[94] Hilary Mantel, *Giving Up The Ghost*, 75.

are inter-as-well-as-intra-generational. Gendered scholarship scripts and tales from those who did *not* climb up the examination ladder show the attenuation of class relations in the context of gender and race. They trouble our concepts of social mobility and make us question the idea of a meritocracy. How schooling was (and is) experienced by children depends on many things, but a generational analysis of autobiographical material suggests school conformists and rebels, and society in general has much to gain from the equal treatment of qualities coded as feminine and those coded as masculine.

BIBLIOGRAPHY

PRIMARY SOURCES

ARCHIVAL SOURCES

Helen Taylor's papers and letters, Mill-Taylor Collection. LSE archives and special collections.

AUTOBIOGRAPHIES, MEMOIRS, DIARIES, LETTERS, OBITUARIES

Albertine, Viv. *Clothes, Clothes, Clothes, Music, Music, Music, Boys, Boys, Boys.* London: Faber & Faber, 2016.
Ashworth, Andrea. *Once in a House of Fire.* London: Picador, 1998.
Avery, Valerie. *London Morning.* London: Pergamon, 1967.
Baker, Danny. *Going to Sea in a Sieve: The Autobiography.* London: Phoenix, 2013.
Bawden, Nina. *In My Own Time: Almost an Autobiography.* London: Virago, 1997.
Baylis, Trevor. *Clock This: my life as an inventor.* London: Headline Book Publishing, 1999.
Beckham, Victoria. *Learning to Fly: the autobiography.* London: Penguin, 2001.
Berg, Leila. *Flickerbook.* London: Granta, 1998.
Brady, Karren. *Strong Woman: The Truth About Getting To The Top.* London: Collins, 2012.
Brand, Russell. *My Booky Wook.* London: Hodder & Stoughton, 2008.
Brittain, Vera. *Testament of Youth.* London: Virago, 1986.
Chaplin, Charlie. *Charlie Chaplin: My Autobiography.* London: Penguin, 2003.
Chorley, Katherine. *Manchester Made Them.* London: Faber and Faber Ltd, 1950.
Church, Richard. *Over the Bridge.* London: The Reprint Society, 1956.
Collins, Andrew. *Where Did It All Go Right? Growing Up Normal in the 70s.* London: Ebury Press, 2003.
Dash, Paul. *Foreday Morning.* London: BlackAmber Books, 2002
Davenport-Hill, Matthew. *Eton and Elsewhere.* London: John Murray, 1928.
Duffy, Maureen. *That's How It Was.* London: Virago, 2002.
Essex, David. *Over the Moon.* London: Random House Books, 2012.
Flintoff, Jean-Paul. *Comp.* London: Victor Gollancz, 1998.
Foakes, Grace. *Four Meals for Fourpence.* London: Virago, 2011.
Forster, Margaret. *Diary of an Ordinary Girl.* London: Chatto & Windus, 2017.
Garnett, Tony. *The Day the Music Died: a Life Lived Behind the Lens.* London: Constable, 2016.

Goody, Jade. *How It All Began: My First Book*. London: John Blake Publishing, 2006.
Gerrard, Stephen. *Gerrard: My Autobiography*. London: Bantam Press, 2006.
Hanley, Lynsey. *Respectable: Crossing the Class Divide*. London: Penguin, 2017.
Hattersley, Roy. *A Yorkshire Boyhood*. London: Abacus, 2008.
Haythorne, Evelyn. *On Earth to Make the Numbers Up*. Castleford: Yorkshire Art Circus, 1991.
Heren, Louis. *Growing Up Poor in London*. London: Orion Books, 2001.
Johnson, Andrew. *This Boy*. London: Corgi, 2013.
Kuhn, Annette. *Family Secrets: Acts of Memory and Imagination*. London: Verso, 1995.
Lee, Laurie. *Cider with Rosie*. Harmondsworth: Penguin, 1971.
Lindsay, Robert. *Letting Go*. London: Thorogood, 2009.
King, Ledley. *King: Ledley King My Autobiography*. London: Quercus, 2013.
Mantel, Hilary. *Giving Up the Ghost*. London: Fourth Estate, 2013.
McKay, Margaret. *Generation in Revolt*. London: William Heinemann, 1953.
Mitchell, Hannah. *The Hard Way Up*. London: Virago, 1977.
Morley, Edith. *Before and After*. Reading: Two Rivers Press, 2016.
Parkinson, Michael. *Parky*. London: Hodder & Stoughton, 2008.
Patch, Harry with Richard Van Emden. *The Last Fighting Tommy*. London: Bloomsbury, 2014.
Powell, Margaret. *Below Stairs*. London: Pan Books, 2011.
Roberts, Robert. *A Ragged Schooling*. Manchester: Manchester University Press, 1976.
Rodaway, Angela. *A London Childhood*. London: Virago, 1985.
Rolph, C.H. *London Particulars*. Oxford: Oxford University Press, 1980.
Rowse, Alfred L. *A Cornish Childhood*. Truro: Dyllansow Truran, 1998.
Scannell, Dorothy. *Mother Knew Best: Memoir of a London Girlhood*. New York: Pantheon Books, 1974.
Southgate, Walter. *That's the Way it Was: a working-class autobiography 1890–1950*. Surrey: New Clarion Press, 1982.
Spender, Stephen. *World Within World*. New York: St Martin's Press, 1994.
Street-Porter, Janet. *A Baggage: My Childhood*. London: Headline Books, 2004.
Thompson, Flora. *Lark Rise to Candleford*. London: Penguin, 1973.
Whitehorn, Katherine. *Selective Memory*. London: Virago, 2007.
Widdecombe, Ann. *Strictly Ann*. London: Orion Publishing, 2014.

SECONDARY SOURCES

Hoggart, Richard. *The Uses of Literacy*. Harmondsworth: Penguin [1957] 1971.
Mannheim, Karl. "The problem of generations". In *Studying Aging and Social Change*, edited by Melissa Hardy, 22–65. London: Sage Publications, 1997.
Steedman, Carolyn. *Landscape for a Good Woman*. London: Virago, 1986.
Walkerdine, Valerie and Helen Lucey, Helen. *Democracy In The Kitchen: Regulating Mothers and Socialising Daughters*. London: Virago, 1989.
Williams, Raymond. *The Long Revolution*. Letchworth: Broadview Press, 2001.

CHAPTER 8

Students

> *The electric lights had already been turned on in the school and a great shaft of light blazed out across the pavement from the main doorway. It was early and no one else was entering. I looked up at the stone steps, hollowed out by hundreds of feet, through the hall and up the staircase to the second floor. The welcoming doorway was my hoping door; the worn stone steps my ladder to the stars. Kind hands, earnest people, were there to help me up them. I bared my yellow teeth in a smile of pure happiness, charged across the threshold and galloped up the stairs.*
> —Helen Forrester, *Twopence To Cross The Mersey*
> (London: HarperCollins, 2016), 224

Helen Forrester was the pen name of June Bhatia. The oldest of seven children of middle-class parents who lost everything during the Depression, her father moved the family to Liverpool (which was his birthplace) in the hope of finding work, but instead of the bustling, wealthy city he remembered, they found a dismal place, blighted by unemployment and poverty. Much of the burden of looking after her siblings fell upon June, who was kept out of school, and it was the memory of these years of hardship that she embedded in her first volume of autobiography *Twopence to Cross the Mersey*. Eventually, June staged a rebellion, and her parents agreed to let her attend evening school. She spent seven years in local authority classes and managed in each subsequent year to win a small scholarship to cover the cost. My epigraph shows her enthusiasm for learning, and the meaning she attached to the imaginative possibility of intellectual and cultural transformation. This chapter will use individual stories to explore the change higher education made at a personal level, uniting male and female lives to deepen understandings of institutional life brought together with class and gender culture and constructs of masculinity and femininity.

© The Author(s), under exclusive license to Springer Nature Switzerland AG 2022
J. Martin, *Gender and Education in England since 1770*, Gender and History, https://doi.org/10.1007/978-3-030-79746-1_8

Using their own words extracted from autobiographies and memoirs in published anthologies written by individuals born between 1850 and 1974, supplemented by interviews from the *Does Work Still Shape Social Identities and Social Action* project funded by the Economic and Social Research Council, I unlock the impact of higher education to see how and in what ways it changed lives. This includes a glimpse into the world of the historical university with a focus on gendered student sub-cultures at Oxford and Cambridge, often described as places for a gentleman's education, in culture, civilisation and national identity, but also places of counter-cultural behaviour among the student body, characterised by the donning of unorthodox fashions, excessive drinking and violence.[1] Without making claims for these voices as 'typical' or entirely representative, educational biographies help us understand higher education institutions as sites for the making of gendered subjectivities, focusing in particular on the experience of communal living, sociability and communities of masculinity and femininity practice in specific institutional settings.

The perspective is that of looking at intellectual history from the receiving end. Working across spatial and temporal lines, the objective is to give an interpretative account of educational experience. Cases selected illuminate class and gender relations including cultural reproduction in the education of the Oxbridge male, plotting continuity in gendered identity-making in relation to the formation of elite masculinity. We note the growing number of female students, and the importance of a gendered historical perspective for understanding and evaluating a twenty-first century men as minority in higher education phenomena. We see that the experience of former scholarship winners resonates with the accounts of subsequent generations of working-class students in elite universities, who encounter cultural dissonance as they face the challenge of the unfamiliar and find themselves 'strangers in paradise.'[2]

To set the context, I start with a short history of widening participation in learning and teaching. Where higher education is concerned, the historiography has tended to focus on institution building as related to the historical world of the university and the campus experience. I aim to widen the aperture and think more deeply about the experience of those we might now call 'commuter students,' to consider what working people and women gained by attending evening lectures and/or by being a pupil-teacher and perhaps going on to teacher training college. Their historic invisibility is specifically classed,

---

[1] ESRC Identities Programme project *Does Work Still Shape Social Identities and Social Action* (RES-148-25-0038); Heather Ellis, "Foppish Masculinity, Generational Identity and the University Authorities in Eighteenth-Century Oxbridge," *Cultural and Social History*, 11, no. 3 (2014), 367-384.

[2] Diane Reay, Gill Crozier and John Clayton, "Strangers in Paradise? Working-class Students in Elite Universities," *Sociology*, 43, no. 6 (2009), 1103-1121.

racialised and gendered, and I intentionally scope a more inclusive canvas here to include the intellectual histories of people from backgrounds who are traditionally under-represented at university.

HISTORICISING WIDENING PARTICIPATION

The Mechanics' Institute movement was the main adult education movement of the early nineteenth century, which provided lecture courses, libraries and in some cases museum facilities initially to working men. Rather by default, they did open their doors to women when it was discovered that they weren't *not* allowed to go.[3] Beyond this, teacher training colleges and colleges for working men and working women were being founded; there were post-school educational organisations like local authority evening schools and lectures being advertised under the auspices of the University Extension movement. In towns and cities all over England, lists of prospective students were signed up, and if there was sufficient money to subsidise a visiting lecturer, peripatetic professors were engaged. This pattern of activity included initiatives involving the Langham Place circle and the North of England Council for Promoting the Higher Education of Women, which saw the founding of women's colleges in Cambridge and Oxford.

Before 1869, there was no university-level college for women in England. The vision Barbara Bodichon had of changing this went back to 1848 when her brother entered Jesus College, Cambridge.[4] In 1862, Emily Davies made informal enquiries to Oxford and Cambridge about the possibility of extending a 'local' or 'middle-class' examination designed to provide boys' secondary schools with standards for their graduates to girls. Oxford refused but Bodichon and Davies began the process of institution-building after Cambridge officially opened local examinations to girls. Although some supporters, notably Anne Jemima Clough and Henry Sidgwick, parted company with Davies over her insistence on proving the intellectual equality of the sexes by following the existing University of Cambridge syllabus and the foundation being nominally Anglican, Bodichon did not. By virtue of her initial donation and the £10,000 left in her will, she was the college's principal financial benefactor.[5]

The first students went to Hitchin, where Davies rented in 1869 a building for herself and five other women to live together, to learn together and become the first women to study for a degree course at any English university. With the support of Cambridge professors, they went on to take the Cambridge Tripos examinations, and in 1872, a permanent college opened at Girton village, about two miles from Cambridge. Meanwhile, Newnham College, the Clough and Sidgwick initiative opened first as a boarding house in 1870, then in 1876

---

[3] Jana Sims, "Mechanics' Institutes in Sussex and Hampshire: 1825-1875," unpublished PhD thesis, Institute of Education, University of London, 2010.

[4] Pam Hirsch, *Barbara Leigh Smith Bodichon 1827-1891: Feminist, Artist and Rebel* (London: Chatto and Windus, 1998), 31.

[5] Op cit, 249.

as a college espousing 'separate but different' secular education for women. Traditional middle-class ideals about femininity were evident in the 'special' examinations for women and enthusiasm for public social service that flourished at Newnham, where entry into the teaching profession was also encouraged. By the 1880s, Girton and Newnham had developed into fully fledged women's colleges at Cambridge, in new purpose-built buildings. Outside, rather than integrated into, the university, their students took the university's degree examinations, though the question of actually awarding degrees to women provoked bitter controversy with three votes on the issue in 1897, 1921 and 1947. Until 1948, their students had to make do, at best, with mailed university certificates.[6]

Institution-building happened in an atmosphere of reform prompted by royal commissions set up to investigate the ancient universities and subsequent legislation in 1854 and 1877, which ended the Anglican monopoly and allowed dons to marry. The 1854 Oxford Act made substantial changes to how the University was run, including a more centralised university authority that encouraged the establishment of private halls to accommodate female students. Lady Margaret Hall and Somerville opened in 1879, followed by St Hugh's in 1886 and St Hilda's in 1893. Until 1820, the Anglican universities of Oxford and Cambridge had a duopoly in England. In London, University College was established on non-denominational lines in 1826 and the Anglican King's College followed in 1829. These later became the founding colleges of the University of London that admitted women to all degrees except medicine in 1878. After this, Anglican Queen's and the non-denominational Bedford College were drawn into university work, although Queen's, unlike Bedford, did not become an official part of the university establishment. London established two more women's colleges in the 1880s—Westfield and Royal Holloway, in addition to Bedford College and King's College for Women. By 1900, 169 women had graduated, representing around 30 per cent of the total.[7]

Elsewhere co-educational colleges were being established. Before 1898, London University was solely an examining body, and any higher level teaching institution with staff and students could apply to award its external degrees. Consequently, newly established colleges of higher education realised that they could class themselves as vicarious universities, and attract students, by subscribing to London's matriculation and final exams. Thus, Nottingham became a university college in 1881, Reading in 1892, Sheffield in 1897 and Exeter in 1901. The first of the Durham colleges, University College, was founded in 1832. It was situated in Durham Castle, located in a building dating back to Norman times, and did not admit women to degrees until 1895. In 1881, the civic colleges in Leeds, Liverpool and Manchester formed their own collective

---

[6] Rita McWilliams-Tullberg, *Women at Cambridge* (Cambridge: Cambridge University Press, 1998).

[7] Figures quoted in Claire G. Jones, "'All your dreadful scientific things': women, science and education in the years around 1900," *History of Education*, 46, no. 2 (2017), 164.

degree-granting body, called Victoria University, and admitted both men and women. University College, Bristol, existed from 1876 to 1909 and was the precursor to the University of Bristol. All its courses, except in medicine, were open to men and women on the same basis.

Some dedicated working-class autodidacts obstinately fought their way into tuition. There is a need to write the history of this neglected tradition as those who valued the pursuit of knowledge as an end are unwittingly forgotten amidst the celebration of meritocracy and upward social mobility that suggest being working class is something to get away from.[8] What historical research like that of June Purvis and Jonathan Rose has shown is that working-class men and women cited intellectual independence as a goal of education, believing the radical dictum 'knowledge is power.' Some, like Jude Fawley, the boy who talks to the crows he is supposed to be scaring away, with his eye on Oxford, in Thomas Hardy's 1895 novel *Jude the Obscure*, were less fortunate. Self-educated and with a thirst for knowledge, Jude drifts from crow-scaring to stonecutting with his dreams of higher learning shattered by an Oxford don who advises him to stick to his own trade. Impulsively, Jude chalks a biblical verse along the College wall: '*I have understanding as well as you; I am not inferior to you: yea, who knoweth not such things as these?*'[9]

Pupil teaching was attractive for Mary Bridges Adams who was born into a small Welsh working-class family but grew up in industrial Newcastle. Adams started her working life in schools organised under the 1870 Education Act, fought her way into tuition at Bedford College where she was charged £21 for two terms and took classes in history, mathematics, English language and literature, French, Greek, and Latin. For comparison, the fees for students in the Oxford and Cambridge women's colleges were then around £105 per annum, including tuition, board and lodging. Brilliant at ancient Greek, in 1882 she passed the Intermediate London B.A. examination in the Arts and continued her studies within local reading groups. Clearly, she both valued education and the qualification, which Oxbridge women were not yet entitled to. In 1897, she was elected as an Independent Labour Party candidate for the Greenwich division of the London School Board and became well known for her educational activism.[10]

The state system introduced in 1846 was a predominantly school-based model of training for the elementary school teacher. Apprentice teachers had

---

[8] Owen Jones, *Chavs. The Demonization of the Working Class* (London: Verso, 2012), 96-8.

[9] June Purvis, *Hard Lessons: the lives and education of working-class women in nineteenth-century England* (Minneapolis: University of Minnesota Press, 1989); Jonathan Rose, *The Intellectual Life of the British Working Classes* (Yale: Yale University Press, 2001); Thomas Hardy, *Jude the Obscure* (Harmondsworth: Penguin, 1998), 118.

[10] Bedford College, Student Register, Easter terms 1882, College Calendar; Greenwich Heritage Centre, "Vincent's Newscuttings," Volume 6, 108; Jane Martin, *Making Socialists: Mary Bridges Adams and the Fight for Knowledge and Power, 1855-1939* (Manchester: Manchester University Press, 2013); Carol Dyhouse, *No distinction of sex? Women in British universities 1870-1939* (London: UCL Press, 1995), 28.

to be of 'good moral character' with examination passes in general and religious knowledge plus maths and mechanics for boys, and cooking, knitting, laundry and needlework for girls. Indeed, female pupil teachers were also expected to help with school cleaning as part of their continuing 'education.' After a five-year apprenticeship, it was anticipated they would compete for a government scholarship which meant that those successful were qualified to teach a class of 50 children or go on to further study at a training college for two years at the student's own expense (where female trainees continued to study domestic subjects).[11] Certification was normally the highest qualification for an elementary school teacher, and Mary Bridges Adams, who became a headteacher by the age of 30, was unusual.

After 1890, the setting up of day training colleges tied to a university college and, from 1910, grants for prospective schoolteachers helped widen female participation in higher education. Whereas many middle-class male teachers in the public and endowed schools scorned the idea of vocational training, this was less true of their female counterparts. Hence, the fee-paying girls' schools and universities trained women to be secondary *schoolmistresses* since they disdained the title of teacher for its associations with the elementary sector.[12] The 1902 Education Act allowed local authorities to develop their own teacher training colleges alongside those of the religious bodies that already existed. These were to be independent of the elementary schools and not connected with the day courses run by the universities. In 1907, the Liberal government introduced maintenance grants for students at training college, which no longer came under the elementary Code of Regulations.

Students whose degree courses and further training were financed by scholarships from the Board of Education had no alternative but to teach since the conditions stipulated at least three years in the classroom. So, Ellen Wilkinson accepted 'signing the pledge' as a condition of going to Manchester University in 1910. 'At the University I began to live life to the full, as I had always dreamed of living it... books unlimited, lots of friends, interesting lectures, stimulus of teamwork.'[13] At Bristol, in 1933, Kathleen Uzzell remembered being sent 'into a room where we were told we had to swear an oath to teach for five years, but it was pointed out that it was a "moral" not a "legal" oath... The promise to teach for five years meant a promise not to marry as there were no married female teachers except war widows.' Mrs Day, who graduated from Manchester in Classics in 1937, summed up the aspirations of many working-class girls perfectly. 'From the time I could speak I was told that I wanted to be a teacher. To my parents, poor and working class, it was the only way to lift us

---

[11] Miriam E. David, *The State, the Family and Education* (London: Routledge & Kegan Paul, 1980), 106-7, 128-9; Meg Gomersall, *Working-Class Girls in Nineteenth Century England: Life, Work and Schooling* (Basingstoke: Macmillan, 1997), 85.

[12] Miriam E. David, *The State, The Family and Education*, 124-5.

[13] Ellen Wilkinson, "Ellen Wilkinson," in *Myself When Young By Famous Women of Today*, ed. Margot Asquith (London: Frederick Muller, 1938), 416.

into a better life... We never questioned. I sometimes wonder how my father would have taken it if we had not been clever. So it was purely pragmatic.'[14]

The multiplication of institutions played their part in incremental change. The redbrick University of Birmingham received its charter in 1900 and Bristol in 1909. Civic universities including Exeter, Leicester, Newcastle and Southampton grew from associate colleges of longer established universities (Durham, London and Oxford) in the early 1900s. No more universities opened before 1945. The proportion of the age group attending university (age participation ratio) was 1.5 per cent in England and Wales (compared with 3.1 per cent in Scotland) in 1938. One in four male undergraduates studied at Oxbridge, whereas the number of women was less than one in ten.[15]

The age participation ratio was still under 4 per cent in the 1950s, and it remained harder for girls to secure financial support. This was because boys' public schools had close connections with Oxbridge colleges and boys endowed schools were richer and better placed to fund scholarships than the girls' schools. Secondly, the universities offered more scholarships and bursaries to boys. Finally, the recipients of local authority awards (available from the 1880s) and state scholarships (after 1920) were generally male.[16] In 1945, the Minister of Labour persuaded university vice-chancellors to prioritise recruitment of ex-servicemen. Unless deemed of 'exceptional ability,' female school leavers were more likely to receive an offer of financial assistance to take two-year teacher training courses and help address a shortfall of teachers.[17]

Whereas the university training departments were masculinist workplaces, the women's teacher training colleges were segregated from other forms of higher education with low status. In fact, the McNair Report of 1944 described them as lagging in current thought and practice, staffed by over-burdened lecturers who had no time for reflection and academic research. But more recent historical studies suggest this was an unfairly gendered characterisation, which neglects the dedicated professional/vocational commitment of many female educators, including women like Mary Miller Allan and Lillian de Lissa foundation principals of Homerton College and Gipsy Hill Training College. Nevertheless, McNair's main proposals were for a three-year certificate (introduced in 1960) and closer links with the universities to address the historical 'stigma' of teacher education.[18]

[14] Carol Dyhouse, "Signing the Pledge? Women's Investment in University Education Before 1939," *History of Education*, 26, no. 2 (1997), 217, 218.

[15] Carol Dyhouse, "Going to University in England between the Wars: access and funding," *History of Education*, 26, no. 2 (1997), 1; Carol Dyhouse, "Signing the Pledge? Women's Investment in University Education Before 1939," 211.

[16] Carol Dyhouse, "Signing the Pledge? Women's Investment in University Education Before 1939," 209-10.

[17] Celia Briar, *Working for Women? Gendered Work and Welfare Policies in Twentieth-Century Britain* (London: UCL Press 1997), 97, 111.

[18] Christine Heward, "Men and women and the rise of professional society: the intriguing history of teacher educators," *History of Education*, 22, no. 1 (1993), 27; Elizabeth Edwards, "Mary Miller Allan: The Complexity of Gender Negotiations for a Woman Principal of a Teacher Training

Decisions by the University Grants Committee, responding to a lack of university places for those with the entry qualifications, resulted in the creation of seven new campus universities (East Anglia, Essex, Kent, Lancaster, Sussex, Warwick and York). Referred to as 'plate-glass' universities on the basis of their modernist architecture, they established a reputation as go-ahead and unstuffy in comparison with England's earliest universities Oxford (1096) and Cambridge (1209) and the 'red-brick' universities founded in the industrial cities in the nineteenth century. Sussex, for example, was rarely out of the newspapers, often in the gossip columns, helped by the presence among its 1964 student intake, of the Jay twins. Catherine and Helen, the photogenic daughters of a Labour Cabinet Minister, became the faces of the swinging decade. Photographed by David Bailey in their Courréges boots and mini-skirts, written about in the *Tatler* magazine, appearing in the 1966 film *Alfie* starring Michael Caine, they were the epitome of what 1960s students, as far as tabloid newspapers were concerned, were supposed to be about—Sussex, sex and sociology.

Guaranteed grants for students accepted on a university course became available in 1962 with no differentiation made between male and female entitlements. Fees were paid in full by local authorities, and there was a means-tested annual grant of up to £340 to cover living costs. Parents were expected to contribute towards the grant according to their level of income, the contribution being stipulated by the local authority. With nearly 70 per cent of students receiving grants almost wholly from public funds, the experience of 'going to university' was reshaped in important ways, not least because more young people could afford to choose universities away from home. As the habit of going to university became more firmly established, women made up 25 per cent of undergraduates overall but 15 per cent in Oxford and 10 per cent in Cambridge where single-sex colleges prevented the admission of women, as did quotas in medicine until 1975.[19]

Expansion continued through the creation of 30 'polytechnic' institutions to provide more vocationally oriented, sub-degree qualifications, and the Open University to take advantage of new opportunities in distance learning which, from 1969, created opportunities for men and women of all ages to combine studying with family and/or employment responsibilities. It remained the case that superior resources, prestige and expectations were the reward of academic men. In 1971, for example, state subsidy ranged from £1284 per student at male-dominated universities, to £920 in colleges of education and £720 in advanced courses in further education. Teacher education policy saw the

---

College," in *Practical Visionaries: Women, Education and Progress 1790-1930*, ed. Mary Hilton and Pam Hirsch (Harlow: Longman, 2000), 149-194; Kay Whitehead, "Contesting the 1944 McNair Report: Lillian de Lissa's working life as a teacher educator," *History of Education*, 39, no. 4 (2010), 507-524.

[19] Carol Dyhouse, "Troubled Identities: Gender and Status in the History of the Mixed College in English Universities since 1945," *Women's History Review*, 12, no. 2, 2003, 173.

exclusion of women from senior posts as colleges became mixed sex, larger and more complex and finally part of university training departments.[20]

Growing central control by the state following the abolition of the University Grants Committee saw the freezing of maintenance grants at existing levels in 1990, to be topped up by loans. The 1992 Further and Higher Education Act granted 35 polytechnics full university status, increasing the number of universities by 50 per cent and doubling the number of university students but the formation of the Russell Group of self-proclaimed 'leading' universities soon showed the new system as unitary in name only. Means-tested tuition fees of £1000 were introduced in 1998–99 which rose to £9000 per year for undergraduates in 2012. Five years later, figures from the university admissions service showed UK women were a third more likely to go to university than men; more likely to complete their degrees and achieve 'upper' degrees.[21]

Going to university is generally seen as a marker of social mobility but male decision-making may be consistent with rational choice theory in a labour market where 'real men,' who do well in the world, can do so without going to university. In 2016, for instance, a report by the Young Women's Trust found that male apprentices earn as much as £2000 a year more than their female counterparts earn and are more likely to get a job. Some young men are resistant to university life. The academy is a social field in which working-class males may feel alienated, a space they perceive as feminised, middle-class and culturally 'uncool' in the sense of its association with learning.[22] Links between student and institutional cultures are complex. Individual histories therefore are vital. I focus first on a sample of non-traditional students composed of some of the first students at Ruskin College, Oxford, and prospective teachers in training colleges, drawing on published autobiographies and oral testimony from interviews conducted between 2005 and 2008. Both groups are generally ignored and forgotten in histories of widening participation, relegated to separate studies of adult and teacher education of which there is a dearth.

To Be Educated and Share with My People

Wil Jon Edwards began work in 1900 as a 12-year-old collier's boy in South Wales. In his autobiography, *From the Valley I Came*, he recalls the passionate autodidact culture of his male working community. Before the day's work, miners would sit down for a chat in the Double Parting, a spacious area like a

---

[20] David Rubinstein and Colin Stoneman, "Introduction" in *Education for Democracy*, ed. David Rubinstein and Colin Stoneman (Harmondsworth: Penguin, 1972), 9; Christine Heward, "Men and Women and the Rise of Professional Society", 23.

[21] *The Guardian*, 28 August 2017.

[22] Carolyn Jackson, "'Laddishness' as a self-worth protection strategy", *Gender and Education*, 14, no. 1 (2002), 37-50; Carolyn Jackson, Steve Dempster & Lucie Pollard, '"They just don't seem to really care, they just think it's cool to sit there and talk': laddism in university teaching-learning contexts," *Educational Review*, 67, no. 3 (2015), 300-314.

junction, where trains of trams were made up to be filled with coal and drawn by horses from the working faces.

> I know that it was during these little meetings that I heard the most extraordinary subjects discussed in a most intelligent way, or so it seemed to me. Such subjects would range quite naturally through Science, Art, Religion, Philosophy and Economics. I used to look forward eagerly to these discussions during food spells: I loved to hear the talk, and I had a keen desire to learn. I recall one morning in particular when, after we had eaten our bread and cheese and shut our tin food boxes, a discussion began on two poets and their poetry, Meredith and Kipling.[23]

Studying correspondence classes after days spent working in the mine, he remembers the thrill of winning a scholarship at Ruskin College. 'I was now going to Oxford to be educated and I would, I believed gain much; but whatever I gained it would be shared with my people as I worked to raise their status.'[24]

Ruskin aimed to provide university-standard education for working-class people to empower them to act more effectively on behalf of their community. A conscientious scholar, Edwards was determined to use his learning to build a more socially just society for 'his people.' He attended lectures faithfully but felt patronised for being poor, taught as if he were back at elementary school, the only thing missing being the cane. The appointment of Henry Sanderson Furniss as a lecturer in economics made matters worse. Furniss lacked experience and had barely 'spoken to a working man except gardeners, coachmen, and gamekeepers' before coming to Ruskin. Edwards read his comments on his work—'a jolly good essay spoilt by discussing the Marxian theory of value'—and was furious. When he asked to be excused from attendance at the Furniss lectures, he found he was the 38th student to do so. In response, another worker student, miners' leader and political theorist Noah Ablett began leading unofficial classes in Marxist political economy. In 1909, Ablett led a revolt at Ruskin College to form the Marxist education group Plebs.

In Oxford, the Ruskin men were social and political outsiders. A set apart from 'town' (the non-academic population) and 'gown' (the academic community), Edwards recalled that dress marked them out on the city streets. 'Our strong rough shoes, our good enough best suits, our shirts with their neckbands gripped by ties which had hitherto only seen the light of day on Sundays and holidays, all joined in proclaiming that we were socialists, working men, "reds," in the eyes of townsmen and gownsmen.' Occasionally, tensions spilled over such that culturally, the learning experience included fights with male students from different social backgrounds. Things turned nasty when Labour leader Arthur Henderson came to speak in Oxford town hall. Cries of 'Ruskin

---

[23] Wil John Edwards, *From the Valley I Came* (London: Angus and Robertson, 1957), 46.
[24] Op cit, 161.

Reds' triggered pitched battles as crowds of male undergraduates marched to the College and lobbed bricks through its windows.²⁵

Before 1919, Ruskin was an all-male community. Early students spoke of a bond of brotherhood and the unorthodox gender and social roles that were allotted to them. To keep running costs to a minimum, students took turns to cook and clean. Durham miner Jack Lawson was funded on a trade union scholarship. The language Lawson used to describe domestic labour suggests he did not see it as unmanly and effeminate and that he considered work inside the home as *real* work (his wife was in domestic service). Each student had to clean his own room and make his bed, besides doing daily housework.

> At the weekend you put on an apron, took a bucket of water, soap, and scrubbing-brush, and thoroughly scrubbed such steps or passages as had been allotted to you. In this way the College and all buildings connected with it were scrubbed from top to bottom every week and cleaned daily also. The Scrub List was just as important as the Lecture List—and its educational value was not less. These humble duties were changed round every week, so that in a year you had scrubbed every portion of the buildings inside and out, had learned to cook porridge, bacon and eggs, make the tea, wash the dishes, and be responsible for the proper performance of all duties for the sixty students. It was a great experience, an amazing experiment and amazingly successful.²⁶

This was a very different gender socialisation to that within the ancient universities where domestic staff did everything. As they did in the women's residential colleges. In Cambridge, the only housework a 1900s Newnhamite did was to make her bed on the servants' day off. 'She did not even have to wash up the crockery etc. used in her own room. Shoes were put outside the door to be cleaned by Bowen, the Clough Hall porter, and he filled the coal-scuttles.'²⁷

We turn now to the experience of those who attended teacher training establishments including those residential colleges under the control of the churches. Born in 1902, elementary school child Marjorie Brewer was unusual in winning a scholarship to a public boarding school, Christ's Hospital, in Hertford. Denied special privileges given to other girls because the headmistress took a dim view of her illegitimacy, her experience was an unhappy one. Despite excellent examination results, she was duly refused a university grant on the grounds that she had not 'contributed much to the life of the school.' Her hopes of studying medicine dashed, Marjorie followed the traditional pathway mapped out for an academically able working-class girl instead. She

---

²⁵ Op cit, 165, 179.
²⁶ Jack Lawson, *A Man's Life* (London: Hodder & Stoughton, 1933), 96.
²⁷ Dorothy Thacker, 'Women in Laboratories', in *A Newnham Anthology*, ed. Ann Phillips (Cambridge: Cambridge University Press, 1988), 78. See Laura Schwarz *A Serious Endeavour: gender, education and community at St Hugh's, 1886-2011* (London: Profile Books, 2011) for a discussion of the domestic staff known as 'scouts' at St Hugh's, Oxford.

took up a local authority grant enabling her to go to London's Furzedown Teaching Training College, which marked a decisive shift for her. 'They treated you like adults, they didn't care about your ancestry; if you did a good job and worked hard, that was it.'[28]

Future union leader Ronald Gould was a former scholarship boy who became a teacher in the 1920s. A change in his father's employment meant his parents could afford to pay for him to attend Westminster College, founded in 1851 as a training institute for teachers for Wesleyan Methodist schools. Ronald remembered the 'ragging' of new students in the first term, including a fake exam, public humiliation at mealtimes, sodden beds, stolen pyjamas and water poured over them from chamber pots, culminating in an initiation ceremony in an unlit lecture theatre. First, a white shrouded figure appeared on the stage, followed by another carrying a poker that he then heated with a blow lamp, at which point the two were joined by nine more shrouded figures dragging with them the juniors' elected leader. 'One of the nine explained in sepulchral tones that the chairman was to be branded on the forehead with "W" for Westminster and that he would suffer on behalf of all of us. The chairman was dragged behind a screen, and soon loud, anguished yells assailed our ears, and the smell of burning flesh our nostrils.' When the 'branded' student reappeared, they were ordered to march in single file on the stage and have a 'W' inscribed on their forehead with red greasepaint. What they really smelt was the poker singeing a pig's tale.[29]

Oral narratives of men and women from working-class backgrounds, who went to teacher training college in the 1950s and 1960s, show the meshing of class, gender and occupational identities. Susan's parents encouraged her to become a teacher, and in 1950, she attended a residential women's training college where the culture of femininity resembled that of a girls' boarding school. She loved her hostel, which was 'like a big family,' domestic intimacies drew them together and her friendship circle enjoyed going out for coffee and cake. Susan recalled the prospective teachers were closely watched with great concern taken to ensure they were morally exemplary, 'it wouldn't be liked if you were not suitably dressed or anything like that, you know. You had a certain responsibility.'

Recruited as a mature student at a time of teacher shortage, Paul went to a Catholic teacher training college in his hometown after completing National Service. Unlike Susan, he lived at home. Limited finances meant he had to stay put and study within commuting distance. 'I used to just go, there was quite a few of us, you know. We used to meet on the bus in Manchester, go there and back, and it was a case of going there, listening to the lectures, coming home, doing your essays at the last minute on a Sunday night, it had got to be handed in on a Monday.'

---

[28] Marjorie Pollitt, *A Rebel Life* (Ultimo: Red Pen Publications, 2007), 4-6, 7.
[29] Ronald Gould, *Chalk Up The Memory* (Birmingham: George Phillip Alexander, 1976), 24.

Bricklayer's son Edward was part of the second male intake at his teacher training college in the early 1960s. Most of the students were female, and he thought the woman principal ran the college like a girls' high school. Many women tutors were unmarried. 'In fact, the joke going around was that they knew everything about children except how to have them. One lady bored us for six months, she talked about the development of the child from birth to the age of six months, and it was like real time.' The college was in a remote location, with little public transport, and his experience of communal living was insular and claustrophobic. 'We used to walk to the village, to the pub, in all weathers, and walk back again at the end of the evening, and we were really isolated, so any social life, we had to make between ourselves. I suppose that gave good team spirit, but then it wasn't, it's not like the life of Riley that some students tend to lead today.'

Serving teacher Richard, in his 30s when interviewed in the 2000s, had an early ambition to act, but there were class and gender anxieties. 'I'd always done drama but on the council estate you didn't do drama. You were gay or something like that and you really felt, you know, oh, I'd better not do it because they might think, yeah, I'm a bit, I'm a bit funny like.' After various short-term jobs, he went back to college. 'There sort of my life changed because I met people that had foresight that had parents that pushed them, that they understood the world, not just through the way I understood it.' After an English and Theatre Studies degree, he used the Graduate Teaching Programme, which offered salary-based training from 1998 to 2012, as a stepping-stone to a teaching career.

When former student teachers spoke of how they were socialised into workplace identities at training college, gendered language was intertwined with social class. The desire to be valued, to make good and make a difference, and values of nurturing, pride and respect were important themes which predisposed those from working-class backgrounds to choose teaching as an occupation. As the first in their families to experience higher education, they did not see teacher training as a second-rate education or career, but there is a sense in which institutional cultures and the wider society encouraged a gendered construct of the caring teacher as something women are 'naturally' good at, and a relegation of teacher training to an inferior status, either consciously or unconsciously. What about the nature of class and gender cultures, identities and formation within the most elite spaces? It is to these that we now turn.

Cultural Reproduction in the Historical World of the Ancient University

In 1892, Edith Morley's father was comfortable with her enrolment at the Ladies Department of London's King's College in Kensington Square, because it was a 20-minute walk from the family home. A suffragette, she wondered if later generations felt 'the thrills of adventure and fulfilled desire which were granted to us, to whom the comradeship of work and play had hitherto been unknown and to whom the disciplined training to surmount intellectual difficulties was at once a stimulus and a revelation.'[30] Edith revelled in newly founded clubs and societies, a student common room, discovering the joys of team sport, and the freedom associated with cycling.

Communal living in the early women's colleges was governed by regulations and obligations. No one should put their head above the parapet, and all should behave impeccably, keep quiet and work hard. This must have been hard for a woman in her 20s like Mary Paley who announced to her family, rather than requested, that she intended to 'go in' for the new Cambridge examinations. One of the first women to study at Cambridge during the beginnings of Newnham College, she thought its Liverpudlian principal, Anne Jemima Clough, treated them like 'schoolgirls.' Another early Newnhamite commented acidly, in a letter home, of a change of mind about cricket. 'Well, yesterday evening we were just going to play, when Miss Clough came out and said she was sorry, but she could not possibly let us play. She said it would spoil the grass.' Several generations of Newnham students were required to wear a hat and gloves in central Cambridge, banned from smoking or riding a bike in the main streets, entertaining male friends in their rooms and going on the river in term-time unless accompanied by a chaperone.[31] Mostly they dismissed it as part of the Victorian attitude to women since college life was interesting and less restricted than life at home. Friends warned Shena Simon about 'a group of Cambridge ladies—wives of Professors—who kept an eagle eye on our behaviour, and every lapse would be immediately reported to the University and would delay the granting of equal rights.' But Shena's main concern was for the chaperone forced to accompany her to boring economics lectures at Trinity.[32]

Salford birth control pioneer Charis Frankenburg went to Somerville College, Oxford, in 1912 with few illusions. 'We realised that we were in Oxford on probation and that to attain what we all hoped for—complete recognition by the University—it was up to us to provide no ammunition for the die-hards.' She recalled of a request to invite a College Fellow to tea. 'Alone?' Somerville principal Emily Penrose asked. 'Yes, he's very shy, and he asked me to tell you that he is over seventy and was my father's tutor.' Penrose, the first woman to gain a first-class degree in Classics at Oxford and instrumental in securing the admission of women as full members in 1920, reflected. 'I should *think* you might... Yes, you may.' Charis's father was an alumni of Trinity College, Oxford, who went on to become a Professor of English, principal of

---

[30] Edith Morley, *Before and After* (Reading: Two Rivers Press, 2016), 50.

[31] Mary Paley Marshall, "71 Regent Street," in *A Newnham Anthology*, ed. Ann Phillips (Cambridge: Cambridge University Press, 1979), 3-5; M. de G. Verrall, "Innocent Gaiety," in *A Newnham Anthology*, 5-8.

[32] Shena Simon, "To Trinity Unchaperoned," in *A Newnham Anthology*, 58-9.

Borough Road Training College, inspector of schools and Chief Inspector of Teacher Training for the Board of Education.[33]

Future historian Dorothy Marshall arrived at Girton in 1918 following six years at Park School in Preston, a state secondary school run on feminist lines by Alice Stoneman, a former North London Collegiate pupil and Girtonian. Girton's pioneer period was over with the main buildings complete, but Dorothy was shocked to find it weak on 'mod cons' like flushing toilets:

> On each floor except the ground floor there was a room divided into discrete cubicles fitted with the usual seating arrangements except for the lack of water. A lever released a flow of either sand or sawdust, I cannot remember which'. Every afternoon at tea time, when the young ladies were in Hall, munching, if I recollect correctly, bread and margarine, or some equally unattractive substance, a party of men used to come up in the service lift and empty the stinking buckets.[34]

At first, Dorothy found Girton an alien community. Social lives revolved around private bedroom parties dedicated to cocoa and nicknamed 'JUG' after the jug of milk the servants left in each student's room after dinner. 'For the fresher who came up as I did without friends it was the time when one became most conscious of how lonely one was. This was accentuated by the ease with which the product of boarding schools, used to mingling with their kind and often with a school mate to keep them company could form little groups.' The culture of femininity was upheld in the manner of middle-class customs and strictures. So, the rules of 'The Prop' meant a 'fresher' or first-year could only be on first name terms with her peers but had to wait for the honour of being 'propped' (shorthand for 'May I propose to call you by your Christian name?') by a senior.[35]

Viewed through the prism of Dorothy Marshall's experience, chaperones were less of a requirement and mixed dances became as much a part of social life as they had not been for the first Girtonians. The arrival of officers in the American army, university men, sent to get a taste of English life was momentous. 'They were unencumbered either by the necessity of taking their academic obligations seriously or by the conventions of English society and the female company on which they normally relied was on the other side of the Atlantic.' When Vera Brittain returned to Somerville after working as a nurse for much of the First World War, she accepted the traditions of her social class. She knew that Oxbridge was the training ground for the powerful, and she wanted to enter the world of men, but chaffed at the confines of the female community, while recognising they were founded out of the exclusionary policies of the men's colleges.[36]

---

[33] Charis Ursula Frankenburg, *Not Old Madam, Vintage!* (Lavenham: Galaxy Press, 1975), 60.
[34] Dorothy Marshall, *The Making of A Twentieth Century Woman* (London: Blazenbooks, 2003), 45.
[35] Op cit, 47.
[36] Op cit, 81; Vera Brittain, *Testament of Youth* (London: Virago, 1986).

The vestiges of the chaperone system still operated when Peggy Jay went to Lady Margaret Hall in the 1930s, although she and her contemporaries no longer had 'to wheel their divans into the corridor at weekends when young men were allowed to call.' Jay's reminiscences illustrate the panoptic surveillance built into the institutional architecture. Whereas the traditional Oxbridge college was built around staircases, with students' rooms clustered vertically, women's colleges were organised around corridors. This made it easier to keep an eye on students.[37] Some women objected to feeling as if they were in the historical world of the university almost on sufferance. 'They do you such a favour, these colleges,' wrote Leila Berg. 'You have to be so grateful because there are some special colleges they're *allowing* girls to go to. I don't want special favours. Boys can go to any place they want to, even if they haven't got the marks I have.' Teacher training college was the default option, and Berg agreed to go for one term but spent her time writing and organising aid to Spain during its civil war. She left before she could be expelled but got a second chance by studying for a diploma in journalism.[38]

Reminiscences and vignettes collated by Newnham Fellow Ann Phillips include an outsider perspective on undergraduate life. Ultimately, most are privileged women, but some voices trouble the dominant narrative of happy, carefree times. Miss Reed was a 1930s Scholarship Girl from a working-class home in south-east London. At Newnham, she was an unhappy misfit who could not disabuse peers of the notion that her parents were remarkably enlightened in sending her to an elementary school.

> Newnhamites never seemed quite real to me. They all seemed to come from the professional classes and from quiet homes in the country. They didn't seem to know what life was all about. I joined the Labour Party, or Club, or whatever it was called. *They* didn't know either, though they tried terribly hard. I remember once listening to an impassioned talk by some good soul, who was horrified because there were households in Britain where the only hot water was obtained by boiling kettles. I'd been filling my weekly bath that way all my life.[39]

Miss Reed's account shows her frustrations. She had strong economic grounds for going to university but struggled to get a job, and there is little evidence of personal enrichment. She had known freedom and independence in the city, heard the speakers at Hyde Park Corner, attended lectures and visited museums and art galleries. The undergraduate curriculum, designed for public schoolgirls who, as far as she could see, had read nothing, fell short of the measuring rod of her state secondary school. However, the cultural transmission of upper-middle-class values—how to eat asparagus, the clothes and amount of lipstick to wear, the social season and the classist implications of

---

[37] Peggy Jay, *Loves & Labours* (London: Weidenfeld & Nicolson, 1990), 35; Laura Schwarz, *A Serious Endeavour*, 47.

[38] Leila Berg, *Flickerbook* (London: Granta, 1997), 145.

[39] K.A. Rees, "I Didn't Like Newnham," in *A Newnham Anthology*, 177.

courtship etiquette—was incessant. 'I didn't know you had to be introduced to a man before you could get to know him; at home we picked up our boyfriends on the street corner, just outside the Public Library,' and it was all perfectly respectable.[40]

Similarly, meanings of elite manliness in the ancient universities relied on stereotypes of gender difference. Witness poet John Betjeman who 'went up to' Oxford in 1925 and recalls social segregation attached to symbols of dress and manner. 'Aesthetes' had long hair and wore suits, plain silk ties and cream or strawberry-pink flannel trousers when in vogue. 'Hearties,' on the other hand, 'were good college men who rowed in the college boat, ate in the college hall, and drank beer and shouted. Their regulation uniform was college tie, college pullover, tweed coat and grey flannel trousers.' Betjeman's fellow 'aesthete' Stephen Spender rejected the prejudices of those who had been privately educated: 'who thought that not to come from a public school was as ridiculous as to be a foreigner. To them, my interest in poetry, painting and music, lack of interest in games, and eccentricity in dress and personal appearance, were symptoms of insanity.' On sunny days, Spender took a cushion into the quadrangle and read poetry.[41]

The son of affluent Quaker parents, A.J.P. Taylor went to Oriel College, Oxford, to study modern history in 1924. Rubbing shoulders with men who saw Oxford 'as a place that would give them the necessary social stamp for well-paid jobs in the civil service,' he recognised the university as a distributor of elite jobs and status. Oxford contemporary, John Innes Mackintosh Stewart saw the gendered segregation as a hangover from schooldays for public school entrants. '"Womanizing" of a low sort classed a man as an unspeakable; romantic attachments and even cautious physical experiments—but all preferably disastrous—with girls in distant places and during vacations were admitted an occasioned mild awe; but one risked ridicule by a bare mention of the women's colleges.'[42]

In the early 1930s, Nevill Mott went from Cambridge student to 27-year-old Professor of Physics at Bristol. 'One of the great satisfactions of research is setting young men on the road to a successful career themselves and the lifelong friendships that result. Cambridge was able to give me this experience early,' he wrote in the 1970s. Balliol man Nigel Nicolson knew women were around on the perimeters, 'somewhere in the outer suburbs, convents loosely linked to our great monastery, but unvisited, and from which no visitors came.' But when sexism manifested itself in the form of a male don refusing to lecture to '*undergraduettes*,' the men walked out. This was no demonstration of university solidarity, said Nicholson, 'more a gesture of romantic chivalry on which

---

[40] Op cit, 178.
[41] John Betjeman, "John Betjeman," in *My Oxford*, ed. Ann Thwaite (London: Robson Books, 1977), 65; Stephen Spender, *World Within World* (New York: St Martin's Press, 1994), 33.
[42] Alan John Percival Taylor, *A Personal History* (London: Hamish Hamilton, 1983), 69; John I.M. Stewart, "J.I.M. Stewart," in *My Oxford*, 81.

we flattered ourselves, and a noble excuse for avoiding a lecture which we expected to be dull. None of us ever spoke to the girls whose champions we had so unexpectedly become.'[43]

Novels embellish the image of interwar Oxbridge as finishing schools for young gentlemen. Just as testimony from actors who attended drama schools in the 1920s and 1930s suggest they performed the same function for 'society' girls in this era.[44] Charles Ryder, the narrator of E.M. Forster's novel of 1945, *Brideshead Re-Visited*, evokes the 1920s Oxford habitus of dreaming spires and quadrangles. Cousin Jasper, president of the Junior Common Room (undergraduate body of the College), visits Ryder in his large, ground-floor rooms in the front quadrangle, with deeply recessed windows and eighteenth century panelling. He commends him for reading History, 'A perfectly respectable school. The very worst is English literature and the next worst is Modern Greats. You want either a first or a fourth.' In matters of attire he suggests, 'Dress as you do in a country house… go to a London tailor; you get better cut and longer credit.' Ryder's Oxford was a man's world, which he likened to the aristocratic season. In his second year, he has no desire to 'impress the new freshmen who, like their London sisters, were here being launched in Society.'[45]

How was gender formation mediated within the context of higher education in the 1940s and beyond? Biographical sources support the argument that a gendered redistribution of educational credentials in a context of comprehensive re-organisation of secondary education in English schools challenged but did not necessarily remove the principles of gender classification and hence elite power relations in the twenty-first century.[46]

CHANGES AND CONTINUITIES: THE SITUATION AFTER 1940

The Oxford Nina Bawden entered in 1943 was a peaceful, privileged oasis. A university restored by war to a strange and timeless silence. No bells rang, by official order, and there was almost no traffic. She thought her generation unique in so far as there appeared a relative classlessness. 'The austerity of war concealed social and financial differences. Since we were all poor and shabby, neither poverty nor shabbiness troubled us. Since we expected to be recruited into the services when we went down, we were not fretted by personal ambition.' Bawden also records an argument she had with Margaret Thatcher, a contemporary at Somerville who also came up on a state scholarship and who she urged to support the vision of a post-war welfare state. 'Of course, she admitted the Labour Club was more *fashionable*—a deadly word that immediately reduced my pretensions—but that in a way suited her purposes. Unlike

---

[43] Nevill Mott, "Nevill Mott," in *My Cambridge*, ed. Ronald Hayman (London: Robson Books, 1977), 25; Nigel Nicolson, in *My Oxford*, 134.
[44] Flora Robson, "Flora Robson," in *My Drama School*, ed. Margaret McCall (London: Robson Books, 1978), 17-31.
[45] Edward Morgan Forster, *Brideshead Re-Visited* (Harmondsworth: Penguin, 2000), 21, 98.
[46] Madeleine Arnot, *Reproducing Gender?* (London: Routledge, 2002).

me, she was not "playing at politics". She meant to get into Parliament and there was more chance of being "noticed" in the Conservative Club.'[47]

Bawden's contemporary, Brian Cox, put a rather different inflection on things. Looking back on life at Cambridge in the 1940s, he said his state secondary schooling made him feel 'very superior to grammar and public school boys who were tongue-tied when a girl came into the room.' When John Stewart returned to Oxford as a lecturer in 1949, he was pleased to find the men's colleges no longer 'cluttered up with hopelessly thick or even incorrigibly idle youths from privileged homes.'[48] Still, there was no reason for thinking that upper-class masculinity would disappear.

In the early 1950s, sociologist Dennis Marsden was the first of his family to go to university. He wrote about his experience in *Breakthrough*, a 1968 collection of accounts Ronald Goldman commissioned to show how men and women who were born into working-class homes scaled the ladders of educational opportunity. 'I didn't make many friends,' Marsden says of his time at Cambridge. 'Yet how quickly all those very large Public Schoolboys called Charles or Miles or Giles or Jeremy, struck up acquaintance and hailed one another loudly across street and quad!' Another counter-cultural memory was of his landlady's approving stories of his fellow lodgers, with their Indian Army fathers, who 'liked to come out into the kitchen to play cards with her. These, her eyes seemed to say, were *real* Cambridge men: what kind of creature are you?'[49]

Public school voices boomed across the tables at Caius when Bernard Barker started his Cambridge career in 1965. Educated at a pioneering London comprehensive school, Eltham Green, he recalled 'I learned quickly but painfully that my home in south London would not feel the same again. I should never really belong to this alternative universe of scarlet gowns, ancestral portraits and chapel services.' His future wife Ann was a student at the University of York, which opened in 1963. On his first visit, Bernard arrived in time for supper in Ann's college canteen where you collected food from a counter. 'There was no high table and there were no portraits, no gilded crests, no gong and no grace… The women serving food and wiping tables were very cheerful but did not behave like our college servants. There was no sign of deference, no hint of formality.' People came and went as they liked, eating and talking in groups around contemporary, light wood tables.[50]

Before 1970, anyone under the age of 21 was legally a child and the university authorities *in loco parentis*. Women trod a tightrope of double standards in

---

[47] Nina Bawden, "Nina Bawden," in *My Oxford*, ed. Ann Thwaite (London: Robson Books, 1977), 155, 165-6.

[48] Brian Cox, *A Great Betrayal*. London: Chapmans Publishers, 1992) 42; John I.M. Stewart, "J.I.M. Stewart," 85.

[49] Dennis Marsden, "Dennis Marsden," in *Breakthrough: autobiographical accounts of the education of some socially disadvantaged children*, ed. Ronald Goldman (London: Routledge & Kegan Paul, 1968), 120.

[50] Bernard Barker, *Busking Latin* (Stamford: The Stamford Press, 2019), 64, 152.

relation to the policing of acceptable sexuality and sexual practice. Antonia Pakenham followed in her mother's footsteps to Lady Margaret Hall in 1950. Rules were a vestigial of the past. Since coming home from dances after curfew was an infringement, she would return for breakfast wearing a veil to suggest she had been to early Mass. Despite all the evidence to the contrary, female morality was unimpeachable among Pakenham's set. 'It was tacitly understood that one could survive the most delightful experiences untouched: perhaps we were like the Aga Khan, on whose lips wine turned to water. At any rate what we firmly believed of ourselves, we naturally believed of our best friends.' Sheila Rowbotham went to St Hilda's College, Oxford, where the authorities expelled one girl discovered in bed with her boyfriend. Whereas she lost her grant and failed to get into any other university, the boy was simply sent away from his college for two weeks. However, because sex and Oxford women proved newsworthy, the attendant unwelcome publicity produced a shift in the regime.[51]

Hunter Davies, future author and husband of Margaret Forster the 'ordinary schoolgirl' we met in Chap. 6, grew up on a Carlisle council estate. In 1954, he went to University College, Durham, with his fees paid and an annual maintenance grant from his local education authority. Imitating Oxbridge, Durham had University policemen called bulldogs, college servants and a High Table butler, but few public school boys. His male peer group was predominantly lower-middle-class northern grammar schoolboys, the first in their families to go to university. All of which made them socially acceptable to female teacher education students at college dances, to which the university authorities bussed the male students. If romance blossomed, the object of desire would get an invitation to the Castle, in itself a big attraction, as was a male undergraduate, considered a 'notch-up' from a prospective teacher. So, 'you would buy crumpets…perhaps steal some jam from the table at breakfast, straighten the bedclothes, open the bedroom window to let out the pong, tidy the desk and prepare your lair.' When Davies returned to do a postgraduate teaching qualification, he was elected president of the Junior Common Room. As 'Senior Man,' he got the best rooms, free sherry and a typewriter.[52]

Grammar-school educated Alan Coren won a scholarship to Wadham College, Oxford, in the 1950s. In an autobiographical vignette, he described another side to Oxbridge class and sexual politics of the era with overtones of the 1928 D.H. Lawrence novel, *Lady Chatterley's Lover*, notorious for its story of the emotional and physical relationship between an upper-class-woman and working-class man. 'It was a general principle among privately educated male undergraduates that one walked about holding hands with well-born gels whom one planned eventually to marry, but screwed nurses; whereas the rest

---

[51] Antonia Fraser, "Antonia Fraser," in *My Oxford*, ed. Ann Thwaite (London: Robson Books, 1977), 174-5; Sheila Rowbotham, *Promise of a Dream: Remembering the Sixties* (London: Penguin Press, 2000).

[52] Hunter Davies, *The Co-Op's Got Bananas! A Memoir of Growing Up in the Post-War North* (London: Simon & Schuster, 2016), 198.

of us walked about holding hands with nurses whom we planned eventually to marry and screwed well-born gels.' Coren recalled tales of men 'who, at fever pitch' allegedly shouted to their privately educated female victim 'And this one's for Jarrow!'[53]

In her memoir *A Woman's Place*, published in 2016, Labour politician Harriet Harman describes another form of sexual harassment. Harman left home to go to York University in 1969. As she neared the end of her studies, she claims a male academic offered to guarantee her a better degree if she would have sex with him. She rejected his advances, but a friend did not. Unlike Harman, she felt powerless to refuse: 'she had worked hard, was from a working-class family living in a small town and all her family's hopes were riding on her. She didn't dare risk returning home with a 2:2.'[54] A working-class girl who made it to university, Jane Thompson expressed her desire for a different world.

> I wanted such a life. I did not think that I would have to beat men at their game or compete with them. I thought I could merely join in. I knew that it would mean renouncing the company of women for the most part, as friends and confidantes, because women, on the whole, did not go to university, or want careers, or expect in those days, to travel the world and to be making history.[55]

Only then did she learn how patriarchy works and that being schooled like a 'middle-class boy' was insufficient grounds for becoming an equal in the world of men. The breakthrough of which she writes is of a different order to those in Goldman's edited collection. An outsider on the grounds of class and gender, Thompson became a feminist.

Former secondary modern schoolboy Robert Lindsay attended Nottingham's Clarendon College to gain the qualifications needed to take the teacher training course at Rose Bruford drama school in Kent. He really wanted to become an actor, but his father was outraged at the prospect. 'Why don't you go right over the top and become a bloody hairdresser!' He won a grant to study drama at perhaps the world's most ambitious drama school, the Royal Academy of Dramatic Art (RADA), which meant an interview at the local authority offices to secure his funding. The assessors were stuffy and condescending, and he wanted to drop out, but a teacher talked him out of it. As a drama student, he felt out of place in his hometown where people looked at him as if he was a bit of a 'weirdo.' This was the era of 1960s hippy sub-culture, and he looked the part—long hair, Afghan coat, desert boots and speaking fluent 'flower-power.'[56]

Change happened but constancy also. Ann Widdecombe gained a place at Birmingham University in the 1960s. Her account of undergraduate life harks back to the cocoa parties England's first women students enjoyed. 'At the end of each day's lectures and a stint in the library we returned to hall for supper

---

[53] Alan Coren, "Alan Coren" in *My Oxford*, 195.
[54] Harriet Harman, *A Woman's Work* (London: Allen Lane), 7.
[55] Jane Thompson, *Women, Class and Education* (London, Routledge, 2000), 23.
[56] Robert Lindsay, *Letting Go.* (London: Thorogood, 2009), 49

and then worked in our rooms. After that we brewed up coffee in the communal kitchen and talked for hours, sometimes crowding into each other's rooms or into the small lounge that was provided on each floor.' Her father funded her second degree at Lady Margaret Hall, Oxford, while incredulous his daughter was more ambitious than his son. Contrasting the high culture of the two institutions, she found difference in a readiness to articulate ambition. 'At Birmingham a few of us wanted to be MPs, at Oxford people talked with perfectly straight faces about who might be Cabinet material.'[57]

Andrew Mitchell read History at Cambridge in the 1990s. His 2012 autobiography, *Back Story*, conjures shades of the eighteenth century myth of effortless male achievement that Michèle Cohen identified. The habitus Mitchell describes is one of getting up late and going to the pub, confident that two hours of work per day and cramming for exams got you a good degree and hence the requisite credentials.[58] Mitchell's story, as he tells it, supports recent research on the 'uncool to work' and 'effortless achievement' discourses among male undergraduates in England. Dave, a middle-class, white, student Steven Dempster interviewed at Westchester University, an old campus university, rejected women's conscientious approaches to coursework. Unlike them, Dave said he went close to the wire, working to an imminent deadline and achieving strong results without all the unnecessary 'tweaking' and 'faffing.' In his words, writing an essay due in on Friday morning at 10 o'clock, 'I started at 5 o'clock on a Thursday night. I sat back on my computer, just typing away with a bottle of whisky next to me, and by half past ten I've done the work, emptied the bottle of whisky, and I'm in the pub for last orders.'[59]

This is a very different undergraduate experience to that of Viv Albertine who gains access to higher education at the age of 40. 'I work hard,' she says, 'I never miss a lecture. I try and overachieve, like all mature students. People given a second chance know the value of their reprieve.' Absorbing the message about manmade language on her film and photography degree, she rebels with 'righteous indignation' once outside the lecture hall. Working systematically through the Dewey system in the college library, she takes each book off the shelf, adding, in black biro '"/she" and "/woman" to every "he" and "man".' Her task is vast and unfinished: 'there is hardly one book in the whole library that doesn't use the generic male pronoun. As if only men think and feel and discover and read.'[60]

---

[57] Ann Widdecombe, *Strictly Ann* (London: Orion Publishing, 2014) 66, 70.

[58] David Mitchell, *Back Story* (London: Harper, 2012); Michèle Cohen, "'A Habit of Healthy Idleness': boys' underachievement in historical perspective," in *Failing Boys? Issues in Gender and Achievement*, eds. D. Epstein, J. Elwood, V. Hey and J. Maw (Buckingham: Open University Press, 1998), 19-34.

[59] Carolyn Jackson and Steve Dempster, '"I sat back on my computer… with a bottle of whisky next to me": constructing "cool" masculinity through "effortless" achievement in secondary and higher education', *Journal of Gender Studies*, 18, no. 4 (2009), 347.

[60] Viv Albertine, *Clothes, Clothes, Clothes, Music, Music, Music, Boys, Boys, Boys* (London: Faber & Faber, 2016), 261-2.

Research on the twenty-first century student experience suggests male undergraduates recognise their status as a minority category in higher education but do not feel disadvantaged by it, neither during their studies nor in relation to post-degree life chances.[61] Whether they will in the future is an empirical question, which it is too early to test. However, concerns about lad cultures in higher education contexts proliferated in the UK print media in 2013 and after, with cases of sexual violence against women on campus. In contrast to the segregated experience of pioneer undergraduate women, two-thirds of female students who responded to studies by the National Union of Students reported having experienced some form of verbal or non-verbal harassment.

Besides drunkenness, public rowdiness and sexual harassment, pervasive features of lad culture include sexist, harassing and sometimes abusive practices to degrade, humiliate and objectify women. British film *The Riot Club* (2014) tells the story of ten Oxford students who belong to an exclusive dining society, inviting comparisons with the Bullingdon Club, a private all-male dining club for Oxford University students, whose past members include Conservative politicians David Cameron, Boris Johnson and George Osborne. Often depicted within sections of society without money and power, the script renders gang culture, misogyny and violence part of the 'domain of the sayable,' to use the language of Judith Butler, within elite university communities.

Conclusion

In living memory, the idea of continuing one's education has moved from the margins to the mainstream of public life. While a female undergraduate no longer seems a travesty of common sense, plotting a gendered history of students is not a simple linear telling. If going to university now appeals more to women than to men, we need to ask why. Perhaps the answer lies in contemporary aspects of lad culture. Very different from the 1920s 'hearties' John Betjeman wrote about, does the myth of effortless achievement and the 'uncool to work' discourse defined in opposition to the book-learning and academic regulation of the universities, deter young men who do not value the credentials bestowed by obtaining a degree? For those choosing to enter traditionally male occupations the financial imperative is weaker than it is for those making equally gendered career choices and taking up jobs traditionally labelled as women's work.

Elements of the current gender order in tertiary education may be different, but the retrieval of subjugated knowledge helps us appreciate gendered trends and disrupt taken-for-granted normative assumptions about the student body. The voices brought together here unlock more nuanced understandings of gendered learning journeys, without losing sight of our heterogeneity and individual uniqueness. While there is not space to delineate all these, I end with an uplifting discourse of hope, flagging a love of learning as an end and/or as

---

[61] Ruth Woodfield, "The gendered landscape of UK higher education: do men feel disadvantaged?," *Gender and Education*, 31, no. 1 (2019), 15-32.

a source of social change, to address the unfulfilled desires of people's lives. For Eleanor Lodge, going to Lady Margaret Hall in 1890 was the moment her real life began. 'The very fact of having a room of one's own, a place where one not only could work, but was expected to work, the possibility of independence, of arranging one's time for oneself, of getting up and going to bed according to one's own ideas and not those of others, made each day an adventure and joy.' She did well. In 1928, Eleanor became the first woman to obtain the degree of DLitt from Oxford University and a CBE in 1932.[62]

BIBLIOGRAPHY

PRIMARY SOURCES

ARCHIVAL SOURCES

Bedford College Papers, Royal Holloway Archives and Special Collections, University of London.
"Vincent's News Cuttings," Volume 6, Greenwich Heritage Centre.

AUTOBIOGRAPHIES, MEMOIRS, DIARIES, LETTERS, OBITUARIES

Albertine, Viv. *Clothes, Clothes, Clothes, Music, Music, Music, Boys, Boys, Boys*. London: Faber & Faber, 2016.
Barker, Bernard. *Busking Latin: A memoir by Bernard Barker*. Stamford: The Stamford Press, 2019.
Bawden, Nina. "Nina Bawden." In *My Oxford* edited by Ann Thwaite, 153-167. London: Robson Books, 1977.
Berg, Leila. *Flickerbook*. London: Granta, 1997.
Betjeman, John. "John Betjeman." In *My Oxford* edited by Ann Thwaite, 59-71. London: Robson Books, 1977.
Brittain, Vera. *Testament of Youth*. London: Virago, 1986.
Coren, Alan. Alan Coren In My Oxford edited by Ann Thwaite, 181-199. London: Robson Books.
Cox, Brian. *A Great Betrayal*. London: Chapmans Publishers, 1992.
Davies, Hunter. *The Co-Op's Got Bananas! A Memoir of Growing Up in the Post-War North*. London: Simon & Schuster, 2016.
Edwards, Wil Jon. *From the Valley I Came*. London: Angus and Robertson, 1957.
Forrester, Helen. *Twopence to Cross the Mersey*. London: HarperCollins, 2016.
Frankenburg, Charis Ursula. *Not Old Madam, Vintage*. Lavenham: Galaxy Press, 1975.
Fraser, Antonia. "Antonia Fraser." In My Oxford edited by Ann Thwaite, 169-181. London: Robson Books.
Gould, Ronald. *Chalk Up the Memory*. Birmingham: George Phillip Alexander, 1976.
Harman, Harriet. *A Woman's Work*. London: Allen Lane, 2017.
Jay, Peggy. *Loves & Labours*. London: Weidenfeld & Nicolson, 1990.
Lawson, Jack. *A Man's Life*. London: Hodder & Stoughton, 1933.
Lindsay, Robert. *Letting Go*. London: Thorogood, 2009.
Lodge, Eleanor. *Terms and Vacations*. London: Oxford University Press, 1938.

---

[62] Eleanor Lodge, *Terms and Vacations* (Oxford: Oxford University Press, 1938), 41.

Marsden, Dennis. "Dennis Marsden" in *Breakthrough: autobiographical accounts of the education of some socially disadvantaged children* edited by Ronald Goldman, 106-123. London: Routledge & Kegan Paul, 1968.
Marshall, Dorothy. *The Making of a Twentieth Century Woman*. London: Blazenbooks, 2003.
Marshall, Mary Paley. "71 Regent Street." In *A Newnham Anthology* edited by Ann Phillips, 3-5. Cambridge: Cambridge University Press, 1979.
Mitchell, David. *Back Story*. London: Harper, 2012.
Morley, Edith. *Before and After*. Reading: Two Rivers Press, 2016.
Mott, Nevill. "Nevill Mott." In *My Cambridge*, edited by Ronald Hayman, 15–26. London: Robson Books, 1977.
Nicholson, Nigel. "Nigel Nicholson." In *My Oxford* edited by Ann Thwaite, 125-138. London: Robson Books, 1977.
Pollitt, Marjorie. *A Rebel Life*. Ultimo: Red Pen Publications, 2007.
Rees, K.A. "I Didn't Like Newnham." In *A Newnham Anthology* edited by Ann Phillips, 177-8. Cambridge: Cambridge University Press, 1979.
Robson, Flora. "Flora Robson." In *My Drama School*, edited by Margaret McCall, 17-31. London: Robson Books, 1978.
Rowbotham, Sheila. *Promise of a Dream: Remembering the Sixties*. London: Penguin Press, 2000.
Simon, Shena. "To Trinity Unchaperoned." In *A Newnham Anthology* edited by Ann Phillips, 58-9. Cambridge: Cambridge University Press, 1979.
Spender, Stephen. *World Within World*. New York: St Martin's Press, 1994.
Stewart, John I.M. "J. I. M. Stewart." In *My Oxford* edited by Ann Thwaite, 73-88. London: Robson Books, 1977.
Taylor, Alan John Percival. *A Personal History*. London: Hamish Hamilton, 1983.
Thacker, Dorothy. "Women in Laboratories." In *A Newnham Anthology*, edited by Ann Phillips, 78-9. Cambridge: Cambridge University Press, 1979.
Verrall, M. de G "Innocent Gaiety." In *A Newnham Anthology* edited by Ann Phillips, 5-8. Cambridge: Cambridge University Press, 1979.
Widdecombe, Ann. *Strictly Ann*. London: Orion Publishing, 2014.

OTHER CONTEMPORARY BOOKS AND PAMPHLETS

Hardy, Thomas. *Jude the Obscure*. Harmondsworth: Penguin Classics, 1998.
Rubinstein, David and Stoneman, Colin. "Introduction." In *Education for Democracy*, edited by David Rubinstein and Colin Stoneman, 7-13. Harmondsworth: Penguin, 1972.

SECONDARY SOURCES

Arnot, Madeleine. *Reproducing Gender?* London: Routledge, 2002.
Cohen, Michèle. "'A Habit of Healthy Idleness': boys' underachievement in historical perspective." In *Failing Boys? Issues in Gender and Achievement*, edited by Debbie Epstein, Jeanette Elwood, Valerie Hey and Janet Maw, 19-34. Buckingham: Open University Press, 1998.
David, M. E. *The State, the Family and Education*. London: Routledge & Kegan Paul, 1980.
Dyhouse, Carol. *No distinction of sex? Women in British universities 1870-1939*. London: UCL Press, 1995.

Dyhouse, Carol. "Signing the Pledge? Women's Investment in University Education Before 1939," *History of Education*, 26, no. 2 (1997): 207-223.
Dyhouse, Carol. "Going to University in England between the Wars: access and funding," *History of Education*, 31, no. 1 (2002): 1-14.
Dyhouse, Carol. "Troubled Identities: Gender and Status in the History of the Mixed College in English Universities since 1945," *Women's History Review*, 12, no. 2 (2003): 169-194.
Dyhouse, Carol. *Students: a gendered history*. London: Routledge, 2006.
Edwards, Elizabeth. "Mary Miller Allan: The Complexity of Gender Negotiations for a Woman Principal of a Teacher Training College." In *Practical Visionaries: Women, Education and Progress 1790-1930*, edited by Mary Hilton and Pam Hirsch, 149–194. Harlow: Longman, 2000.
Ellis, Heather. "Foppish Masculinity, Generational Identity and the University Authorities in Eighteenth-Century Oxbridge," *Cultural and Social History*, 11, no. 3 (2014): 367-384.
Heward, Christine. "Men and women and the rise of professional society: the intriguing history of teacher educators," *History of Education*, 22, no. 1 (1993): 11-32.
Hirsch, Pam. *Barbara Leigh Smith Bodichon 1827-1891: Feminist, Artist and Rebel*. London: Chatto and Windus, 1998.
Jackson, Carolyn. "'Laddishness' as a self-worth protection strategy," *Gender and Education*, 14, no. 1 (2002): 37-50.
Carolyn Jackson, Steve Dempster & Lucie Pollard. "'They just don't seem to really care, they just think it's cool to sit there and talk': laddism in university teaching-learning contexts," *Educational Review*, 67, no. 3 (2015): 300-314.
Jackson, Carolyn & Steve Dempster. "'I sat back on my computer… with a bottle of whisky next to me': constructing "cool" masculinity through 'effortless' achievement in secondary and higher education," *Journal of Gender Studies*, 18, no. 4 (2009): 341-356.
Jones, Claire G. "'All your dreadful scientific things': women, science and education in the years around 1900," *History of Education*, 46, no. 2 (2017): 162-175.
Martin, Jane. *Making Socialists: Mary Bridges Adams and the Fight for Knowledge and Power, 1855-1939*. Manchester: Manchester University Press, 2013.
McWilliams-Tullberg, Rita. *Women at Cambridge*. Cambridge: Cambridge University Press, 1998.
Purvis, June. *Hard Lessons: the lives and education of working-class women in nineteenth-century England*. Minneapolis: University of Minnesota Press, 1989.
Reay, Diane, Crozier, Gill & Clayton, John. "Strangers in Paradise? Working-class Students in Elite Universities," *Sociology*, 43, no. 6 (2009): 1103-1121.
Rose, Jonathan. *The Intellectual Life of the British Working Classes*. Yale: Yale University Press, 2001.
Schwarz, Laura. *A Serious Endeavour: gender, education and community at St Hugh's, 1886-2011*. London: Profile Books, 2011.
Sims, Jana. "Mechanics' Institutes in Sussex and Hampshire: 1825-1875." PhD thesis, University of London, 2010.
Whitehead, Kay. "Contesting the 1944 McNair Report: Lillian de Lissa's working life as a teacher educator,"' *History of Education*, 39, no. 4 (2010): 507-524.
Woodfield, Ruth. "The gendered landscape of UK higher education: do men feel disadvantaged?," *Gender and Education*, 31, no. 1 (2019): 15-32.

PART III

Teachers and Teaching

CHAPTER 9

Women in Teaching

> *Of course, teachers cannot "keep out" of politics—no one can. From cradle to grave the lives of all of us are ordered directly and indirectly by Parliament. The registration and vaccination of infants, the education of children, marriage and divorce laws, the size of our incomes, the purity of our food, the safety of our streets, the sanitation of our houses, the pollution of the very air we breathe and the conditions under which we are buried and cremated are all affairs which concern and are regulated by Parliament. For good or ill we are all in politics and when people tell us to "keep out" they only mean they wish us to be passive and to take no active part in the ordering of our own lives, and those of our compatriots. More than this they would rather we did not take too much notice of the way in which they themselves are performing the task. Ours is not to reason why!*
> —Florence E. Key, *Woman Teacher*, 26 October 1934, 24

This is the voice of an elementary school teacher caught up with the gender politics of the early twentieth century. Like most women teaching working-class children, she taught infant and girls' classes. More unusually, she joined the women's suffrage movement and was active in the creation of the Federation of Women Teachers, a pressure group within the NUT, with the goal of achieving equal pay between men and women teachers. The case of this English teacher trade unionist highlights the importance of teaching as the site on which a women's politics has been conducted, working against cultural and social assumptions about gender conveyed through the taken-for-granted or naturalized discourse of the caregiver. As a young woman living out radical ways of being a woman teacher, the respect and recognition of her peers brought Florence Ellen Key (1887–1965) to the fore within teacher trade unionism and her political vision, principles and ideas flowed out into and across the everyday world of girls and women.

© The Author(s), under exclusive license to Springer Nature Switzerland AG 2022
J. Martin, *Gender and Education in England since 1770*, Gender and History, https://doi.org/10.1007/978-3-030-79746-1_9

The argument of this chapter is that former and present-day women teachers produced a discourse of democratic civic professionalism based on the affective domain of caring about children and community, mobilising the belief that all children matter and celebrating the potential to be effective, to make a difference in the world. Therefore, I attempt to bring theory and research into dialogue by way of an empirical mapping of the changing iconographies of education and politics and the people who inhabit the classrooms, in a range of historical moments. In developing this agenda, I examine hegemonic framings of professionalism (based on white, male, and middle-class norms) and a gendered division of labour as major issues underlying teachers' work. My purpose is to use a range of sources to illuminate a congruency between how gender, class and professional identities were shaped and conceived, the development of teacher professionalism and professional expectations and involvement in wider reform movements. Suggesting that there is much value in understanding the teacher identity/social action relation in the past and tracing how the present and future resonates with continuities and difference.

There is an extensive literature that examines the increasing demand for elementary school teachers and the significant numbers of strong, imaginative women who found teaching posts in Victorian England.[1] For working-class and later girls from the middle classes, a teaching career offered a specialised training, lifelong career and attractive salary, professional identity and important public work. We see this in the writing of D.H. Lawrence, the first major English novelist to have direct experience of our state schools. Lawrence got his education on scholarships and went on to teach in an elementary school in Croydon. For Ursula Brangwen, a character in Lawrence's 1915 novel *The Rainbow*, teaching was a way into a full and interesting life. 'She had a standing ground now apart from her parents. She was something else besides the mere daughter of William and Anna Brangwen. She was independent. She earned her own living. She was an important member of the working community.'[2]

Elementary teaching offered working-class girls a living wage and a respectable way to earn a living. Once a system of payment by results was introduced in 1862 and central government increasingly controlled pay and conditions, women were increasingly relied on to ensure an adequate supply of teachers. Large numbers worked as untrained supplementary teachers (the only requirement being that they should be aged 18 or over and vaccinated against smallpox), but the story of stonemason's daughter Sarah Jane Bannister born in 1858, shows what an ambitious and dedicated woman might achieve as part of a large public sector labour force. Bannister completed her teacher-training at

---

[1] See, for example, Dina M. Copelman, *London's Women Teachers: Gender, Class and Feminism, 1870–1930* (London: Routledge, 2014); Alison Oram, *Women Teachers and Feminist Politics, 1900–39* (Manchester: Manchester University Press, 1996); Frances Widdowson, *Going Up Into the Next Class: Women and Elementary Teacher Training 1840–1914* (London: Women's Research and Resources Centre Publications, 1980); Jane McDermid, *The Schooling of Girls in Britain and Ireland, 1800–1900* (London: Routledge, 2012).

[2] D.H. Lawrence, *The Rainbow* (Harmondsworth: Penguin, 2007), 390.

a college in Tottenham and went on to obtain work as London's only female principal of a pupil-teacher centre, in Stepney, before leading a new, non-residential day training college at Moorfields, London.[3] Aged 23, she married a widowed teacher 15 years her senior. She had one child and in the 1880s, she and her husband were selected as mentors for Inner London's pupil teachers. She later served on a government committee on teacher education and became an alderman in the London Borough of Hendon. By 1914, when she led Moorfields, elementary teaching was women's work both statistically and by reputation.

The fact that women joined the workforce in increasing numbers suggests elementary teaching was not a gender neutral sphere of paid work but defined as a feminised occupation characterised by stereotypical features of femininity (being caring, facilitative, supportive). In England, the numerical gender balance of the state-maintained school workforce has been remarkably stable for over a century, and as a policy issue, it has been linked to an institutional culture which is biased towards females. Today, 26 per cent of teachers are male (38 per cent of secondary and 15 per cent of primary school teachers). As a result, there have been various calls for more male teachers on the grounds that teaching staff should reflect the make-up of the wider society, or to provide role models or 'father figures' to address the issue of underachieving boys in the education system and maintain discipline in the classrooms. In fact, research suggests that male teachers do not necessarily enhance academic outcomes or motivational levels of boys.[4]

The analysis of the teacher's world presented here derives from an ESRC-funded project focusing on work-derived identities and their relation to social action. The study was qualitative, based on in-depth interviews made between 2005 and 2008, and documentary research using a range of archival sources including personal papers and institutional records.[5] Central to the project, in terms of methodology, were 40 semi-structured interviews, with female and male teachers in both the primary and secondary sector, from both city and country schools. They all volunteered to take part and represented a broad spectrum of professional and biographical profiles in terms of age, experience, personal history, levels of the promotional structure and domestic arrangements. The individuals profiled here are similarly located in terms of their experience of a field of action constituted by their shared participation in schooling

---

[3] Wendy Robinson, "Sarah Jane Bannister and Teacher Training in Transition 1870–1918," in *Practical Visionaries: Women, Education and Social Progress 1790–1930*, ed. Mary Hilton and Pam Hirsch (Harlow: Longman), 131–148.

[4] Joanne McDowell and Revert Klattenburg, "Does Gender Matter? A Cross-National Investigation of Primary Class-room Discipline," *Gender and Education*, 31, no. 8 (2019), 947–965.

[5] ESRC Identities Programme project *Does Work Still Shape Social Identities and Social Action* (RES-148-25-0038).

processes. Teachers' accounts illuminate Bourdieusian notions of habitus embedded within everyday actions in a highly feminised occupation in the sense of a high proportion of women.

I start with a word or two about educational contexts, changes, and continuities. The use of a precise historical chronology would be too monolithic and deterministic because formations of professionalism are historically contingent and depend on the sector within which they emerge and the relations that underpin that sector.

Feminisation and the Culture and Politics of Teachers' Work

Gerald Grace has identified four broad phases intended to be indicative of the teachers' lives/policy interpellation understood as the moment and process of recognition of interaction with organisational policy, within which characterisations of a teacherly self can be constituted. However, his analysis of the political development of teacher's professional lives tends to render women and gender invisible. In this respect, a focus on class cultural condescension as *the* hallmark of 1900s policy-making overlooks the ways in which teachers' work was mediated by the gendered policies of governments. Neglecting the fact that the 1920s were a period of reaction to feminist gains made during and immediately after World War One, when the rights and safeguards of women workers came under attack and the marriage bar was only the most tangible of the obstacles placed in the way of women's advancement.[6]

Members who split away from the NUT to form the NUWT in 1920 wanted an alternative trade union to one whose role had been defined by men, an association which would reflect their political and educational outlooks and help them challenge the inequalities they perceived in society, offering a support network to help them in their struggle against what would be called everyday sexism today. For them, equal pay for equal work was a precondition of professional status. The argument being that since women teachers performed the

---

[6] Gerald Grace, "Teachers and the state in Britain: A changing relation," in *Teachers: The Culture and Politics of Work*, ed. Martin Lawn and Gerald Grace (|Abingdon: Routledge, 2012), 193–228.

same job as men, paying them less undermined the status and reward of all teachers, encouraging local authorities to employ women because they were cheaper.[7]

In contrast, the aim of the NAS, which had the motto 'Men teachers for Boys,' was to oppose equal pay and a growing practice of substituting women teachers for men in boys' departments in state-maintained schools as a way of saving money. The men who joined the NAS did not want to work under female bosses and tried to attract male teachers by carving out a 'masculine' niche.

> Let women take charge of the infants indiscriminately by all means, for there they are more fitted for the task, but as soon as the boys begin to be segregated into male classes, their teachers should be of their own sex. This is especially necessary in their games, exercises and physical training, and the general public will learn with a sense of absurdity that it is necessary for the men to protest against women being put in charge of this department.[8]

Besides the argument that men provide a role model for male pupils and enact tough discipline, women's eligibility for the inspectorate was a source of aggravation among workers who disliked having women assess the standard of their teaching. With an exclusively male membership until 1975, Alison Oram considers their attitude that of a 'macho' industrial trade union using breadwinner ideology as a bargaining lever while fostering anxiety that a female workforce produced an inappropriate femininity of culture in schools.[9]

In some localities, authorities met demands for equal pay, but this changed after national Burnham scales were introduced in 1920. Women teachers in the state system had the highest pay cuts under austerity measures in the 1920s and 1930s and were increasingly likely to be required to resign on marriage. Other gender issues included the impact of co-education as amalgamations to form mixed departments saw their virtual exclusion from school leadership in the elementary system, and female exclusion from the inspectorate, besides monitoring teacher quality in respect of needlework. In supporting married women teachers, the NUWT used egalitarian arguments (see Text Box 9.1).

---

[7] The NUWT had eight aims. (1) To collect and express the opinions and wishes of women teachers to secure their combined action. (2) To secure better pensions and earlier optional retirement. (3) To secure equal pay and equal increments for men and women teachers of the same professional status. (4) To secure the maintenance of each girls' and infants' department under its own headmistress. (5) To secure representation of women on all education authorities. (6) To secure direct effective representation of women teachers' interests in Parliament. (7) To secure that all the higher educational posts shall be open equally to men and women and with equal remuneration. (8) To convene conferences on educational subjects and to promote such questions as have for their object the well-being of women and children.
[8] *The Birmingham Mail*, 23 January 1934, UWT/D/68c/1.
[9] Alison Oram, *Women Teachers and Feminist Politics*, 151–6.

Text Box 9.1 Memorandum Sent by the London Unit of the NUWT on the Employment of Married Women as Teachers

In the belief that the London County Council is actuated by a desire to maintain the greatest efficiency in its schools and to promote the greatest good of the children attending them, the London unit of the National Union of Women Teachers begs to lay before the Council the following considerations with regard to the employment of married women as teachers. The dismissal of women on marriage:

1. Deprives the schools of the services of trained and experienced teachers just at the time when they are approaching the period of maximum efficiency in their profession.
2. Necessitates the employment of an unnecessarily large percentage of young and inexperienced teachers and thus injuriously affects the school organisation.
3. Involves a waste of public money through the training of large numbers of teachers who, by reason of the compulsory curtailment of their professional careers, are prevented from making an adequate return to the community for the expense it has incurred in their training.
4. Makes teaching for women, a 'blind-alley' occupation. Parents will, therefore, be unwilling to incur expense in training their girls for it, and the field of selection will thus be injuriously restricted.
5. Tends to encourage a lower standard of qualification and efficiency on the part of entrants, the majority of whom will naturally be looking forward to a comparatively short scholastic career if marriage is to mark its termination.
6. Robs the children of the invaluable contribution made to their training by those women who, through marriage, have experienced a wider and fuller life.

We feel also that a great and influential representative body like the London County Council cannot be deaf to the claims of justice:

1. The enforcement of celibacy as a condition of employment is an unwarrantable encroachment on individual liberty. A woman should be free to decide for herself how best she can serve her home, her family and the community of which she is a part.
2. Since this condition is not and cannot be universally applied in other professions and forms of employment, it amounts to a special disability for those working in public service.
3. Condemns to celibacy many self-sacrificing men and women who have heavy financial responsibilities on account of dependent relatives.[10]

---

[10] EO/STA/2/12 Married Women Teachers.

Operating against a background of backlash against feminism, the Women's Co-operative Guild argued the marriage bar was unfair not only to the teachers and the parents who maintained their daughters in pursuit of this goal but 'the nation which is deprived of the services of the woman just when she is becoming of real value.'[11] A charity worker at a settlement in West Ham wondered if an exception might be made in the case of a young wife who had just left her violent husband. Should he advise her to apply for a divorce? Would she 'be eligible to apply for a post under your Council or under the Council of any other county or district?' An unbending metropolitan official simply wrote NO.[12]

Grace characterises the era as a period when some organised teachers sought empowering identities as trusted professionals, while radical movements in the state sector such as the Teachers' Labour League presented perspectives for reform based on direct popular control of education. By 1939, he considers state schoolteachers had achieved respectable white collar/white blouse security as one of the accepted lesser professions associated with what he calls an *ethic of legitimated professionalism*. If so, this did not translate into career gains for women as opportunities for advancement dwindled. Nevertheless, the NUWT secured a notable victory when their elected representative, Agnes Dawson, persuaded the Labour controlled London County Council to remove the marriage bar on women teachers in 1935.[13]

Councillor Shena Simon who we met as a Newnham student in Chap. 8, took a lead in attacking attempts to clamp down on the employment of married women in Manchester. Serving alongside Shena was Hannah Mitchell who deliberately limited her fertility to that she could pursue a life outside the domestic sphere. Hannah was at that time serving on a welfare committee and had one point ready-made.

> When an unemployed man applied for relief, the first question he was asked was whether his wife was working, and if she wasn't, the second question was 'Why not?' In reply to the 'two-incomes-in-one-home argument' I asked what was the difference between a couple bringing two hundred and fifty each, and a man who brings five hundred into the home, except that in one case the woman renders service to the community. I quoted from the prayer-book: 'Marriage is an honourable institutions', but, I said, the supporters of this resolution seemed to be making it look like a dishonourable thing, for which a woman must be penalized by losing her job, and sacrificing the career she has worked hard to fit herself for.[14]

---

[11] London County Council Education Committee: Employment of Married Women Deputation to urge the amendment of SO 354, received by the Chairman of the Education Committee 15 January 1926, EO/STA/2/12 Married Women Teachers.

[12] J. Wells-Thatcher, Counsel for the Poor to the Education Officer, The Given-Wilson Institute, London Road, Plaistow, 1 December 1926, EO/STA/2/13 Married Women Teachers General Papers 1923–1934.

[13] NUWT. 1935. 'Another victory—The removal of the marriage bar'; *Woman Teacher* 1919–1960.

[14] Hannah Mitchell, *The Hard Way Up* (London: Virago, 1977), 218.

Shena felt the same when a male councillor said 'how dreadful it would be for the children, if, just when the "scholarship" examination was being held, all the women teachers in junior schools were away having babies.' She thought better of saying she was sure they would manage things differently given the taboos around contraception and birth control. The resolution was defeated, but some men grew petulant and ill-tempered as Hannah recalled. One female councillor who began her speech by saying she thought woman's place was in the home was disconcerted by the interruption in a 'very powerful male voice: "What are you doing here then?"'[15]

The third phase of teacher-state relations Grace identifies is from 1940 to the mid-1970s. Despite the lifting of marriage bars, gender norms encouraged mothers to take a career break and return part-time when their family commitments allowed. Men outnumbered women in the emergency teacher training colleges established to address the post-war issue of teacher supply, and the proportion of men in junior and secondary modern schools (the former elementary sector) grew by 10 per cent in the 1950s. Regarding teachers' professionalism, Grace sees this as the heyday of teacher autonomy, albeit generally confined within the limits of their own classrooms, since they often had little control over school goals and administration; while the value placed on public examinations traditionally exerted a check on teacher agency at secondary level. Equal pay was phased in between 1955 and 1961 and the NUWT disbanded, but a new career structure favoured those in full-time posts with no gaps in employment and there were more promotion posts in the then male dominated secondary sector. Nevertheless, the NAS resisted all implementation of equal pay while promoting a new Union of Women Teachers said to be for member's wives.[16]

If we consider Grace's final period from the late 1970s/early 1980s, we can see how, amid talk that something had gone badly wrong with education and the British welfare state, teachers saw the return of a politics of confrontation. At school level, a growth in the size of secondary schools was the motor of significant bureaucratisation. External pressures at the behest of government also affected routine practices that had previously been informal in style like records of achievement, profiling of student progress, staff appraisal and inspectors' reports.[17] Arguably, national accountability, with detailed directives on chief subject areas, rates of development and modes of assessment, the

---

[15] Joan Simon, *Shena Simon: Feminist and Educationist. Based on the Correspondence and Writings of Lady Simon of Wythenshawe* (privately printed, 1986), III, 11–11a; Hannah Mitchell, *The Hard Way Up*, 218.

[16] Asher Tropp, *The School Teachers: The Growth of the Profession from 1800 to the Present Day* (London: Macmillan, 1957), p. 62; Margaret Littlewood, "The 'Wise Married Woman' and the Teaching Unions," in *Women Teachers: Issues and Experiences*, ed. Hilary De Lyon and Frances Widdowson (Buckingham: Open University Press, 1989); Mike Ironside and Roger Seifert, *Industrial Relations in Schools* (London: Routledge, 1995).

[17] Roy Lowe, *Schooling & Social Change 1964–1990* (London: Routledge, 1990), 135–146.

introduction of league tables for GCSE and A levels, and Standard Assessment Tests, turned teachers into the most controlled group of professionals in the country.

The neo-liberal social policy and marketisation of education instigated by the Conservative governments of the 1980s and 1990s was developed with enthusiasm by the 'New Labour' administrations of Tony Blair and Gordon Brown (1997–2010) as a way of improving institutional, group and individual standards and effectiveness in schooling. Within this policy movement of emphasising quality in terms of performance, standards and accountability, students became educational clients, with parents the consumers of education systems. Metrics in the shape of publicly available league tables of results, and a more stringent school inspection process (set up in 1992) were used to 'measure' standards, with an unprecedented emphasis on the phenomenon of the failing school. Increased levels of public spending accompanied further years of mandated reform, and promotion of change implementation by external interest groups (including government agencies and corporate bodies) as opposed to educator groups. Related to this, some interpret the introduction of performance management systems modelled on 'best' commercial practice (e.g. based on calculative, competitive, individualistic, and hierarchical norms and values) as a masculinisation of teaching as an activity and organisational structure.[18]

What does this mean, then, for the temporal constitution of perceptions of gender, the 'teacher' occupational identity, and social action across the broad sweep of historical time considered here? I will focus first on a reconstruction of the working lives of Kate Dice (née Johnson, 1872-1959) and Florence Key (née Adams) chosen because they represent seemingly discrepant cases – married women teachers, pioneering suffragettes, feminists, and socialists with a powerful drive for a life that transcended the domestic sphere. As young women they completed teacher training and went on to obtain work as city teachers, earning on average around half as much as their male counterparts.

The final section focuses on the oral testimony of eight women who became teachers in the 1950s and beyond. Thickly layered descriptions reflect the complexity of several realities that teachers simultaneously balance. For example, socialisation into expected gender roles comes up again and again, as part of the socio-cultural reproduction into late-modern society. Male teachers were more likely to self-identify as career teachers. Married women teachers mostly took time out of teaching to nurture their biological children, which broke the occupational narrative. The dual career marriage and gendered qualities of the 'good teacher' persist with emergent themes of caring, commitment, community, dedication, selflessness and respect.

---

[18] Mary Thornton and Patricia Bricheno, *Missing Men in Education* (Stoke-on-Trent: Trentham, 2006).

Pedagogies of Resistance: The Making of Kate Miriam Dice

One of eight children, Kate Dice was born in the maritime locality of Rotherhithe on the south bank of the river Thames, where her father worked as a contractor until his death sometime in the 1880s. Kate became a pupil teacher and when tensions with her widowed mother escalated, went to live with her elder sister and her husband, who were teachers and socialists. Kate's socialism was initially because of their influence.[19] They supported her additional training at the British Society's Stockwell College (Fig. 9.1) where the typical student was an academically gifted daughter of the labour aristocracy or lower middle class.

Stockwell was a progressive institution, which used Froebelian practice, such as clay modelling, painting and games and storytelling for teaching young children. Under the leadership of Quaker Lydia Manley, the college developed an

Fig. 9.1 Stockwell College, undated, [c. late nineteenth century]. (Courtesy of Brunel University London Archives)

---

[19] With thanks to Colleen Morrison for sharing this personal information.

[20] Linda Mahood, *Feminism and Voluntary Action: Eglantyne Jebb and Save the Children, 1876–1928* (Basingstoke: Palgrave Macmillan, 2009), 80–81; Stockwell College Student List 1892; K. Dice to P. Ibbotson, 9 May 1955, National Association of Labour Teachers.

autonomous female sub-culture, giving students the feeling that they were a professional group, and the friendships they made stayed with them throughout their professional lives. Stockwell had a college magazine and a flourishing literary society, with elements of a liberal education and a direct influence from specific bodies of research into child development and pedagogy. Kate topped all her exams, and as a newly qualified teacher, she went where she was needed at one of Stockwell's training schools teaching a class of 80.[20]

Kate's letters amongst the papers of the National Association of Labour Teachers show the links between the elementary school world and the metropolitan intelligentsia as she reflected upon events that had occurred many decades earlier. She honed a public political identity as secretary of the Beckenham branch of the Women's Social and Political Union but broke away and joined another suffrage organisation called the Women's Freedom League in 1907.

In the workplace, Kate found shared values, and her public life reveals the importance of group memberships and social networks (Text Box 9.2). Trade unionist Agnes Dawson was on the staff at Crawford Street and Kate worked with fellow socialist Mary O'Brien Harris (who we met in Chap. 6) at Southwark Road. In 1902, Kate married policeman's son Albert Dice, then principal of London's Kennington and New Cross pupil teacher centre. Albert was a former scholarship boy who went to Cambridge University and worked in municipal secondary schools before he retired in 1933.[21]

Text Box 9.2 The Teaching Career of Kate Dice
- 1894, assistant mistress, Galleywall Road School, Southwark
- 1896, assistant mistress, Crawford Street School, Camberwell
- 1899, assistant mistress, Southwark Road pupil-teacher centre
- 1905, assistant mistress, Sydenham Hill School, joins suffragettes
- 1908, joins Fabian Women's Group
- 1909, founds London Married Woman Teachers' Association
- 1913, addresses suffrage meeting on the fringe of the NUT annual conference
- 1914, writes chapter on elementary teaching for the Fabian Women's Group
- 1919–32, head teacher, Waller Road Girls' School

[21] Cambridge University Alumni, 1261–1900.

Teaching played a pivotal role facilitating access to politics, but Kate's friendship with Barbara Drake was a different incubator for her widening horizons. It was through Drake that she established links with an impressive network in the Fabian Society's Women's Group who were exploring how the daily lives of women had been excluded from the historical record. Ideas passed back and forth as Kate sustained a 'chatting acquaintance' with Barbara's aunt, Beatrice Webb, and corresponded with Charlotte Shaw. Thus, Kate Dice's political trajectories focused on reform circles that combined an interest in surveying and mapping a newly conceived space of 'the social' and sought to relate their findings to proposals for practical action. Between 1909 and 1913, for example, she participated in a Fabian project to record the finances and everyday lives of working-class families in Lambeth, London. *Round About a Pound a Week* helped to unlock the story of how women, particularly, got by and argued for government reforms including school meals and health clinics.[22]

During the 1900s, members of the Fabian Women's Group can be seen arguing for equal pay and married women's right to work. Along with Mary O'Brien Harris, Kate Dice wrote for a 1914 Fabian publication, *Women Workers in Seven Professions*.

> Progressive women today resent the social system which requires them to be economically dependent upon others. They realise that social service needs labour of a highly skilled variety and they therefore demand training for their work as a guarantee of their efficiency in its performance and, on the other hand, monetary payment and security of tenure as guarantees to them of their independence. As a natural corollary of women's lack of political power, there are no spheres of professional work in which prevailing conditions are in these respects completely satisfactory. Perhaps the teaching service in the State schools comes nearest to complying with progressive demands: at any rate Government recognises the need for training and, to a large extent meets its cost. A salary, more or less adequate, is paid in return for the teaching given and security of tenure is, with few exceptions assured.[23]

In 1909, Kate helped to found the London Married Women Teachers' Association, which had four goals. (1) To safeguard the interests of married women teachers. (2) To gain security of tenure and compensation for unjust dismissals. (3) To secure compensation for loss of pensions of breakdown allowances. (4) To afford opportunities for married women teachers to interchange opinions and take action where necessary on subjects of educational importance. An early president and later honorary secretary, the climate in which she operated was hostile.[24]

---

[22] Sally Alexander, *Women's Fabian Tracts* (London: Routledge, 1988), 161.
[23] Kate Dice, "Elementary Teaching," in *Women Workers in Seven Professions*, ed. Edith Morley (London: George Routledge and Sons, 1914), 38–39.
[24] Herbert Delauney Hughes and Geoffrey Frederick Brown, *The W.E.A. Education Year Book 1918* (Nottingham: University of Nottingham, 1981), 457.

Kate Dice had no children but she was fighting against deeply held cultural assumptions that mothers ought to be occupied with their homes and families. As an anonymous writer to the *Morning Post* put it, 'Why on earth should a woman who does not love her children sufficiently to tend them and care for them, who is not sufficiently interested in child nature to study it and spend hours with it when she has it within the four walls of her own home, be considered so eminently suitable to tend other people's children?' Others thought it preposterous 'that the wives of well-to-do professional men, well able to support them, should occupy positions in our public schools (it is not permitted in any other branch of the civil or public service), to the exclusion of their unmarried sisters, who have to depend upon their own resources for a livelihood.' With a membership of about 250, the Association had an uphill struggle. As president, Kate successfully challenged the legality of attempts to exclude suffragettes from trade union activities, but it was hard work.

In London, the proportion of married women teachers varied between 30 and 10 per cent. Mounting unemployment meant attitudes hardened. In this scenario there were those who argued every married woman teacher 'should be taught unselfishness and should manage at home on their husband's wages, other people have to. It is only taking bread out of younger one's mouths. They forget they were young once.' As we read local authority correspondence, we are forced to the realisation that some were prepared to snitch on working women. 'I myself know of two,' wrote E. West of Camden, 'one in 56a Tufnells Park Road, Mrs Camps, and another in 333 Camden Road, Mrs Turner neither of these men did anything in the war. Trusting you will see your way to put this before the Committee.'[25]

London's marriage bar did not affect Kate personally (the authority did not sack married women teachers already in their employ when the ban was introduced), but she thought it patriarchal. In 1913, she addressed a suffrage rally on the fringe of the male-controlled NUT conference, and the National Federation of Women Teachers asked her to join them.[26] Subsequently, supporters printed her speech against a proposal for a referendum on women's suffrage from the Women's National Anti-Suffrage League, which she feared might enable governments to postpone votes for women indefinitely. To show how opinions change, she said mass schooling is now described as *popular education* but was decidedly *unpopular* in the past. 'I remember well how early in my career as a teacher I had to evade sundry missiles thrown at me by irate parents who would rather have had their children running errands and washing up things in the home than wasting their time in school on such a thing as learning.'[27]

---

[25] EO/STA/2/13 Married Women Teachers; E. West to R. Blair, 28 September 1922, EO/STA/2/12 Married Women Teachers.

[26] *Minutes*, 26 April 1913; 28 January 1914; 19 November 1922.

[27] *The Referendum*, Women Teachers' Franchise Union.

In 1919, Kate Dice was promoted to a post as head teacher at Waller Road elementary school, within walking distance of her home. Founded in 1888, unlike most city schools, Waller Road was a two-storey building as neighbours successfully objected to the proposed three-storey design at the planning stage. Former pupil Hilda Medora recalled:

> Mrs Dyce wore long dresses down to the ground. She kept her handkerchief in a pocket in a likewise long petticoat. If she needed it, a child was 'privileged' to stoop down, extract the handkerchief and pass it up. When she wanted, unannounced an assembly, she played the Soldiers' March from Faust with a heavy hand. The staff knew the signal: work stopped immediately, and we all filed silently into the hall.[28]

Looking back, Kate said she ran Waller Road School on what they would now call 'workers control' lines. Whilst her attempt to form a democratic learning community may not have been apparent to the pupils, she wrote the secretary of the National Association of Labour Teachers of her concern to give staff a greater role in decision-making, her criticism of centralisation and bureaucratisation and delegation of key roles and responsibilities. 'All letters sent to me were read by all members of the staff… If HMI's or Local Inspectors asked me to tell the staff this or that… I always insisted on their meeting the members of the staff themselves to whom their suggestions were to be conveyed.'[29]

As a leader she remained a classroom teacher, initiated communal meals and non-contact time as routine practice and advised her 'flabbergasted' colleagues to 'Go up and have a rest and smoke if you feel you want it.' School policy was to abolish the cane, but parents sometimes took issue with alternate disciplinary practices such that staff had to 'rescue' a child and give advice on 'proper' punishment. There was a Parents Committee to coordinate opposition to proposed cuts in education spending, and official hostility escalated when she allowed parental representatives to question the award of a local authority scholarship to a police officer's daughter with a poor examination performance. At the time, grass roots activists challenged the favouritism evidenced in a bias towards the children of police officers among scholarship winners pulling out a broader issue about the fallacy of meritocratic discourse (indeed Kate's father-in-law was a former policeman whose sons were scholarship winners). Kate resented bureaucratic interference but recognised that her demands always got a quick response. She called this the 'the reward of "guts"—ugly word, nevertheless the best for my purpose.'[30]

Waller Road School attracted attention from people of influence including the Duchess of Atholl who was a Parliamentary Secretary to the Board of

---

[28] Edmundwaller.lewisham.sch.uk/schoolHistory.php accessed 22 November 2018.
[29] K. Dice to P. Ibbotson, 21 November 1953.
[30] Ibid.

Education during the 1920s. Atholl, who was known for her concern about the quality of the school environment, created a favourable impression on Kate, and she confided her fear that the authority framed her social-reconstructionist form of progressive education as obstructionist, retrograde, and barred her from promotion. The Duchess promised to visit the school and the logbook records that she went in February 1930. The NUT censured Kate for having spoken with the Duchess, and she disappears from the official record after. Presumably, she retired in 1932 after the separate schools for boys and girls at Waller Road amalgamated.[31]

Tracing the career profile of Kate Dice suggests she was both troublesome and troubling to the authorities. As a teacher, she brought together a conception of professionalism rooted in masculine rewards—scope for the intellect, a decent salary, service to the state and access to citizenship—but without having to reject the idea of teaching as a maternal and feminine sphere of work.

Education and Democracy: The Making of Florence Key

The daughter of a publican, Florence Key undertook college training at St Margaret's in Ripon before returning to take up a post in the East London working-class community in which she grew up (and where her father belonged to a masonic lodge). Appointed as secretary of the East London branch of the Women's Freedom League and a volunteer nurse during the First World War, she married Charles Key in 1917. The two had met at the Dempsey Street Elementary School in Stepney, where she was an assistant teacher and he taught in the boys' department. The pair were united by a commitment to socialist causes, and as newly-weds, they lived in what was described as a 'workman's flat' over the local railway. In common with Kate and Albert Dice, the Keys had no children, and Florence kept on working.

When Poplar Labour Party won control of Poplar borough council in 1919, Charles Key was one of the victorious politicians. Two years later, Charles was deputy mayor and at the centre of the Poplar Rates Rebellion when 30 Labour councillors went to prison for their refusal to collect Poplar's poor rate. Faced by a rating system that discriminated in favour of wealthy boroughs, Poplar's Labour councillors wanted the burden of poor relief spread more evenly across London as a whole. Just as 'Poplarism' became synonymous with a participatory, 'bottom-up' radical politics, so the NUWT motto proclaimed, 'she who would be free herself must strike the blow.' As Agnes Dawson's editorial of the first *Woman Teacher*, their weekly journal stated, they sought 'to proclaim from the housetops our judgement on things that matter vitally to education.'[32]

---

[31] Robin Betts, Parliamentary Women: Women ministers of education, 1924–1974," in *Women, Policy-Making and Educational Administration in England: Authoritative Women since 1880*, ed. Joyce Goodman and Sylvia Harrop (London: Routledge, 2000), 175–180; Visitors Book, Division 6, Waller Road 1888–1958; LCC Education Particulars, 1919–1932.

[32] *The Woman Teacher*, 26 September 1919, 1.

Fig. 9.2 Portrait of Mrs Florence E. Key, Member of the Council 1927–51 and President 1932, UWT/G/1/14, from the records of the National Union of Women Teachers. (Courtesy of UCL Institute of Education Special Collections)

Political work included financial support for NUWT candidates in local elections, deputations and lobbying, questionnaires to MPs and co-operation with other feminist organisations with the aim of spreading the doctrine and practice of equality. Part of the union leadership from the early 1920s, Key was elected president in 1932 (Fig. 9.2). For over 30 years, her 'Watching Brief' column occupied a regular slot in the *Woman Teacher*, where her campaigning journalism offered a platform for women's voices and concerns. Gendered social policy certainly presented her with much to criticise, including the perception that most working-class girls were headed for domesticity and only temporary workers in unskilled, low-paid employment. Not only this, she demanded free secondary education for all and the raising of the school-leaving age also.

The Keys pulled together as a political couple and support for equal pay shows this. Florence attacked NAS advocacy of the family wage—noting that single men teachers were paid as much as married, and some women were responsible for the financial maintenance of family members. Poplar's Labour council upheld the principle of equal pay, and Charles stressed the danger of cheap female labour. Addressing a rally in Trafalgar Square, he accused the NAS of suffering from an 'inferiority complex, for they most evidently fear the competition of women on equal terms.' Florence observed the importance of political engagement.

We women teachers, who strove for Equal Citizenship realise that equal pay for equal work must be our next objective, but we must bear in mind that unequal pay is not only a question of prejudice and custom, it is also part of an economic structure, and the advent of justice in the payment of women depends largely on how much we do our share in solving the economic problems in which the world is involved.[33]

Florence Key thought women should carry on working when they married. She thought it wrong for 'cultured women to have to look out for some rich man to keep them nice or nice men to have as wives women who cared only for housework.' Not only did she stress the pleasure and satisfaction wage earning brought but the economic self-determination and autonomy to be gained from controlling a separate income. 'We must get away from the idea that women were working only to earn a living. It was a question of freedom, but we did not want freedom only for spinsters, for we demanded the right of every woman to go forward on her own feet with equal opportunities!'[34]

In era when public discourse on sexuality and eugenics influenced a strong negative reaction against single women, she did not deviate from upholding the heterosexual norm but argued vehemently for all women to be able to shape their own lives. 'As long as local education authorities could dictate women in matters concerning their own private lives the teaching profession would not attain the dignity which was its right.' She also strongly censured men who objected to female leadership. 'A man whose mind was so obsessed by sex that he could not think of a woman except in terms of sex and could not regard her as a colleague and work with her or under her, was totally unfit to have dealings with little children and the sooner such men left the profession the better.' Challenging gender binaries, she demolished the idea of 'manly virtues' saying, 'sturdy independence and self-reliance were as admirable and desirable in a woman as in a man.'[35]

Feminist elementary teachers saw society as divided on social class lines as well as by gender. Armed with these beliefs, Florence renounced underlying assumptions about girls in interwar educational policy, and the NUWT was the only teacher union or professional association to maintain a consistent critique of the content, quality and approach of the teaching of domestic subjects. It was seldom that the NUT displayed its hand thus far. In the words of a contemporary recruitment post seeking to appeal to teachers as workers, 'The National Union of Teachers is professional and is neither pro-feminist nor anti-feminist. Be professional and join a professional organisation.' Undaunted, Key and the NUWT saw themselves as educationalists fighting for a progressive policy for all. They were well aware of the impact of austerity measures in these

---

[33] *East London Advertiser*, 2 January 1932.
[34] *Woman Teacher*, 10 January 1930.
[35] *Woman Teacher*, 18 January 1924; 20 January 1933; 19 January 1934.

years, arguing for the right of all children to an equal chance of the best education the community can provide irrespective of social status or financial standing of their parents.[36]

In 1937, Florence resigned her teaching post and became a full-time salaried union official and editor of *The Woman Teacher*. She often represented the NUWT at meetings of other feminist organisations such as the Six Point Group,[37] and supporters helped her mount an election campaign when she stood unsuccessfully for the London County Council in 1946 on a Labour Party platform. In her view, 'no party was 100 per cent feminist and it was very necessary to have a member on the London County Council who could watch the interests of women teachers and the children and voice their desires.' At a meeting of the Open Door International in Denmark in 1947, she applauded the attempt to ensure women got a 'square deal from the United Nations and are not relegated to some sub-human category when human rights are under consideration.'[38]

The notion that women were being exploited as 'cheap labour' is a key message of Jill Craigie's 1950 film *To be a Woman*.[39] The NUWT and the Equal Pay Campaign Committee sponsored the film, which featured prominently in their campaigning activities during the 1951 general election, called just 18 months after the Labour Party won the 1950 election with only a five-seat majority. Campaigners like Florence Key saw this as a prime opportunity for concerted cross-party lobbying, and the film explained the need for equal opportunities against a backdrop of newsreel shots of marching suffragettes accompanied by 'The March of the Women,' which was the anthem of the women's suffrage movement. Besides the then NUWT president, other women are seen working in their homes, in factories, nursing, and teaching, in politics and in the professions.[40]

---

[36] Felicity Hunt, *Gender & Policy in English Education 1902–1944* (London: Harvester Wheatsheaf, 1991), 106; Patricia Owen, "She who would be free," 93.

[37] The Six Points were: (1) Satisfactory legislation on child assault. (2) Satisfactory legislation for the widow. (3) Satisfactory legislation for the unmarried mother and her child. (4) Equal rights of guardianship for married parents. (5) Equal pay for teachers. (6) Equal opportunities for men and women in the civil service. The Open Door Council, established in May 1926, was a British organisation pressing for equal economic opportunities for women. It opposed the extension of 'protective legislation' for women, regarding such legislation as 'restrictive' and arguing that it effectively barred women from better-paid jobs such as mining. In 1929, an international version was established, Open Door International.

[38] NUWT London Unit *Minutes*, 5 November 1945, 21 and 31 January 1946; *Woman Teacher*, May 1947.

[39] Jill Craigie (1911–1999) was an English documentary film director and screen writer: the first British woman film director to achieve a combination of critical acclaim, publicity and wide distribution. A socialist and feminist, she was married to the Labour politician Michael Foot for 50 years (1913–2010).

[40] Carl Rollyson, *To Be a Woman: The Life of Jill Craigie* (London: Aurum Press, 2005), 129–133.

Florence Key saw the NUWT as feminism in action. Members applauded 'her trenchant arguments on equal pay and opportunities, on the married women's right to separate assessment and taxation of income, as well as her defence of children's rights to the best possible educational facilities.' Always she conceptualised teaching as important public work, espousing a professional ideal in which democracy was both a goal and a method of instruction. As she put it in 1925, 'the greatest work of a teacher lies, not in the impartment of instruction, but in the happy training of the individuality of the child and in helping it to express itself as a happy and useful member of the community.'[41] As this account of her working life shows, she recognised her solidarity with all those the culture defines as lesser or marginalised, seeking to enhance the woefully deficient elementary education available to the children of the working poor to equip them for a life of public service.

For a little over 40 years, the NUWT offered work and community to women building a path towards advocacy and resistance in fighting for social change both for themselves and for others (Fig. 9.3). *The Woman Teacher* was a vital component that helped spread the excitement among younger sisters who read copies brought home by pioneering older siblings: 'There was no thought of material gain or personal advantage in the work which they undertook,' but it 'gave us experiences and memories which will enrich us to the end of our lives.'[42] If teaching as public work gave Kate Dice and Florence Key access to a social life as well as to political and professional activity, what about our sample from the generations of women teachers who came after?

Fig. 9.3 UWT/H/10, cover of Emily Phipps 'History of the NUWT,' 1928, from the records of the National Union of Women Teachers. Institute of Education Special Collections. (Copyright UCL Special Collections)

[41] *Woman Teacher*, May 1952.
[42] *Woman Teacher*, March 1961, 67.

Gender and Teaching in the Second Half of the Twentieth Century

In this section, we move out of the archive into living history. Despite the prevailing ideology of domesticity, a significant number of wives had paid jobs in post-war England. Earlier marriages and smaller families meant that the average woman would complete childbearing and rearing by the age of 35 or 40, leaving her 20 years or more of productive working life, a pattern commonly referred to as the 'dual role.' One-third of all women teachers were married in 1952. Eight years later, this proportion had reached 42 per cent.[43] Mapping the gendering of school work offers an analytical thread linking past, present and future lives in education.

Oral testimony shows the impact of the past in the present. Conventional qualities of the 'good teacher' persist with emergent themes of caring, commitment, dedication, selflessness and respect. However, teachers' talk suggests a dissonance surrounding the emergence of new occupational identities that support Martin Lawn's post-1980s understanding of the 'good teacher' as a competent employee experiencing a diminishing sense of agency or control. Lawn's ideas take us beyond the 'modern times' charted by Grace, suggesting that there are continuities in teacher vocation, but that occupational stereotypes and the gendered meanings of a 'good teacher' are reconfigured within successive policy settlements. Life stories are used to make narrative sense of this conjunction of continuity and change within the broader context of their situation as public sector employee.[44]

The framing of care for children as 'women's work' appeared in many of the life-history interviews. Susan's testimony illustrates this. A retired primary school teacher from a working-class background, we first heard from Susan in the previous chapter, recalling her experiences of teacher training college in the early 1950s. An only child, Susan received every encouragement to do well at school, and her parents sent her to a fee-paying Catholic secondary school. The nuns encouraged her, and she admired her maths teacher who may have acted as a role model. She would like to have become a librarian but assumed her parents could not afford the four-year university course that this required and saw teaching as 'one of the jobs a girl could do.' That or banking. A preference for connectedness, said to be more characteristic of women than men, is central to Susan's account, although her teacher identity is contingent, detailed as a matter of class and gender.

Susan's entry into working life was hard. Her mother had just died, and she returned home to live with her father and started teaching in a mining community like the one in which she grew up. Built in the 1930s, her first school

---

[43] Miriam David, *The State, the Family and Education*, 168–169.
[44] Martin Lawn, *Modern Times? Work, Professionalism and Citizenship in Teaching* (Lewes: Falmer Press, 1996).

was designed around three sides of a quadrangle housing infants, boys and girls. There were seven classes segregated (Susan's word) into two streams—an A and B. She had the so-called 'bottom' class.

> You'd got the bulk who'd been in 1B and weren't going to shine. You'd got one or two who'd been in 2A and hadn't shone so they'd got kicked out and you'd got some who'd been in the class the year before. That's not a good introduction when you're straight from college, particularly if you've got a head that wasn't really helpful. But by the following summer I'd, I'd got out and got round it.

Susan's father was protective and made her a wooden pencil holder after the head reprimanded her. 'Fifty pencils standing straight up, all sharpened. And she came in and she was you haven't got enough pencils there… and she stood there and counted them. She didn't attack me on pencils after that.' Established female B-stream teachers helped her find her way to becoming a teacher, and she explained they 'sort of mothered you.' She expressed a deep concern for the children in her care developing her pedagogy, particularly nature study, to match their interests. One girl 'knew where wild daffodils grew; and she brought me some. Now I suspect that she didn't get a full meal every day. But she would bring that in for her teacher because she knew that I would like it, you know, that kind of thing.'

Susan explained her decision to join the NUT by saying she was 'not too keen on the NUWT at all.' She met her future husband at a union function, and the sexual division of household labour was the reason she did not seek promotion.

> I made the decision that I would stay as a classroom teacher because I wanted to be able to encourage my own children, have time for my own children and my husband… Because I've seen so many times where you've got a man and a woman, they're both teaching, and the woman decides she's going up in the scale and somewhere along the line everything falls to pieces; and I didn't want that to happen.

Gendered discourses recur in her account. She changed jobs to work for the same authority as her husband and later swopped schools when he joined her school as deputy head. She was unsure the head wanted them to work together and sensed he had concerns about a married couple on the staff. 'They don't get lost, you know, the two of them could be troublemakers, you know, cause trouble I suppose was his feeling.' As a wife and mother, she stopped going on school trips after she returned to teaching and only attended union conferences as a delegate's wife. Asked if she would choose to become a teacher if she had her life over, she said she might have gone into office work, which was something else girls did in the 1950s.

Harriet trained as an infant schoolteacher in the 1970s. She associates professionalism in early childhood practice with a gendered ethics of care discourse. 'I think there's an awful lot of females go into it thinking that they're lovely little children, and that's what they want to do. They just want to teach all the little children. It's like, you play it for years, and you think that's what you're going to carry on doing, you know.' Harriet re-entered formal education after marriage, when her children were young and graduated from the Open University. Articulating her motivation, she implies teaching took her heart: 'feeling you're doing something worthwhile… You can actually see, as well, physically sort of, what you have done over time. Because a lot of the children I have for two years and you can see a huge difference in, in how they've sort of matured and grown and advanced in two years.'

Harriet's story includes many tensions, centred on workload, educational leadership and discipline. Her first school was in a place of high unemployment, cheap housing and many single parent families who could not afford to live anywhere else. Children would 'come into school not being able to read, not being able to tie shoelaces, no social skills at all hardly.' The staff 'had a lot of problems with behaviour, so a lot of what I was doing was actually socialising, social management, with the children rather than teaching. Um, and it was very, very hard, but I enjoyed it.' In contrast, she finds her current school 'a haven of peace and calm. Basically, we teach the children and they listen to us. You have the odd bother, you know, a child who misbehaves, they are not all saints and angels, but I must spend, I must spend about 98 per cent of my time teaching.' She tries to compartmentalise her public and private worlds, arriving at work early and leaving late to do her marking and lesson preparation in school, but has sleepless nights towards the end of the summer holidays. 'I'm planning things in my head for the rest of the next year and things, so you can't put it off completely.'

This group of women teachers spoke at some length about the gendering of professional cultures and identity irrespective of the education sector in which they worked or had worked. Some of those who became teachers in the 1990s reflected on the classroom as a space for doing and being in the construction of professional identities based on gendered discourses of caring. At the time of her interview, Alison was teaching Art in in an urban secondary school in the north-west of England. Alison's father was a mechanical engineer, and she grew up in the 1980s in what she described as an affluent suburb, attending local Roman Catholic schools, followed by university and a one-year teacher training course. She met her future husband, at university, at the Christian Union. Whilst her decision to go into teaching got positive affirmation during work experience, she stressed she was 'always seen, within my family, as a sort of mother earth type character. I was always left to look after all the children [laughs], you know. So, it was something that came quite naturally really. Something that I decided to do and I never really wavered from it.' Her first school was in a deprived inner-city community with a strong gang culture, and she took pride in the fact that her second cohort of GCSE students was the highest achieving the school had ever seen. She also became active in extra-curricular initiatives, putting on school productions in the face of negativity from many colleagues, coaxing the children with sweets and biscuits to stay after school.

Alison's testimony preserves a deep sense of seeking and striving hard towards the promotion of active, creative individuals and a harmonious learning community. She was invested in a definition of a good teacher as 'someone who cares,' and she evaluated the effectiveness of her teaching on that basis: 'Showing the children that you care. And if they know that you care you gain a certain level of respect and with a lot of difficult children that's what comes first really. And then they want to then achieve for you and they want to listen to you and show you what they've done.' It is telling that she uses her pedagogical skills to nurture a sense of being worthy, of possessing creative, inventive and critical capacities, to give pupils dignity. 'That's quite important to me, so if I've got a group of children who tend to be under confident, I will give them something that I know will be quite wow, like projecting work from a projector that they can trace out and then giving them a medium that has instant, fantastic, wow results.'

After she qualified, she reports her family combined pride in her professional achievements with judgements that she was 'working too hard' and questions like 'when are you going to have children, when are you going to start taking time for your family.' Now mothering a biological son and foster child, she must reinvest in the discourses of caring to maintain her place in the moral order.

> And that's how I get up every morning, the fact that I'm needed by my family and the children in this school. That's why it never occurs to me not to come to school. And that's not because I particularly enjoy every day, because some days are horrible. But you don't enjoy every day at home when you're cooking and doing the ironing and things like that, but it doesn't occur to me not to do it. It's the same thing really.

Caring and commitment prompted her to foster a 16-year-old Bangladeshi girl who disclosed in school that she was going through the arranged marriage process. An action that also opened feelings of guilt. 'There are far more needy children in this school that I wouldn't take home and sometimes I feel quite guilty because there are children in this school now who are so neglected. And behaviour problems are so bad that they desperately need someone to love them and care for them.' Alison speaks of 'living and breathing' work. She articulates an idea of education as a collective practice that is community-based, lifelong and directed towards social equality. As she put it, 'I'd like to see school, what I call a full-service extended school with doctors' surgeries and health clinics, dentists, child-care, even a shop on site.'

The themes of caring and commitment can define work identities and the development of the 'teacherly self' I have been arguing. We see this in another example. Hannah was deputy head of an inner-city secondary school in Northern England. Her father was in business administration, and her mother worked part-time. Like Alison, she felt compelled to work in urban schools in working-class areas. For both, this came down to a sense of duty, a notion of commitment. Hannah's testimony preserves a deep sense of 'ability' labels and their effects on pupils in school. She experienced insecurity, uncertainty and confusion at grammar school, and this helped shape her professional identity. 'I suppose I just felt as if, you know, if I'm feeling like this, then somebody else must be… you know, there's kids that have been written off, before they've even tried. And I don't know; I think I just did things differently, just without knowing it.' She taught using children's interests and experiences as starting points—to 'liven things up, and, you know, to make people interested.'

Hannah transgresses gendered stereotypes about the form of leadership that is being imported, refined and developed within schools. In struggles over positioning, her ability to discipline boys was critical to her promotion to senior management. 'I had a particular knack, for some reason, of being able to deal with naughty boys. I don't know why. But I'd a group that were just no hopers, really, and dragged them through.' She went on to talk about the everyday sexism she encountered as a young female leader.

> You knew who not to talk to, because you knew they would just think, oh the young upstart, woman as well. The first conversation I had with a member of staff was, oh, they've only employed you so that you can make them tea and coffee. They'll have a job, I said, because I don't drink it, and I certainly don't make it for anybody else either. So that was the first thing that any member of staff said to me. And I got a lot of hostility from Senior Management. Sexist stuff: ageist stuff, the fact that I was younger than them.

This shows how embodied the work of a teacher is. Hannah was negatively positioned within a set of power relations reflective of the school's single-sex past, and the newly co-educational school showed little sign of repudiating its masculinist culture. Female staff colluded through participation in the 'old boys' kind of stuff,' senior male colleagues patronised her. Things escalated when she was passed over for an acting deputy post. She went to see the acting head. 'Because I think he was so blasé about giving his two mates a job, and he didn't think it would affect anybody else. Nobody else had questioned it, apart from me. So, I was, by that time I had just got up and walked out. I could hardly speak. My heart was in my throat, you know, and I thought, well, I had to say something.' Ultimately, she secured a deputy headship elsewhere.

Mary was a mature entrant to teaching after completing the business of childbearing and rearing. Her mother, aunts and uncles were all in education, and as an 18-year-old, she made a deliberate choice not to enter the profession. Now in her 50s, she thought her age helped her maintain authority in the classroom. In contrast to younger teachers for whom overfamiliarity can be a problem, she could joke and laugh with pupils and play the maternal role. 'I mean the amount of children that call me Mum all the time… I've never really had problems with discipline at all, and I think it is to do with age. I know it doesn't always work that way, but I do think a lot of it is. I think children are less likely to do anything if you're older.' She combined teaching with caring for parents and grandchildren, and in her account, the links with social action were through religion and politics, and school events. Her aim in teaching is to make children love maths, and she doesn't want to get out of the classroom, 'I've actually had a kid come to me and say I'm a maths teacher now because of you. Things like that. I mean I suppose that's what makes it all worthwhile.'

Historically, the 'naturalness' of the woman teacher and the related construction of the occupation as women's work is reflected in the caring and nurturing that characterise acts of teaching. It was found in the words, action and practice of a young female primary school teacher in her mid-20s. As a child, Emma loved playing schools.

> I used to write all my teddies and my dolls names down on an A4 piece of paper and I would just do the register, then pretend it was a new day, and do the register again… The children have found me a bit, not maternal, because obviously I'm not their mother but really approachable and you know, I love hearing their wacky stories and you can't help but become part of their family for that time you're teaching them really… I can tell them what to do and the results they produced from what I told them to do, it's just a great sense of satisfaction for me, a sense of achievement.

In the case studies discussed in this chapter, there was a continuum of caring discourses ranging between the more specific definitions of caring, such as caring as parenting, and the most inclusive, caring as commitment can be seen to have prevailed. Such discourses were a common feature of what constituted the making of a good teacher past and present. In an important sense, the teacherly self and professional habitus in the education field rest on a nurturing, familial vocabulary. Oral testimony suggests the persistence of gender stereotypes as teachers forge a 'teacherly' self in moments of time and maintain and amend this over the course of a working life and beyond. The importance of emotional labour suggests that 'feeling' acts as a vital mode of cognition helping encode experience as a value-laden expression where meaning becomes embedded in forms and intonations that reflect gendered practice.

CONCLUSION

Let us re-visit the quote with which I started. The feminism of the women who joined the NUWT was their response to a perceived injustice. They did not keep out of politics but saw themselves as part of major historical change. Other women in teaching may have had greater inhibitions when it came to self-identifying as feminists, but there is a shared sense in which the emotional labour underpinning the meaning of teaching as work lay in the mesh experienced between ordinary, everyday life and the political and the public. Oral and written testimonies from different teaching generations demonstrate what difference having access to this form of employment made, suggesting a pattern of ambitions for themselves and for their pupils that made a significant contribution to attempts to forge new forms of community through advocacy work. They suggest the tensions between freedom and autonomy underpinning the job and the difficulties of trying to articulate a gender-free professionalism when the activities and interaction of the teaching workforce were and are powerfully gendered.

The specific utility of Kate Dice and Florence Key as historical subjects is to show the salience of lived experience for a feminist tradition of thought and practice that has been neglected in studies focused on the development of teaching as a profession. Belief in critical thinking, discussion and education is very apparent in Kate's writing as is her desire to create progressive spaces within school walls. Florence crystallised in her work situation a political consciousness rooted in the demand for total equality on the same terms as men, above all for economic equality. Participation in a group solidified mutual affinity, and they probably agreed with one of the best-known early Fabians, the novelist H.G. Wells, who declared: 'The Socialist movement *is* teaching, and the most important people in the world from the Socialist's point of view are those who teach.'[45]

Former Secretary of State for Education Shirley Williams reflected on how becoming a teacher should be a very 'impressive' life path and regretted that the 'status now goes to the headteacher, but it doesn't really go to the teacher.'[46] In the struggle for equal pay and professional autonomy, the women who turned to the NUWT claimed teacher gender does not matter, but teachers' work is still seen to be a feminised role such that professional identity is bound up with gender identity and specific discourses underpin and assist this 'normalizing' and 'naturalizing' process. Women's experiences cannot be subsumed within conventional narratives centred upon male career paths as a recent increase in the gender pay gap at England's largest multi-academy trusts, with women paid 55p for every pound earned by men at two chains, shows.[47]

Florence Key's vision was of the teacher as a trusted professional, modelling active citizenship, ready to engage in an informed way with parents, local community, and in national debates. Taking the long view shows the importance of understanding teaching as a gendered vocation. It shows defining professionalism involves fluid encounters between government regulation, identity politics and everyday life. All the members of the teaching generations represented here connected education to democracy and wanted an educative relationship between schools, teachers and local communities that worked in both directions. We may discern clear signs of concern with a notion of the person-centred school as the driving force of the educative encounter in order to cultivate social change and combat inequalities.

---

[45] H.G. Wells, *New Worlds for Old* (London: Macmillan, 1909), 265.
[46] Shirley Williams, *Climbing the Bookshelves* (London: Virago, 2010), 35.
[47] John Dickens, "England's largest academy trusts see gender pay gap widen," schoolsweek.co.uk, 5 April 2019.

Bibliography

Primary Sources

Archival Sources

Stockwell Training College (STC) List of Students 1861–1924, Records of the British and Foreign Schools School, Brunel University.

STC OSA [Old Students' Association] List 1892–1893 compiled by B. Hildersley Stevens and Miss H.M. Kidd 1936 to post 1948, Brunel University.

EO/DIV 6/WAL/MISC/1 Waller Road School, Deptford, Visitors Book 1888–1958, London Metropolitan Archives.

EO/STA/2/12 Married Women Teachers, London Metropolitan Archives.

EO/STA/2/13 Married Women Teachers General Papers, London Metropolitan Archives.

London County Council Education Service Particulars 1910–1935, London Metropolitan Archives.

Joan Simon, *Shena Simon: Feminist and Educationist. Based on the Correspondence and Writings of Lady Simon of Wythenshawe* (privately printed, 1986), Manchester City Council, Archives, Rare Books and Collections.

National Association of Labour Teachers papers, London Metropolitan Archives.

Fabian Society, LSE Archives.

Records of the National Union of Women Teachers, UCL Institute of Education Archives and Special Collections.

Autobiographies, Memoirs, Diaries, Letters, Obituaries

Williams, Shirley. *Climbing the Bookshelves*. London: Virago, 2010.

Newspapers and Periodicals of the Period

The Women Teacher, 1919–1961.

Other Contemporary Books and Pamphlets

Lawrence, David Herbert. *The Rainbow*. Harmondsworth: Penguin, [1915] 2007.

Pierotti, Muriel. *The Story of the National Union of Women Teachers*. London: Publishers for the NUWT, 1963.

Tropp, Asher. *The School Teachers: The Growth of the Profession from 1800 to the Present Day*. London: Macmillan, 1957.

Wells, Herbert George. *New Worlds for Old*. London: Macmillan, 1909.

Secondary Sources

Copelman, Dina M. *London's Women Teachers: Gender, Class and Feminism, 1870–1930*. London: Routledge, 2014.

David, Miriam E. *The State, The Family and Education*. London: Routledge & Kegan Paul, 1980.

Grace, Gerald. "Teachers and the State in Britain: A Changing Relation." In *Teachers: The Culture and Politics of Work*, edited by Martin Lawn and Gerald Grace, 198–223. Lewes: Falmer Press, 1987.

Hughes, Herbert Delauney and Brown, Geoffrey Frederick. *The W.E.A. Education Year Book 1918*. Nottingham: University of Nottingham, 1981.

Ironside, Mike and Seifert, Roger. *Industrial Relations in Schools*. London: Routledge, 1995.

Lawn, Martin. *Modern Times? Work, Professionalism and Citizenship in Teaching*. Lewes: Falmer Press, 1996.

Littlewood, Margaret. "The "Wise Married Woman" and the Teaching Unions." In *Women Teachers: Issues and Experiences*, edited by Hilary De Lyon and Frances Widdowson, 180–190. Buckingham: Open University Press, 1989.

Lowe, Roy. *Schooling and Social Change 1964–1990*. London and New York: Routledge, 1990.

Mahood, Linda. *Feminism and Voluntary Action: Eglantyne Jebb and Save the Children, 1876–1928*. Basingstoke: Palgrave Macmillan, 2009.

McDermid, Jane. *The Schooling of Girls in Britain and Ireland, 1800–1900*. London: Routledge, 2012.

McDowell, Joanne and Revert Klattenburg, Revert. "Does Gender Matter? A Cross-National Investigation of Primary Class-room Discipline." *Gender and Education*, 31, no. 8 (2019): 947–965.

Mitchell, Hannah. *The Hard Way Up*. London: Virago, 1977.

Oram, Alison. "A Master Should Not Serve under a Mistress: Women and Men Teachers 1900–1970." In *Teachers, Genders and Careers*, edited by Sandra Acker. Lewes: Falmer Press, 1989.

Oram, Alison. *Women Teachers and Feminist Politics 1900–39*. Manchester: Manchester University Press, 1996.

Robinson, Wendy. "Sarah Jane Bannister and Teacher Training in Transition 1870–1918." In *Practical Visionaries: Women, Education and Social Progress 1790–1930*, edited by Mary Hilton and Pam Hirsch, 131–148. Harlow: Longman.

Rollyson, Carl. *To Be a Woman: The Life of Jill Craigie*. London: Aurum Press, 2005.

Thornton, Mary and Bricheno, Patricia. *Missing Men in Education*. Stoke-on-Trent: Trentham, 2006.

Widdowson, Frances. *Going Up into the Next Class: Women and Elementary Teacher Training 1840–1914*. London: Women's Research and Resources Centre Publications, 1980.

CHAPTER 10

Gender Struggles

When I was a girl I wished dreadfully that I had been born earlier so that I could have been a suffragette. Now I wish I had been born later, to involve myself in the essentially youthful ferment of Women's Liberation. This seems less odd to many of my contemporaries than to many women young enough to be my daughters, who are apt to mutter that they have all the freedom they need, thank you, and what is there worth fussing about? Well, what is the Women's Liberation fuss about? It is a search for an identity as a human being; a deeply felt, often inarticulate protest at being typecast by sex from birth to death.
—Mary Stott, 15 January 1971 *Women of the Revolution: Forty Years of Feminism*, ed. Kira Cochrane (London: Guardian Books, 2010), 3.

The words of Mary Stott, who founded the *Guardian* women's page, focus attention on the development of women's rights and feminism. Reconstructing the habitus Stott occupied, this chapter tells a story of radical innovation that is often left unsaid. Twenty years after scholar-activist Diana Leonard wrote that 'current initiatives to improve boys' achievement are not crediting the contribution of feminist work of the 1980s to improvement of girls'—and boys'—academic performance,' this chapter will excavate histories of social action that helped put questions of gender and sexual relations on public agendas.[1] The distance of time gives us the opportunity to reflect on events with a fresh eye, to locate progressive initiatives produced by women teachers

---

[1] Diana Leonard, "Teachers, femocrats and academics: Activism in London," in *Whatever Happened to Equal Opportunities in Schools?* ed. Kate Myers (Buckingham: Open University Press, 2000), 181.

and politicians in their larger history. Work on equal opportunities and sexism inside state schools during an era in which people were increasingly insistent about defining and claiming their individual rights, identities, and perspectives, is presented and analysed as cases from modern educational and political history.

We have seen that feminist teachers from the suffrage generation thought politics governed their whole lives. Teacher feminism entered the elementary educational system as well as the more prestigious secondary world of middle-class girls' high schools and the pre-1944 municipal secondary schools, but here I take up the story in the 1970s and 1980s, mapping networks of feminist educators and their educational aspirations and achievements. Individual stories challenge interpretations that shape the actions and imaginations of the present, showing these women's concerns with the relation between education and the gender order were remarkably prescient. For this generation of feminist teachers, the formulation of demands for equal pay and opportunity into legislation was the spur for campaigns to create gender-just learning communities where girls might learn to recognize themselves as equal and resist discrimination, and boys might learn to deconstruct a patriarchal conception of masculinity, and construct egalitarian beliefs. They campaigned on the basis of equal opportunities (female access to a male world) and/or anti-sexist (changing the world) perspectives.

To evoke these gender struggles, emphasis is placed on events in Britain's second most important institution of representative democracy, the Inner London Education Authority (ILEA). As previous chapters have shown, women in teaching, politics and policy-making made an important contribution to education in the capital city. Historian Asa Briggs, giving evidence to the Royal Commission on Local Government in Greater London in 1959, certainly thought so. In the main, he said, women had been 'among the most active members' of the London County Council, sustaining an important role. From 1928 onward, they never represented under 20 per cent of London's councillors, peaking at 35 per cent in 1952. Infuriated by Labour's near monopoly of power at London's County Hall, the Conservative government of 1959–63 created a new local elected body consisting of the Greater London Council (GLC) and the Inner London Education Authority (ILEA), established as a permanent, quasi-autonomous committee of the Council.

The GLC was the first English council to set up a Women's Committee (1981), and ILEA the largest education authority with equal opportunities policies. Sylvia Denman became the ILEA's first black senior officer as principal equal opportunities officer and later deputy director of education and Herman Ouseley, in the newly created post of director of equal opportunities and policy co-ordination, brought to two the number of black senior officers ever appointed by the authority in 1986. It was responsible for a number of groundbreaking reports into racism and sexism in the mid-1980s, but conservatives were very good at convincing middle England it was dominated by the 'loony left.' Frances Morrell was its first and only woman leader (1983–87). She took another woman, Ruth Gee, with her as deputy.[2]

ILEA extended over 12 London boroughs until its abolition as part of the 1988 Education Act. The costs of education in the capital were higher than elsewhere, and right-wing politicians deemed the Authority expensive and educationally ineffective. Here I am concerned to document how the so-called sexual revolution played out in gendered civic involvement and democratic renewal in the ILEA in the context of the passage of time marked by three phases of liberalism. (1) The era of social liberalism. (2) The phase after 1979 when early Thatcherism was characterised by a determined focus on the money supply, public spending reduction, a return to nineteenth century liberalism and an emphasis on individual responsibility. (3) The phase of neoliberal globalisation treated as a set of practices over the past 30 years, which promote markets over the state and regulation and individual advancement/self-interest over the collective good and common wellbeing: reconfiguring relations between governing and the governed and power and knowledge.[3]

This is a local study but one from which we can learn broader lessons since Inner London was England's largest education authority, a place where electorally, women were notably successful, and the location of most political initiatives on the question of equality policy. In his 1989 book *Assessing Radical Education*, Nigel Wright says 'the history of education may be viewed as the history of policies which failed to achieve their aims.' He also identifies the 1890s, 1920s and 1960s as favourable decades for radicals because their ideas had the ear of politicians and policy-makers.[4] My argument is that issues relating to feminist pedagogies and organisational policy in the lifetime of the ILEA, 1965–90, form an important part of a particular radical tradition in English education, historically and politically, in this case a progressive one. Addressing the silencing of this social innovation and the way in which it has fallen from memory, is to address the practices of social misrecognition that the new metrics of the 1990s and the numbers game of so much Gap Talk sometimes inspired.[5]

WOMEN'S LIBERATION: THE BREAKTHROUGH GENERATION?

Jill Tweedie, principal columnist on the *Guardian's* women's page, upbraided the nascent women's liberation movement when she expressed the view that the 'explicit' demands of equal educational opportunities for both sexes and childcare for pre-school children were all acceptable to the old-established

---

[2] Sarah Olowe, *Against the Tide: Black Experience in the ILEA* (London: Inner London Education Authority, 1990), 11; Daniel Stilitz, "Sylvia Denman: Obituary", *Guardian*, 30 May 2019.

[3] See Nancy Fraser, *Justice Interruptus: Critical Reflections on the "Post-socialist" Condition* (New York: Routledge, 1997).

[4] Nigel Wright, *Assessing Radical Education* (Buckingham: Open University Press, 1989), 182.

[5] Angela McRobbie, *The Aftermath of Feminism: Gender, Culture and Social Change* (London: Sage, 2009).

women's organisations. 'The only new ingredient Women's Lib ever had to offer was the intellectual recognition of an imprisoned psyche and the realisation that when the inner battle is fought and won, concrete injustices crumble at the roots. And that is not done by being nice.'[6] For Tweedie, the personal *was* political. It was a point she took care to stress in her life writing.

Growing up in wartime, Tweedie came to understand gender inequality through the habit in middle class families to send sons to boarding school. 'Unquestioningly I accepted that my brother, being a boy, had to be saved from German bombs and I must take my chances.' Entanglements of gender and social class evident in an angry exchange of fire between Tweedie and her mother. He doesn't *have* to go, Tweedie says. He could stay at home and go to Whitgift on the bus with me." "Whitgift?" says Mother, "but that's not a public school." "Whitgift?" says Robbie, "that's for oi-guys." "It's all right for me, though… I can go to school with oi-girls but not precious Robbie."' Once she has done with high school, her grandparents pay for her to attend a Swiss finishing school. She gets married but her first baby dies and when her husband disappears with their two living children and her efforts to trace them fail, she moves to London via Amsterdam and husband number two, starting work as a journalist. Occupational identity mattered. There was a strong sense 'that anything the male sex had or did was by definition the best on offer, and men didn't go in for Little Jobs, to be picked up and dropped as the fancy took them. Men had careers, and therefore careers were *ipso facto* desirable and my right too.'[7]

For Tweedie's generation of women, the hardships of post-war austerity had given way to a new consumerism which meant that everything from cars to fridges, televisions, vacuum cleaners and washing machines were increasingly in evidence.[8] The contraceptive pill was introduced for married women in 1962 and by 1969 was freely available to all women. At the same time, the numbers of young women involved in university education grew. Miriam David describes how politically this was an exciting time.

> It could be argued that political involvement was the stamp of my generation of students, in ways completely different from current generations of students. Searching for meaning amongst various political and social movements was a significant process, although there were a number of different, often conflicting, left political groups within the broader movement for social change. Nevertheless, another significant hallmark was the extent to which most of the groupings were to the left and were about the growing politics of liberation.[9]

---

[6] Jill Tweedie, "Why nice girls finish last," in *Women of the Revolution: Forty Years of Feminism*, ed. Kira Cochrane (London: Guardian Books, 2010), 10.

[7] Jill Tweedie, *Eating Children with an Unfinished Memoir Frightening People* (Harmondsworth: Penguin, 1994), 16, 98, 351.

[8] David Kynaston, *Modernity Britain 1957–62* (New York: Bloomsbury, 2015).

[9] Miriam David, *Personal and Political: Feminisms, Sociology and Family Lives* (Stoke-on-Trent: Trentham Books, 2003), 30.

The student movement erupted in 1968, with protests in Paris, across the United States and in London, against the Soviet invasion of Czechoslovakia, and against American involvement in the Vietnam War. Also in 1968 there was an outburst of women's militancy in the labour movement. Bristol women bus conductors struck for pay parity. Hull women campaigned on safety issues for trawler men at sea, and nearly 200 female workers walked out of the Ford car plant at Dagenham in protest at sexual discrimination.[10] The Ford women were sewing machinists who made seat covers for the cars produced and wanted an end to the traditional differential between male and female wage rates (they were placed in the union's B grade of unskilled workers when men who did the same level of work were placed in the semi-skilled C grade).

In government, Prime Minister Harold Wilson promoted women. Barbara Castle entered Wilson's Cabinet as first Minister for Overseas Development (1964–65; Minister for Transport, 1965–68 and first Secretary of State for Employment, 1968–70). As Secretary of State, Castle met with the Dagenham women and took up their cause as the 2010 British film *Made in Dagenham* shows. She never doubted that she was as good as her male colleagues because a belief in sex equality was part of socialism for her.

> We had our quota of macho-males, but we had come into office as the standard bearers for the caring society and that was a society from which women would benefit most. And in Harold Wilson we had a Prime Minister who believed in women and positively enjoyed promoting them. So, although there were plenty of reactionary males lurking in Cabinet, it was easy to win feminist arguments. It was symbolic, for instance, that David Steel was able to get his abortion law reform through Parliament and put the 1967 Abortion Act on the statute book because government gave it time.[11]

A powerful woman in a pre-Twitter storm era, Castle aroused the resentment of the 'macho-motorist' who objected to her 'invasion' of his male space. A woman in charge of transport was bad enough, but one who could not drive was intolerable. In 1967, resentment turned into fury when she introduced the breathalyser as a way of testing a person's blood alcohol level. Instantly, it became 'open season.' Publicans threatened to refuse to serve her, and men who were happiest playing darts in the pub sent her abusive, threatening letters. 'Thank you' was the verdict of one woman whose letter Castle would not forget. The writer felt she had returned her husband to her. 'He used to go to the public house alone. Now he takes me with him to drive him home.'[12]

---

[10] Contemporary interest in feminist history grew after the making of the commercial cinema film *Made in Dagenham* (2010) (a stage musical version opened at London's Adelphi Theatre in 2014), and Sarah Gavron's 2015 film *Suffragette*.

[11] Barbara Castle, "No Kitchen Cabinet," in *Very Heaven: Looking Back at the 1960s*, ed. Sara Maitland (London: Virago, 1988), 53.

[12] Ibid.

On the other side of the Atlantic, a group of young women at a protest meeting against the concept of beauty contests in Atlanta City responded to a call to dump their bras and girdles into a 'freedom trash can.' A reporter covering the event added the flames and so started the myth of the burning bra.[13] At home in London's Holland Park in the spring of 1970, comprehensive campaigner Caroline Benn was reading Betty Friedan as her husband noted in his political diary. 'Easter Day. Had a lie-in. Caroline is reading a book called *The Feminine Mystique* about the new Women's Liberation Movement which is beginning to develop strongly in the States and even in Britain.'[14] Friedan attended the all-female Smith College in 1938 and wrote about what she termed the 'problem that has no name.'

> As she made the beds, shopped for groceries, matched clip-cover material, ate peanut butter sandwiches, chauffeured Cub Scouts and Brownies, lay beside her husband at night, she was afraid to ask even of herself the silent question: 'Is this all?'[15]

Friedan was not alone in acknowledging that she herself had become a victim of the 'mystique.' Her liberal, reformist feminism analysing the frustration she and other middle-class white women felt with their work in the home as a wife and mother had a profound influence, but alongside it sprang up more radical groups that grew off the new libertarian left politics and grass-roots movements like the Campaign for Nuclear Disarmament.

Teaching in London after graduating from St Hilda's College in Oxford, Sheila Rowbotham published an article that is widely regarded as a key founding document of British women's liberation in the left-wing paper *Red Dwarf* in 1969. A heightened awareness of subjective identity passed into women's liberation, which re-remembered 'the personal is political' as the community of women in the NUWT faded into oblivion with the gaining of equal pay for women teachers. In collaboration with Sally Alexander and Anna Davin, Sheila helped organise the founding conference at Ruskin College, Oxford, with over 600 female delegates and a crèche uniquely staffed by men, including the sociologist Stuart Hall. Ten more national conferences took place between 1970 and 1978 producing demands for equal pay, equal educational and job opportunities, free contraception, abortion on demand, free 24-hour nurseries, financial and legal independence, an end to all discrimination against lesbians and a right to a self-defined sexuality.[16]

[13] Mary Stott, *Before I Go* (London: Virago, 1985), 21.
[14] Tony Benn, *Office Without Power: Diaries 1968–72* (London: Arrow Books, 1989), 257.
[15] Betty Friedan, *The Feminine Mystique* (Harmondsworth: Penguin, 2010 edition), 5.
[16] Mary Kennedy, "One Woman's Reflections on the Ruskin Conference, 'celebrating the Women's Liberation Movement thirty years on,' Ruskin College, Oxford, 18 March 2000," *Women's History Review*, 10, no. 2 (2001), 349–352.

Sue Bruley joined the socialists and the feminists when she went to the LSE as a student in 1970, joining marches and protests including the notorious Miss World demonstration. She was a working-class girl and former secondary modern school pupil all at sea at an elite university and trying to make sense of her experience of 'left-wing posturing' and sexism among a predominantly white middle-class male student body. In 1974, by this time a teacher in a further education college, she joined a local women's group and became heavily involved in consciousness-raising, 'the process by which women come together, talk about their experiences, try to put them into some sort of context and develop a feminist orientation and practice.' Sue's circle discussed bodies and self-image, childhood, work, relationships, love, jealousy, anger, children and sexuality. Two were single mothers, two had wealthy backgrounds, six were in working-class jobs and two experienced social mobility through education.[17]

Looking back over more than 40 years, Sue observed that she wanted to include the experiences of grassroots activists and hitherto marginalised voices in the historical record. For example, Karla had a London working-class background. She expressed the opinion that most of us 'were angry and resentful about how we were treated, as women in the world around us' whether it was in jobs, human relationships or the distribution of responsibility for childcare and domestic work in the home. 'I would have said I was going because socialist politics weren't enough and that was true. But I think at a deeper level my need was to be with other women who were like me, to have some of the same feelings as I did. That I wanted a different frame of reference for my relations with men. I wanted a different world.' Consciousness raising was life-changing for her, but she also recognised that the implications of Black feminism were not really understood until later in the 1980s.[18] Witness bell hooks's critique of Friedan's solution to the problem she described, 'She did not discuss who would be called in to take care of the children and maintain the home if more women like herself were freed from their house labor and given equal access with white men to the professions.'[19]

Australian-born Lynne Segal migrated to London in 1970, where she lived in Islington, in a house bought with her sister. She recalled the 1970s as the friendliest decade there had yet been for western women, especially independent young white females like her who were also accidentally mothers. Before the growing number of one-parent families had given rise to alarmist predictions and blamed for everything from the rising crime rate to the decline of civilisation, she and her contemporaries escaped the stigma as 'fallen' or 'abandoned' women. Still too few in number and too far out from the norm to have been labelled 'as the selfish, male-ejecting go-getters responsible for

---

[17] Sue Bruley, "Consciousness-Raising in Clapham; Women's Liberation as 'Lived Experience' in South London in the 1970s," *Women's History Review*, 22, no. 5 (2013), 718–719.

[18] Sue Bruley, "Consciousness-Raising in Clapham," 725, 733–734.

[19] bell hooks, *Feminism is for Everybody: Passionate Politics* (London: Pluto Press, 2000), 1–2.

"disturbing the nest."'[20] Islington's radical habitus and the openings created by social movements included feminist spaces. In these circumstances, she recalled, independent young mothers in the 1970s were often the early heroines, the immediate beneficiaries and, so it soon seemed, the ultimate success stories, of the early years of women's liberation. 'Women with children,' as Sheila Rowbotham later observed, 'were our equivalent to the Marxist proletariat.'[21]

These were heady days. Involvement in 1960s radicalism offered 'an excellent breeding ground for feminism,' declared Anna Coote and Beatrix Campbell. 'Men led the marches and made the speeches and expected their female comrades to lick envelopes and listen.'[22] How did the gender struggles of women's liberation translate into the education field? As studies became available, research with girls as the focus began to stress the failure to address what Felicity Hunt suggests is one of the most powerful messages girls received in schooling in the first six decades of the twentieth century—that femininity signified subordination 'in virtually every sphere with the possible exception of being allowed to enter a room first and walk on the inside of the pavement.'[23] Even this did not extend to those growing up working-class like my mother who was told to give way to 'her betters' in school assembly.

Co-education: The Real Issue?

As provision of comprehensive schooling in the state system increased, so did the number of co-educational schools, but there was minimal discussion of the issue after the NUWT disbanded in 1961. An exception was R.R. Dale's three-volume study of 1969–74 comparing mixed and single-sex schools that suggested co-education had social advantages for boys. More cautious about the impact on girls, he assumed everyday contact with both sexes was a good thing, helping to smooth the 'natural' process of maturation towards heterosexuality. In what set out to be a work of 'objective' social science, he went on, 'It will help a young man to mix easily with women when he enters the world, but it will not guarantee him a happy marriage. It will help a young woman to understand men, but she may still try to drive instead of using her art of persuasion.'[24]

---

[20] Lynne Segal, *Making Trouble: Life and Politics* (London: Serpents Tail, 2007), 3. According to the 1990 General Household Survey, the proportion of lone parents headed by an unmarried mother rose from 4 per cent of all households in 1987 to 6 per cent, from 5 per cent to 7 per cent by a divorced mother and from 2 per cent to 4 per cent by a separated mother. Figures cited in Sue Lees, *Sugar and Spice: Sexuality and Adolescent Girls* (Harmondsworth: Penguin, 1993), 147.

[21] Lynne Segal, *Making Trouble*, 4.

[22] Anna Cootes and Beatrix Campbell, *Sweet Freedom: The Struggle for Women's Liberation* (London: Pan Books, 1982), 13.

[23] Felicity Hunt, *Gender & Policy in English Education 1902–1944* (New York: Harvester Wheatsheaf, 1991), 143.

[24] R.R. Dale, *Mixed or Single-Sex School? Volume 1, A Research Study in Teacher-Pupil Relationships* (London: Routledge, 1969), 237.

Educationist Robin Pedley relegated single-sex schools 'to the thought and practice of a by-gone age.' He reckoned co-education to be a progressive move and could no more defend 'segregation of the sexes' than he could segregation for reasons of class or intellectual 'ability.'[25]

Mathematician Kathleen Ollerenshaw was a Conservative member of Manchester city council who worried that any move to mixed-sex schooling in 'working-class schools' was predicated on the argument that girls help to 'civilize' boys. At the same time, she noted the many working-class girls in single-sex secondary modern schools who not only spent less time on mathematics than their male counterparts but were denied access to science because of the lack of facilities in many girls' schools. On balance, she favoured the retention of choice and regretted decision-making based on administrative convenience and cost, noting single-sex education was strongly associated with elite education, whereas research suggested it was the 'less able' girl, and the girl whose home background was least secure, who gained the most from it.[26]

For sociologist Barbara Cowell, support for single-sex schools and support for selective education stemmed from personal experience. At elementary school, she was made to sit between two illiterate boys so she could teach them to read and write. 'They made my life a misery, pulling my plaits, kicking my shins and generally convincing me that boys were uncouth and insufferable. The County Scholarship to the local Girls' High School which I won at ten was my passport to freedom from Sam Cross and Billy Whitwell.' Cowell feared comprehensive education meant the only 'bright,' 'ambitious' and 'intelligent' girls 'who can hope to escape are those whose parents can afford to send them to independent schools—as long as such schools are permitted to exist!'[27]

By the 1980s, several studies questioned whether the move from single-sex to co-educational comprehensive schools really offered equal opportunities to girls. In fact it was argued that whereas the former may provide a basis for shared gender solidarity, mixed comprehensive schools had not encouraged any real structural change in female-male power relations. Others wondered whether we might construct new masculinities, which were not dependent on the devaluing of women and absolute polarisation from femininity. Examples showed sexual harassment was commonplace and that girls resented a policy of being let out of school ten minutes before the boys to allow them time to get clear of the building. 'I don't care if I lose school time, it's the principle of the thing I object to. If this work is supposed to be worth doing then we're missing out. Anyway did you hear about that second year? She was sexually assaulted by six boys last week and that was at break—how are they going to stop that, lock us up?'[28]

---

[25] Robin Pedley, "The Comprehensive School: England," *FORUM*, 5, no. 2 (1962), 5.

[26] Kathleen Ollerenshaw, *Education for Girls* (London: Faber and Faber, 1961), 66–67.

[27] Barbara Cowell, "Mixed and Single-Sex Grouping in Secondary Schools," *Oxford Review of Education*, 7, no. 2 (1981), 171.

[28] Madeleine Arnot, "How shall we educate our sons?" In *Co-Education Reconsidered*, ed. Rosemary Deem (Milton Keynes: Open University Press, 1984), 37–56; Pat Mahony, *Schools for the Boys? Co-education Reassessed* (London: Hutchinson, 1985), 48.

Fear and anxiety about teenage pregnancy was another argument in favour of single-sex schooling. Interviewed by the author in 2015, Anne Page recounted a story in circulation when she joined the governors of Islington Green Comprehensive School, London, in the 1970s. Parents would not dream of sending their daughters there, given the stories of sex in the basement gym, on a floor covered in soft mats. Added to which, people saw prams lined up outside, first thing in the morning. On her first visit, Page was keen to see this den of iniquity.

> No basement. The school had no basement. So, I said 'Well, where is this basement then?' The head or whoever was showing me around: 'Basement? We've got a bit of a lower area where the gym hall is'. So, we went down there, and it was a perfectly ordinary gym hall. Bit of a sprung floor even. It was just a bit lower level… There were no gym mats all over or anything. So, I said 'Why has this myth grown up about sex here in the gym and prams outside?' They all burst out laughing and said: 'We run a mother's club in the youth centre, which was empty during the day'. There were rooms set aside at the youth centre and so there was community education going on… I was instantly dispelling this which had been allowed to fester.[29]

AnnMarie Wolpe carried out an investigation at a new comprehensive school in Greater London whose first intake of 180 pupils was in 1972. Most boys and girls were in favour of co-education on the basis of the advantages they got in social interaction. Typical of the comments made by 12-year-old girls were 'When you are in a girls' school it gets boring and you get fed up with seeing other and fight.' 'You get to know nice boys and that. You wouldn't meet any boys and be keen on boys.' However, the boys were slightly more effusive in their preference for mixed school in terms of overcoming boredom and widening their horizons. One boy went further. 'If I was in an all boys' school, I would hate it. Now and again if you have got any problems and you look round and see a girl sitting there… it just takes your mind off it, well in my eyes it does.'[30]

Caroline Benn and Brian Simon found no evidence of increased sexual promiscuity in mixed comprehensive schools. Cracking open school timetables, however, they found pupils did not appear as non-gendered subjects into whom teachers wanted to induct knowledge with obvious examples of gender differentiation in the distribution of school knowledge. Half the schools surveyed excluded girls from specific curriculum areas and 49 per cent excluded boys from catering, dance, domestic science, hygiene, jewellery making, nursing and pottery. Feminists and pro-feminist comprehensive campaigners put the issue of subject choice on the agenda. Attempts to break down the gender

---

[29] Interviewed by the author, 1 July 2015.
[30] Annmarie Wolpe, *Within School Walls: The Role of Discipline, Sexuality and the Curriculum* (London: Routledge, 1988), 85.

inequality led Jane Marshall to observe: 'It was concluded that girls could now learn woodwork and boys could become a bit more domesticated. Bright girls could perhaps take sciences, competing alongside boys for high status professions. Boys could relax, take it easy and at last do some girls' subjects without losing face.'[31]

At Haverstock Comprehensive School in north London, feminist teacher Kate Myers undertook to monitor sex-stereotyped option choices pupils were making and gendered patterns of academic achievement in the late 1970s. Some, like journalist Michael Wharton, expressed their fear in hyperbole. Under the headline 'Totalitarian Days' he wrote:

> They [the pupils] should reflect that the cult of 'equal opportunities' is, in one respect, potentially more drastic than National Socialism or Communism. It does not stop at eliminating books written by people of a hated race, class, religion or ideology. Since men and women will have different and varying functions for as longs [*sic*] as they reproduce their kind, every book about human beings can be banned as 'sexist'.[32]

Academics, advocacy groups, governors, teachers and ILEA representatives attended when Haverstock ran a conference on equal opportunities; feminist publishing houses and the Equal Opportunities Commission sent representatives also. Discussion centred on the content of education (both the official and the hidden curriculum), the content of the textbooks and language in which school subjects are pursued, the subjects that the pupils either choose or are entered for and the gendered labour market. Gender difference was constructed in terms of the operation and effects of 'sex-role', 'stereotyping' and 'socialisation', which were some of the key analytic concepts for 1970s feminism.

Myers became Equal Opportunities Organiser for the London borough of Ealing in January 1987. In common with Brent, Haringey and Inner London, Ealing was significant both in its support of equality initiatives through policy development, availability of resources and targeted funding, and acceptance of gender equality as a legitimate professional development issue for teachers. In post, Myers aimed to (1) seek out the good practice and support already in existence, (2) initiate and encourage good practice, (3) publicise and coordinate good practice, (4) establish support networks, (5) establish an understanding that good equal opportunities practice equals good educational practice.[33] Throughout this period, sensationalist media coverage fuelled deep

---

[31] Gaby Weiner, *Feminisms in Education: An Introduction* (Buckingham: Open University Press, 1994), 75; Jane Marshall, "Developing Anti-Sexist Initiatives in Education," *International Journal of Political Education*, 16, no. 2 (1983), 113–137.

[32] Cited in Kate Myers, "How did we get here?" in *Whatever Happened to Equal Opportunities?* ed. Kate Myers (Buckingham: Open University Press, 2000), 5.

[33] Kate Myers, "Did it make a difference? The Ealing Experience 1987–9," in *Whatever Happened to Equal Opportunities?* ed. Kate Myers (Buckingham: Open University Press, 2000), 109.

prejudices like that which appeared in *The Sun* as early as 17 May 1987, entitled 'Loonies ban sexist Robin Redbreast!' According to which, one primary school head reported having been forced to 'dump' 21 sacks of books following a spot check by roving 'loony' equal opportunities staff.[34]

Like the parked prams outside Islington Green, the Robin Redbreast story was untrue but became received wisdom. Newspaper and television coverage of this type illustrate what Myers calls equiphobia. That is, an irrational hatred and fear of anything to do with equal opportunities. Writing for *Comprehensive Education* edited by Caroline Benn in 1985, she called for a fresh approach.

> We cannot afford (both financially and morally) to allow our children to neglect vital areas of educational experience in the name of specialization. We know that the areas they neglect are largely dependent on their gender not their ability or aptitude. This is indefensible and incompatible with the aims of comprehensive education. It is time to base our education system on the philosophy of equality of outcome as well as opportunity.[35]

All of which was controversial. At Ealing, the politics of place intervened. Sections of the media were anxious to tarnish the borough's reputation since it was home to the then leader of the opposition, Labour MP Neil Kinnock. Within 48 hours of the Labour Party losing control of the borough, in May 1990, victorious Conservatives disbanded the Ealing gender equality team and redesignated their posts.

Sometimes, sentiments making a direct causal connection between the sense that the social, economic and power relations of the sexes at work were wrong and that the education system had simply reproduced this imbalance translated into practical policies. Launched in September 1979, the Manchester-based scheme entitled 'Girls into Science and Technology' (GIST) was geared to bringing girls up to male standards of achievement and set about the task by introducing new, female-defined, values into schools. This was a form of gender policy-making designed to convince girls (and their teachers) of their potential in 'subjects' as we conceive it with inherently masculinist biases and to open career opportunities through persuasive work with employers. Less familiar projects that sought to offer an equal education to boys and girls were conceived within a now closed all-boys' inner-city comprehensive school in London's Hackney and at Stantonbury Campus comprehensive school in Milton Keynes, a new town in Buckinghamshire developed after the 1950s. The rest of the county managed to resist the introduction of comprehensives and the academically selective grammar school system fully remains.[36]

---

[34] Kate Myers, "Did it make a difference? The Ealing experience 1987–9," 111.

[35] Kate Myers, "Inequality in the Curriculum. How to Fail Most of Our Pupils without Really Trying", *Comprehensive Education*, 49 (summer 1985), 17.

[36] Richard Harris and Samuel Rose, "Who Benefits From Grammar Schools? A Case Study of Buckinghamshire, England," *Oxford Review of Education*, 39, no. 2 (2013), 151–171.

Inside the Comprehensive Secondary School: Programmes for Boys

Frances Magee and Lynn Raphael Reed have described the promotion of a gender initiative in Hackney Downs School for Boys, the first school to have been taken over by an Educational Association set up under the 1993 Education Act and subsequently closed after a long and acrimonious battle between staff, parents and governors on the one hand and the officers of the local authority on the other. Magee was a deputy head teacher with a responsibility for curriculum but left the school in 1985, while Reed was a teacher in the school from 1983 and 1990 and interviewed a number of staff retrospectively as part of a project recording life histories of teachers committed to social justice.

From the late 1970s, Hackney Downs was in the forefront of the promotion of equal opportunities initiatives including supposedly homogenous 'ability' grouping, integrated humanities, and policies for anti-racism, sex equity and anti-sexism. The idea for the latter came from a school women's group set up as a space in which to share understandings and experiences. It was taken forward by a mixed staff working party who pioneered the teaching of what came to be called the Skills for Living course—a response to 'the paucity of provision of education for sexual self-definition, relationships between the sexes, parenthood and domestic responsibility.'[37]

Discipline was part of the impetus for creating the course but it was also premised on giving boys the opportunity to learn domestic skills to help them become more self-sufficient and aware of the inequality and sexism around them. It was hoped that boys would learn to question 'common sense' notions about who does the housework and childrearing and such aspects of gender expression as the aggressive and violent interpretation of masculinity. Emphasis was very much on helping 'boys to develop a repertoire of expression and ways of relating which included intimacy, trust, cooperation, mutual supportiveness, taking responsibility for their own and each other's emotional well-being' through discussion-based approaches. Progressive practice meant trying to break down tough talking, and they soon learned boys were ready to share first-hand knowledge and thoughts on family life if asked 'Do any of you know a baby of one year? What toys does it like to play with?' Painfully silent if the question became 'What toys do one-year-old babies like to play with?' Besides role-play, Skills for Living pioneered new perspectives on sex education that went beyond the normative biological model. Instead of facts about human bodies cornered into the science curriculum, the emphasis was on friendship

---

[37] Frances Magee, "Working with Boys at Hackney Downs School 1980–4," in *Whatever Happened to Equal Opportunities in Schools? Gender Equality Initiatives in Education*, ed. Kate Myers (Buckingham: Open University Press, 2000), 156–165; Lynn Raphael Reed, "'Zero tolerance': Gender performance and school failure," in *Failing Boys: Issues in Gender and Achievement*, ed. Debbie Epstein, Jannette Elwood, Valerie Hey and Janet Maw (Buckingham: Open University Press, 1998), 56–76.

and intimacy in relationships, sexual and non-sexual, and reassurance about body differences being normal.[38]

In 1982, Hackney Downs staff presented at the first local authority sponsored conference on programmes for boys in schools in England—the ILEA's 'Equal Opportunities—What's in it for Boys?' What these teachers wanted was to enable boys to 'acquire a more accurate and honest view of themselves; recognize and understand the causes of bias evident in images of society and history and contribute positively to a more just society.' Frances Morrell, ILEA's new leader, was supportive.

> Hackney Downs is the first of the Authority's all boys' schools to make the issue of gender explicit in the curriculum. It is essential for schools to find ways to challenge sexist attitudes and values. Hackney Downs sets an example of attitudinal education which, while raising issues, is not coercive but which extends very positively the range of choices that pupils have not only in curriculum content but also in the formation of their attitudes and values. It is, in our opinion, a valuable example of real education for a better society.[39]

Curriculum innovation at Hackney Downs not only found expression in publication but garnered the school an international reputation for anti-sexist approaches. Indeed, the Labour-led ILEA's last full inspection report includes the following assessment. 'The school is to be congratulated upon developing highly positive relationships between pupils and staff and also within the staff. This is a school with a most civilised and humane working environment that is a credit to the whole staff.'[40]

However, the opening of a mixed comprehensive school nearby had a negative impact on recruitment. Hackney Downs had a continual drop in roll from 1985 on and press coverage became more hostile. Initially, anti-sexist campaigns were greeted in a rather tongue in cheek way: 'Baby care—a job for the boys. An all-boys' school has added a fourth R to its syllabus. Rearing babies has joined reading, writing and arithmetic.'[41] Now the school's well-organised and militant staff were castigated for their actions over pay and working conditions, as was ILEA for a lack of commitment to challenge racism. Hostility escalated with the degenerative forces beginning to polarise staff into apparently irreconcilable oppositions.

> One very striking opposition that emerged was that between white feminists who were characterized as 'soft' and 'liberal', and black anti-racists, characterized as 'macho' and 'traditionalists'. A vitriolic attack was launched by a small group of black parents, governors and staff on the anti-sexist programme with boys, Skills for Living, and what was called 'approaches around doing work on gender that

---

[38] Pat Mahony, *Schools for the Boys*, 158.
[39] Lynn Raphael Reed, "'Zero tolerance': Gender performance and school failure," 68.
[40] Ibid.
[41] *Daily Express*, 11 January 1983, op cit, 162.

fail our male youth'. At the same time there was an increase in the sexual harassment of female staff, and an increase in violent and authoritarian practices in some classrooms, under the adage that 'what black boys need is strict discipline and stern teaching of the subject'.[42]

In the background to the school closure were a rapidly changing locality in terms of wealth and social composition, rising unemployment and a constantly altering racial mix. Gendering the story another way, as pupil numbers fell, the local authority proposed that Hackney Downs become a mixed establishment 'to make it less aggressive.'[43] Ten years later, it was gone, swiftly and controversially closed in December 1995.

Clashes about aspects of anti-sexist education in Hackney Downs School should be seen as exemplar actions in the continuing ideological battle of educational ideas over comprehensive schooling in this era. An all-boys school founded by the Worshipful Society of Grocers in 1876, it was set up for the middle classes. Thirty years later, it became a municipal secondary school accepting fee payers and scholarship holders, opting to go comprehensive (and abolish caning) in 1969.[44] Former pupils like Alfred Sherman, whose ideas were important in undermining the post-war social democratic consensus, criticised the 'comprehensivisation' of a school which had been a flagship of opportunity for talented children, many of whom were very poor: 'We East European immigrant Jews in particular benefited from this aspect of the opportunity society,' he said.[45] Today Mossbourne Academy stands on the site of the original school.

Stantonbury Campus was Milton Keynes's first purpose-built comprehensive school established in 1974. The second largest comprehensive school in England and the first not to require a uniform, it was organised around two mixed schools, with state-of-the-art facilities including a theatre and sports centre shared with the local community. The curriculum featured interdisciplinary work, the arts were central in school life and teachers and pupils were on first-name terms. Founding director Geoff Cooksey said later it struck him as 'strange that people called Stantonbury Campus radical. It always seemed to us as immensely normal. You actually treated children in the same way that you treat your own kids… and you treated parents in the same way that you treat your neighbour.'[46] Rosemary Deem, who became a governor of the school in 1980, recalled gender 'was also part of that debate about what

[42] Lynn Raphael Reed, "'Zero tolerance': Gender performance and school failure," 70.

[43] Maureen O'Connor, Elizabeth Hales, Jeffrey Davies and Sally Tomlinson, *Hackney Downs: the School That Dared to Fight* (London: Cassell, 1999).

[44] Peter Medway, John Hardcastle, Georgina Brewis and David Crook, *English Teachers in a Postwar Democracy: Emerging Choice in London Schools* (Basingstoke: Palgrave Macmillan, 2014), 47–48.

[45] *The Independent*, 28 July 1995.

[46] (https://www.livingarchive.org.uk/content/local-history/people/geoff-cooksey/geoff-cooksey-1925-2012).

kind of state school should you have at secondary level and what are the ways of ensuring that gender doesn't have to become a problematic factor in giving a good education.'[47]

At Stantonbury, new teachers advertised a woman-only consciousness-raising meeting that 15 women attended, despite jokes and snide comments, determined to establish a Stantonbury Campus Sexism in Education Group. After this, a mixed group of teachers took up the issue of gender discrimination within the school while a female-only consciousness-raising group of teachers met outside the school. Sexist assumptions in the curriculum and the dominance of knowledge which was only about men meant staff prioritised the need to change the transmission of a restrictive 'sex-role' to girls, to avoid sexism and make subjects more 'girl-friendly.' How to resolve a tendency to spend more time and effort trying to address the poor learning of visibly and vocally inattentive boys as a means of maintaining classroom discipline proved more problematic. Experiments which showed that girls benefitted and made progress in single-sex mathematics sets, for example, were felt to be at odds with Stantonbury philosophy *'that the education of all children is held to be intrinsically of equal value.'* Although some felt that fudged over the real position, which for people who wanted change was 'not only for girls to feel more comfortable with the mathematics content of the school day, but also to enable boys and girls to develop skills in areas not normally seen as being their domain.'[48]

The 'Be a Sumbody' event staged in Easter 1983 was particularly successful, directed at making maths more relevant, interesting and comprehensible for girls. The day included a drama workshop and careers convention with local women representatives of mathematically based jobs. Integrated Science was another innovation introduced as part of a common core curriculum for all pupils up to the age of 16. Teachers produced their own non-sexist learning resources (including booklets and worksheets) that rarely passed unremarked upon by at least some pupils. Nevertheless, two years after the introduction of Integrated Science, the conventional sex-segregation of subject choice within the three sciences (more boys choosing physics, more girls choosing biology) had disappeared.

Consciousness sharpened, but within marked limits. The Group quote the research of a 16-year-old pupil who surveyed 45 of her contemporaries. 'Although Stantonbury does not encourage discrimination,' she concluded, '74 percent of girls and 64 per cent of boys said they were treated differently. Girls are allowed to do the same subjects as boys, but they are treated quite differently in the classroom.'[49] Others came to similar to conclusions,

---

[47] Interviewed by the author, 9 February 2015.
[48] Jenny Shaw, "The politics of single sex schools," *Co-Education Reconsidered*, ed. Rosemary Deem (Milton Keynes: Open University Press, 1984), 21–36; Stantonbury Campus Sexism in Education Group, Bridgewater Hall School, "The realities of mixed schooling," in *Co-Education Reconsidered*, ed. Rosemary Deem (Milton Keynes: Open University Press, 1984), 66.
[49] Op cit, p. 69.

suggesting teachers can be seen to 'collude' in essentialism. Valerie Walkerdine for example in her critique of the application of psychoanalytic pedagogy to nursery school describes how a woman teacher who has been taught that free expression is all-important in teaching young children does not contest demeaning sexual abuse from a tiny boy, on the grounds that it is 'natural.'[50]

Overall, the desire to challenge what Sara Ahmed calls 'gender fatalism' (boys will be boys, girls will be girls) was evident among pro-feminist practitioners who questioned the hierarchy of human attributes and sought to educate boys and girls for a society where gender divisions are less relevant and men and women share in paid work and caring.[51] At Hackney Downs, various factors contributed to the evolving Skills for Living programme but there was also considerable support and pressure from the ILEA for such an initiative. In contrast, the local authority was hostile to Stantonbury Campus, opposing 'progressive' teaching methods and comprehensive schooling. Ultimately, Stantonbury became a grant-maintained school under the 1988 Education Act, opting out of the then Conservative-controlled local authority and funded directly by a grant from central government. Moving on from discussion of feminisms in education in the everyday life of two relatively sympathetic schools, I turn to policy originated and carried through by the only woman leader of England's largest educational authority—the ILEA.

Policy Strategies: The Feminist Touch?

Frances Morrell (née Galleway) represents the generation who came into education feminisms during the era of social liberalism. Born into the working-class in 1937, she passed the 11-plus and progressed to a grammar school and then to Hull University. Looking back, Morrell underscored the affinity between her political beliefs and her experience of selective education. Its meaning distilled in a memory of a school trip to the Rowntree chocolate factory in York where her parents worked.

> Our guide paused beside a young woman who was packing chocolates into boxes at incredible speed… She was wearing a white turban and overalls: I was dressed in my school uniform of navy blazer with its badge and Latin motto, ugly brown lace-up shoes and unbecoming berets. We recognised each other at once, though we had not met since we were 11 year olds: we had shared a desk at junior school. She did not speak to me. I did not know how to speak to her.[52]

Interviewed by Beatrix Campbell for *Marxism Today*, Morrell noted her feminism came from her first forays in the political sphere. She'd arrive late, untidy and agitated for a meeting with a group of 'highly polished men, beautiful clothes, frightfully organised, the conflict really between my life and the fact

---

[50] Valerie Walkerdine, *Schoolgirl Fictions* (London: Verso, 1990).
[51] Sara Ahmed, *Living a Feminist Life* (Durham and London: Duke University Press, 2017).
[52] Frances Morrell, *Children of the Future* (London: Hogarth Press, 1989), 13–14.

that they simply didn't have the responsibilities I had. They would all glare at me disapprovingly as I took my seat slightly breathless. And I realised you know that class wasn't the only issue.' A key driving force in the women's action committee that played a decisive role in integrating feminism into socialist politics, she pressed for women candidates in winnable seats. Again, she argued this based on her experience of candidate selection for several Labour seats in the 1979 general election (among them Birkenhead and Manchester Blackley).[53]

Morrell started work as a teacher in 1960; married Brian Morrell (in 1964) and had a child. She went on to become press officer for the Fabian Society and the National Union of Students and met Labour politician Tony Benn. For 13 years, she worked as Benn's political adviser including five years in government. She was elected to the Greater London Council and ILEA to represent Islington South and Finsbury in May 1981. This was the moment 1980s municipal feminism gained expression in radical inner-city policies in Britain. Former participants Irene Bruegel and Hilda Kean suggest that it built alliances with the new urban left and the trade union movement to pursue an agenda that confronted male power through feminist critiques of hierarchical management. Although she herself was critical of the institutions of the local state, I argue Morrell was a 'femocrat' because she was a feminist leading the carriage of 'recognition' and equal opportunity policies inside the local state bureaucracy.[54] Initially chair of the Schools Committee, she became the Authority's leader in 1983 with the motive, means and opportunity to work on equal opportunities.

The ILEA was England's largest and poorest education authority. Equity and justice were key political issues and Morrell introduced a major new policy framework to investigate the relationship between pupils' achievement and social class, gender or ethnic origin. She first proposed this programme to the ILEA Labour Group when deputy leader and chair of the Schools Sub-Committee with the support of a core group of five members who acted together to carry out their goals. All were from working-class backgrounds, experienced in public life and well informed about current policy debates (e.g. Ruth Gee was a qualified teacher with children in ILEA schools). However, their position was made more difficult because the policy 'challenged the assumption of the ILEA senior managers that a good enough job was being done by the authority so far as academic standards were concerned. The preoccupation with improvement in achievement led to an emphasis on accountability which challenged notions of leaving matters to the professionals.' In all this,

---

[53] Beatrix Campbell, "Labouring Women: An interview with Frances Morrell," *Marxism Today*, July 1985.

[54] Bruegel, I. and Kean, H. (1995) 'The moment of municipal feminism: Gender and class in 1980s local government,' *Critical Social Policy*, 147–169; Cynthia Cockburn, *In the Way of Women: Men's Resistance to Sex Equality in Organizations* (Basingstoke: Macmillan, 1991).

it had something in common with the Great Debate launched by then Labour Prime Minister James Callaghan, during a speech at Ruskin College, Oxford, in October 1976. Concerns about the need to monitor the use of resources in order to maintain a national standard of performance were important trends of the time.[55]

After 1979, two strands of thought that had the ear of central government were free market economics as played out in right-wing think tanks (Sherman's Centre for Policy Studies and the Selsdon Group), and the educational ideas put forward in *The Black Papers*. The shift in political mood and ideas illustrated by the Selsdon Group's second manifesto (1977) which argued that 'What the public wants should be paid for by people as consumers rather than by taxpayers… the function of government should be not to provide services but to maintain the framework within which markets operate.'[56] At national level, possibilities for gender change were not a political priority, but at subnational levels work on equal opportunities and anti-sexism was undertaken with the support of a number of inner-city, Labour-controlled, authorities.

For London's socialists, there were political tensions with the Conservative governments led by Margaret Thatcher. The central authority tried unsuccessfully to abolish the ILEA in 1980 and wanted to when it abolished the GLC in 1983 but considered London boroughs were not yet ready to run education services. ILEA became instead the only directly elected education committee in the country and Frances Morrell's new policy framework broke with traditional approaches. First, the initiative came from newly elected members, rather than officers. Second, the underlying thesis was concerned with institutional arrangements as opposed to remedying deficiencies in the children. Third, the local Inspectorate remit was pastoral rather than to appraise performance and request improvement. Fourth, the initiative was political and finally, it was quite new.[57]

In making the case for a prototype educational initiative based on equal opportunities, Morrell drew on research findings that showed economic equality of opportunity—meaning equality of access to all children irrespective of family income—was not enough to make a difference with regard to equality of outcome. Previously Morrell had acted as adviser to the National Children's Bureau at the time of the publication of *From Birth to Seven*, a longitudinal study that followed every child born in the week of 3–9 March 1958 throughout their school lives. The information from this and other studies, describing learning processes inside schools and variations in performance with particular

---

[55] Frances Morrell, "An episode in the thirty years war: Race, sex and class in the ILEA 1981–90," in *Whatever Happened to Equal Opportunities in Schools? Gender Equality Initiatives in Education*, ed. Kate Myers (Buckingham: Open University Press, 2000), 83–84.

[56] Quoted in Frances Morrell, *Children of the Future*, 17.

[57] Frances Morrell, "An episode in the thirty years war: Race, sex and class in the ILEA 1981–90," 82.

reference to intersectionality influenced her. For Morrell, the question was why these patterns existed and what the educational conclusions were. In response, she argued that 'unless those who supported comprehensive education reformed it for themselves, it would be reformed from outside in ways its supporters would not like.'[58]

In the autumn of 1981, all head teachers and a representative of their teaching staff were invited to join the Authority at the Festival Hall on London's south bank to hear Peter Mortimore (director ILEA research and statistics branch) present research findings about school achievement, prepared jointly with his wife, Jo. In the 1983 publication *Race, Sex and Class 1: Achievement in Schools*, Morrell reminds readers that 'Spending, allocation of resources and numbers of staff within the Authority's schools are according to the Education Priority Area index, reflecting the principle that the most socially deprived school should have proportionately the most support.' Culled from reports of researchers and practitioners, the professional development guidance aimed at challenging teachers to implement non-sexist education on democratic educational grounds. In a direct response to sociologist Basil Bernstein's 1970 phrase, 'Education cannot compensate for society' which implied there was a limit to what schools could achieve; the publication concludes: 'Girls will still be pressured to think of marriage rather than a career. Privilege will remain. But for many individual pupils there will be benefits. Education may not compensate for society, but schools can and do help individual pupils. We must now find ways of helping them *all*.'[59]

Morrell's programme also included changing local political structures and culture. Under her leadership, the ILEA established an Equal Opportunities Sub Committee with two subsidiaries, an ethnic minorities section and a caucus of women members. New regulations permitted women members to claim baby-sitting and attendance allowance to challenge a political system 'set up for managerial men.'[60] The culture war illustrated when a Conservative councillor told the press that she used an official car to take her nine-year-old daughter, Daisy, to school. This was a lie but Morrell's refusal to comment saw her reported to the Ombudsman for investigation. While friends noted privately how some of the best-known male politicians on the GLC with a tendency to stray into national politics and were 'not normally publicity-shy, failed to spring to her defence over the matter of the car,' she refused to be drawn. Instead, she called out the barriers to women's political participation: 'the women with children are challenging the system and the men with children aren't because they have something called wives. The House of Commons is run by men in the interests of men and so is County Hall.'[61]

---

[58] Frances Morrell, "An episode in the thirty years war: Race, sex and class in the ILEA 1981–90," 85.

[59] *Race, Sex and Class 1: Achievement in Schools* (London: ILEA, 1983), 5.

[60] Beatrix Campbell, "Labouring Women: An Interview with Frances Morrell," *Marxism Today* July, 1985, 37.

[61] Ruth Lister, *Times Educational Supplement*, 11 March 1983, 7.

Feminism, combined with a distinctive, very powerful leadership style made Frances Morrell a kind of marmite person, causing a strong liking or disliking. One unnamed senior official commended her power as an orator, coming across 'with great conviction and eloquence.' Within the Authority, she mobilised a female caucus to ensure the policy-making process considered views of women's organisations and individual women. Misogynist opponents grumbled women now ran ILEA in their interest. 'Some of the male teachers, indeed some of the officers in County Hall, have been taken aback and a little disgruntled at the speed in which she wishes to see policy change.'[62] In a press release in February 1983, Morrell declared 'The first stage of an equal opportunities policy is equal opportunity to make that policy. We recognise the fact that women are under-represented, both at senior levels of the Authority and in our normal consultative machinery, so we are taking special measures to remedy this.' A newly set up Equal Opportunities Inspectorate offered specialist advice to the schools.

One of the beneficiaries in career terms was Carol Adams who held the post of ILEA Inspector for Equal Opportunities—gender. In common with Morrell, she was from a white, working-class background (in Hackney). A former scholarship girl who attended Christ's Hospital girls' school, Hertford, and subsequently read History at the University of Warwick followed by a spell at the University of Berkeley, California, enjoying 'flower power and radical politics.'[63] Like Morrell, as a feminist within a state bureaucracy, Adams was a femocrat. Again, like Morrell, she was married and a mother. Unlike Morrell, she got divorced. Teaching history at ILEA comprehensive schools in the 1970s, Adams pioneered women's history, editing the *Women in History* series for Cambridge University Press—the first time a mainstream publisher got involved in this kind of work. With a commitment to non-sexist teaching, she went on to manage one of the authority's specialist teachers' centres with advice on classroom strategies, everyday teaching practices and curriculum materials to challenge the values and practices of patriarchy/androcentricity. As she put it, 'It's now considered "good practice" to ask, "How reliable is the Bayeux tapestry as a source of evidence?" It's high time we started asking "who did the sewing?"'[64]

Activist souvenirs in boxes in education archives capture the dynamism that was in the air. Take the programme for London women's history week in March 1985, for example. It includes performances, events and exhibitions involving the archives, library and museum services, theatre groups, schools and ILEA resource centres for teachers. The Imperial War Museum, for instance, screened documentaries and wartime propaganda films (e.g. *A Day in the Life of a Munitions Worker, Jane Brown Changes her Job, Mrs John Bull Prepared, Night Shift, They Also Serve* and *They Keep the Wheels Turning*). There

---

[62] Ibid.
[63] Yvonne Roberts, "Carol Adams," *Guardian*, 19 January 2007.
[64] Carol Adams, "Who did the sewing? The hidden half of history," *Clio* 1 (1981), 24.

was a lecture on the changing experience of women from Sally Alexander and Age Exchange Theatre performances of *What Did you Do in the War Mum?* The Museum of Mankind, the largest anthropological museum in the country, produced worksheets detailing women's contribution to the cultures on display in their galleries. Sociologist Dale Spender spoke at the launch party at the History and Social Science Teachers' Centre.[65]

Diana Leonard joined London's Institute of Education (now UCL IoE) as a Sociology lecturer in 1976. There she established the Centre for Research on Education and Gender in 1984 and in the language of sociological policy network analysis, became an 'individual interlocker' who straddled sectors, fields and settings including the Equal Opportunities Commission, the School Curriculum Development Committee (SCDC) and local government.[66] She also belonged to the founding collective of the Feminist Library, which started life as the Women's Research and Resources Centre in 1975, helping to build a centre that combines activism and radical thought, as well as being an archive and material resource. *Genderwatch* (1987) was the product of the SCDC *Equal Opportunities in Education Development Project* to which Leonard was a contributor. Aimed at teachers and school leaders who wanted to do something about discriminatory practices, the initial run of 800 copies quickly sold out.[67] Leonard also acted as advocate for teacher-led change aimed at gender equality through a Women and Education group. Her influence encompassed curriculum and teachers' professional development, running in-service education and training sessions in collaboration with Carol Adams and others to make a difference, to be transgressive.

Reflecting on the question of legacy, Bruegel and Kean suggest the funding of feminist initiatives and the incorporation of equal opportunity measures into the ILEA bureaucracy 'had the perverse effect of drawing municipal feminism into the mainstream rather more than it feminized the mainstream agenda,' concluding that the idealism of the great liberating moment got subverted.

In London, under what Shirley Williams considered Frances Morrell's 'gifted and radical leadership' of the ILEA, the Authority required institutions to change their governing bodies to include more women, people from ethnic minorities and with disabilities. In advocating the publication of school results to give parents more informed understanding of the often-secret world of education, Morrell set a new standard. So much so that 'what was at the time the exception is now enshrined in practice. Without her energy, drive and determination, and her work in particular on race, sex and class, the world of education would today be less equal place.'[68]

---

[65] London Women's History Week 4–9 March 1985 programme, Kate Myers papers.

[66] Stephen J. Ball and Sonia Exley, "Making policy with 'good ideas': Policy networks and the 'intellectuals' of New Labour," *Journal of Education Policy*, 25, no. 2 (2010), 151–169.

[67] Kate Myers, "Still Watching…' in *Genderwatch: Still Watching…*, ed. Kate Myers, Hazel Taylor with Sue Adler and Diana Leonard (Stoke-on-Trent: Trentham Books, 2007), xi.

[68] Irene Bruegel and Hilda Kean, 1995, 151; Shirley Williams, *Climbing the Bookshelves* (London: Virago, 2010), 174; George Nicholson and Linda Payne, "Frances Morrell: Politician and activist

Conclusion

My reading of these feminists' narratives suggests that they were advocates of a cultural praxis that involved reforming institutions to change the trajectory of political consciousness in late-twentieth-century Britain. Looking at schooling as an arena of social interaction, my argument is that studying their political commitments and practices is critical to the work of gendering the masculinist historiography of a radical tradition in English state education. These educator activists belong to a long line of women trying to build a culture of democracy through radical approaches to curriculum and pedagogy, affirming the possibility of human betterment.

Under Frances Morrell, equity became an important issue in ILEA's policies. For 1980s municipal feminists, identity politics and 1960s radicalism fed into a belief that they were re-making their own world, hence the articulation of concerns for educational work on gender with boys, grappling with hegemonic masculinity and machismo in such a way as to break the circulation of patriarchal values and male control. Witness the words of Kate Myers recalling the thrill of the feminist experience for her gender and generation:

> My main memories of this time are the excitement of working on this initiative that had political (local) and much school-based support; working with stimulating and committed people, both colleagues in the advisory team and heads and teachers in schools; trying to ensure that equal opportunities was seen as a professional issue and dealt with in that way; being ridiculed by the media and consequently having to be ultra-careful about everything that was said, written and done; the occasional feeling of being attacked on all sides and not being able to please anyone (too soft and liberal for the 'hard' left and too extreme for the right); and finally tensions between people working on equality issues, particularly about race and gender.[69]

In tandem with feminist literature, feminist pedagogy introduced the female human agent in an otherwise male-dominated analysis of the education system. The particular emphasis on 'sex-role,' 'stereotyping' and 'socialisation' had limitations, and conceptually, understandings of the sex/gender distinction were revised with growing attention to intersectionality. Marina Foster highlights the silencing of Black voices while acknowledging recognition that we cannot separate sexism, sexual exploitation and sexual oppression from racism was a significant step.[70] We have to go beyond the idea of monolithic groups facing discrimination, separate out different kinds of femininity, and different

---

who worked with Tony Benn and Led the Inner London Education Authority," *The Independent*, 19 January 2010.

[69] Kate Myers, "Did it make a difference? The Ealing experience 1987–9," 122.

[70] Marina Foster, "A Black perspective," in *Whatever Happened to Equal Opportunities in Schools? Gender Equality Initiatives in Education*, ed. Kate Myers (Buckingham: Open University Press, 2000), 189–200.

kinds of masculinity, to track the organic connections and dissonances between structure and agency.

This chapter helps demolish a simple idea of history as progress and constant movement. Thinking of history as pattern making is a useful metaphor for understanding shift in social change because the patterns look different according to which way you look at them. We need a dialogue between past, present and future and heuristic models of feminist 'waves' get in the way of this. As do ahistorical popular iterations with a lack of awareness of former attempts to deal with the shifting shape of patriarchy and the contemporary relevance of late-twentieth-century initiatives promoting gender equality in schools. Women's social action is missing from standard histories and more reactionary and recuperative men's right stances today. After the Authority was abolished Geen Bernard, the ILEA's first black politician (in 1981), said her 'time on the ILEA was a great experience. I would do it again. But, since Frances Morrell left, nothing has been done for black kids.'[71]

Reconstructing the deeds of activists and early participant histories shows what feminism managed to achieve. It shows also how media trashing of feminist and left leaning urban educational initiatives and the structural destruction of their networks by central government served to distort debate about ILEA's effectiveness and the contribution of labouring women like Frances Morrell. For some, she represented a 'beacon of certainty,' exuding confidence as a woman in power. But she aroused much hostility and revealed the hidden injuries of class and gender for daring to make her voice heard: 'criticism to wound has to come from a source you respect. I don't respect the position of a lot of journalists so it can damage me, but it doesn't hurt me. But on another level the knowledge that virtually never will the person you are, and the kinds of strength and weaknesses you have, ever be conceded… well, yes, that can be very painful.'[72] Ridicule helped to disparage and silence feminist ideas and actions, distorting the nature of a female contribution that for all its contradictions and limitations had a desire to make a fairer and more democratic public education at its heart.

Bibliography

Primary Sources

Archival Sources

Caroline Benn papers, UCL Institute of Education
Diana Leonard papers, UCL Institute of Education
Kate Myers papers, UCL Institute of Education

---

[71] Geen Bernard, "The First Black Politician," in *Against the Tide*, ed. Sarah Olowe (London: Inner London Education Authority, 1990), 44.

[72] Campbell, *Marxism Today*, 37.

Autobiographies, Memoirs, Diaries, Letters, Obituaries

Benn, Tony. *Office Without Power: Diaries 1968–72*. London: Arrow Books, 1989.
Bernard, Geen. "The First Black Politician," in *Against the Tide*, edited by Sarah Olowe, 41–45. London: Inner London Education Authority, 1990.
Castle, Barbara. "No Kitchen Cabinet." In *Very Heaven: Looking Back at the 1960s*, edited by Sara Maitland, 47–58. London: Virago, 1988.
David, Miriam E.. *Personal and Political: Feminisms, Sociology and Family Lives*. Stoke-on-Trent: Trentham Books, 2003.
David, Miriam. "Diana Leonard: Obituary." *Guardian*, 9 December 2010.
Nicholson, George and Payne, Linda. "Frances Morrell: Politician and Activist Who Worked with Tony Benn and Led the Inner London Education Authority." *The Independent*, 19 January 2010.
Olowe, Sarah. *Against the Tide: Black Experience in the ILEA*. London: Inner London Education Authority, 1990.
Roberts, Yvonne. "Carol Adams: Obituary." *Guardian*, 19 January 2007.
Segal, Lynne. *Making Trouble: Life and Politics*. London: Serpents Tail, 2007.
Stilitz, Daniel. "Sylvia Denman: Obituary." *Guardian*, 30 May 2019.
Tavers, Tony. "Frances Morrell: Obituary." *Guardian*, 14 January 2010.
Tweedie, Jill. *Eating Children with an Unfinished Memoir Frightening People*. Harmondsworth: Penguin, 1994.
Williams, Shirley. *Climbing the Bookshelves*. London: Virago, 2010.

Newspapers and Periodicals of the Period

Comprehensive Education
FORUM for New Trends in Education
Marxism Today

Other Contemporary Books and Pamphlets

Adams, Carol. "Who Did the Sewing? The Hidden Half of History." *Clio*, no. 1 (1981): 22–25.
Arnot, Madeleine. "How Shall We Educate Our Sons?" In *Co-Education Reconsidered*, edited by Rosemary Deem, 37–56. Milton Keynes: Open University Press, 1984.
Bruley, Sue. "Consciousness-Raising in Clapham; Women's Liberation as 'Lived Experience' in South London in the 1970s." *Women's History Review*, 22, no. 5 (2013): 718–719.
Coote, Anna and Campbell, Beatrix. *Sweet Freedom: The Struggle for Women's Liberation*. London: Pan Books, 1982.
Cowell, Barbara. "Mixed and Single-Sex Grouping in Secondary Schools." *Oxford Review of Education*, 7, no. 2 (1981): 165–172.
Dale, R.R. *Mixed or Single-Sex School? A Research Study in Teacher-Pupil Relationships: Volume 1*. London: Routledge, 1969.
Foster, Marina. "A Black Perspective." In *Whatever Happened to Equal Opportunities in Schools? Gender Equality Initiatives in Education*, edited by Kate Myers, 189–200. Buckingham: Open University Press, 2000.

Leonard, Diana. "Teachers, Femocrats and Academics: Activism in London". In *Whatever Happened to Equal Opportunities in Schools?* edited by Kate Myers, 166–186. Buckingham: Open University Press, 2000.

Magee, Frances. "Working with Boys at Hackney Downs School 1980–4." In *Whatever Happened to Equal Opportunities in Schools? Gender Equality Initiatives in Education*, edited by Kate Myers, 156–165. Buckingham: Open University Press, 2000.

Mahony, Pat. *Schools for the Boys?* London: Hutchinson, 1985.

Marshall, Jane. "Developing Anti-Sexist Initiatives in Education." *International Journal of Political Education*, 16, no. 2 (1983): 113–137.

Morrell, Frances. *Children of the Future*. London: Hogarth Press, 1989.

Morrell, Frances. "An Episode in the Thirty Years War: Race, Sex and Class in the ILEA 1981–90." In *Whatever Happened to Equal Opportunities in Schools?* edited by Kate Myers, 77–92. Buckingham: Open University Press, 2000.

Myers, Kate. "Inequality in the Curriculum. How to Fail Most of Our Pupils without Really Trying", *Comprehensive Education*, 49 (summer 1985), 14–17. Benn Papers, Box 199.

Myers, Kate. "Did it make a Difference? The Ealing Experience 1987–9." In *Whatever Happened to Equal Opportunities?* edited by Kate Myers, 106–124. Buckingham: Open University Press, 2000.

Pedley, Robin. "The Comprehensive School: England." *FORUM*, 5, no. 2 (1962), 4–22.

Raphael Reed, Lynn. "'Zero Tolerance': Gender Performance and School Failure." In *Failing Boys: Issues in Gender and Achievement*, edited by Debbie Epstein, Jannette Elwood, Valerie Hey and Janet Maw, 56–76. Buckingham: Open University Press, 1998.

Shaw, Jenny. "The Politics of Single Sex Schools." In *Co-Education Reconsidered*, edited by Rosemary Deem, 21–36. Milton Keynes: Open University Press, 1984.

Stantonbury Campus Sexism in Education Group, Bridgewater Hall School. "The Realities of Mixed Schooling." In *Co-Education Reconsidered*, edited by Rosemary Deem, 57–70. Milton Keynes: Open University Press, 1984.

Stott, Mary. "The Second Sex." In *Women of the Revolution: Forty Years of Feminism*, edited by Kira Cochrane, 3–5. London: Guardian Books, 2010.

Tweedie, Jill. "Why Nice Girls Finish Last." In *Women of the Revolution: Forty Years of Feminism*, edited by Kira Cochrane, 9–11. London: Guardian Books, 2010.

Wolpe, Annmarie. *Within School Walls: The Role of Discipline, Sexuality and the Curriculum*. London: Routledge, 1988.

PUBLISHED REPORTS

ILEA. *Race, Sex and Class: 1. Achievement in Schools*. London: ILEA, 1983.

SECONDARY SOURCES

Ahmed, Sara. *Living a Feminist Life*. Durham and London: Duke University Press, 2017.

Ball, Stephen J. and Exley, Sonia. "Making Policy with 'Good Ideas': Policy Networks and the 'Intellectuals' of New Labour." *Journal of Education Policy* 25, no. 2 (2010): 151–169.

Bruegel, I. and Kean, H. "The Moment of Municipal Feminism: Gender and Class in 1980s Local Government." *Critical Social Policy* (1995): 147–169.

Cockburn, Cynthia. *In the Way of Women: Men's Resistance to Sex Equality in Organizations*. Basingstoke: Macmillan, 1991.
Fraser, Nancy. *Justice Interruptus: Critical Reflections on the "Post-socialist" Condition*. New York: Routledge, 1997.
Harris, Richard and Rose, Samuel. "Who Benefits from Grammar Schools? A Case Study of Buckinghamshire, England." *Oxford Review of Education*, 39, no. 2 (2013): 151–171.
hooks, bell. *Feminism is for Everybody: Passionate Politics*. London: Pluto Press, 2000.
Hunt, Felicity. *Gender & Policy in English Education 1902–1944*. New York: Harvester Wheatsheaf, 1991.
Kennedy, Mary. "One Woman's Reflections on the Ruskin Conference, 'Celebrating the Women's Liberation Movement thirty years on,' Ruskin College, Oxford, 18 March 2000." *Women's History Review*, 10, no. 2 (2001): 349–352.
Kynaston, David. *Modernity Britain 1957–62*. New York: Bloomsbury, 2015.
Lees, Sue. *Sugar and Spice: Sexuality and Adolescent Girls*. Harmondsworth: Penguin, 1993.
McRobbie, Angela. *The Aftermath of Feminism: Gender, Culture and Social Change*. London: Sage, 2009.
Medway, Peter, Hardcastle, John, Brewis, Georgina and Crook, David. *English Teachers in a Postwar Democracy: Emerging Choice in London Schools*. Basingstoke: Palgrave Macmillan, 2014.
Myers, Kate. "Still Watching...." In *Genderwatch: Still Watching...*, edited by Kate Myers, Hazel Taylor with Sue Adler and Diana Leonard. Stoke-on-Trent: Trentham Books, 2007.
O'Connor, Maureen, Hales, Elizabeth, Davies, Jeffrey and Tomlinson, Sally. *Hackney Downs: the School That Dared to Fight*. London: Cassell, 1999.
Ollerenshaw, Kathleen. *Education for Girls*. London: Faber and Faber, 1961.
Saint, Andrew, ed. *Politics and the People of London: The London County Council, 1889–1965*. London: Hambledon Continuum, 1989.
Walkerdine, Valerie. *Schoolgirl Fictions*. London: Verso, 1990.
Weiner, Gaby. *Feminisms in Education: An Introduction*. Buckingham: Open University Press, 1994.
Wright, Nigel. *Assessing Radical Education*. Milton Keynes: Open University Press, 1989.

CHAPTER 11

Conclusion: Constancy and Change in the Twenty-First Century

> *Shirley (not yet Mrs King) arrives at Peckham School for Boys and Girls a former Victorian workhouse with two rectangular blocks of concrete attached incongruously to both ends of it approached by what was once called the Paupers' Path leading up to its castle-sized doors… her parents, Winsome and Clovis, are proud of her for making it to university to read History and thereafter gaining a Certificate in Education she's the one who made it not her older brothers who didn't have to do any housework or even wash their own clothes, whereas she had to spend her Saturday mornings doing both who were given first helpings at meals they never had to cook, and extra portions because they were growing lads, including mega-helpings of the most desirable desserts who weren't punished for speaking their mind, whereas she was sent to her room at the slightest sign of insurrection, keep your thoughts to yourself, Shirl and while it's true they got the strap and she didn't—for going out without permission or not coming home on time from school—it was only because she never broke the rules.*
> —Bernadine Evaristo, *Girl, Woman, Other* (Harmondsworth: Penguin, 2019), 217–218

Mrs King is an education success story. As Shirley, she won a place at a single-sex grammar school with a pipeline to the professional classes. She believes in making society more equal for her pupils and feels the pressure to be a great teacher *and* an ambassador for every black person in the world. Carole, the teen Super Geek who goes off the rails after she is gang raped, is Mrs King's 'first and greatest achievement.' Under her wing, the 'talented, fallen' protégé becomes the first child in the school's history to make it to Oxbridge and reignites the reason why she went into teaching in the first place, which is the power of education to change lives. Mrs King, who remains committed to giving Peckham kids a fighting chance, has come far through meritocratic selection and hard work. Her daughters could go further. For five years, she and her husband attend church every Sunday to get them into Grey Coat Hospital, a highly academic state-funded secondary school in Westminster. A school that hit the headlines in 2015 when David and Samantha Cameron chose it for their eldest daughter, Nancy, making Cameron the first serving Conservative prime minister in history to send his child to a state secondary school.

Mrs King's utility as a literary subject is to show the strong grasp ideas of 'merit' and 'meritocracy' have on the creation of everyday narratives of value and power. At school, her mission is 'to make history *fun* and *relevant* because we need to avoid repeating the mistakes of the past and to deepen our understanding of who we are as the human race, don't we, class?' The boys with swastikas brandished on their blazers she deals with by educating them about Hitler's Final Solution. She 'tries not to succumb to the paranoia that comes from thinking every negative reaction is due to her skin colour.'[1] Most of her playmates on the municipal housing estate where she grew up were not subject to the same gravitational pull, neither were the children she taught. For Mrs King, a difficulty was that as the 1980s became history, the 1990s brought more problems than solutions. Issues like more children at school from families struggling to cope, more unemployment, poverty, addiction and domestic violence. By the millennium, things have degenerated to the point of pupils with large knives in school rucksacks, pistols hidden down socks and more young people joining the gangs that tout for members on the streets outside.

Evaristo experiments with form and uses the intergenerational stories of 12 female characters to explore how race, sexuality, gender, history, and social class intersect and raise timeless questions about agency and resistance within a patriarchal society that help us put the present into perspective, which is what this book has tried to do. This conclusion will make connections, drawing threads together in order to consider the historical specificity of our current gender system and how it interacts with other systems, like race, social class and 'ability.' Reflecting on what has changed and what has remained the same across the span of time considered here, I will select some key themes beginning with a focus on discourses of difference pertinent to understanding issues of gender, culture and power.

In the 1780s, evangelical educators like Hannah More were beginning to construct sets of mental traits distinctive to boys/men and girls/women based on the belief that male and female bodies were homologous with their minds. A narrative which meant that if a girl child was quicker and more advanced, this was unlikely to be read as a mark of genius, whereas the conspicuous 'dullness' of the male child was construed as incommensurable potential. By the 1880s, medical opinion would declare that his 'natural' mental superiority placed the upper-class boy 'at the apex of evolution,' a mark that 'distinguished him not just from all girls but from lower-class boys.'[2] Therefore, it was not grades and

---

[1] Bernadine Evaristo, *Girl, Woman, Other* (Harmondsworth: Penguin, 2019), 221, 224.
[2] Michèle Cohen, "'A habit of healthy idleness': Boys' underachievement in historical perspective," in *Failing Boys: Issues in Gender and Achievement*, ed. Debbie Epstein, Jannette Elwood, Valerie Hey and Janet Maw (Buckingham: Open University Press, 1998), 25.

academic performance but individual 'character' that was at the heart of education in Eton and other public schools, and the illusion of excellence fostered there made 'effortless achievement' an important concept in the aristocratic attitude to education. An ethos of manliness not only constructing the superior mental power of the English gentleman but his 'Other,' the swot, whose hard work is the very evidence of a lack of 'natural' intellect.

Perhaps this is the narrative Boris Johnson spun back on himself when he was London Mayor in 2013 and branded his brother, Jo, and David Cameron as 'girlie swots' for gaining first class degrees at university, when he had to make do with a 2:1. Or when as prime minister it was revealed that Johnson referred to Cameron as 'a girly swot' for a second time in a 2019 cabinet paper and appeared to insult the Labour leader Jeremy Corbyn after footage of his first prime minister's questions seemed to show him gesticulating towards Corbyn saying 'Call an election, you great big girl's blouse.' Which is the greater insult journalist and author Lucy Mangan reflected—to be feminine or to be hard working? Whatever the whys and wherefores of Johnson's sexist language and his exploitation of a more generalised campaign against 'political correctness' and liberal values on issues of gender, race and sexuality, Mangan assembles an impressive line-up of powerful women from Brenda Hale, Britain's first female law lord, to climate activist Greta Thunberg to speculate the time of 'girly swots' may be now. 'We've tried it the other way and frankly it has not gone well,' she says.[3]

While Johnson gave the boys' boarding school lingo a political life, perhaps his rear guard machismo suits a 'climate of ideas' or structure of feeling the downside of which includes forms of hatred and anger, such as misogyny that seem to be on the rise. A point in time and space when it is argued a fear of feminisation and a hunt for manliness has seen retro ideas of what it means to be a strong man (and dreams of power) go mainstream in the western world.[4] Johnson won a sweeping victory in the general election in December 2019, and it was among 35-to-54-year-old men in semi-skilled and unskilled manual occupations where the Conservatives won the biggest swing from Labour. These were the descendants of generations of men carried along by urbanisation and Victorian economic growth, who saw male wages rise with mass production and entered a world of industrial work where the tradition of on-the-job training meant that progression was not governed by examinations and qualifications gained prior to starting work, but by the experience of work itself. Men who grew up in families where the breadwinner was one for whom technological change and the disappearance of manufacturing jobs and the coal mines that fuelled industries like steel and heavy engineering brought them into the category of the 'left-behind' living in post-industrial districts in northern England and in coastal areas in southern England.

[3] Peter Walker, "Boris Johnson calls David Cameron 'girly swot' in leaked note," *The Guardian*, 6 September 2019; Lucy Mangan, "How 'girly swots' came back to bite Boris Johnson," *The Guardian*, 25 September 2019.
[4] Pankaj Mishra, *Age of Anger: A History of the Present* (Harmondsworth: Penguin, 2017).

The implication of a crisis of masculinity is a long tradition. In England today, the classed and racialised discourse touches on difficulty in school with many citing a need to do more for underperforming white working-class boys. Indeed, the feminisation of schooling is one thing that the rhetoric holds responsible for the alleged crisis of male failure. Yet if we look closely, we see that academic achievement far from becoming feminised in today's schools has been feminine for a long time. Indeed, gendered 'gap talk' was carried along by the development of formal education systems and the history of the College of Preceptors set up in 1846 to raise the poor standard of teaching in private schools shows this.

Specifically concerned to professionalise teaching, the Preceptors pioneered a number of innovations over the Victorian period including the introduction of public examinations for secondary schoolchildren. This had the strong backing of early members like pioneer educators Frances Buss and Jane Chessar who coached their female pupils for entry, but it was the apparent reluctance on the part of teachers to submit themselves to examination that led the Preceptors to extend their examinations to schoolchildren. Consequently, the first ever public examination of English school pupils took place under their auspices in 1850, and the female candidates quickly achieved better grades. 'I am ever careful to avoid throwing an apple of discord,' bemoaned one Preceptor, but 'I can hardly forbear saying on the present occasion… that the ladies have done themselves more credit than the gentlemen.'[5] By 1880, the proportion of female candidates outstripped the male, and they maintained their lead in performance, notably at first-class level where there was a percentage difference of 16 per cent in 1883.

Explanations for the gender gap varied. First, it was noted that boys were on average younger at the date of examination and second that they were obliged to take more difficult subjects. It was adduced then and after that subjects favoured by boys were harder than subjects favoured by girls. Twice the schemes of work were changed to ensure the curriculum was not biased in favour of females, but no one questioned male underachievement as such. Thus children were failed because the deep structure of Western culture's educational thought, to use the terminology of Jane Roland Martin, legitimated the labelling of subjects such as maths and science as 'masculine' or 'hard' in comparison with others such as English and modern languages which were defined as 'feminine' or 'soft.' Perhaps this logic helps explain why girls were permitted a lower standard in maths in the annual examinations of elementary school pupils during the era of payment-by-results.

---

[5] Quoted in Andrea Jacobs, "'The girls have done very decidedly better than the boys': Girls and examinations 1860–1902," *Journal of Educational Administration and History*, 33, no. 2 (2001): 120–136.

By the 1920s, government reports had institutionalised a notion of a habit of 'healthy idleness' that protected boys from overuse of mental energy in contrast to their female peers who were thought to be in greater danger of working themselves too hard. Psychologists and teachers agreed that there were greater intellectual differences between individuals than between boys and girls but that boys and girls were very different in terms of emotion and temperament. Educationally these binaries were mapped on to stereotypical subject choices reflected in a male predilection for science and mathematics and female for the aesthetic and literary subjects. This constituted a serious situation but academically, male under-performance in examinations was actually represented as an index of their mental health. Girls, on the other hand, were viewed as industrious and conscientious and therefore especially vulnerable to exam stress that could, in extreme circumstances, interfere with their capacity for healthy maternity.

Boys did worse in the 11-plus examinations by which post-war children were selected for secondary schooling. Not because of any intrinsic deficiency it was argued, but because their early development lags behind girls. Few questioned the conventional wisdom in the 1940s, but as time passed, questions were raised about the legality of weighted selection procedures in some English authorities. Limited data suggested girls achieve better grades than boys at all examination levels, and the ILEA, for example, abandoned its policy of treating boys and girls differently when it assessed the results of tests taken by pupils in their final primary year in 1983. It was anticipated the move would mean that about 5 per cent more of girls than of boys would fall into the top band of the authority's three broad 'ability' bands with grave implications. 'If more girls are perceived as being band one material, the speculation goes, then those girls might achieve more. Conversely, boys seen as band three material might not do as well as they would have done, had they got into band two.' As attempts were made to make opportunities more equal, the ILEA faced concerted criticism. A male head said: 'It's a definite advantage to be a woman at this moment. We will be watching the situation closely and we'll be worried if there is an imbalance in any way.'[6]

Knowledge that the stereotype of the diligent girl who works too hard and her counterpart the 'healthily' unconcerned boy is nothing new helps us put the present into perspective. What differs nowadays is the greater cultural visibility of twenty-first century school girls as a metaphor for meritocratic social change. Thus the greater presence of young women in higher education as evidenced by entry figures, dropout rates and degree performance statistics becomes a yardstick for arguments which presuppose that boys as a group underachieve. Simultaneously, access to education remains gendered by prestige of institution and field of study. Thus male enrolments are associated with entry to the highest-tariff institutions, to science and engineering courses and

---

[6] "ILEA ends adjustment for sex," *Times Educational Supplement*, 18 November 1983, papers of Kate Myers; Pat Mahony, *Schools for the Boys?* (London: Hutchinson, 1985), 15, 24.

to research degrees. Added to which, the gains women have made do not carry through into society and the economy since women are over-represented in poorly paid jobs.

Rather than asking why boys underachieve, which presupposes that they do, the more sensible lines for action would be to focus on the question of access alongside that of the content of education and what counts as school knowledge and why. The question of social and cultural power is of vital importance in determining how far children fulfil their potential both in school and afterwards. We need to ask who is responsible for 'choice' and to recognise that equal treatment might not be enough to overcome deep-seated structural disadvantage. This includes thinking critically about the school curriculum and our system of public examinations, the culture of teaching and pressure on children and youth to gain acceptance in peer groups. As well as about the family as a site and source for the operation of control, the importance of teacher expectations and attention to violence as learned behaviour. There is plenty of evidence to show the persistence of male monopoly of linguistic and physical space, for example, as well as teacher attention that can have negative connotations when associated with questions of discipline and issues of classroom control. These are large historical questions and ethnography, memoirs, personal testimonies and statistics can help reveal how we are where we are.

Although positive net lifetime returns from higher education have been larger for female graduates than for male, this is because non-graduate women typically earn less than non-graduate men do. There remains a variety of explanations for this. The feminisation of occupations, women taking time out to have children and in some cases, institutions continuing to pay women less for the same work. The position of women in the higher education sector where they represent a high proportion of workers but are mostly in non-academic posts and under-represented at the senior level illustrates this. Despite women representing 46 per cent of the academic workforce, for example, women hold 28 per cent of professorships (up from 23 per cent 5 years ago) and the majority of women who do gain promotion are white. Thus Nicola Rollock's research showed there were just 25 Black women professors in the UK in 2019.[7] Women are more likely to be teaching in the less prestigious post-1992 universities, more likely to be on part-time contracts and in specific subject areas like nursing and teaching.

To a large extent, the gender biases and stereotypes that exist in society are invested in our institutions and in our knowledge traditions, gendering an invidious divide between vocational and academic knowledge. As a result, those boys/girls, men/women who enter sex-stereotyped intellectual fields

---

[7] Sean Coughlin, "Only 1% of UK University Professors are Black," *BBC News*, 19 January 2021 https://www.bbc.co.uk/news/education-55723120; Nicola Rollock, "Staying Power: The career experiences and strategies of UK Black female professors," UCU, February 2019; "Portraits of Female Black Professors," *BBC News*, 9 March 2020, https://www.bbc.co.uk/news/in-pictures-51800467.

can look and feel like space invaders. A critical question in this book has been whether the elite Western tradition has the intellectual resources within to transform itself and come to terms with the historical effects and traces of 'really useful' working-class educational knowledge, racism and sexism to reflect the range and complexity of our cultural wealth. Sara Ahmed calls attention to the problems of gender and reflects, 'Women's studies as a project is not over until universities cease to be men's studies… To build women's studies is to build in an environment that needs to be transformed by women's studies; the point of women's studies is to transform the very ground on which women's studies is built.'[8]

The question of gender equity became mainstream when anxiety began to be expressed about boys' under-achievement in the context of the language of meritocracy. But behind the cultural pull of populist rhetoric that men are facing an identity 'crisis,' we need to remember that not all boys/men, girls/women are the same. The concept of 'crisis' does not accurately describe the reality, while the traditionalist discourse on men and children that often surfaces in the arguments of those campaigning for fathers' rights and traditional family values assumes that gender roles are relatively fixed. We see this in the worry about where children are going to get their male role models from if the proportion of men in teaching keeps falling and the inherent sexism implicit within the stereotypes around which the role model idea revolves including assumptions about men and computers or engaging in football talk. But the real ongoing crisis is about the number of teachers rather than their sex. Teaching skills have no gender, and role modelling is a genderless matter since what matters is signalling the value of kindness, respect, resolve and such like.

Enough work has been done for us to recognise that stereotypical 'boy-friendly' practices could reinforce a problem of how boys are schooled. Over and again we have heard the voices of boys like Shaun—a hard-working, well-behaved, white, inner-city working-class boy who wants educational success while simultaneously trying to maintain his standing within the male peer-group culture. Shaun's aspirations are the cause of much trouble and turmoil around the contradictions of combining white, working-class masculinities with academic achievement. In the end, his struggle against the educational context he finds himself in (a school that was over 95 per cent working class, with 47 per cent of children on free school meals and a huge staff turnover) becomes intolerable. He leaves school at 16 with minimal exam passes.[9]

Schools have often been seen as masculinity-making devices. Matthew Arnold saw his renovated Rugby as a means of forming a Christian gentleman, and cultural constructs of 'character' have long been essential to the formation of elite English masculinity. Other reformers besides Arnold have given other

---

[8] Sara Ahmed, *Living a Feminist Life* (Durham, North Carolina: Duke University Press, 2017), 112.

[9] Diane Reay, *Miseducation: Inequality, Education and the Working Classes* (Bristol: Policy Press, 2017), 156–162.

schools the task of forming a sober and industrious working man—the ideal breadwinner. At the time of writing, Boris Johnson is the 20th British prime minister to be educated at Eton College, and there remains an irrefutable link between certain single-sex public schools, culture and power. Commenting on David Cameron's claim that being a former Etonian didn't affect his understanding of people, a former pupil opined that it was utterly risible. 'When I attended Eton in the 1990s pupils practised foxhunting on bicycles and went scuba-diving in PE. Some dined annually with the Queen. I made toast for a Saudi royal and shared classes with Prince William. Eton is not simply "a particular school"—it is a peculiar school.'[10]

Above all else, hegemonic masculinities still dominate English schooling much as they do British public life. Boys' private schools remain extraordinarily powerful patriarchal channels of elite reproduction, offering an inside track to social capital for a few. Let us consider a role-play underpinning a Scholarship Examination Question set by Eton College, cited by Danny Dorling:

> The year is 2040. There have been riots in the streets of London after Britain has run out of petrol because of an oil crisis in the Middle East. Protesters have attacked public buildings. Several policemen have died. Consequently, the Government has deployed the Army to curb the protests. After two days the protests have been stopped but twenty-five protesters have been killed by the Army. You are the Prime Minister. Write the script for a speech to be broadcast to the nation in which you explain why employing the Army against violent protesters was the only option available to you and one which was both necessary and moral.[11]

The question included a quote from Machiavelli's *The Prince* and was worth 25 marks. Five marks for summarising the quote, 5 for noting any reservation you might have about sending in the Army and 15 for putting this authoritarian policy into practice. With only 20 per cent of the marks allocated for critical thinking, the social commentator who drew attention to the question noted: 'that's training, not education.' At the time of writing, it costs £42,511 a year to send a boy to Eton College, with parents charged over £14,000 a term (excluding 'extras' like music lessons).

White male dominance of scientific/technological spheres, high-status professional work and managerial positions of authority and control, academic and economic capital is intact. English newspaper columnist, political commentator and writer Owen Jones suggests a low-paid, part-time, female shelf-stacker as an appropriate symbol for the twenty-first century in his study of the demonisation of the working class.[12] Cultural assumptions about male and female identity not only have a powerful impact but a double entanglement of a post-feminist, neoliberal politics that holds up the 'successful' girl and female

---

[10] Alex Derber, "Eton and the Masses," *The Guardian*, 14 March 2010.
[11] Danny Dorling, *Inequality and the 1%* (London: Verso, 2015), 98–99.
[12] Owen Jones, *Chavs* (Harmondsworth: Penguin, 2012), 167.

celebrity within academia as motif, obscures spaces of contradiction notably within everyday sexism including verbal insults and in some cases physical molestation in a wide variety of schools, colleges and universities.

Warnings about increased sexualised behaviour, the influence of internet pornography and the role of mobile devises as tools of abuse have been ignored. In 2017, research commissioned by the National Education Union found 24 per cent of girls reported unwanted touching in school, compared with 4 per cent of boys. In March 2021, more than 100 schools were named in an outpouring of harrowing testimony on the Everyone's Invited website, which was set up to expose misogyny, harassment and assault. Tragically, survivors drew attention to a lack of redress and support for many victims in a high number of cases, some of which stretched back as far as the mid-1980s. Amid concerns over a 'rape culture' within specific institutions (including historically all-boys' private schools such as Eton, St Paul's and Westminster) and warnings of a UK epidemic of child sex abuse, there were calls for best practice resources for schools on delivering relationships and sex education as well as guidance for primary school teachers on how to handle questions related to sex that go beyond the relationships education curriculum. Reminiscent of feminist concerns following the move from single-sex to co-educational schools in the state sector, it appears that private schools that were previously boys' schools, some of which only admit girls post-16, may have a particular problem.[13]

A conceptualisation of agency as free will is central to those who would wish away structural discrimination and suggest aspiring to equality means treating people equally rather than differently. UK women and equalities minister, Liz Truss, gave a speech called *The Fight for Fairness* in December 2020 in which she talked about the need to switch focus from 'fashionable' issues like race and gender to poverty and geographical inequalities. 'Too often, the equality debate has been dominated by those who believe people are defined by their protected characteristics and not by their individual character,' she said in a much-trailed foray into current culture wars and the politics of identity. 'While we were taught about racism and sexism,' she reflected on her state schooling in 1980s Leeds, 'there was too little time spent making sure everyone could read and write' (although it didn't prevent her winning a place at the University of Oxford). Truss's speech is important because of the work it does in helping to reconceptualise class as a cultural identity rather than as about economic relationships or access to capital. Yet the fact is that UK poverty still wears a largely female face.

In the period this book covers, women have changed their lives to move into paid work in greater numbers and at every level, but men have never taken on the equivalent responsibility for unpaid childcare and housework, even as women's employment rate reached a record high, at 72 per cent compared with 78 per cent for men. After March 2020, the impact of the coronavirus (COVID-19)

---

[13] Mahony, *Schools for the Boys?*, Haroon Siddique, "DfE warns schools could be closed over 'rape culture' claims," *The Guardian*, 31 March 2021.

pandemic increased inequality with more vulnerable labour market groups most strongly affected by job and earning losses so far. For example, women outnumber men by three to one in sectors including key workers—health care, schools, social care and supermarkets—but are more likely than men in those sectors to earn less than the real Living Wage an independently calculated rate based on living costs like food, clothing and bills. In schools that is true of 22 per cent of women and 8 per cent of men. Female business owners are more likely to have found the pandemic stressful, while the lives of female health workers were put at risk by having to wear ill-fitting personal protective equipment designed for men.[14]

With schools in England closed during national lockdowns, surveys showed that home-working landed women with a disproportionate workload in childcare and home schooling. At the same time, trades union research found that more than seven out of ten requests from working mothers through the job furlough scheme (an unprecedented experiment in retaining people's social status while they have been out of work) have been rejected. One working mother thought 'We like to say we've progressed, but we haven't. In my mum's day, girls were expected to leave school and cook and clean and look after the little ones. I don't think we've moved on as much as we think.' Despite feeling crushed by everything, she had not had a conversation with her husband. 'There's no point. His dad was the provider of money and not of care. He has fallen into that same stereotype. He will never change.'[15] Representative of her gender and generation, this woman is a public sector keyworker, juggling on-going disparities in housework.

COVID-19 has impacted men and women in different ways. Data shows that men were more likely to be infected with the disease and more likely to die from it, and that most Black and South Asian groups remained at higher risk than White British people. Overall, men had a higher risk of severe illness and death, while women's well-being was more negatively affected than men's during the first year of the pandemic. The impact on victims of domestic abuse was also profound with services reduced as the impact of COVID-19 infection hit staffing and safe spaces. Much of the care burden fell to women, and the impact of school and nursery closures saw women losing jobs or hours. Women's groups argued the UK's response to the pandemic suffered from the lack of a female perspective, and a committee of MPS concluded government policies have 'repeatedly skewed towards men.' Committee chair Caroline Noakes spoke of a 'very blokey mentality at the top' of government, which had suffered from 'the predominance of single-sex education around the cabinet table.' Nearly half those polled in a Mumsnet survey for International Women's Day 2021 expected gender equality to go into reverse, while the chief executive of the Fawcett Society accused the government of ignoring mounting evidence of a crisis in gender equality. 'It's like we're on this freeway heading in the wrong direction, and we keep missing the

---

[14] Alexandra Topping, "International Women's Day: Experts discuss Covid's impact on gender equality," *The Guardian*, 8 March 2021, https://www.theguardian.com/world/2021/mar/08/women-need-policies-designed-for-them-say-campaigners.https://www.livingwage.org.uk/news/women-have-long-been-trapped-essential-work-pays-too-little-its-time-make-amends (accessed 19 August 2021);

[15] Natasha Walter, "How COVID brought mothers to breaking point," *The Observer*, 28 February 2021, 8–11.

exits,' she said. 'We urgently need investment in childcare, we need employers reporting on sex-disaggregated redundancies data—we need a really serious focus on women. But without women in the room, without women in positions of power, it is just not going to happen.'[16]

Yet a belief in meritocracy is firmly entrenched in the British psyche. Recent survey data suggest that ideas about hard work, ambition and equal opportunity remain ingrained. Thus 76 per cent of the British public see hard work as essential or very important in determining success. More important than, say, knowing the right people or coming from a wealthy family. Just 36 per cent thought being born a man or woman was essential or very important whilst support for authoritarian populism is strongest among those who have seemingly failed the 'merit' test. This in the midst of a global pandemic whose effects in health terms are light years away from a reflection of 'merit' and when recent evidence has suggested the risk of precarious work, and its intensification during the ongoing pandemic, are not random but highly dependent on gender, ethnicity, class and how they intersect.[17]

Boris Johnson pledged that his government will lead a 'levelling up' of prosperity across the UK with the emphasis largely on spatial inequalities. As Liz Truss's speech indicated, discussion at the individual level is focused on character with populist rhetoric about the 'problem' of white working-class boys mobilised to control the gender agenda. But this is a massive simplification of who is struggling in schools today, which ignores other deep-seated structural disadvantages and appears to separate the interconnected domains of education, employment and family. To illustrate, it remains the case that white working-class boys with lower educational qualifications and a lower likelihood of going to university have higher employment rates and higher social mobility than working-class people of ethnic minority background.[18]

The fight for gender equality has come a long way since the Georgian era at the start of this book, but we still need a reform agenda that is concerned to equalise gender orders. By gendering the educational landscape, my history writing offers a space from which to challenge long-standing biases and omissions that limit how we understand politics and society. Alternate futures are possible. We need to build back fairer after the pandemic so that the way we

---

[16] https://www.livingwage.org.uk/news/women-have-long-been-trapped-essential-work-pays-too-little-its-time-make-amends (accessed 19 August 2021); Alexandra Topping, "Half of women in UK fear equality is going back to the 1970s: Survey," *The Guardian*, 8 March 2021, https://www.theguardian.com/world/2021/mar/08/half-of-women-in-uk-fear-equality-is-going-back-to-1970s-survey?CMP=Share_iOSApp_Other; BBC News, "Covid: Support 'repeatedly skewed towards men', say MPs," 9 February 2021, https://www.bbc.co.uk/news/uk-politics-55978335

[17] Arnand Menon and Alan Wager, "How the language of meritocracy has transformed British politics," *The Guardian*, 4 March 2021, https://www.theguardian.com/commentisfree/2021/mar/04/britain-meritocracy-research-pandemic; https://wbg.org.uk/analysis/uk-policy-briefings/how-has-the-risk-of-precarious-work-evolved-in-the-covid-19-uk/

[18] Peter Walker, Aamna Mohdin and Alexandra Topping, "Downing Street suggests UK should be seen as a model of racial equality," *The Guardian*, 31 March 2021.

'educate' young people is better for all. Achievement in public examinations is not the only index by which we ought to be measuring the quality of educational life. Above all, personal accounts show how much bullying, friendship, peer pressure and the messages children receive about themselves through the formal and hidden curricula of schooling matter too.

We need to face up to certain things both in education and society as a whole. We need all educational establishments to be gender-sensitive spaces in which everyone can be seen learning together as equals, with respect and empathy. We need a cultural context where learners and teachers look beyond common sense understandings such that they can identify that the history they are learning is *a* story, for example, and where all pupils and students can see their past reflected in the curriculum. We need to incorporate perspectives of class, gender and 'race' into what counts as school knowledge and to help break down the traditional vocational/academic divide. We need a vision of gender democratisation that has commitment from everyone. To challenge not only everyday sexism, misogyny, homophobia and gender stereotypes but also a discourse of cisnormativity. Cultural ideas like the definition of being a 'real' man and 'true' masculinity can be so destructive with boys themselves arguably the first victims. We need to believe in political power as the ability to be effective, to make a difference and to educate young people for civic participation to address the forces of gendered power that have shaped our past and present so the different generations don't face the same world tomorrow as they did yesterday.

Bibliography

Primary Sources

Archival Sources

Kate Myers papers, UCL Institute of Education

Newspapers and Periodicals of the Period

BBC News
The Guardian
The Observer

Secondary Sources

Ahmed, Sara. *Living a Feminist Life*. Durham, North Carolina: Duke University Press, 2017.
Cohen, Michèle. "'A Habit of Healthy Idleness': Boys' Underachievement in Historical Perspective." In *Failing Boys: Issues in Gender and Achievement*, edited by Debbie

Epstein, Jannette Elwood, Valerie Hey and Janet Maw, 19–34. Buckingham: Open University Press, 1998.
Dorling, Danny. *Inequality and the 1%*. London: Verso, 2015.
Evaristo, Bernadine. *Girl, Woman, Other*. Harmondsworth: Penguin, 2019.
Jacobs, Andrea. "'The Girls have Done Very Decidedly Better than the Boys': Girls and Examinations 1860–1902." *Journal of Educational Administration and History*, 33, no. 2 (2001): 120–136.
Jones, Owen. *Chavs*. Harmondsworth: Penguin, 2012.
Mahony, Pat. *Schools for the Boys?* London: Hutchinson, 1985.
Mishra, Pankaj. *Age of Anger: A History of the Present*. Harmondsworth: Penguin, 2017.
Reay, Diane. *Miseducation: Inequality, Education and the Working Classes*. Bristol: Policy Press, 2017.
Rollock, Nicola. "Staying Power: The Career Experiences and Strategies of UK Black Female Professors." UCU, February 2019.

Appendix: Important and Influential Public Events

1779
Nonconformist Relief Act gives religious dissenters the right to teach without needing to be licensed by their local Church of England bishop.

1791
Roman Catholics Relief Act gives Catholics the right to open schools on condition that an oath of allegiance to the monarchy is sworn.

1792
A Vindication of the Rights of Woman by Mary Wollstonecraft published.

1808
Society for Promoting the Lancastrian System of Educating the Poor is formed (renamed the British and Foreign Schools Society for the Education of the Labouring and Manufacturing Classes of Society of Every Religious Persuasion in 1814).

1811
National Society for Promoting the Education of the Poor in the Principles of the Established Church (the Church of England) is formed.

1833
Factory Act prohibits the employment of children under nine in factories and textile mills.

1834
Poor Law Amendment Act sets up the workhouse system designed to make certain that nobody in receipt of relief was at any advantage over those who were in some kind of work, assumes all women dependent on men.

1845
Frances Buss co-founds a private day school with her mother renamed the North London Collegiate School for Ladies (1850): the first fee-paying girls' day school to offer male academic standards and attempt to create a schoolgirl community.

© The Author(s), under exclusive license to Springer Nature Switzerland AG 2022
J. Martin, *Gender and Education in England since 1770*, Gender and History, https://doi.org/10.1007/978-3-030-79746-1

1848
Queen's College, London, established for women who intend to teach.
1860
Eton Volunteer Corps founded: a volunteer rifle battalion that went to become the most famous of the public school corps.
1862
Payment by Results is introduced in elementary education: each child is expected to pass the annual test, and for girls only, plain needlework is an examinable obligatory subject.
1865
The University of Cambridge is the first English university to open its local examinations to girls.
1866
Female suffrage societies started in London and Manchester.
1868
Public Schools Act gave public schools independence from direct jurisdiction or responsibility of the Crown, the established church or the government.
1869
Endowed Schools Commission established to redistribute educational endowments.

First college offering advanced tuition and examinations of the Pass Degree and Honours standards of Cambridge for women founded at Hitchin (moves to Girton in 1874).

Municipal Reform Act gives women the vote in local elections.
1870
Lydia Becker, Emily Davies and Elizabeth Garrett Anderson are the first School Board women.
1872
Girls' Public Day School Company founded.

Elizabeth Garrett Anderson founds the New Hospital for Women in London's Euston Road, staffed entirely by women.
1873
First ever government appointment of a woman: Mrs Nassau Senior is appointed as an Assistant Inspector of Workhouses.
1875
Elizabeth Garrett Anderson is the first woman to join the British Medical Association.

Martha Merington is the first female Poor Law Guardian.

First female clerks employed by the Post Office Savings Bank.
1878
The University of London is the first English university to open all its examinations and degrees to women.

Domestic economy becomes a compulsory subject for elementary school girls.
1882
Married Women's Property Act allowed married women to own and control property in their own right.

1883
Women's Co-operative Guild is established.
1885
Criminal Law Amendment Act raises the age of sexual consent to 16 for females.
1887
Agnata Ramsay (Girton) is the only person placed in the top division of the first class in Classics at Cambridge.
1888
Clementina Black secures the first equal pay resolution at Trades Union Congress (TUC).

Seven hundred women matchmakers strike over poor wages and dangerous conditions.
1893
Oxford University abolishes chaperonage for women attending lectures.
1897
National Union of Women's Suffrage Societies (NUWSS) is founded.
1903
Emmeline Pankhurst forms Women's Social and Political Union (WSPU).
1904
Equal Pay League formed within the National Union of Teachers (renamed the National Federation of Women Teachers in 1906).

Report of the Interdepartmental Committee on Physical Deterioration advocates the teaching of domestic subjects to girls.
1905
Militant acts in support of women's suffrage begin to occur.

Maude Lawrence is the first Chief Woman Inspector.
1907
Reina Lawrence is the first woman to serve on a local council (Hampstead, London).

Women's Freedom League is founded.
1914
War is declared. Both the NUWSS and WSPU cease campaigning.
1918
Women over 30 who met certain property qualifications or were graduates voting in a University constituency could vote for Parliament.

Education Act brought in a standard school-leaving age of 14 for all.

Countess Constance Markievicz is the first woman elected to Parliament. As a member of Sinn Fein, she does not take her seat.
1919
Nancy Astor is the first woman to take a seat in Parliament.

Sex Disqualification (Removal) Act admits women to the legal profession, higher grades of the Civil Service and the magistrature.

National Association of Men Teachers formed within the National Union of Teachers (NUT).

1920
National Federation of Women Teachers break away from the NUT to become the National Union of Women Teachers.
Women are admitted to Oxford University as full members.
1921
Eugenicist Marie Stopes opens Britain's first family planning clinic in London.
1922
National Association of Men Teachers break away from the NUT to become the National Association of Schoolmasters.
Law of Property Act allows both husband and wife to inherit property equally.
1923
Matrimonial Causes Act makes grounds for divorce the same for women and men.
1928
Women are given universal suffrage on the same terms as men.
1929
Margaret Bondfield (Labour) becomes Britain's first female Cabinet Minister and Privy Counsellor.
1939
War is declared.
1940
British government introduced food rationing to ensure fair shares for all (ends 1954).
1942
Girls Growing Up by Pearl Jephcott published, which allows for the possibility that girls' experiences may be different from boys.
1943
Dame Anne Loughlin becomes the first female President of the TUC.
1944
Abolition of marriage bar on women teachers.
Board of Education becomes a Ministry of Education.
1945
Ellen Wilkinson (Labour) becomes Britain's first British female Minister of Education.
1947
All British medical schools become co-educational.
Women are made eligible for full membership and degrees from Cambridge University, but the statute limited the numbers of women to one for every ten men.
Compulsory schooling extended to 15.
1948
Founding of the National Health Service to ensure free health care for all at the point of need: previously only the insured (usually men) benefitted.
Married women in work could choose between paying the full national insurance rate and the lower 'married woman's stamp' (until 1977).

National Service Act put peacetime conscription into place: Healthy males aged 17–21 years were expected to serve in the armed forces for 18 months and remain on the reserve list for four years unless conscientious objectors or working in exempted occupations.

Women admitted to Cambridge University as full members.

1949

First coin-operated launderette is opened in London.

1951

Festival of Britain.

1953

Women teachers are awarded equal pay.

The Second Sex by Simone de Beauvoir is published in English for the first time.

1955

Mary Quant opens a boutique called Bazaar on the King's Road, Chelsea.

Barbara Mandell becomes the first female newsreader on English television.

Baroness Sharp becomes the first female Permanent Secretary within the Civil Service.

1957

The *Guardian* starts its women's page.

1958

Hilda Harding becomes the first female bank manager.

Stella Isaacs, Marchioness of Reading, Baroness Swanborough, is the first Life Peeress.

1960

The L-Shaped Room by Lynne Reid Banks published, a sensational and shocking bestseller: describes the stigma of unmarried motherhood.

1961

Contraceptive Pill first became available on the NHS.

1962

Dame Elizabeth Lane became Britain's first female County Court judge.

1963

Last national servicemen leave the armed forces.

The first Beatles LP released.

1965

Barbara Castle (Labour) becomes Britain's first female Minister of Transport.

1967

Abortion Act gives women in Britain (except Northern Ireland) abortion rights with certain conditions.

Homosexual acts, between consenting adults in private, decriminalised.

NHS (Family Planning) Act allows health authorities to give contraceptive advice regardless of marital status, and the Family Planning Association (FPA) follows suit.

1968

Grosvenor Square demonstrations against the Vietnam War.

Marlborough College became the first leading public school to admit female pupils.

Women at the Ford car factory in Dagenham strike over equal pay.

1969

No-fault divorce proved only by the 'irretrievable breakdown of relationship' legalised.

1970

Britain's first National Women's Liberation Conference is held at Ruskin College, Oxford.

Equal Pay Act makes it illegal to pay women lower rates than men for the same work.

Age of majority reduced from 21 to 18 years.

1971

World's first safe house for abused women and children set up in Chiswick, west London.

1972

Children Act sets the minimum school-leaving age at 16.

National Health Service (Family Planning) Amendment Act allows local authorities to perform vasectomy services on the same basis as other contraceptive services.

1974

Founding of the National Women's Aid Federation.

1975

First Rape Crisis Centre opens in London.

Sex Discrimination Act outlawed direct and indirect discrimination in work, education and training.

1976

Domestic Violence Act enables women to obtain a court order against their violent husband or partner.

Equal Opportunities Commission comes into effect.

Race Relations Act outlaws discrimination on the grounds of 'colour, race, or ethnic, or national origins' in public places.

1978

The Organisation of Women of African and Asian Descent is set up: the first black women's organisation in Britain to organise at a national level.

1979

Margaret Thatcher (Conservative) becomes Britain's first female Prime Minister.

1981

Baroness Young (Conservative) became the first woman leader of the House of Lords.

Greenham Common Women's Peace Group begins.

1984

First National Black Feminist Conference is held.

1987
Diane Abbott (Labour) becomes the first black woman elected to Parliament.
1988
Introduction of a National Curriculum in state schools.
Section 28 of the Local Government Act makes it illegal for any council or government body to 'intentionally promote homosexuality, or publish material with the intention of promoting homosexuality' (abolished 2003).
1992
Betty Boothroyd (Labour) becomes the first woman Speaker of the House of Commons.
1993
Parity between men and women in higher education enrolment is reached.
1994
House of Lords ruling gives equal rights to part-time workers.
Rape in marriage is made a crime.
1997
Marjorie Scardino becomes the first female Chief Executive of a FTSE 100 company.
1999
New rights to maternity and parental leave conferred.
Sex Discrimination (Gender Reassignment) Regulations make it illegal for employers to discriminate against trans people.
2003
Employment Equality (Sexual Orientation) Regulations are introduced to protect people against discrimination based on their sexual orientation.
2006
Margaret Beckett (Labour) becomes Britain's first female Foreign Secretary.
2007
Jacqui Smith (Labour) becomes Britain's first female Home Secretary.
2008
Education and Skills Act requires participation in some form of education or training until the school year in which the child turned 17, raised to the person's 18th birthday (in 2015).
2010
Equality Act protects against discrimination by employers, businesses and organisations which provide goods or services, health and care providers, someone you rent or buy a property from, schools, colleges and other education providers, transport services and public bodies. The nine protected characteristics in the Act are age, disability, gender reassignment, marriage or civil partnership (in employment only), pregnancy and maternity, race, religion or belief, sex, and sexual orientation.
2015
Libby Lane becomes the first female Bishop to the Church of England.
2019
General election on 12 December returns the highest number and proportion of female MPs ever recorded: 220 (34 per cent) of 650 MPs are women.

Index[1]

A
Ablett, Noah, 198
Abu-Lughod, Lila, 36
Adams, Carol, 265, 266
Agutter, Catherine, 85
Ahmed, Sara, 127, 261, 279
Alberti, Johanna, 29
Albertine, Viv, 166, 172, 175, 210
Alexander, Sally, 31, 153, 154, 250, 266
Allan, Mary Miller, 195, 195n18, 196
Allen, Sheila, 154
America, 31
Anderson, Elizabeth Garrett, 140–142
Anglican, 8, 58, 59, 63–65, 68, 71, 172, 191, 192
Arnold, Matthew, 147, 279
Arnold, Thomas, 54, 55
Arnot, Madeleine, 39, 98, 100, 112, 122
Ashworth, Andrea, 166
Assessment, 30, 110, 111, 120, 122, 124–126, 129, 154, 156, 224, 235, 258
Assisted Places Scheme, 112
Association of Head Mistresses, 135
Astor, Nancy, 11
Attlee, Clement, 15, 87, 88
Austen, Jane, 52, 53
Austerity, 123, 206, 221, 233, 248
Autobiography, 1, 19, 33, 42, 47, 52, 58, 73, 163, 164, 186, 189, 190, 197, 210
Avery, Gillian, 1
Avery, Valerie, 183

B
Baker, Danny, 166, 183
Baker, Kenneth, 110, 111
Baldwin, Stanley, 72
Ball, Stephen, 27, 113, 118–120
Balls, Ed, 123
Bannister, Sarah, 218
Barker, Bernard, 207
Battersby, Audrey, 153
Bawden, Nina, 166, 176, 178, 206, 207
Baylis, Trevor, 182, 183
Beale, Dorothea, 59–61, 136
Beard, Mary, 35
Beckham, Victoria, 176
Bedales school, 101
Bedford College, London, 59, 153, 192
Bell, Andrew, 63
Bell, Susan Groag, 29
Benn, Caroline, 94, 103, 250, 254, 256
Benn, Tony, 262
Bennett, Judith, 27, 52

---

[1] Note: Page numbers followed by 'n' refer to notes.

Benson, Sheila, 34
Berg, Leila, 164, 204
Bermondsey, 43, 45, 46, 84, 85, 185
Bernard, Geen, 268
Bernstein, Basil, 264
Betjeman, John, 205, 211
Beveridge Report, 15, 150
Birmingham, 6, 70, 88, 99, 108, 142, 154, 185, 210
Birmingham, University of, 195, 209
Black Papers, 17
Blackstone, Tessa, 108
Blair, Tony, 117, 225
Bluestocking Society, 63
Board of Education, 71, 83, 86, 135, 144, 147, 194, 230
Bodichon, Barbara, 191
Boer War, 11, 66, 144
Borough Road Training College, 203
Bourdieu, Pierre, 40–42, 147
Bowlby, John, 45, 88
Boyle, Edward, 92
Bradford, 69
Brady, Karren, 166, 176
Brand, Russell, 176
Breadwinner, 6, 7, 14, 27, 31, 92, 102, 221, 275, 280
Brent, 255
Brewer, Marjorie, 199
Bridges Adams, Mary, 80, 193, 194
Brighton, 58
Bristol, University of, 193
British Sociological Association (BSA), 32, 154
Brittain, Vera, 165, 167, 203
Brougham, Henry, 54
Brown, Gordon, 225
Bruegel, Irene, 262, 266
Bruley, Sue, 251
Bryce Commission, 1895, 70
Bulcraig, Clara, 84, 85
Burt, Cyril, 86
Burton, Antoinette, 32
Buss, Frances, 59–61, 72, 136, 137, 140, 146, 276
Butler, Judith, 2, 211
Butler, Samuel, 54
Butterfield, Herbert, 28
Byers, Stephen, 117

C
Callaghan, James, 263
Cambridge, 3, 28, 30, 56, 70, 135, 168, 190–192, 196, 199, 202, 205, 207, 210
Cambridgeshire, 81
Cambridge, University of, 34, 137, 191, 227
Camden School for Girls, 72
Cameron, David, 123, 125, 211, 275, 280
Campaign for Nuclear Disarmament, 250
Campbell, Beatrix, 252, 261
Capitalism, 3–7, 30
Carlisle, 145, 208
Carr, E.H., 28
Castle, Barbara, 249
Catholic, 63, 64, 178, 185, 200, 236, 238
Central Schools, 83, 84, 166, 170
Centre for Contemporary Cultural Studies, 16, 36
Centre for Policy Studies, 263
Chaplin, Charlie, 174
Charity School movement, 62
Charterhouse school, 54
Chartism, 8
Cheltenham Ladies College, 136
Chessar, Jane, 140, 276
Chorley, Katharine, 165, 167, 168
Christie, Agatha, 59
Church, Richard, 165, 173, 174
Churchill, Winston, 15, 58, 86, 88
City Technical Colleges, 112
Clapham Sect, 62
Clapton County Secondary School for Girls, 148
Clarendon Commission, 56, 71
Clark, Alice, 29, 30
Clarke, Mary Gavin, 135, 158
Clarricoates, Kathleen, 97
Clough, Anne Jemima, 191, 202
Cobbe, Frances Power, 58
Cohen, Michèle, 39, 60, 136, 210
College of Preceptors, 276
Collet, Clara, 61
Collins, Andrew, 184, 185
Common, Jack, 73
Connell, Raewyn, 38

Consciousness raising, 251, 260
Conservative governments, 70, 72, 109, 129, 225, 246, 263
Cookery, 2, 66, 108, 142–144, 150, 152, 153, 184
Cooksey, Geoff, 259
Cooper, Gordon, 64, 82
Co-operative movement, 8
Coote, Anna, 252
Corbyn, Jeremy, 275
Coren, Alan, 208, 209
Cornish, 169, 174
Corrigan, Phillip, 98
Cotswold, 170
Coventry, 93
Covid, 282
Cowell, Alice, 140
Cowell, Barbara, 253
Cox, Brian, 79, 207
Cox, Roger, 114
Craigie, Jill, 234, 234n39
Creak, Edith, 70
Crosland, Anthony, 93
Cross Commission on Elementary Education, 66
Crowther Report, 1959, 88, 92
Culture, 1, 2, 5, 8, 9, 16, 19, 26, 34, 36, 37, 39–41, 40n48, 43, 61, 70, 71, 80, 84, 85, 98, 99n65, 107, 108, 117, 121, 122, 129, 135–159, 164, 177, 180, 181, 189, 190, 197, 200, 201, 203, 210, 211, 219–225, 235, 238, 240, 264, 266, 274, 276, 278–281
Curriculum, 19, 44, 53–56, 69, 74, 80, 87, 92, 94, 97, 99, 102, 110, 111, 114, 115, 117, 129, 135–159, 164, 166, 177, 183, 204, 254, 257–260, 265–267, 276, 278, 281, 284

D
Dale, R.R., 252
Dash, Paul, 166, 183
David, Miriam, 112, 122, 136n2, 153, 154, 248
David Lister High School, 94
Davidoff, Leanore, 32

Davies, Emily, 56, 57, 60, 140–142, 191, 288
Davies, Hunter, 208
Davies, Lynn, 37
Davin, Anna, 35, 250
Dawson, Agnes, 223, 227, 231
Dayus, Kathleen, 142
De Lissa, Lillian, 195
Deem, Rosemary, 154, 259
Delamont, Sara, 100
Dempster, Steven, 210
Denman, Sylvia, 246
Department for Education and Skills, 122
Department of Education, 110
Derbyshire, 167
Dice, Kate, 225–231, 235, 242
Dickens, Charles, 9
Domesticity, cult of, 7, 137
Dorling, Danny, 280
Drabble, Margaret, 153
Drake, Barbara, 228
Drill, 66, 144
Duffy, Maureen, 166, 179, 186
Durham, 72, 195, 199, 208
Durham University College, 192, 208
Dyhouse, Carol, 2, 43

E
Ealing, 82, 255, 256
East Anglia, University of, 196
Eckhard, Edith, 43
Education, 1, 26, 52, 79, 108, 137, 164, 190, 246, 273, 288
Education Act, 1870, 65, 138, 193
Education Act, 1880, 65
Education Act, 1902, 10, 71, 194
Education Act, 1918, 81
Education Act, 1944, 79, 86, 147
Education Act, 1988, 110, 116, 166
Education feminisms, 122, 261
Edwards, Wil Jon, 197, 198
Elementary schools, 10, 46, 61, 63–66, 69–72, 81, 83, 84, 138, 142, 144, 145, 148, 150, 169, 171–174, 177, 179, 193, 194, 198, 199, 204, 218, 219, 227, 230, 253, 276, 288
Eleven-Plus, 182

Employment, 5, 8, 9, 13, 15–19, 44, 46, 47, 59, 61, 62, 64, 80, 82, 90, 93, 95, 102, 103, 109, 115, 116n24, 123, 129, 141, 145, 150, 154, 166, 196, 200, 222, 223, 232, 241, 281, 283, 287, 293
Enlightenment, 3–7, 27
Equality Act, 2006, 122
Equality and Human Rights Commission, 128
Equal Opportunities Commission (EOC), 17, 112, 113, 152, 255, 266, 292
Equal Pay Act, 1970, 17, 292
Essex, David, 166, 182, 183
Essex, University of, 196
Ethnicity, 26, 33, 108, 113, 114, 116, 128
Ethnography, 1, 27, 37, 47, 99, 278
Eton College, 56, 86, 280
Europe, 6, 15, 86
European Union (EU), 18
Evangelical, 62, 63, 67, 274
Evans, Mary, 156
Evaristo, Bernadine, 274
Examinations, 18, 54, 57, 58, 60, 61, 66, 70–72, 79, 81, 99, 101, 107, 112, 113, 116, 124, 125, 136, 137, 141, 146, 147, 149, 156, 165, 166, 168, 170, 177–184, 186, 187, 191–194, 199, 202, 224, 230, 275–278, 284, 288
Exeter, University of, 192, 195

F
Fabian Women's Group, 228
Factory Act, 1878, 65
Farndon, Reginald, 82
Fawcett, Millicent Garrett, 25
Fawcett Society, 123, 128, 282
Feminization, 6, 116, 220–225, 276, 278
Femocrat, 262, 265
Fine, Cordelia, 127
First World War, 10, 11, 52, 73, 82, 85, 138, 168, 203, 220, 231
Flintoff, John-Paul, 184, 185
Foakes, Grace, 171, 172, 174

Forrester, Helen, 189
Forster, E. M., 206
Forster, Margaret, 145, 163, 186, 208
Frankenburg, Charis, 202
French Revolution, 3, 136
Friedan, Betty, 250, 251
Fuller, Mary, 36
Furniss, Henry Sanderson, 198
Further and Higher Education Act, 1992, 197
Furzedown Teaching Training College, 200

G
Garnett, Eve, 84
Garnett, Tony, 179
Gavron, Hannah, 153
Gee, Ruth, 247, 262
Gender, 1, 25, 52, 79, 107, 137, 164, 189, 217, 245, 274, 293
Gender codes, 39, 47, 64, 98, 103
Gender norms, 6, 89, 126, 224
Gender order, 38, 53–62, 84, 126, 129, 186, 211, 246, 283
Gender regime, 38
General Certificate of Secondary Education (GCSE), 112, 113, 120–122, 124, 125, 147, 186, 225, 238
Gerrard, Stephen, 166
Gewirtz, Sharon, 113
Gillborn, David, 121
Gipsy Hill Training College, 195
Girls' Public Day School Trust, 60
Girton College, 30, 81, 135
Godolphin School, 81
Goldman, Ronald, 207, 209
Gomersall, Meg, 111
Goody, Jade, 185
Gould, Ronald, 200
Gove, Michael, 123
Governesses' Benevolent Institution, 59
Grace, Gerald, 220, 223, 224, 236
Grammar schools, 53, 55, 56, 70, 71, 82, 87–91, 93–95, 99, 100, 102, 126, 137, 147, 150, 157, 163, 168, 169, 171, 179, 181–184, 208, 240, 256, 261, 273
Gramsci, Antonio, 38, 39

Great Depression, 11, 79
Greater London Council (GLC), 246, 262–264
Green, Mary, 93, 94
Green, William, 141, 178
Greening, Justine, 124
Greenwich, 140, 193
Greenwood, Walter, 72
Grey, Maria, 60, 61
Griffin, Christine, 99
Griffin, Gabrielle, 157
Griffiths, Morwenna, 37
Grimsby, 79

H
Hackney, 68, 148, 256, 265
Hackney Downs School, 257, 259
Hadow, Henry, 86
Hadow Reports, 150
Hale, Brenda, 275
Hall, Catherine, 32
Hall, Stuart, 16, 250
Hammond, Barbara, 29
Hammond, Lawrence, 29
Hanley, Lynsey, 185
Hardy, Thomas, 193
Hare, Augustus, 54
Haringey, 255
Harman, Harriet, 122, 209
Harris, Mary O'Brien, 138, 147–150, 227, 228
Harrow school, 54
Hastings, Frances, 142
Hattersley, Roy, 166, 178
Haverstock Comprehensive School, 255
Haythorne, Evelyn, 165, 171
Headmasters' Conference, 56
Heath, Edward, 109
Henderson, Arthur, 198
Hennegan, Alison, 90
Heren, Louis, 166, 170, 176
Heterosexuality, 252
Hewitt, Cecil Rolph, 166, 171
Hill, Matthew Davenport, 165, 173
Hill, Rosamond Davenport, 143
Hinds, Lily, 145
Holland Park Comprehensive School, 181

Homan, Ruth, 143
Homerton College, 195
hooks, bell, 251
Hughes, Molly, 136, 145
Hull, 94, 249
Hunt, Felicity, 252
Huxley, Thomas, 140, 141

I
Identity, 2, 7, 10, 18, 19, 26, 33, 36, 38, 39, 55, 58, 71, 84, 85, 108–116, 120, 127, 128, 136, 144, 146, 159, 164, 186, 190, 200, 201, 218, 219, 223, 225, 227, 236, 238–240, 242, 246, 250, 267, 279–281
Ideology, 5, 7, 28, 32, 38, 39, 73, 83, 90, 92, 129, 136, 138, 141, 146, 221, 236, 255
Ilkeston, 182
Imperial Darwinism, 55
Independent Labour Party, 193
Industrial revolution, 153
Inner London Education Authority (ILEA), 246, 247, 255, 258, 261–268, 277
Institutional Darwinism, 55
International Working Men's Association, 65
Islington Green Comprehensive School, 254

J
Jackson, Brian, 89
Jardine, Lisa, 34
Jay, Catherine and Helen, 196
Jay, Peggy, 204
Jephcott, Pearl, 43–46, 146, 154
Johnson, Alan, 166, 176, 181, 183
Johnson, Boris, 211, 275, 280, 283
Jones, Owen, 280
Jones, Robert, 85, 86

K
Keele, University of, 90
Kennington and New Cross Pupil Teacher Centre, 227

Kent, University of, 156
Key, Charles, 231, 232
Key, Florence Ellen, 217, 225, 231–235, 242
Khan, Sadiq, 25
Kidbrooke school, 93
Kimmins, Grace, 85
King, Ledley, 166, 185
King Edward VI Girls' High School, Birmingham, 70
King's College London, 59, 90, 192, 201
Kinnock, Neil, 256
Kitch, Chris, 157
Knightley, Keira, 31
Knowledge, 1, 4, 7, 19, 32, 36, 47, 64, 85, 94, 97, 98, 110, 115, 125, 136, 138, 141–145, 147, 154, 156–159, 170, 193, 194, 211, 254, 257, 268, 277–279, 284
Knowles, Lilian, 30, 31
Knox, Vicesimus, 53
Kuhn, Annette, 155, 166, 179, 181
Kynaston, David, 88

L

Labour governments, 14, 88
Lady Margaret Hall, Oxford, 81, 192, 204, 208, 210, 212
Lake District, 184
Lambart, Audrey, 98
Lancashire, 7, 64, 70, 145
Lancaster, 63, 196
Lancaster, University of, 196
Langham Place Circle, 59, 191
Laski, Marghanita, 15
Latin, 54, 56–58, 63, 74, 91, 94, 136, 136n2, 137, 182, 193, 261
Lawn, Martin, 236
Lawrence, D.H., 29, 208, 218
Lawrence, Maude, 289
Lawson, Jack, 199
Lee, Laurie, 166, 170
Leeds, 6, 31, 154, 177, 184, 192, 281
Lees, Sue, 101, 114, 157
Leicester, University of, 154
Leonard, Diana, 58, 154, 157, 158, 245, 266

Leverhulme Numeracy Research Programme, 120
Liberal, 122, 138–140, 142, 147, 158, 194, 227, 258, 267, 275
Lincolnshire, 79
Lindsay, Robert, 166, 182, 186, 209
Liverpool, 6, 14, 166, 189, 192
Lodge, Eleanor, 212
London, 3, 25, 30, 31, 36, 51, 53, 59, 61, 65, 70, 83, 84, 93, 100, 101, 114, 115, 139, 143, 148, 157, 181, 192, 193, 206, 207, 222, 223, 228, 229, 231, 247–251, 255, 263, 265, 266, 280
London County Council, 45, 169, 182, 222, 223n11, 234
London Married Woman Teachers' Association, 227
London School Board, 66, 80, 138, 139, 144, 193
London School of Economics, 9
London, University of, 148, 153, 192, 195
Lucey, Helen, 113
Lucraft, Benjamin, 65, 66, 69, 142, 144
Lumb, Nora, 82

M

Mac an Ghaill, Máirtín, 114
Macrae, Sheila, 118–120
Magee, Frances, 257
Maguire, Meg, 118–120, 118n32
Maitland, Emma, 140
Major, John, 112
Malthus, Thomas, 62
Manchester, 6, 17, 84, 87, 166, 168, 192, 194, 200, 223, 256
Mangan, J.A., 55
Mangan, Lucy, 275
Manley, Lydia, 226
Mann, Jessica, 153
Mannheim, Karl, 164
Manpower Services Commission, 109
Mantel, Hilary, 166, 169, 172, 176, 186
Marsden, Dennis, 89, 207
Marshall, Dorothy, 30, 203
Marshall, Mary Paley, 3
Marshall, Sybil, 81
Marshall, T.H., 42, 43, 46

Martin, Jane Roland, 37, 255, 276
Martin, Leslie, 182
Marylebone, 140
Maurice, Frederick Denison, 59
Mayfield Comprehensive School, 94
Maynadr, Mary, 155
McCarthy, Margaret, 169
McNair Report, 1944, 195
McRobbie, Angela, 36, 99
Mearns, Andrew, 9
Mechanics Institute movement, 191
Medora, Hilda, 230
Melody, June, 113
Merchant Taylors' School, 54
Meritocracy, 19, 59, 89, 91, 129, 181, 187, 193, 274, 279, 283
Methodist, 79, 200
Milburn, Alan, 122
Miles, Margaret, 94, 207
Mill, John Stuart, 67
Miller, Florence Fenwick, 142
Miller, Jane, 26, 100, 101
Mirza, Heidi Safia, 114
Miss World, 31, 153, 251
Mitchell, Andrew, 210
Mitchell, Hannah, 223
Mitchell, Juliet, 26, 31, 34, 153
Moi, Toril, 42
Mokyr, Joel, 62
Monnow Road School, 84
More, Hannah, 63, 274
Morley, Edith, 164, 165, 167, 201
Morrell, Brian, 262
Morrell, Frances, 247, 258, 261–268
Mortimore, Peter, 264
Mott, Nevill, 205
Müller, Henrietta, 142, 143
Myers, Kate, 255, 256, 267

N
National Association of Schoolmasters (NAS), 83, 221, 224, 232
National Children's Bureau, 263
National Council for Civil Liberties, 96
National Curriculum Council, 111
National Educational Union, 65
National Education League, 65
National Education Union, 281
National Service, 93, 200
National Society, 64
National Union of Teachers (NUT), 12, 83, 217, 220, 227, 229, 231, 233, 237, 290
National Union of Women Teachers (NUWT), 12, 83, 86, 102, 151, 220–224, 221n7, 231–235, 237, 241, 242, 250, 252, 290
Needlework, 2, 64, 66, 142, 147, 150, 152, 184, 194, 221, 288
Newcastle, 73, 193, 195
Newcastle Commission, 56
Newnham, 3, 153, 192, 202, 204
New Right, 17, 166
Newsom, John, 123, 138, 150–152
Newsom Report, 1963, 92
Nirenstein, Minnie, 149
Noakes, Caroline, 282
Nonconformist, 64
Norfolk, 64, 170
Northampton, 184
Northcote-Trevelyan Report, 1854, 59
North London Collegiate School, 136, 287
North of England Council for Promoting the Higher Education of Women, 191
Norwood Report, 1943, 87
Not in Employment, Education or Training (NEET), 123
Nottingham, 182, 192, 209
Nottingham University College, 43
Notting Hill and Ealing High School, 81

O
Oakley, Ann, 26, 43, 45
O'Connor, Maureen, 93
Office for Standards in Education (OFSTED), 112
Ollerenshaw, Kathleen, 138, 152, 253
Open University (OU), 101, 158, 196, 238
Oram, Alison, 221
Osborne, George, 211
Osler, Audrey, 114
Ouseley, Herman, 246
Oxbridge, 71, 190, 193, 195, 203, 204, 206, 208, 273

Oxford Act, 1854, 192
Oxfordshire, 167, 183
Oxford, University of, 183, 195, 196, 211, 212, 281

P
Page, Anne, 254
Pakenham, Antonia, 81, 208
Pankhurst, Emmeline, 10, 52
Panorama, 116, 117
Parkinson, Michael, 180
Pascall, Gillian, 114
Patch, Harry, 172
Pedersen, Joyce Senders, 35
Pedley, Robin, 253
Perez, Caroline Criado, 2, 25
Phillips, Ann, 204
Pinchbeck, Ivy, 35
Plummer, Gillian, 99
Politics, 1, 8, 9, 14, 19, 27–40, 47, 56, 62, 65, 108–116, 136, 139, 140, 153, 156, 158, 159, 170, 208, 217, 218, 220–225, 228, 231, 234, 241, 242, 248, 250, 251, 262, 264, 265, 267, 280, 281, 283
Poplar, 231, 232
Potter, George, 142
Powell, Margaret, 168, 186
Power, Eileen, 30, 31
Power, 1, 2, 5, 8, 14, 16–19, 26–28, 31, 33–38, 40–42, 55, 57, 70, 72, 79, 80, 85, 87, 88, 91, 92, 97, 108, 117, 119, 121, 126, 129, 136–138, 146, 154, 159, 167, 177, 182, 184, 186, 193, 206, 211, 228, 240, 246, 253, 256, 262, 265, 268, 273–275, 278, 280, 283, 284
Psychosocial, 19
Public Schools Act, 1868, 57, 288
Pupil teachers, 64, 70, 80, 82, 148, 190, 194, 219, 226, 227
Purvis, June, 193

Q
Quaker, 147, 205
Queen's College, 59, 157

R
Race, 3, 9, 26, 36, 55, 84, 116, 128, 150, 187, 255, 266, 267, 274, 275, 281, 284
Ragged School movement, 54
Ranke, Leopold von, 28
Rathbone, Eleanor, 14
Reading University College, 192
Reay, Diane, 119
Reed, Lynn Raphael, 257
Reed, Miss, 204
Reid, Elizabeth Jesser, 59
Resistance, 3, 7–15, 36–38, 42, 98, 99, 108, 155, 174, 177, 186, 226–231, 235, 274
Resolution Foundation, 123
Richardson, Mary, 140
Ringrose, Jessica, 122, 122n43
Roberts, Robert, 172
Rodaway, Angela, 166, 178, 186
Rollock, Nicola, 278
Rose, Jonathan, 193
Rose Bruford drama school, 209
Rowbotham, Sheila, 31, 32, 208, 250, 252
Rowe, Albert, 94
Rowse, Alfred, 166, 169, 174
Royal Academy of Dramatic Art (RADA), 186, 209
Royal Holloway College, London, 192
Rugby school, 279
Ruskin College, Oxford, 158, 197, 198, 250, 263

S
Salford, 72, 172, 202
Salter, Emma Gurney, 81
Sayers, Janet, 156
Scannell, Dorothy, 145, 169, 173, 186
Scholarship, 27, 28, 30, 31, 34, 52, 57, 58, 60, 70–73, 79–87, 89, 102, 135, 145, 149, 155, 159, 165, 166, 168, 169, 171, 177–179, 181, 187, 189, 190, 194, 195, 198–200, 204, 206, 208, 218, 224, 227, 230, 259, 265
School, 1, 27, 52, 79, 163, 189, 218, 273

School Board Chronicle, 140
School Curriculum Development Committee (SCDC), 266
Scott, Joan, 33, 38
Scrutton, Thomas, 68, 69
Second World War, 15
Segal, Lynne, 34, 251
Selsdon Group, 263
Sex Discrimination Act, 1975, 17, 31, 80, 97
Sexual abuse, 19, 124, 261
Sexual division of labour, 3–7, 27, 38, 166
Sharp, Evelyn, 51, 73, 84
Shaw, Charlotte Payne-Townshend, 30
Shaw, Jenny, 156
Sheffield, 178, 192
Sheffield, University of, 86
Sherman, Alfred, 259, 263
Sidgwick, Henry, 191
Simon, Brian, 94, 254
Simon, Shena, 87, 202, 223
Six Point Group, 14, 234
Skills for Living, 257, 258, 261
Smith, Adam, 5
Smith, Bonnie G., 27, 28
Smith, Dorothy, 41, 47
Smyth, Thomas, 66
Social class, 27, 33, 52, 56, 57, 70, 72, 73, 84, 88, 107, 108, 121, 122, 129, 137, 146, 201, 203, 233, 262, 274
Socialism, 7, 8, 51, 226, 249
Social mobility, 62, 91, 102, 122, 136, 181, 187, 193, 197, 283
Sociology, 45, 99, 124, 153, 154, 156, 196, 266
Somerset, 63, 172
Somerville College, Oxford, 102, 202
Southampton, University of, 195
Southgate, Walter, 169, 176
South London Working Men's College, 140
Southwark Road Pupil Teacher Centre, 227
Spender, Dale, 32, 155, 266
Spender, Stephen, 169–170
Spens Report, 1938, 86
Stanley, Julia, 72, 107–109, 164

Stantonbury Campus, 256, 259–261
Stanworth, Michele, 97
Steedman, Carolyn, 33, 34, 181
Steedman, Hillary, 137
STEM subjects (science, technology, engineering and mathematics), 113, 124, 126
Stereotype, 45, 97, 110, 113, 128, 150, 205, 236, 240, 241, 277–279, 282, 284
Stewart, John Innes Mackintosh, 205, 207
Stewart-Murray, Katharine Duchess of Atholl, 230, 231
St Hilda's College, Oxford, 208, 250
St Hugh's College, Oxford, 192
Stirling, Alice, 30
Stockwell College, 226
Stoneman, Alice, 203
Stott, Mary, 10, 11, 13, 14, 245
St Paul's Industrial School, Limehouse, 68
St Paul's School, London, 68
Street-Porter, Janet, 166, 179
Suffolk, 64
Suffolk, Earl of, 54
Suffrage, 14, 30, 51, 65, 217, 227, 229, 234
Sullivan, Alice, 101
Sunday Schools, 8, 62
Sunderland, 82, 98
Surr, Elizabeth, 142
Sussex, 168, 196
Sussex, University of, 156
Swindells, Julia, 34

T
Taunton Commission, 56, 60, 136
Tawney, R.H., 31
Taylor, A.J.P., 205
Taylor, Helen, 67–69, 142, 173
Taylor-Mill, Harriet, 67
Teachers, 1, 26, 52, 79, 107, 141, 165, 190, 217, 273, 290
Teachers Labour League, 223
Technical and Vocational Educational Initiative (TVEI), 110
Technical schools, 71, 87, 88

Thatcher, Margaret, 17, 102, 110, 111, 119, 206, 263, 292
Thompson, E.P., 7, 29, 35
Thompson, Flora, 167
Thompson, Jane, 90, 91, 94, 209
Thring, Edward, 56
Thunberg, Greta, 275
Titmuss, Richard, 43, 46
Tom Brown's Schooldays, 55
Tottenham, 70, 166, 219
Toynbee Hall, 143
Trades Union Congress (TUC), 13, 123, 289, 290
Truancy, 67, 68, 98, 100
Truss, Liz, 281, 283
Tweedie, Jill, 247

U
UCL Institute of Education (IoE), 266
Ungerson, Clare, 156
United Nations (UN), 152, 234
University College London (UCL), 192
University Colleges, Bristol, 193
University Colleges, Durham, 208
University Colleges, London, 192
University Extension movement, 191
Uppingham School, 55
Upton House Truant School, 68
Uzzell, Kathleen, 194

V
Victoria University, 193
Vincent, Kerry, 114
Vlaeminke, Meriel, 69, 71, 137

W
Wadham College, Oxford, 208
Walkerdine, Valerie, 102, 113, 261
Wallasey Education Committee, 88
Waller Road School, 230
Warwick, University of, 35, 265
Watkins, Peter, 111
Waugh, Evelyn, 58
Webb, Beatrice, 9, 30, 228
Webb, Sidney, 70
Wedderburn, Dorothy, 34

Weiner, Gaby, 112, 122, 136, 154
Welfare, 11, 14–17, 35, 43, 102, 129, 143, 166, 168, 206, 223, 224
Wells, H.G., 242
Westfield College, London, 192
Westlake, Alice, 140, 144
Westminster School, 274, 281
Westminster Teacher Training College, 200
West Riding, 70, 93, 136n2
Whitehorn, Katharine, 168
Widdecombe, Ann, 166, 168, 209
Wilkinson, Ellen, 13, 87, 194
Willetts, David, 123
Williams, Raymond, 39, 40, 47, 138, 141, 146, 158, 164
Williams, Shirley, 242, 266
Willis, Paul, 36, 98, 108, 110
Willmott, Phyllis, 64
Wilson, Harold, 15–17, 93, 103, 249
Winchester College, 54
Windrush, 166, 181
Winrow-Jones, Jo, 158
Wintringham, Margaret, 11
Wolf, Alison, 123
Wollstonecraft, Mary, 4, 14, 35
Wolpe, AnnMarie, 101, 155, 254
Women's Budget Group, 123
Women's Co-operative Guild, 289
Women's Freedom League, 227, 231, 289
Women's Research and Resources Centre, 266
Women's Social and Political Union (WSPC), 10, 227, 289
Woodhead, Chris, 117
Woolf, Leonard, 58
Woolf, Virginia, 41
Wright, Alice Mary, 2
Wright, Nigel, 247

Y
Yorkshire, 145, 180
York, University of, 154, 158, 207
Young, Michael, 91

Z
Zangwill, Edith Ayrton, 10

GPSR Compliance

The European Union's (EU) General Product Safety Regulation (GPSR) is a set of rules that requires consumer products to be safe and our obligations to ensure this.

If you have any concerns about our products, you can contact us on

ProductSafety@springernature.com

In case Publisher is established outside the EU, the EU authorized representative is:

Springer Nature Customer Service Center GmbH
Europaplatz 3
69115 Heidelberg, Germany

www.ingramcontent.com/pod-product-compliance
Ingram Content Group UK Ltd.
Pitfield, Milton Keynes, MK11 3LW, UK
UKHW051120170425
457525UK00003B/34